Karen + Tommy,

May God
bless & keep
you & your
loved ones!
With the love
of Christ,
C. Read

Walking With The Enemy

A TESTIMONY

C. Read

True Light
Publications®

"I know that, whatsoever God doeth,
It shall be forever:
Nothing can be put to it, nor any thing taken from it:
and God doeth it, *that* men *should fear before Him.*
That which hath been is now;
and that which is to be hath already been;
and God requireth that which is past."
Ecclesiastes 3:14-15

Hard Cover / Fourth Edition
ISBN 0-9672825-8-6

Book Cover Designs by Sarah

All Scripture quotations have been taken from the Authorized Version of the King James Bible originally published in 1611. One characteristic of this version is *its use of italics,* which is used to indicate words supplied by the editors to help clarify the meaning and better relate the original language into English. It should be noted, that these words were not in the original manuscripts, and at times, it does change the meaning and intentions of The Author.

An interesting quote from the Apocrypha[1] states: "For the same things uttered in Hebrew, and translated into another tongue, have not the same force in them..." In other words, in the translation process of the Holy Scriptures, the true meaning is not always accurately conveyed because there is not a corresponding word. Moreover, the Holy Bible cannot truly be understood unless the true Author, who is the Holy Spirit of the LORD God Almighty, genuinely gives you the ability to fully comprehend what He has written.

PRINTED IN THE UNITED STATES OF AMERICA

CONTENTS

ACKNOWLEDGEMENTS

I WOULD LIKE TO ACKNOWLEDGE MY FATHER IN HEAVEN,

WHO IS THE LORD GOD ALMIGHTY!

THE MOST HIGH GOD!

THE GREAT I AM!

ALL PRAISE, HONOR, AND GLORY UNTO HIM

AND HIS BELOVED SON, JESUS CHRIST THE LORD!

WHO IS MY SAVIOR, MY REDEEMER, AND MY FRIEND!

AND IT IS ONLY BECAUSE OF HIM,

THAT I AM ALIVE AND LIVING!

PRAISE HIS HOLY NAME!

FOREVER AND EVER.

AMEN!

In Dedication to All God's People

SPECIAL THANKS

I would like to express my thankfulness
to the LORD God Almighty for the beautiful family that
He has so graciously given me during my Time here on this earth.
Especially for sending us Elijah—the LORD knew we needed him!
I Am truly grateful for the One that God has joined me with,
and for my precious Gifts. I love them all so very much,
and I Am thankful for the love they have given me.
May Almighty God abundantly bless them
with His love, joy, and peace
always and forever!
Amen!

IN ADDITION

I praise God for all who have helped
or encouraged me in this awesome endeavor.
I will always be eternally grateful to the Holy One of Israel
for His beloved servants that He has put in my path,
and also for the ones that I Am yet to meet...

PREFACE

I believe we are embarking on a Time in History that will be like no other. The world is changing so fast that at times it is hard to keep up, but praise God the Eternal Truth of His Holy word is Timeless.

We *really* need God on our side in these difficult and trying times in which we are living, because the Devil is out to lead astray whosoever he is able to deceive or manipulate into believing his lies.

Satan's primary goal is to steal, kill, and destroy God's creation, but if God's favor is upon you, He can intervene on your behalf, which is why God's grace, mercy, and forgiveness is so important.

In the beginning, this Testimony was only sent to a select few, but I truly believe God desires for *all* men to have an opportunity to see and hear what the LORD God has revealed to me by His Holy Spirit.

I Am certain that everything in connection with this work is under the faithful care and guidance of the LORD God Almighty, and it is *only* through Providence[2] that God made sure that I had my first perfect bound book on 28 February 1995—exactly two years to the very day in which the "True Light" pierced the Darkness!

One day all of God's people will see exactly what has taken place in the Darkness, and then they will realize how Almighty God has been working among so many others to have His will accomplished.

I have to say that I have endured much opposition from within and without, but I Am determined to share what the LORD God has so graciously allowed me to write down. And *only* by His grace will I fulfill the call that the Most High God has placed upon my life.

It is really not my desire to bring attention to myself or to others, and for that reason I have changed or deleted names and places so as not to identify specific individuals and their whereabouts.

The deception I was involved in could happen to anyone, anywhere in the world. In fact, it is going on at an alarming rate! The only consolation is, it has been foretold in the Holy Scriptures.

Since my translation from the Darkness into His glorious Light, I see that dates and events are extremely important with the LORD, despite the fact that my Enemy has tried to get me to believe otherwise. And looking back, I see just how significant they really are.

When I started the Preface to the Third Edition of this book on 22 July 1999, I did not fully realize the great importance of this day. The corresponding Jewish date for that day was 9 Av 5759, also known as "Tisha B'Av," which is a very solemn day for many religious Jews.

According to tradition, both of the Jewish Temples in Jerusalem were destroyed on the 9th Day of Av! Reportedly, the first one was burned by a Babylonian general during Nebuchadnezzar's reign in the year 586 BC, and the second Temple was completely destroyed by the Romans under the command of Titus during the Jewish revolt in 70 AD.

These magnificent buildings represented God's presence in the midst of His chosen people; and because the destruction of these Holy sites were to have occurred on this day, the 9th Day of Av is justifiably a day of great mourning for all who memorialize this day.

As you read this Testimony, may you see and understand that we no longer need man-made buildings to experience the presence of Almighty God in our lives. And if you genuinely allow the LORD to purify your heart, He may choose to make His habitation with you!

But it can only happen through Emmanuel, the Messiah—the Holy One of Israel! And in order for God to cleanse and forgive you of your sins, you must accept His great sacrifice when God gave up His only begotten Son as the ultimate offering for the "sin" of this world.

We are at a turning point in the war between God and the Devil, and it won't be too long before Death will finally be swallowed up in Victory! Praise the precious and mighty name of Yeshua HaMashiach,[3] the LORD Jesus Christ, the *true* "Anointed One!"

The coming of the LORD has indeed inflicted a most serious and fatal blow to the Enemy; and by God's direction, the Testimony of Jesus will be the contributing factor in the downfall of Satan's Kingdom.

My hope in publishing this incredible book that I have been given the awesome privilege to be a part of, is that it will cause the LORD God Almighty to be beloved in the eyes of His people more and more.

May the peace of God be upon you as you seek to sincerely love the Holy One who made the Heavens and the earth, with all your heart, soul, mind, and strength! He is a faithful Creator. Always!

20 Tevet 5761 / Sunday, 14 January 2001

Addendum To The Preface

In Light of the horrific events of 11 September 2001, may this book offer solace, knowledge, and understanding in these very difficult and trying Times in which we are living.

May we never forget those who willingly give up their own lives to save the lives of others; and most especially the Holy One who gave His precious Life, so that all "men" may have Eternal Life!

1 Tevet 5762 / 15 December 2001

INTRODUCTION

The following transcript is a brief excerpt from a program on a contemporary "Christian" Radio station that was broadcast the day after the Branch Davidian[4] compound in Waco, Texas went up in flames.

While the world looked on in horror, close to eighty people, including women and children, were completely destroyed by the fire on the 19th of April 1993 at the place that was called Mount Carmel.[5]

Due to my experience of *Walking With The Enemy*, I Am able to understand how a person like the late David Koresh was capable of manipulating, seducing, and totally deceiving his followers into believing his outrageous lies, even though I have never personally met the "man."

My situation involved totally different people and places, but it's the same as a man once wrote after I sent him *Walking With The Enemy*: "It would take a while to share with you all that I found to be in common with your story, though they are different, the similarities are undeniable. It's amazing how the Enemy's signature is the same."

As you read this Testimony, you will see several things that coincide with some of the bizarre events surrounding Waco, Texas. My only explanation: THIS IS A WAR BETWEEN GOD AND THE DEVIL!

The hosts of this radio station were very instrumental in some aspects of writing this book, but they probably had no idea that they were being used by God in such a way as to help expose the hidden agenda of the Devil himself. Which is: The Peaceful Eradication of Mankind!

This dialogue was my first encounter with the hosts of WWAR,[6] and even though they were discussing an extremely serious subject, after reading this transcript, you will have to admit that the LORD God has such a wonderful sense of humor.

GUEST SPEAKER: WELL KNOWN PROPHECY & CULT EXPERT
20 APRIL 1993

Host "Let's go to Cathy...Thanks for being patient. And go ahead with your question or your comment."

Cathy "...I was just wanting to mention I had just been delivered from a cult, and actually it happened on 28 February 1993."[7]

Host "What took place? What kind of cult was this? Can you give the name of it, Cathy?"

Cathy "The name of the ministry was La'el Ministries. I was with them a little over three years."

Host "[Doctor], is there a question you would like to ask of Cathy, maybe to find out what kind of a cult this was?"

Guest "Yeah, Cathy, uh, first of all, I rejoice that you have been delivered."

Cathy "Oh, me too. It's wonderful actually!"

Guest "And I can tell by the sound of your voice that you thank God that you weren't beguiled totally and completely into this thing, but something of the clear word of God got to you so that you came to Christ. Right?"

Cathy "Oh yeah!"

Guest "...That is a great testimony, Cathy. I'd be interested to know, did someone come and preach, or did—"

Cathy "Oh no. The LORD actually came down by His Spirit into my living room."

Guest "Do what?"

Cathy "It was a real fascinating experience."

Guest "Oh my!"

Cathy "He, uh— It's kind of a whole long story."

Guest "Cathy, stop right there! Did you say someone, or something, came down and materialized in your living room?!"

Cathy "The Holy Spirit manifested in a person and spoke. And that person actually happened to be me.

And I hate to—I don't hate to say me, but for some reason it's almost like I Am boasting if I claim that the LORD actually spoke through me. But He did...He spoke in a very mighty way, and it happened that same day...

The main thing about it, is that our leader—my ex-leader, was. . .supposedly a very godly man.

And it was through deception, and seduction, and many things were involved."

Host "Cathy, can I encourage you when we get through with our conversation with our guest to give him a telephone call there at his ministry, and you all can discuss this?

I'm sure you have some questions relative to what Cathy is talking about.

And Cathy, if you would jot down that telephone number and call him. We have another caller waiting, and since you said it is a long story then maybe he can find time to discuss it with you."

Cathy "OK."

Guest "And we'll be happy to send this book, *The Marks of a Cult,* to all who call and request it. So we will welcome your call."

I DID CALL HIM AFTERWARDS, and I was surprised that he took my phone call. I went into detail about some of the things that took place during my time with La'el Ministries, and he seemed quite intrigued.

He mentioned that the LORD may be able to use my experience as a ministry for others, however at the time I did not realize that God would have me develop a book that would explain exactly how I was able to be deceived into thinking that I was walking with followers of the LORD Jesus Christ, when in truth, I was *Walking With The Enemy.*

This book is a collection of very personal letters and transcripts that I have written and received since being delivered from the Enemy which will give an honest, straightforward, and detailed account of how I came to be in such a vulnerable and dangerous situation.

In the editing process, I have revised the wording of various letters to bring greater clarity, but I have not altered the overall contents. Moreover, I did not make changes to actual transcripts or letters from others, except for obvious errors, selected omissions, and name changes.

One letter in particular, dated 5 June 1993, is one I sent out to several churches and individual Christians as I was directed to by the LORD. This was to be the first of many letters that God would be asking me to send to those whom He had laid on my heart.

Most of the original letters I sent were signed, sealed, and notarized at the Chancery Clerk's office by direction of the LORD. I realize this practice is somewhat unorthodox, and I have not done it in the past, but then again, I Am not the same as I was before.

Since the night of 28 February 1993 my relationship with the LORD God Almighty has taken on new purpose and meaning, and the overwhelming desire of my heart is to please my Heavenly Father.

I greatly desire to obey God whether or not I fully understand or know all the reasons why. You may not understand it all either, but I hope you will receive what the LORD has revealed to me by His Spirit.

May you truly grasp what you are about to read, and may God grant you the grace, knowledge, and wisdom you will need in order to comprehend and apply these wonderful Truths to your individual life.

My purpose in sharing my story, is so that others may gain a better understanding of this war that we are in. However, you might be completely unaware of the danger, or you may possibly be one who does not even acknowledge God or Satan, but it is so important that you find out whose side you are on, before it is too late.

Sadly, the name of Jesus Christ has been, and continues to be, misused and abused for personal, political, and financial gain; and the memory of Jesus and all that He has done for mankind has become so tainted with evil! It has even gotten to the point where you must have a very guarded approach to those who claim to be a "Christian."

Apostasy, hypocrisy, and compromise is bringing churches down and destroying God's people! The LORD said that many would come in His name, claiming to be of Christ, yet they are ravenous wolves dressed in sheep's clothing seeking to kill, steal, and destroy. Therefore, we must pay very close attention to what a person does, not just what they say.

You also need to keep in mind that the Enemy does not want you to become aware of any of this, since this Testimony will expose him for who he really is. And he will try any means possible to divert your attention away from this book, but I hope you will persevere if you really want to know the Truth of what I have learned about his tactics.

Moreover, it is imperative that you come to terms with the fact, that as long as you are living in this present world, you too are at great risk of *Walking With The Enemy*. And only by *Walking in the True Light* will you ever be able to recognize who the true adversary really is.

And please realize that the true condition of your heart will affect how you will respond to the words that Almighty God has given. Only the sincerely humble will fully appreciate The Message.

If you happen to find out that you are on the wrong side, my sincere hope and prayer for you is that this Testimony will persuade you to get on the side of the LORD, while there is still time.

And if you are truly one who is seeking God with all your heart, my most earnest prayer for you is that you will come away from here with more of a love, and a deeper appreciation for God the Holy Father, Jesus Christ His Son, and the Holy Spirit of the Most High God!

Churches

"I Jesus have sent Mine angel
to testify unto you these things in the Churches.
I Am the root and the offspring of David,
and the Bright and Morning Star."
Revelation 22:16

To Whom it May Concern, 5 June 1993

I Am sorry this is such an impersonal salutation, but I will be sending this letter to various people who are related to, friends with, or have had associations with those of La'el Ministries.

I will also be sending this letter to those who have not even heard of them, but really need to. My objective is to enlighten those who are unfamiliar with this type of ministry and its practices.

La'el Ministries was originally a prayer group that evolved into a Bible study group, and ultimately became a "Church" with a listing in the Church Directory of the local newspaper. [As of this writing.]

Many have come and gone over the last four years, but the main leaders are "Pastor" Huff; Liz, assistant-pastor; and Cindy, teacher.

I was with them for the last three years, and initially I only met with the group on Thursday nights, but I eventually joined the meetings that were held on Wednesday and Sunday nights.

They presently hold meetings, which are open to the public, in their home. They were held in my home for the last two years; that is, up until the incredible night of 28 February 1993.

Soon before I left the group they also started a ministry for the children, with Liz as the main teacher, and Cindy as a substitute.

So, by all outward appearances, this seemed to be a perfectly harmless group of people getting together to study the Bible and to serve and worship the LORD Jesus Christ in song, word, and prayer.

Interestingly, Huff and Liz claimed to be Jewish, as well as prophets that had been sent by God to preach His word in Truth. They also considered me the "weakest" member, which is why they said I needed them to discern the "word" properly. My gift was the ministry of "helps," rather than "discernment," according to Liz.

I walked with these people for three years really believing that they were my friends, and that they actually loved and cared about me. I grew to love and trust them completely, and would have done anything in my abilities to be a true friend.

Everything that I ever did for them I did as unto the LORD and never expected anything in return. I see why it is so important to have that frame of mind in light of everything I know now.

I truly felt they were sent by God into my life to help me to learn of Him and His ways; and I have to admit that I did learn very much from my associations with these people. *That* is what I would like to share, as much as I Am able to disclose at this time.

This letter explains some of my feelings after our separation.

Dear Pastor Huff and Liz, *11 May 1993*

I received a letter from Cindy the other day and she is wondering why I have chosen not to speak to her, but as I mentioned to you, I just cannot deal with any of you right now. The wounds of what you all have done are too deep, and I Am going through a healing process.

I know when I saw you two at the store there was such a sadness that came over me, and I spent the rest of the day crying over all this. I did not realize seeing both of you would cause such a reaction in me.

You know, it really bothers me that I could have special friends like you for three years, and come to find out you really weren't the type of friends I thought you were. I tried to write you a letter a few weeks after our break-up, but I just could not finish the letter. Besides, my Husband kept pestering me until I came to bed. He has expressed that he does not want me to talk with any of you unless he knows about it.

I do want you to know that I hate it that things turned out this way. I really had no idea that it would. I never thought that I would be rejected by all of you. I figured I would walk with you forever. It was a very hard thing to accept for a while.

Even when I spoke to you on the phone Liz, I still had a lot of sadness in my heart concerning the loss of our friendship. I really felt like you two cared about me in a way that nobody ever has in my whole life.

I still care about what happens to you, and I really do not desire anything bad for you regardless of what you might think or what it seems like. And I know in your hearts you do believe that.

I Am not writing this letter to gain your sympathy. I do not want yours or anybody's for that matter. I take complete responsibility for what I do in this body of mine, and I know I will reap the effects of what I sow.

I just want you to know, that no matter what the Enemy says to you, I Am following Jesus! He is my LORD and my God! And Him alone do I serve! I know you have said that when people walk away from you that they will no longer walk with Jesus, and for some that is very true, but I think you will be wrong in my case.

I hope that one day you will see the complete Truth and walk in the True Light. That is my greatest desire. And I hope you will share this letter with everyone, even the children, because that is truly my greatest desire for them too. I don't know if you will, but would you please tell the children that I love them even though they do not see Me right now?

I will continue to pray for all of you as the LORD directs me. After all, He does know what is best for us, as He is the only One who truly knows our hearts' intent. And by the way, I have not judged you people. I do not know exactly what your true intent is. I only know to the extent of what you have spoken. But God commands that we look at our behavior, and that of our brothers and sisters, and that is all I have done.

I know you think that I Am under attack by the Enemy. And I Am! He hates the stand I have made. But that is what this is all about! Light against Darkness! The battle has already been won, we just don't see it yet.

I pray that you, in the end, will be standing on the side of Truth. But only you can decide.

This will probably be my last personal letter to you. I have written many. Do you ever reread them, or have you thrown them all away? I would say they probably never meant anything to you, just as it is obvious that I never meant anything to you either.

My last words to you are these: Purify your hearts! Repent! And turn back to Almighty God so that He can heal you, and make you whole again. He so wants to, but you have to be willing to confess your sin to Him so that He can cleanse you of the unrighteousness, and also confess your sins to one another so healing can begin.

This has been a very hard letter for me to write, and I still have a lot of pain and grief inside that I did not realize was there. But just remember, when I Am in public, the LORD is my Armor, His angels are all around me, His Holy Spirit is inside of me, and I have chosen to yield myself to the LORD God Almighty no matter what kind of fool it makes me look like. This letter is from my heart and there are no evil motives behind it. If you have ears to hear, you will hear!

PS. I just heard you got a summons to appear in court. I have not received one yet, but if I do, don't be concerned—I will only speak the truth with all honesty and sincerity as I always have with you.

Let the LORD'S peace be with you, and I know it will if He truly resides in you. As He has said, "I will never leave you, or forsake you. I Am with you alway[s,] even to the end of the world...

And behold, I come quickly, and My reward is with Me, to give every man according as his work shall be. I Am Alpha and Omega, the Beginning and the End, the First and the Last!"

As I finished writing that letter, I received a phone call from Cindy's ex-husband asking me to appear in court on 17 May 1993. For that reason I added a postscript, but I want to apologize for the sarcastic tone. It was just not a good note to conclude that letter on.

In spite of what they say, I know they are not living in peace. Based on what God has impressed upon my heart, I know they are living in fear and torment, and I Am sorry they have chosen to live that way.

I would think that all the strife, confusion, and anxiety that they are going through would show them who they are *really* following. And it is certainly not the Prince of Peace, who is the LORD Jesus!

My personal relationship with them permanently ended on the night of 28 February 1993. The only dealings I have with Huff and Liz now is as the Holy Spirit leads me into their path.

I will go into some of what happened on that extraordinary February night, so that maybe you will have a clearer understanding as to why I can no longer befriend them, or have anything to do with any of the members of La'el Ministries, unless the LORD directs me.

That was a night that none of us present will *ever* forget, despite the fact that Mr. Huff and Liz would like me to believe that it was an uneventful evening. Furthermore, it is because of what has transpired *since* that night, as to why this has become such an issue.

I know many of you would rather not get involved or wish you did not have to face any of this, and I Am truly sorry for the grief and heartache many of you have gone through, and will continue to go through, because of your relation or associations with some of the members of this Bible study group.

I pray that you will learn to trust the LORD Jesus Christ for every aspect of your life, and allow Him to comfort, encourage, and strengthen you through all of this. You just need a humble and sincere heart, and be willing to receive and obey the Truth.

I would like to address the parents at this time. I know this has to be very hard for you, and if you are a true Christian, you must really be pulled in two different directions. I sincerely hope that you will prayerfully get before the LORD God and earnestly seek Him with all your heart on what you should do, and just do it!

At times, the LORD may ask us to do the hardest things, and we may not necessarily know the outcome, but your obedience can sometimes make the difference between life and death.

I Am speaking of spiritual life and spiritual death, which is so much more important since it will be forever. I pray the LORD will give us all an extra measure of grace to endure what is up ahead.

TWENTY EIGHT FEBRUARY 1993: This was such an unusual day for me, and when Liz saw me for the first time that evening she fell back against a wall in the hallway and a shocked look came across her face.

I asked her what was the matter, and she said, "Oh, nothing." Then she commented on what I was wearing, but it was an old shirt she had seen plenty of times before, and I never got *that* reaction out of her. I knew she was lying, but I just did not know why yet.

Later on that evening, I gave Liz an article from the Sunday morning newspaper on David Koresh and the Branch Davidians. It was just telling about his many wives and his claims that he was "Christ."

[Please note: I was not yet aware of the violent confrontation between the Branch Davidians and the Federal agents, mainly because Cindy had kept me busy all day going out to her house in the country. And looking back I Am sure that it was by direction of Liz and Huff.[8]]

As Liz was reading that article, Huff seemed *very* nervous. It was obvious that he was aware of that situation. After Cindy read the article, I asked her out of hearing range of Huff and Liz if she knew what "spirit" David Koresh operated under. She said, "No." And I said, "The spirit of anti-Christ, the same spirit that is here." She did not say anything, but she looked at me kind of funny.

[I said many things on this incredible night that I did not fully understand or realize the ramifications until later, and I Am still gaining insight on many things pertaining to all of this.]

While we were waiting to get started, I spoke to Wendell, one of the newest members of the group, and I said, "I see the adversary has not kept you away tonight." And he said, "Not that he hasn't tried." And I said, "Well, I Am very glad to see you."

Then I spoke to Thomas, Liz's husband, and I said, "I Am very glad to see you too." And I patted him on the arm.

[This was a highly unusual way for me to be talking to members of the group, but I did not think much about it then.]

The following is some of the words to the song that we were singing when the LORD interrupted our meeting on that unforgettable evening of 28 February 1993—*The* Night To Remember!

"ARISE, O GOD
LET YOUR ENEMIES BE SCATTERED,
FOR YOU ARE EXALTED KING OF ALL THE EARTH!
RIDING HIGH ABOVE THE HEAVENS!
YOUR NAME SHALL BE PRAISED IN THE MIGHTY GATES OF ZION!
YOUR KINGDOM SHALL REIGN FOREVER! AND EVER!"

It was on this memorable night that the LORD God Almighty answered my most earnest prayer, and made His awesome presence known in our midst in such a mighty and supernatural way!

Seventeen people, including women and children, were present, along with the Holy Spirit of the Most High God! And I might add that many demonic "spirits" were also in attendance; however, they did not remain after the LORD showed up! Praise God!

I do not remember what point we were at in the song, but while I was singing my arms were suddenly thrust up into the air, and I began praying as the Holy Spirit gave me utterance. I felt as if Almighty God was pouring Himself into me while my arms shook uncontrollably. Yet, for those who looked on, I did not appear to be shaking at all.

Moreover, there was such anger, rage, and hostility coming from my mouth, and I got so loud that I was drowning out the music. So after a while, they decided to quit singing and playing the musical instruments. [Huff played the guitar and Liz the keyboard.]

To give you a feel for the atmosphere that night, my Husband had a fire going, but it was not cold enough, so He had a door and a window open. So, while the LORD God was pouring out His wrath and indignation through me, it was not just limited to the confines of my living room—It was also for the "prince of the power of the air"[9] to hear!

This went on for a little while, and then I abruptly stood up and walked to the front of the fireplace where "Pastor" Huff usually sat to teach. I turned to face everyone with my hands still held high in the air, and still praying in the "Spirit." Then, I suddenly stopped!

There was a DEAD silence in the room, and every eye was on me. I stood there for just a moment, and without bending my elbows, I suddenly brought my arms down directly in front of me—even with my waist—and with my arms still straight, I forcefully made a sweeping motion to the sides as if to say, ENOUGH!

At that moment, it felt as though I just melted to the floor, and then I bowed down and put my face to the ground. The first intelligible words out of my mouth were, "O Jesus, You are so beautiful!"

I then began praising the LORD God and giving Him all honor and glory. I told Him I Am nothing without Him, and that anything I have that is truly worth having is only because of Him. I told Him that I love and adore Him, and He alone is my LORD and Master.

After that, I lifted my face up from the ground and saw that everyone was staring at me. I started to get somewhat nervous and I began to mumble something about how I really did not like to be the center of attention, and how this really was not like me.

Mr. Huff interrupted and very mockingly said to me, "Well, give the interpretation." I hesitated for maybe a fraction of a second, and I just closed my eyes and said very firmly, "I will."

Usually, I was very intimidated by both Mr. Huff and Liz, but this night was so different. There was such a boldness about me that I was actually intimidating to them!

I had noticed that there had been a real fear growing in them for some time, but I really did not understand why until after this night, and the subsequent meeting we had on 2 March 1993.

I did not have the tape recorder on as I usually did, so I was not able to get the prophecy that was given that night on tape. However, it really didn't matter because the LORD brought everything He addressed at that time back to my memory almost exactly word for word.

As the LORD spoke these words to those who were gathered together in my home on 28 February 1993, it was spoken with love and compassion, but with much boldness and conviction.

Moreover, ever since that night, my Enemy has accused me of not demonstrating the love of God in order to discredit what took place, but it just further proves to me that we do not serve the same "God."

Please prayerful consider these words from *my* God.

Prophecy of 28 February 1993

"Many things you have been taught here has been done in secrecy and in Darkness. You have been taught truth mixed with lies, and the LORD says it will go on no longer!

And you, Mr. Huff, is the one who has taught the lies, and the LORD says it will go on no longer in this home. The LORD is giving you a chance to turn from your sin, and He is so forgiving that He will not hold your sin against you, if you repent. And if you do not, you will die!

He is my Husband, and I love Him with a love that cannot be broken. I love you too, but with a brotherly love. And I beg you to repent!

Everything you have learned here has been tainted with evil, and you cannot hold on to any of it. The only thing that you can hold on to is the fact that Jesus Christ died for you, and by His mighty power, God raised Him from the dead. If you believe that in your heart, and claim Him as LORD, He will put the same Spirit that raised Jesus from the dead inside of you, to lead you and guide you into the Truth!

Light will overshadow Darkness, and Darkness will not be able to stand in the presence of God!"

I went on to say that anyone who wanted to come and pray and read the Bible together would be very welcome, but it would no longer be a two "man" show run by "Pastor" Huff and Liz.

I realized that was all the LORD was giving me to say at that time, but He also said that the remainder of this prophecy would come out later. However, I did not voice that to the group.

I started getting rather nervous again and I said, "Well, that is all that I have." I went to my seat and they resumed singing. Then Mr. Huff got up and preached as if nothing had even taken place!

I got very agitated and was about to respond, but God calmed me down and said, "IT WILL BE ADDRESSED AT THE APPOINTED TIME!"

The rest of this prophecy did indeed come out on the Second of March when my Husband and I got together with some of the members of La'el Ministries, but it was more of a confrontation.

I will not go into all of the details of that particular meeting, except to say, THEY HAVE MUCH TO HIDE.

At this time, I would like to address only family members, friends, and those who are acquainted with me. If you know me very well, you know that I became very committed to the LORD during a temporary assignment to Yuma, Arizona in November of 1979, while I was enlisted in the United States Marine Corps.[10]

I have been a Christian for thirteen years (as of this writing), and I Am very sorry to say that I have been a very prideful, arrogant, and thoughtless person at times. And I would like to express to you that I truly regret if I have ever demonstrated that attitude towards you.

I would never intentionally want to be hurtful to anybody, even when I was not "born again,"[11] but I see where I have been selfish and inconsiderate, and I ask that you please forgive me.

This is truly from my heart, and I Am not saying these things to win back relationships, or to manipulate you in any way. That is really not my intent in confronting you with this.

In fact, I Am not doing so well in the relationships I have in my life now, but with the LORD'S help, I Am sure God will restore whatever needs to be re-established, in His perfect timing.

What is even more heart breaking to me though, is that all the while when I truly thought I was walking with the LORD God I was actually *Walking With The Enemy.* And due to the fact that I was such an improper representative of the LORD Jesus Christ, I Am extremely sorry.

But because the LORD God Almighty is so wonderful, merciful, and forgiving, He will not hold any of my sins against me, especially since I committed them out of ignorance.

I love the LORD God so much, and I just know that He will turn everything around for my good and for the good of others. I Am so very thankful to Him for delivering me out of the Power of Darkness!

And I want to emphasize that what took place on those nights was by the leadership of the Holy Spirit. It was not my doing at all. His anointing does not come as I will it, but only as He wills it.

So do not think I Am anything because He chose to use me in this way. I Am nothing, but Jesus Christ in me is everything! And it is only by the grace of Almighty God that I Am even able to talk about any of this, much less put my experience down on paper.

The overriding desire of my heart is to have a deep, personal, and intimate relationship with our Creator, and I see how sin can separate me from Him, and ultimately kill me whether I Am deceived or not. As He says, "My people perish for lack of knowledge."

My earnest prayer before God is that He will show me anything in my heart that displeases Him, and cleanse me of the unrighteousness, so I can have a pure heart before Him, and see Him more clearly.

One request that I would like to ask of you: If you belong to the LORD, and He brings up my name in your heart, would you please pray for me? And not for me only, but for all God's people, whether they have been "born" into the kingdom of God yet or not. He truly honors the fervent prayers of a righteous man or woman.

Thank you for taking the time to read this. I will always be grateful for your prayers. May the LORD bless you and keep you from the Evil One. He is out there seeking whom he may destroy, and he takes no greater pleasure than to bring down a Christian.

But always remember, "Greater is He who is in me, than he who is in the world!" And the same holds true for you if you are a genuine disciple of the LORD Jesus Christ and God the Holy Father.

I praise the LORD God that He has given me the ability to put these words to paper. And I pray that He receives all the glory and honor for anything and everything I do that is truly worth doing.

BLESSING, AND HONOR, AND GLORY, AND POWER, AND MIGHT,
BE UNTO HIM THAT SITTETH UPON THE THRONE, AND
UNTO THE LAMB, FOREVER AND EVER! AMEN!

I attest this letter to be the Truth as much as the LORD God Almighty
has given me the understanding, ability, and authority to speak.

Signed and sealed in the presence of a witness on the 11th Day of June
in the year of the LORD, One Thousand Nine Hundred and Ninety-Three.[12]

PRIOR TO PUBLISHING THE SECOND EDITION OF THIS BOOK, Liz told me they no longer have Bible study meetings in their home, and that they were attending a "charismatic" church[13] located out of town. The last I heard she is now attending the local United Methodist Church.

The county newspaper has since removed La'el Ministries from their church listings under much protest from Liz I was told, but a year later their Ad showed back up again just as it was before.

After speaking with the Editor about it, he said it was apparently due to an error, and it was promptly removed again. Also worth noting, at the time my second book, *Walking in the True Light,*[14] was published, Cindy was actually working for this particular newspaper.

I Am sure that the Editor had been warned about this group, but he may not have fully understood the danger involved with them. May this Testimony be a wakeup call for all of God's People!

This book was initially published on 2 March 1995, and as you continue reading, you will see that it goes into many details regarding my involvement with La'el Ministries. I Am certain that they do not serve the One whom I serve, but I really take no great pleasure in knowing what their end will be.

However, God knew exactly what was up ahead, and I truly believe He is allowing me to share what I witnessed in order to help those who are walking in Darkness and know not where they are going.

Moreover, the Prophecy of 28 February 1993 was not only for those present, but for all God's people. And I want to stress that His spoken word will never contradict His written word. It will enhance, and it may even fulfill many of the prophecy's that have been written, but any "divine message" that directly opposes what the LORD has already spoken in His word should not be embraced as the Truth.

As Jesus Christ said, many would come in His name claiming that they are of Christ, and some may even say *they are* Christ; but He warned us to be very wary, and test the "spirits" to see if they are of Him.

Only through the "True Christ" can we know the Truth. And only by Walking in the "True Light" can we see what is truly before us. May this book lead you to the One who can truly give you Eternal Life.

And may this Testimony of the LORD Jesus Christ dissuade you from trusting in a man, a movement, or even you own self; and persuade you to call on the name of the LORD from a sincere and repentant heart. I can attest to the fact that He is true and faithful, always!

John 3:33-34 "He that hath received His Testimony hath set to His seal that God is true. For He whom God hath sent speaketh the words of God: for God giveth not the [Holy] Spirit by measure unto Him."

Isaiah 8:20 "To the law and to the Testimony: if they speak not according to this Word, it is because there is no Light in them."

Ephesians 5:8-13 "For ye were sometimes Darkness, but now are ye Light in the LORD: walk as children of Light:

(For the fruit of the Spirit is in all goodness and righteousness and Truth;) Proving what is acceptable unto the LORD.

And have no fellowship with the unfruitful works of Darkness, but rather reprove them. For it is a shame even to speak of those things which are done of them in secret.

But all things that are reproved (or exposed) are made manifest by the Light: for whatsoever doth make manifest is Light."

Acts 17:30-31 "And the times of this ignorance God winked at;[15] (or over looked) but now commandeth all men every where to repent: Because He hath appointed a Day, in the which He will judge the world in righteousness by that Man whom He hath ordained; whereof He hath given assurance unto all men, in that He hath raised Him from the dead."

Joel 2:28-29 "And it shall come to pass afterward, that I will pour out My Spirit upon all flesh; and your sons and your daughters shall prophesy, your old men shall dream dreams, your young men shall see visions: And also upon the servants and upon the handmaids in those days will I pour out My Spirit."

Romans 8:11 "But if the Spirit of Him that raised up Jesus from the dead dwell in you, He that raised up Christ from the dead shall also quicken[16] your mortal bodies by His Spirit that dwelleth in you."

I John 1:5-7 "This then is The Message which we have heard of Him, and declare unto you, that God is Light, and in Him is no Darkness at all.

If we say that we have fellowship with Him, and walk in Darkness, we lie, and do not the Truth:

But if we walk in the Light, as He is the Light, we have fellowship one with another, and the blood of Jesus Christ His Son cleanseth us from all sin."

Psalm 63:11 "But the King shall rejoice in God; every one that sweareth by Him shall glory: but the mouth of them that speak lies shall be stopped."

I Corinthians 4:5 "Therefore judge nothing before the Time, until the LORD come, who both will bring to Light the hidden things of Darkness, and will make manifest the counsels of the hearts:

And then shall every man have praise of God."

Heed The Call

"Take heed therefore how ye hear:
for whosoever hath, to him shall be given;
and whosoever hath not, from him shall be taken
even that which he seemeth to have."
Luke 8:18

Since my release from La'el Ministries, Cindy and Liz are the only ones that have contacted me thus far, and basically they say I Am wrong and that they are right. They are still contending that they are walking with God, and that I Am *Walking With The Enemy*. In essence that can be true if their "god" is the Devil, and their "enemy" is my God.

Four months after our breakup I mailed a taped message to Cindy which generated quite a response from both Cindy and Liz.[17] I truly spoke what was on my heart, and even now, I sincerely hope that I could somehow be wrong in my perceptions of these people that I had grown to love and trust. But deep down inside, I do not feel that I Am.

One very important lesson that I have learned, is that the "spirit" in which something is spoken is so much more important to consider than the words alone. And only through God can we know for certain whether a person's motives be good, or whether they be evil; which is why it is so important to discern His voice perfectly.

Albeit, there is coming a Day, very soon, in which there will be no more room for doubt as to who truly loves and belongs to the LORD God Almighty, and who does not.

The following letter was sent to my former friend whom I once trusted, and I just praise the LORD God Almighty that I Am now walking in the "True Light" with eyes that can truly see!

Dear Liz, 12 July 1993

I would like to discuss with you many things pertaining to all that has been going on since our separation, but true wisdom is knowing what to talk about, to whom to talk with, and when. Nevertheless, I truly want to be very open and honest with you.

I do not have anything to hide, and there really isn't anything that I can't talk about that has gone on in my life. But that is not to say that there are not some things that I Am extremely ashamed of, and would prefer not to speak about. However, I Am very willing to discuss whatever the LORD may permit.

I also want you to know that just because a person inquires information of me, does not mean that I discuss my whole life story with them. I Am trying very hard to be led of God's Spirit, and I Am not so naive to think that there are not people out there, sent by Satan, to try and trip me up and use my words against me.

But even in that, I Am just going to trust the LORD God to show me my mistakes and help me to not make them again.

I pray that in speaking with you, I will be very sensitive to the Holy Spirit and only speak what He would have me say to you. Moreover, I Am fully convinced that only the word of God spoken in Truth is really the only word that is worth hearing or repeating.

I Am not going to try and quote the Scriptures like you and Cindy have done in past letters. I will just speak to you from my heart, and if I speak the word of God to you in Truth, then it will bear witness, if the Spirit of Christ so dwells inside of you.

Last night when you called, I was almost happy to hear from you, but there was a lot of apprehension there also. Liz, if you can believe it, I Am so sorry that we are not walking together. But like you always used to say to me, "How can two walk together lest they be in agreement?" And we have a *major* disagreement going!

I want to believe you when you say you love me, but I Am having trouble trusting anyone these days. I Am not trying to imply that you are lying when you say that you would do anything for me, but I feel that my dependence and complete trust that I used to have for you and Mr. Huff is what got me into the trouble I was in while I was with you. The one I *fully* trust is my LORD and Savior Jesus Christ.

Of course, it is wonderful to have others that are like-minded, so we can worship God together, fellowship with, and even to some degree be accountable to; but I Am firmly convinced that it is the LORD God Almighty who is my strength, my support, and my sustenance, and the *only* One that will supply my every need.

You have stated that you feel I Am very lonely, but you are wrong there. I do feel that I Am standing alone, but I Am far from lonely. I Am very thankful for the ones that God has put in my life, and I do experience great joy in my heart due to some of those relationships, but I actually enjoy being alone with my Heavenly Father. And my preference *is* to be alone with Him.

I Am starting to understand the personality that the LORD has given me, and why I have done certain things all my life. He has been giving me insight on many things and I would like to share some of those things with you if and when the LORD ever allows me.

I believe what I miss most about the relationship I had with you, is being able to talk with someone about your life and feel like they really care, or so I thought. You and Mr. Huff are the only people in this lifetime that I have been so completely trusting of. I shared things with you that I would never desire to speak about with anybody, but for some reason I did with you two. And look what happened!

Since being released from Satan's control God has revealed so much to me about you and La'el Ministries, and I have since found out that you have lied to me about many, many things.

It is a very hard thing to love someone so much, that you would give them all that you are, and everything that you own, just to have that love crushed beneath their feet.

I would think you would understand why I have no desire to put my trust in another human being ever again. That is why I will only put my trust in my LORD God for anything and everything.

However, just because I do not trust you, does not mean the love I had for you is gone. In fact, I Am starting to understand why the LORD has allowed me to love people the way that I do. One day I hope we can share again, but not unless the LORD allows it.

Liz, I Am actually thankful for our relationship, despite the pain I went through, because it has taught me the need to trust only Him. Not that I will not listen to others and be willing to take their advice, but Almighty God and His word is my final authority.

You asked me last night what I meant by the lies and the Truth I referenced in the tape to Cindy, and I would like to go into that as much as the LORD will allow me. The words I spoke on that tape were truly from my heart, and I just felt a need to speak with you so that you might understand that I Am sincere about my feelings towards you all, in spite of what has been revealed since our separation.

TRANSCRIPT FROM 2 JULY 1993 TAPED RECORDING

"This is a very unusual way for me to talk with people. Usually I talk with them face to face or write a letter, but I have never really ever done this where I speak to somebody through a tape. And the LORD has impressed upon me to speak to you Cindy, and to whomever else you decide to share this with.

One thing I want you to realize is that I care about all of you very much. I know you might judge me and look at the things that you have seen me do. The way that I have responded to some of you in public—my seemingly rejection of you, by not calling you, or even by not writing you at times when you have written to me.

You might take that as rejection, that I do not care, and that is not the Truth. If you really knew my heart, you would know that I actually do care about you. Everything that I have ever done with you, with any of you, since I have left that group, has been under the leadership of the Holy Spirit.

...Cindy, you have addressed the issue of the 28th of February; and Liz, you have addressed the 28th of February; and you have both stated that it was not of God. That it was not by the Holy Spirit. That it was of demonic spirits. And it grieves my heart that you could say that. Not because of anything to do with me, but of everything to do with the LORD. My humanness is in much of a grief and sorrow over you folks.

...I Am going to try and not get too emotional where I cannot speak to you, but I Am going to share this song with you that I heard on the radio—the new Christian radio station that came out real soon after we broke-up. It is on the FM station. When I heard this song I thought about you all, and I just want to play it for you...

One last thing I would like to say to each one of you: Cindy, I truly love you. Kim,[18] *I truly love you. Thomas, I truly love you. Wendell, I truly love you. Liz, I truly love you. And Pastor Huff, I truly love you too.*

That love is what God put in my heart for each one of you, and it will not matter whether you hate me or despise me for what the LORD leads me to do. I will do it, because I love Him the most!

I just pray that each one of you will see the Truth and make a decision in your heart that you are going to follow God and not believe the lies. That is my prayer for each one of you.

And I do not know how God is going to show you, but He will get your attention one way or the other. And if it means removing everything He has put in your life to show you that you are not walking with Him, then He will do that. I know that is not the teaching that you have gotten, but God will humble you.

There is such a sorrow in my heart, especially for you, Cindy. I do not really know what is going on in your life. Just by what I feel inside, I feel like you are really, really hurting; and I wish I could do something about it.

But you have got to submit yourself to God, resist the Devil, and he will flee from you. He does not hang around me. I do not have fear, anxiety, or torment. I have a lot of sorrow, and a lot of pain because of lost relationships and that sort of thing, but God is taking care of that. He has replenished that with His strength and His love and comfort.

In all actuality, if I had my greatest desire met, I would prefer to be out in the middle of nowhere, with nobody—just me and the LORD. That is what I would prefer.

I do not have to have human friends anymore. It is nice to have a little support every now and then from people, because God has been leading me into some things that are very hard to do.

He has been speaking through me in ways that would seem like I have a hatred and anger inside of me, but that is His anger and His hatred over the way Satan has so perverted and mocked His word, and has tried so hard to destroy His people.

He is angry about that, and He has displayed that anger through me. That is His pleasure, and that is His will. And my desire is for His will to be accomplished.

I guess this is just my last chance of pleading with you folks to realize, that you are going the wrong way.

And I hope that you will really get before the LORD God and find out what sin is in your life that is keeping you from seeing the Truth. Sin will blind your eyes. It does not matter what it is, it will do it.

I do not want you to go to Hell. I would like to know you in Heaven. However, that is not something I can decide for you.

Liz mentioned in her letter—I have not written her back yet, but I will when the LORD allows me the time to sit down and write her a letter, but she said that I will suffer a lot because of the stand that I have made.

That is probably very true, but I know inside my heart that any suffering I do now, will be for Jesus' sake... The things that I suffered when I was with you folks was because of my own sin and my own ignorance; but now it is so different.

And you know what? I praise God that I Am counted worthy to suffer for His sake. I praise Him for that!! I think it is wonderful that He has counted me worthy...

He answers so many of my prayers. I pray that He might answer the prayer that you will come to the true knowledge of the Truth, and that you will decide to walk in it. That is something you have to decide, but my prayer is that you will see the Truth, and that you make your decision from there as to what you are going to do.

If you do not want the things of God, or want to walk in Truth, then I cannot do anything for you, and neither can God.

I can tell you that if you do decide to walk with Him, you will not be disappointed.

That is all I have to say for right now. Please consider what the LORD is speaking to your heart. It might be your last chance.

And like I asked the Rabbi, 'What if you are wrong?'[19] "

End of Taped Recording

Liz, you know that I Am very willing to be used of the LORD in whatever manner He so chooses. Contrary to what you believe I do not have to be used of the LORD in any obvious way.

Just the fact of being a true follower of the LORD Jesus Christ makes an impact on this evil world system that we live in. But for some reason both you and Cindy think I have some great desire to be used of God in a major way, and that is really not that important to me.

I know I have stated to you in the past that I would truly like to be able to reach other people for Christ, but beyond that, I Am perfectly content in just getting to know my LORD and Master.

It would be a lot easier if I just pretended like I never knew you, and just moved quietly away, never to be seen or heard from again. Obviously, that is not in the LORD'S plan for our lives. After all, He is the one who is in control. Praise God Almighty!! Knowing *that* is what keeps me going every day.

And I want you to know that I really do not take pleasure in creating a scene in public, but if the LORD so desires for that to happen who am I to say "No." I feel like if I was to try and walk away from all of this that the LORD just would not let me go.

I have been a completely changed person ever since the amazing Day of 28 February 1993. The LORD God Almighty poured Himself into me on that night in a mighty and supernatural way, and I do not even want to imply that I fully understand all that took place. I just know that I Am different in a very wonderful way.

Moreover, I do not have any great need to convince you or any other person that it was of God. In your heart you know it is true if the Spirit of Christ resides with you, and if you do not know, then you will; but it will be too late if you wait for the LORD to reveal it before the entire world at the Great White Throne on Judgment Day.[20]

At this point, I do not know if you are truly deceived, or if you are actually aware of all that is going on. But until the LORD God confirms it to me, and establishes it in my heart, I will continue to hope and pray that you are greatly deceived, and that you really do not fully understand what you are saying and doing.

I pray that you are genuinely misguided in your thinking when you say that what took place on the night of 28 February 1993 was under the power and control of demonic spirits.

And I pray that the LORD will have mercy on both you and Cindy for blasphemy against His Holy Spirit if you truly did it out of ignorance.[21] He knows if you truly meant it, and depending on the intentions of your heart will determine your final outcome.

You used to tell me that sometimes you were so afraid that when you stood before the LORD that He would not be able to say to you, "Well done, My good and faithful servant." I just know that if you continue to ignore His pleadings, your worst fear will come upon you. And only God knows for certain if it will indeed come to pass.

You say that you have no doubt that I Am a servant of the LORD. Well if you really mean it, I hope that you, and whoever is still with you, will take heed and seriously consider these words of warning: You are *Walking With The Enemy!* At least he is my Enemy, who is Satan! The great Deceiver! The father of all lies!

I have many other things that I would like to discuss with you, but I do not have the liberty to do that at this time, so I will bring this letter to a close for now.

Nonetheless, I would like to explain some of the accusations I made concerning you and Mr. Huff, but I would prefer to hear his stand on all this. Is it the same as yours? I will not assume that just because you said something, that it goes for him too.

I sincerely hope he does not have the same opinion that you and Cindy seem to have concerning the night of 28 February 1993.

Aside from all that, I still have hope, and I will continue to pray for you as the LORD leads and directs me.

It would be so wonderful if one day we could look back on all we have been through and be thankful to one another, and most especially to Almighty God for delivering us from the Power of Darkness.

Signed and sealed in the presence of a witness on the 14th Day of July in the year of the LORD, One Thousand Nine Hundred and Ninety-Three.

BY THE TIME I HAD SENT THE FIRST EDITION OF THIS BOOK to the publisher in October 1994, I had sent my 5 June 1993 letter to over one thousand different people, most of whom I did not know personally. For all who responded to that letter in a positive way, I sent them a prophecy that God had given me prior to my release from La'el Ministries.

I received two varied responses to that 27 August 1992 prophecy, and there is quite a contrast in their reactions to what the LORD spoke to me on that Day. I have found that since people have varying degrees of the knowledge of the Truth, they can differ greatly in what they believe; thus, they remain divided, as evidenced by the following letters.

I also now understand that if someone is under an evil influence of any kind, it can cause them to reject what God has spoken.

Dear Sister: *July 12, 1993*

I sure do wish you the best, and I have to write to you what I have to write to you—because he is Lord! I am not. "I charge you in Jesus Name"—to leave this stuff alone now.

If you feel God is giving you a prophecy, write it down and leave it there—between you and God. I charge you to submit to your husband, live a quiet life—if he says you should give a prophetic message, do so, but not without his support or approval.

You can glorify God in many ways as you live a quiet and sober life—tending to your housework and teaching your children the fundamentals of faith in Christ. You could consult home-schoolers for materials—you should consult established "Body of Christ" ministries...etc.

You could pursue texts such as "The Blessing"...and other books... And you can pursue many side areas of wholesome Christian living—and you can be a blessing to the body of Christ in so doing.

You can also neglect my words, but your blood is on your own hands because I have given you warning and a sure "charge" in the Holy Spirit. I hope I can talk to you when I don't have to be so bold towards you.

In Jesus Name,
Jonathan

My Dear Sister Cathy, *July 15, 1993*

I bring you glad tidings in the name of our LORD and Savior Jesus Christ. The unspotted Lamb of God, to whom all praises are due Him! For He is worthy to be praised. For truly He is Alpha and Omega, the Beginning and the End.

I received your gift today and your letters. Thank you so very much. For the LORD Jesus truly knows and He does supply our every need. Cathy, I ask the LORD to give it back to you 100 fold—1000 fold. I stand on the blessing of the word of God:

St. Luke 6:38 "Give, and it shall be given unto you; good measure, pressed down, and shaken together, and running over, shall men give unto your bosom. For with the same measure that ye mete, withal it shall be measured to you again."

You have sown abundantly, my dear sister, you shall reap abundantly. Well I have something to share with you my sister, being led of the precious Holy Spirit.

Jeremiah 1:5-10 "Before I formed thee in the belly, I knew thee; and before thou camest forth out of the womb I sanctified thee, and I ordained thee a prophet unto the nations.

Then said I, Ah, LORD God! Behold, I cannot speak: for I Am a child. But the LORD said unto me, Say not, I Am a child: for thou shalt go to all that I shall send thee, and whatsoever I command thee thou shalt speak. Be not afraid of their faces: for I Am with thee to deliver thee, saith the LORD.

Then the LORD put forth His hand, and touched my mouth. And the LORD said unto me, Behold, I have put My words in thy mouth. See, I have this day set thee over the nations and over the kingdoms, to root out, and to pull down, and to destroy, and to throw down, to build, and to plant."

Jeremiah 1:17-19 "Thou therefore gird up thy loins, and arise, and speak unto them all that I command thee: be not dismayed at their faces, lest I confound thee before them.

For, behold, I have made thee this day a defenced city, and an iron pillar, and brazen walls against the whole land, against the kings of Judah, against the princes thereof, against the priest thereof, and against the people of the land. And they shall fight against thee; but they shall not prevail against thee; for I Am with thee, saith the LORD, to deliver thee."

Ezekiel 2:1-9 "And He said unto me, Son of man, stand upon thy feet, and I will speak unto thee. And the Spirit entered into me when He spake unto me, and set me upon my feet, that I heard Him that spake unto me. And He said unto me, Son of man, I send thee to the children of Israel, to a rebellious nation that hath rebelled against Me:

They and their fathers have transgressed against Me, even unto this very day. For they are impudent children and stiff hearted. I do send thee unto them; and thou shalt say unto them, Thus saith the LORD God. And they, whether they will hear, or whether they will forbear, (for they are a rebellious house,) yet shall know that there hath been a prophet among them.

And thou, Son of man, be not afraid of them, neither be afraid of their words, though briers and thorns be with thee, and thou dost dwell among scorpions: be not afraid of their words, nor be dismayed at their looks, though they be a rebellious house.

And thou shalt speak My words unto them, whether they will hear, or whether they will forbear: For they are most rebellious. But thou, Son of man, hear what I say unto thee; Be not thou rebellious like that rebellious house: open thy mouth, and eat that I give thee.

And when I looked, behold, an hand was sent unto me; and, lo, a roll of a book was therein;"

Ezekiel 3:1-27 "Moreover He said unto me, Son of man, eat that thou findest; eat this roll, and go speak unto the house of Israel. So I opened my mouth, and He caused me to eat that roll.

And He said unto me, Son of man, cause thy belly to eat, and fill thy bowels with this roll that I give thee. Then did I eat it; and it was in my mouth as honey for sweetness.

And He said unto me, Son of man, go, get thee unto the house of Israel, and speak with My words unto them.

For thou art not sent to a people of a strange speech and of an hard language, but to the house of Israel; not to many people of a strange speech and of an hard language, whose words thou canst not understand.

Surely, had I sent thee to them, they would have hearkened unto thee. But the house of Israel will not hearken unto thee; For they will not hearken unto Me: for all the house of Israel are impudent and hardhearted.

Behold, I have made thy face strong against their faces, and thy forehead strong against their foreheads. As an adamant harder than flint have I made thy forehead: fear them not, neither be dismayed at their looks, though they be a rebellious house.

Moreover He said unto me, Son of man, all My words that I shall speak unto thee receive in thine heart, and hear with thine ears. And go, get thee to them of the captivity, unto the children of thy people, and speak unto them, and tell them, Thus saith the LORD God; whether they will hear, or whether they will forbear.

Then the Spirit took me up, and I heard behind me a voice of a great rushing, saying, Blessed be the glory of the LORD from His place. I heard also the noise of the wings of the living creatures that touched one another, and the noise of the wheels over against them, and a noise of a great rushing.

So the Spirit lifted me up, and took me away, and I went in bitterness, in the heat of my spirit; but the hand of the LORD was strong upon me. Then I came to them of the captivity at Telabib, that dwelt by the river of Chebar, and I sat where they sat, and remained there astonished among them seven days.

And it came to pass at the end of seven days, that the word of the LORD came unto me, saying, Son of man, I have made thee a watchman unto the house of Israel: therefore hear the word at My mouth, and give them warning from Me.

When I say unto the wicked, Thou shalt surely die; and thou givest him not warning, nor speakest to warn the wicked from his wicked way, to save his life; the same wicked man shall die in his iniquity; but his blood will I require at thine hand.

Yet if thou warn the wicked, and he turn not from his wickedness, nor from his wicked way, he shall die in his iniquity; but thou hast delivered thy soul.

Again, when a righteous man doth turn from his righteousness, and commit iniquity, and I lay a stumbling block before him, he shall die: because thou hast not given him warning, he shall die in his sin, and his righteousness which he hath done shall not be remembered; but his blood will I require at thine hand.

Nevertheless if thou warn the righteous man, that the righteous sin not, and he doth not sin, he shall surely live, because he is warned; also thou hast delivered thy soul.

And the hand of the LORD was there upon me; and He said unto me, Arise, go forth into the plain, and I will there talk with thee. Then I arose, and went forth into the plain: and, behold, the glory of the LORD stood there, as the glory which I saw by the river of Chebar: and I fell on my face.

Then the Spirit entered into me, and set me upon my feet, and spake with me, and said unto me, Go, shut thyself within thine house. But thou, O Son of man, behold, they shall put bands upon thee, and shall bind thee with them, and thou shalt not go out among them: And I will make thy tongue cleave to the roof of thy mouth, that thou shalt be dumb, and shalt not be to them a reprover: for they are a rebellious house.

But when I speak with thee, I will open thy mouth, and thou shalt say unto them, Thus saith the LORD God; He that heareth, let him hear; and he that forbeareth, let him forbear: for they are a rebellious house."

Well my sister, this is what the LORD gave me to give to you. May God continue to use you in a mighty way. I'll be praying for you.

I made this little something for you with love. Silver and Gold, have I none, but such as I have I give unto thee. May the peace of God forever keep you and strengthen you always.

Love,
Sister Deborah

CONTRARY TO WHAT MANY OTHERS BELIEVE, there is only one Truth, only one God, and only One way to get to Him; and if we do not come to Him by way of the True Light we will believe truth mixed with lies.

Should we refuse to allow Almighty God to show us the Truth, we will continue in the Darkness, yet call it the Light. And I contend that many of God's people are in that very condition.

Jonathan suggested that I contact "established 'Body of Christ' ministries" but after prayerful consideration of what many high profile "Christian" organizations and their leadership stands for, they remind me of the Laodicean Church.[22] Not only are they lukewarm, but they are actually furthering the agenda of the Devil by remaining silent on many issues that are adversely affecting the Churches and God's people.

Many of these leaders are promoting the evils of this age by condoning the disgraceful and abominable practices relating to some of the counterfeit "revivals" and "movements," by refusing to make a stand.

Jonathan, did not respond to the following letter that I sent him, but a few years later he did respond to a letter that I had sent out to many different Christians, ministries, and organizations inquiring about the "event" that took place on Father's Day in 1995 at Pensacola, Florida.[23]

My book, *Walking in the True Light,* goes into greater detail regarding this so-called "Pensacola Revival," but essentially, it is very similar to what took place at La'el Ministries, but on a much, much wider scale. It is affecting churches from all the different denominations, various organizations, and many other people—even the non-religious!

It has been reported that as many as ten thousand Southern Baptist churches are even involved in this "movement!" Strangely, many of the established Churches have not even spoken out against it!

I have since addressed specific issues with several Christian leaders and individuals as I was led by the LORD, and even though I was sometimes reluctant about confronting them with what God said to me, I could remain silent and do nothing, or I could *Heed the Call.*

Dear Jonathan, 25 July 1993

I received your letter of 12 July 1993 and first of all, I want to thank you for the concern that you expressed for me. I really do appreciate that very much.

I would also like to say that courage and boldness are very needed qualities in a Christian if they are going to be able to stand against this present evil world system.

I feel that you are truly concerned about me and my family, and I did prayerfully go before the LORD with your concerns; but the words in your letter did not bear witness with the Holy Spirit inside my heart, and with the Truth of the word of God.

I shared your letter with my Husband and he was definitely not in agreement with the following statements that you made.

QUOTE FROM JONATHAN'S LETTER DATED 12 JULY 1993

"I charge you in Jesus' name—to leave this stuff alone now. If you feel God is giving you a prophecy, write it down and leave it there, between you and God...

You can also neglect my words, but your blood is on your own hands because I have given you warning and a sure 'charge' in the Holy Spirit."

My Husband's response to your letter was that I must continue doing what the LORD has called me to do regardless of what other "men" might say. I shared your letter with one of my daughters, and she said, "It sounds like he's on their side." (Referring to La'el Ministries.)

The following Scripture passage is one that the LORD brought to my attention concerning your letter.

Matthew 16:21-23 "From that time forth began Jesus to shew unto His disciples, how that He must go unto Jerusalem, and suffer many things of the elders and chief priest and scribes, and be killed, and be raised again the third day.

Then Peter took Him, and began to rebuke Him, saying, Be it far from Thee, LORD: this shall not be unto Thee.

But He turned, and said unto Peter, Get thee behind Me, Satan: thou art an offense unto Me: for thou savourest not the things that be of God, but those that be of men."

One of the most important lessons that I have learned from my experience with La'el Ministries is that I can trust the Holy Spirit to lead and guide me into all Truth. God's voice will never contradict His word, and it will always bear witness to the Truth. But until we are able to truly discern His voice, we must diligently keep His word and His commandments; and trust God to work in our hearts.

John 16:13 "Howbeit when He, the Spirit of Truth, is come, He will guide you into all Truth: for He shall not speak of Himself; but whatsoever He shall hear, that shall He speak: and He will shew you things to come."

1 John 2:26-27 "These things have I written unto you concerning them that seduce you. But the anointing which ye have received of Him abideth in you, and ye need not that any man teach you:

But as the same anointing teacheth you of all things, and is Truth, and is no lie, and even as it hath taught you, ye shall abide in Him."

I received the following letter from my Husband almost two weeks prior to yours. It states many things that are very prevalent to your concerns of whether I Am in the will of God. And Jonathan, that is truly my greatest desire—to be in the perfect will of God!

My Dear Sister in the LORD, *29 June 1993*

Cathy, I pray the words I write to you, that you will hear them in your heart and not your mind, as I like to do. For He has laid it on my heart to write these words to you now.

I Am truly sorry for my selfish attitudes and emotions that has come forth from my mind and heart. For they have not been of the LORD our God.

For I have been in this earth as swine in a pool of mud. I do seek your forgiveness in all areas of my life, where my lack of sensitivity to the LORD has resulted in causing pain and grief in your life. I will not accept the excuse that I Am just a man trapped in a sinful world, for that would be the easy way out, the earthly way out, and it would not be the Truth.

Cathy, these things were laid on my heart to you concerning myself. I do seek your love and understanding as I continue to grow in the Truth of our Father's love.

I don't seek to drive a wedge between us, or anything that cuts against the grain of your spirit. However, I do realize that is what I have been doing, and I Am truly sorry.

Now, more than ever, is it time to wake up and pay attention to what is going on in this world. Ever mindful to the presence of the LORD in our daily life; and always being sensitive to the gentle and loving guidance of the Holy Spirit that our God in Heaven has provided us with.

But Cathy, in my ignorance I have allowed myself to give into the ways of this world. These very words were spoken by you to me. I did not accept them then, for my pride would not let me hear, but I do now. Thank God!

Cathy, we have to be strong for the causes of God. It would please Satan just fine for you to be defeated and to quit pursuing the mission God has called you to do. For divorce and separation to move into our lives would only enhance Satan and answer the prayers of those who curse and hate our LORD God Almighty.

Cathy, Satan will use whatever means possible to accomplish his goals: your children, your husband, your church, your community, and the law of the land.

So continue to be cautious of others and always to be sensitive to the Holy Spirit and the WILL OF GOD; ever mindful of your responsibility to reprove those things that are not of the LORD.

I truly thank God for His faithful servant placed in my path, that He so graciously gave to me as my wife.

I thank God for using you as an instrument to bring His word into my heart. Praise God!

I didn't fully tell you just how beautiful and touching the card was that you gave me on Father's Day. It really meant a lot to me. It was one of the most touching things that I have ever received. The words you spoke through that card were filled with your love for me and the sweet fragrance of our LORD.

I Am truly sorry that I have questioned your love or motivations. Cathy, I do love you and I do ask you for your patience and understanding in all things. God Almighty and all powerful will lead us through all of our tribulations. Praise God, for He is so wonderful!

Your friend in the LORD,
Your Husband

Jonathan, I do respect my Husband as the authority that God has put over me; and I trust the LORD completely for him. He has been very much of a protection for me, and at times a great comfort.

Moreover, God has used my Husband in many ways to confirm what He has spoken to my heart. He has been in agreement with every letter that I have sent out to other people, and if my Husband opposes anything the LORD leads me to do, I will not proceed until I prayerfully go before my Heavenly Father in His word and by prayer, and seek His counsel on the matter at hand.

I have full confidence that the LORD God will either work in my heart, or in my Husband's, until we are both in agreement, so that the perfect will of the LORD can be accomplished through us.

God also knew I would continue to have much opposition to what He has called me to do, so He used that letter to help strengthen me. And it certainly did! His letter does take precedence over yours, especially since it is in accordance with God's word.

I Peter 3:1-2 "Likewise, ye wives, be in subjection to your own Husbands; that, if any obey not the word, they also may without the word be won by the conversation of the wives; while they behold your chaste conversation coupled with fear."

Although, your letter was also very encouraging for me. It shows me even more that the Devil is very upset about the stand I have made, and he is trying to get to me by using someone that I care about, in an attempt to place doubt in my heart about what God has said to me.

However, I have serious reservations about you at this time. I pray that you will go before the LORD God Almighty and sincerely ask Him why you are so opposed to the "prophecy" that He gave me.

You place much emphasis on the thoughts and opinions of men, but the most important question I have for you is, how much time do you actually take to read God's word with a humble and sincere heart so that He can make it grow into His wisdom and understanding?

I have many scriptures that I would love to share with you, but I do not feel that now is the time for that. However, I have chosen a few verses that I hope you will seriously consider and meditate on.

John 1:1,14 "In the beginning was the Word, and the Word was with God, and the Word was God...And the Word was made flesh, and dwelt among us, (and we beheld His glory, the glory as of the only begotten of the Father,) full of grace and Truth."

Revelation 19:7-13 "Let us be glad and rejoice, and give honour to Him: for the marriage of the Lamb is come, and His wife hath made herself ready. And to her was granted that she should be arrayed in fine linen, clean and white: for the fine linen is the righteousness of saints.

And he saith unto me, Write, Blessed are they which are called unto the marriage supper of the Lamb.

And he saith unto me, These are the true sayings of God. And I fell at his feet to worship him. And he said unto me, See thou do it not:

I Am thy fellow servant, and of thy brethren that have the Testimony of Jesus: worship God: For the Testimony of Jesus is the Spirit of prophecy.

And I saw Heaven opened, and behold a white horse; and He that sat upon him was called Faithful and True, and in righteousness He doth Judge and make War. His eyes were as a flame of fire, and on His head were many crowns; and He had a name written, that no man knew, but He Himself.

And He was clothed with a vesture dipped in blood: and His name is called THE WORD OF GOD."

Jonathan, I Am sorry if I seem prideful or arrogant because that is truly not my intention. If I feel the LORD is leading me to say or do something, I *must* "Heed the Call" whether it pleases men or not.

If I Am wrong in my perceptions of you, I ask for your forgiveness for not being sensitive enough to the Holy Spirit. Although, if I Am right I hope that you will take heed to what I have spoken.

Only Truth will prevail, and I hope and pray that you will be found walking in Truth. If not, you will be so ashamed when you stand before the LORD Jesus Christ on the great and dreadful Day of the LORD.

I Am not beyond being deceived, but because of the lessons that I have learned through my experiences with La'el Ministries I Am very much on guard and extremely cautious about what I believe.

After *Walking With The Enemy* for three years, I Am very much aware of many of Satan's deceptive tactics to worm his way into my thoughts in order to affect my actions; and I praise God that He has allowed His Truth to prevail in my life!

I will always prayerfully consider anything that you have to say, but the LORD God Almighty is my Master, my Redeemer, and my Supreme Judge! And His word is my final authority!

Praise the precious name of Jesus Christ my LORD! May the grace of Almighty God be with you as you walk with Him in Truth!

"AND THE SPIRIT AND THE BRIDE SAY, COME. AND LET HIM THAT HEARETH SAY, COME. AND LET HIM THAT IS ATHIRST, COME. AND WHOSOEVER WILL, LET HIM TAKE THE WATER OF LIFE FREELY."

Signed and sealed in the presence of a witness on the 27th Day of July in the year of the LORD, One Thousand Nine Hundred and Ninety-Three.

THIS NEXT LETTER WAS SENT TO LIZ'S HUSBAND, whom she apparently never considered her God-given husband. They were divorced soon after I sent him this letter, but I really do not know if he was influenced by it.

Dear Thomas, 2 August 1993

God has led me to write you this letter, and I pray you will listen with your heart, and not with your mind. Just from past experience, I know that my mind has lied to me and led me into believing many things that were not of the LORD or in accordance with His word.

It all started with a thought that came from the Devil, and once I gave into his lies, and held onto it as being mine, my heart began to be darkened by the deceitfulness of sin. If someone was to have spoken the Truth to me, I was not able to hear it, so I continued to believe the lies.

When I was finally broken enough by the effects of my own sin, the LORD was able to get through to my unbelieving heart. And I praise God for His mercy and grace, as He is the only One that rescued me!

The passage that says, *"By grace are ye saved through faith; and that not of yourselves, it is the gift of God. Not of works, lest any man should boast,"* has become so real for me, in a way I could have never imagined.

I have always desired to walk with the LORD God Almighty in Truth with all honesty and sincerity, and I believe you know that. I truly love the LORD Jesus Christ immensely, not because of what I have done, but because of Him and everything that He has done.

I have begun to understand what Jesus Christ actually did while He was on this earth, what He is still doing, and what He will do in the future. Thus, there is such a thankfulness in my heart for all that He is!

Moreover, I Am very certain that He desires to do for you what He has done for me. Namely, to set you free to love and worship Him.

I don't know what your feelings are about me, or what you think about the stand that I have made, but since you have not made any attempts to contact me, I can only assume that you are of the same opinion as Liz, since you still seem to be supporting her.

The following is an excerpt from a letter that Liz had sent me which explains what she really thinks about what took place on the night of 28 February 1993. The letter was dated 9 April 1993, but postmarked 13 May 1993. I guess she was not sure about sending it to me.

EXCERPT FROM LETTER TO CATHY FROM LIZ

"When the message in tongues came forth that night, I was awestruck! I have heard demonic tongues before, but never in such intensity! When you stood up and came to the front, I saw something in you that absolutely made me shudder—I saw Ruth.[24] *There she was in living color! At that particular moment, there was such a fear that ripped through me.*

I was already furious at myself for not doing what God had specifically told me to do earlier—To stand up in front of you and command in Jesus' name by what spirit you spoke. At this point, however, I must confess, I was curious!

All during the 'prophecy' you gave—I say 'prophecy' because God's word says that tongues plus interpretation equals prophecy—The word of God kept rising up inside my heart.

I knew there was no stopping you; no way at that particular moment that you would listen to reason. You were under the control of the same demonic spirit that has oppressed you all your life, the same spirit that held you captive that night at Dairy Queen.[25]

All this was nothing more than a continuation of the same events that had occurred all weekend. God specifically warned us to be on guard against the tactics of our enemy, as we were under direct attack.

Cathy, as soon as you believed you had a word from God, you were not even open to reason. During your walk with Jesus, you have so greatly desired the spiritual gifts, the things of the spirit, that the affection and desire for spiritual things has been the very thing that Satan has always used to deceive you."

In case you do not fully understand the statements she made to me in this letter, I will make it a little clearer for you. She has attributed the events that occurred on the night of 28 February 1993 as being from demonic spirits rather than from the Spirit of Christ.

You were there, along with other witnesses, and I hope that you will be very careful about what you say happened in my home on that evening. I Am sure you know that blasphemy of the Holy Spirit is the only unforgivable sin in this world and the world to come.

I do not have a need to convince you that what occurred on that Night was of the LORD, because I Am sure you already know in your heart. Nevertheless, whether anyone believes me or not, God knows, and that is all that matters as far as I Am concerned.

If you are still inclined to believe the lie as stated in Liz's letter concerning that extraordinary evening of 28 February 1993, then you are in danger of eternal separation from the one, true, and only living God! And I do not desire that for you, or for any one else.

Let the word of God be the Light that you use to judge all things to see whether they be of God or not. Please do not allow someone else to steal what the LORD has spoken to your heart.

Since Jesus Christ came to this earth in order to reveal our innermost thoughts and intents, all men will be without excuse on the Day that they will bow before Him at His Throne.

God's people need to understand that the New Covenant that Jeremiah the Prophet had spoke of has been fulfilled because of the obedience of Jesus Christ to the will of His Heavenly Father.

And Jesus proved His awesome love not only to Almighty God, but also to all of mankind, by His willingness to give His life on the cross at Calvary so that we may be reunited with our Heavenly Father.

Jeremiah 31:31-34 "Behold, the days come, saith the LORD, that I will make a New Covenant with the house of Israel, and with the house of Judah:

Not according to the covenant that I made with their fathers in the day that I took them by the hand to bring them out of the land of Egypt; which My covenant they brake, although I was an Husband unto them, saith the LORD:

But this shall be the covenant that I will make with the house of Israel; after those days, saith the LORD, I will put My law in their inward parts, and write it in their hearts; and will be their God, and they shall be My people.

And they shall teach no more every man his neighbour, and every man his brother, saying, Know the LORD: for they shall all know Me, from the least of them unto the greatest of them, saith the LORD: for I will forgive their iniquity, and I will remember their sin no more."

Thomas, you know that I have sincerely loved you with a brotherly love, and I still do very much. That is the reason why I Am earnestly appealing to you right now. I truly care about you, and I do not want to see Satan given the authority to drag you to Hell with him.

The Devil has lied to you so much, and for so long, but it does not have to continue! If you truly submit yourself to God with all your heart, soul, and mind, Satan *must* relinquish his control over you.

The sin that you are allowing to remain in your life is what is blinding your eyes to the Truth, and it will only get worse if you continue in your sin and ignore what I Am saying to you.

I would like to show you an example from God's word of what happens to someone who claims to be walking in the Truth, but is actually submitted to the Devil and the lusts of their own flesh.

And if you ever see this happen in your life, this can be a sign that you are, without a doubt, *WALKING WITH THE ENEMY!*

Romans 1:18-2:2 "For the wrath of God is revealed from Heaven against all ungodliness and unrighteousness of men, who hold the Truth in unrighteousness; because that which may be known of God is manifest in them; for God hath shewed it unto them.

For the invisible things of Him from the creation of the world are clearly seen, being understood by the things that are made, even His eternal power and Godhead; so that they are without excuse:

Because that, when they knew God, they glorified Him not as God, neither were thankful; but became vain in their imaginations, and their foolish heart was darkened.

Professing themselves to be wise, they became fools, and changed the glory of the uncorruptible God into an image made like to corruptible man, and to birds, and four footed beasts, and creeping things.

Wherefore God also gave them up to uncleanness through the lusts of their own hearts, to dishonour their own bodies between themselves: Who changed the Truth of God into a lie, and worshipped and served the creature more than the Creator, who is blessed forever. Amen.

For this cause God gave them up unto vile affections: for even their women did change the natural use into that which is against nature: And likewise also the men, leaving the natural use of the woman, burned in their lust one toward another; men with men working that which is unseemly, and receiving in themselves that recompense of their error which was meet.

And even as they did not like to retain God in their knowledge, God gave them over to a reprobate mind, to do those things which are not convenient;

Being filled with all unrighteousness, fornication, wickedness, covetousness, maliciousness; full of envy, murder, debate, deceit, malignity; whispers, backbiters, haters of God, despiteful, proud, boasters, inventors of evil things, disobedient to parents, without understanding, covenant-breakers, without natural affection, implacable, unmerciful:

Who knowing the judgment of God, that they which commit such things are worthy of death, not only do the same, but have pleasure in them that do them.

Therefore thou art inexcusable, O man, whosoever thou art that judgest: for wherein thou judgest another, thou condemnest thyself; for thou that judgest doest the same things. But we are sure that the judgment of God is according to Truth against them which commit such things."

The wages of sin is death, whether you are deceived or not! Death tried to get its hold on me, but praise God, greater is He who is in me than he who is in the world! And only by the grace of the LORD God Almighty was I delivered from the power of Darkness.

I would love to talk with you about all the ways that Satan tried to steal, kill, and destroy my life, but as long as you are submitting yourself to sin and iniquity, you will not be able to understand.

In fact, you may even start to think that I Am the one who is *Walking With The Enemy,* and that I Am the one who is deceived, and that I Am the one who is in danger of going to Hell.

However, one thing that is very certain, we will all stand before the Judgment seat of Christ on that Day of the LORD, and be required to give an account of our lives to Him.

It will be such a terrible day for those who have chosen to deny the LORD. The two most important questions we need to ask ourselves: Which side will we be standing on? And will the LORD be able to say to you or to me, "WELL DONE, MY GOOD AND FAITHFUL SERVANT?"

Ecclesiastes 12:13-14 "Let us hear the conclusion of the whole matter: Fear God, and Keep His Commandments: for this is the whole duty of man. For God shall bring every work into judgment, with every secret thing, whether it be good, or whether it be evil."

Satan will not go unhindered any longer! In the LORD'S timing, Jesus Christ will crush Satan beneath His feet; and if you happen to be *Walking With The Enemy,* you will get crushed too!

The battle lines are being drawn in this war for the saints. The LORD God Almighty is asking His people to make a stand for Him without compromise. He requires our complete allegiance to Him.

You need to realize that God is giving you a chance to see the error of your ways so that you can turn from your sin. Please notice what God said to King Solomon after the Temple was completed.

II Chronicles 7:14 "If My people, which are called by My name, shall humble themselves, and pray, and seek My face, and turn from their wicked ways; then will I hear from Heaven, and will forgive their sin, and will heal their land."

I know you were taught by Mr. Huff, just as I was for the three years I was with them, that sin is not acts we do or don't do, but sin is simply not *believing* God. That is such a perversion of the Truth and a lie from the father of lies, Satan himself! Don't you know that the devils *believe* God and they absolutely shudder with fear?!

I really don't know what more I can say to you to help you to realize and understand that I Am sincerely concerned about you, and everyone else from La'el Ministries for that matter.

The LORD has been trying to warn all of you to have nothing to do with the works of Darkness, but obviously, the Devil has a very strong hold on you. I hope you see this as your opportunity to be released from the chains that are binding you!

Please do not pass up this chance to be set free from the power of sin, death, and Satan! I Am begging you to REPENT OF ALL YOUR SINS and turn back to the LORD God Almighty! Should you refuse, you will be so ashamed when you bow before the LORD on that Day.

I know that God loves you, and greatly desires for you to walk with Him in peace and righteousness; and to be filled with the joy of His Holy Spirit. After all, that is truly what the kingdom of God is all about.

But the only way to have true peace and to walk in perfect unity, is to humbly allow the LORD to cut away the evil influences in our lives. Otherwise, Satan will still be able to lead our hearts away from God.

God's word is so true, and if you truly submit yourself to the LORD God above, and resist the Devil, he must leave you alone. Not that he won't try some other way to worm his way back into your life, but if you stay before Almighty God in His word and by prayer, He will be your protection, your direction, and your support if you let Him.

Please give *my God* a try! I love you and I really don't want you to die and go to Hell. If you are willing to put your trust in the LORD, He is so faithful to those who love Him. It is so exciting to worship God in Spirit and in Truth. I thought I was when I was with La'el Ministries, but I was *so* wrong. The difference is like NIGHT AND DAY!

I hope you will take heed to my warnings. Your eternal life is dependent on what you do. I have spoken what the LORD has laid on my heart, and I hope you sense the urgency with which I speak. Please listen to what the LORD God may be speaking to your heart.

I Am sorry if I seem prideful or arrogant because that is truly not my intent. If I didn't care I would just be silent and do nothing, but I do care very much for all of you. I will continue to pray for you and the other members of La'el Ministries as the LORD directs me.

Signed and sealed in the presence of a witness on the 4th Day of August in the year of the LORD, One Thousand Nine Hundred and Ninety-Three.

AFTER I FOUND OUT THE TRUTH about La'el Ministries and Mr. Huff, I had such a great burden to warn others. The Devil has tried very hard to stand in my way, but I thank God that Satan has not succeeded.

The following letter was sent to a man who occasionally came to our Bible Study meetings; and even though I really had no idea how to contact him, the LORD amazingly allowed me to meet up with him.

Dear Philip, 10 August 1993

I really want to thank you for calling me the other day. It was wonderful to hear from you. I have had a lot of opposition to the stand that I have made against Satan, and it was very comforting to hear words of support and encouragement instead of condemnation.

I have prayed for you, especially since the LORD revealed the Truth to me about La'el Ministries. I had such a strong desire to get in contact with you, but I really didn't know how.

I had gone through the phone book one day looking for your name and number, but after I could not find it, the LORD told me to just be patient, and that He would put me in touch with you when it was time. So, I did not give it another thought.

While looking through the tapes at the Baptist Book Store[26] I had already decided I was not going to get another one, but for some reason I kept looking. When I heard your voice behind me, and I saw who you were, I knew exactly why I had been delayed there.

The LORD God is so neat! He arranged that meeting! And I know *that* without a doubt! I was so excited when I went out to my car to get my 5 June 1993 letter for you. I was thanking God the whole way! It has been so fascinating to watch the LORD work!! He is so incredible!

I mentioned when you called last Friday that I had sensed you were a little apprehensive about running into me; and I just want to let you know that I understand more than you might think.

I hope you are always very cautious with all "men," and I pray that you will be ever mindful of the presence of the Holy Spirit.

I now realize that even the most honest and sincere person can be deceived into believing a lie, and walk in that lie, while being convinced that it is the truth. I know, because I did it for three years!

Of course, it was due to my own sin that caused me to be blind to the real Truth. And due to my experiences with some of the members of La'el Ministries, I understand the dangers of sin in a very real way.

I also know the saving grace of my LORD Jesus Christ! And I Am certain that Almighty God will deliver anyone that calls upon the name of the LORD from a sincere and repentant heart.

Whether you can believe it or not, I Am actually very thankful for the time I spent with La'el Ministries because my faith in God is so much stronger as a result of the tremendous trials I endured.

He is truly the only reason why I was able to bear the emotional, physical, and spiritual pain that I went through while I was with Huff and Liz for those three years. It is also because of the LORD that I Am even able to discuss any of this with you now.

I praise the LORD God Almighty every day for the safety and protection that He allowed me and my family to walk in, despite the fact that we were *Walking With The Enemy!*

Because I sincerely love the LORD God Almighty, and truly desire to worship Him in Spirit and in Truth, in His perfect timing He delivered me from the power that Darkness had over me.

Praise the mighty name of Jesus Christ my LORD, who is the perfect Lamb of God who came to take away the sin of the world!!!

God is All-Powerful! God is in control! And it does not matter whether anyone else believes it or not. The Truth will prevail one great and glorious Day, and then the whole world will be able to see how the "True Light" has overpowered the Darkness!

It has been so exciting to walk with the LORD God in Truth; and as He reveals Himself to me, I gain more wisdom and understanding of His ways, which causes me to love, worship, and adore Him even more.

My relationship with the LORD and my Father in Heaven is so wonderfully different since the night of 28 February 1993. The word of God has become so real for my life in a way that I could have never thought possible! Praise God!

I have noted a journal entry that I wrote before my association with La'el Ministries was severed to help you to understand. It was written two weeks prior to the confrontation that my Husband and I had with Mr. Huff, Liz, Cindy, and Wendell on 2 March 1993.

EXCERPT FROM JOURNAL 16 FEBRUARY 1993

I had asked the LORD, at the request of Liz, to tell me if I could trust the people He has placed around me.

Liz said that when things get crazy all around here, I can go back to this book and read what the LORD said.

The LORD is so neat! He did not even address anyone else. He said to look at me and take notice of my behavior. He then brought up these two scriptures:

II Timothy 1:7 "For God hath not given us the spirit of fear; but of power, and of love, and of a sound mind."

I Corinthians 13:1-13 "Though I speak with the tongues of men and of angels, and have not charity [which is God's love in us], I Am become as sounding brass, or a tinkling cymbal.

And though I have the gift of prophecy, *and understand all mysteries, and all knowledge; and though I have all faith, so that I could remove mountains, and have not charity, I Am nothing.*

And though I bestow all my goods to feed the poor, and though I give my body to be burned, and have not charity, it profiteth me nothing.

Charity suffereth long, and is kind; charity envieth not; charity vaunteth not itself, is not puffed up, doth not behave itself unseemly,

Seeketh not her own, is not easily provoked, thinketh no evil; Rejoiceth not in iniquity, but rejoiceth in the Truth; beareth all things, believeth all things, hopeth all things, endureth all things.

Charity never faileth: but whether there be prophecies, *they shall fail; whether there be* tongues, *they shall cease; whether there be* knowledge, *it shall vanish away.*

For we know in part, and we prophesy in part. But when that which is perfect is come, then that which is in part shall be done away.

When I was a child, I spake as a child, I understood as a child, I thought as a child: But when I became a man, I put away childish things. For now we see through a glass, darkly; but then face to face:

Now I know in part; but then shall I know even as also I Am known. And now abideth faith, hope, charity, these three; but the greatest of these is charity."

The LORD told me if I do not see these things happening in my life that the Enemy is attacking me and I must put on my armor. He then led me to the following scripture.

Ephesians 6:10-20 "Finally, my brethren, be strong in the LORD, and in the power of His might. Put on the whole armour of God, that ye may be able to stand against the wiles of the Devil.

For we wrestle not against flesh and blood, but against principalities, against powers, against the rulers of the Darkness of this world, against spiritual wickedness in high places.

Wherefore take unto you the whole armour of God, that ye may be able to withstand in the evil day, and having done all, to stand.

Stand therefore, having your loins girt about with Truth, and having on the breastplate of righteousness; And your feet shod with the preparation of the gospel of peace;

Above all, taking the shield of faith, wherewith ye shall be able to quench all the fiery darts of the wicked. And take the helmet of salvation, and the sword of the Spirit, which is the Word of God:

Praying always with all prayer and supplication in the Spirit, and watching thereunto with all perseverance and supplication for all saints; And for me, that utterance may be given unto me, that I may open my mouth boldly, to make known the mystery of the gospel, For which I Am an ambassador in bonds: that therein I may speak boldly, as I ought to speak."

Dear Father, *16 February 1993*

There is one thing I do want to state here and that is this: I thank You for Your love and the wonderful gifts of Your Holy Spirit.

I know this is a real battle that we are in, and it's a matter of life and death. Elisha[27] (Liz) warned me yesterday that I was the one that was wanting to get into this, so I better get ready for the suffering part. But LORD, it's not that I want to get into all this junk. I just realize for right now, it comes along with getting to know You and Your kingdom.

I would never ever want to give back what I know about You. And I know because I chose to walk this path, that I will get to know You in a more real way.

The evil junk I could do without, and one Day I know we will, but all I ask of You, is that You keep pouring out Your mercy and grace and Truth on all of us, and give us Your strength to endure whatever is up ahead.

I Am learning to totally depend on You, and I know if I am going to survive all this I MUST DEPEND ON YOU.

Help us LORD!
Because we so need You!
Cathy

PS. I will never forget what my LORD Jesus did on that Cross and I will always be indebted to Him for that display of love for me, and for the whole world.
End of Journal Excerpts

On Tuesday night, the second of March 1993, my Husband and I met with Huff, Liz, Cindy, and Wendell to discuss what had happened at our previous Bible study on 28 February 1993. I really had no idea what would transpire during that meeting, but praise God He did!

I just knew that Liz said she needed to share some important things with my Husband and I. She really wanted to discuss it privately, but in light of what took place that past Sunday evening at Bible Study, I felt that it was no longer a private matter.

I asked Liz since the LORD had told her that He required her presence when Mr. Huff ministered to another person, did the same apply to her. She said she didn't have a problem with that, but she was still very persistent in trying to discuss the situation.

Finally, I had to insist that I was not going to talk with her about anything until Huff was present. That night, (1 March 1993) Huff had to work with Liz's father, which is why we could not get together then.

Huff, Liz, and Cindy came over the following evening, and I was hoping that they would have invited Thomas, but they did not.

Prior to our meeting, I had called Wendell to see if he would be interested in coming over since we were going to be discussing the events of that previous Sunday night. He was most eager to join us, but he was disappointed that they had not informed him about the meeting.

I told him that I had a feeling they preferred him not to be there, but I wanted him there, and so did God. However, since God told me that they would not come over if they knew he was going to be there, I asked him not to show up until he saw their car in my driveway.

We usually taped all of our meetings except on Wednesday, since we normally just prayed on those nights. I was very doubtful that Mr. Huff would want any of our discussion on tape, but the LORD told me to have the tape player set up anyway.

The following is the transcript of what was tape recorded during the first part of our meeting on that very memorable Tuesday evening, when the "True Light" pierced the Darkness! Again!

TRANSCRIPT OF 2 MARCH 1993

Cathy "I know when I first came to this group that I was crying out to the LORD to relieve me of some of the burdens that were in my heart.

And I know I gave you a letter—" [Speaking to Mr. Huff.]

Liz "I would like to stop you here."

H... "Let her talk please." [Please note: H... is my Husband.]

Cathy "Could you at least—"

Liz "No, I'd like to stop here, cause I have an objection to the taping."

H... "Why?"

Cathy "Why? Is there anything you have to hide Elisha (Liz), as to the reason why you don't want anything on this tape?"

Liz "No, there is not, but everyone in our church is here."

H... "No, they are not."

Cathy "Not everybody. I wish everybody was here, but they're not. And I wish you had addressed this issue Sunday night, but you didn't. And that's because you do have something to hide."

Liz "No, I don't."

Cathy "Then let's tape it."

Liz "No, I'm not in agreement with the taping."

Cathy "Could you state why?"

Liz "Yes, because unless this is for this church which is present here—"

Cathy "Why the secrecy? Why can't the Church know exactly—You told me that—"

Liz "The church *is* here, Cathy."

Cathy "No, you told me—"

Liz "God's word is specific here."

Cathy "No, you told me that anything that you say to me, anything you say to her, (referring to Cindy) could be preached on the house, uh, mountaintops!"

Liz "Yes, it can."

Cathy "So then, what's the problem?"

Liz "Because the only reason you are making this tape is not for this church, but for members outside of this church."

Cathy "That's a lie!"

Liz "And God—"

Cathy "I Am not! I Am not that type of person! And you have known me for three years..."

Liz "Church affairs out of the church..." (Both of us were talking at the same time.)

Cathy "That's crazy! You are lying! I Am sorry. That is not what I— How can you judge the intents of my heart?"

Liz "I'm not judging the intents of your heart."

Cathy "You are saying this is for outside purposes. If there is anything that happened, why would you care? You said the mountaintops! The mountaintops is everywhere!"

Liz "Well, what does God's word say, Cathy?"

Cathy "It says that anything—That any secret thing will be revealed! *Every* secret thing! Thank God!!!"

Liz "It says that things will be taken care of in the church. *That's* what it says."

Cathy "All right."

Liz "It says we're not a part of the world."

Cathy "Thank the LORD I Am not a part of this world!"

Liz "And it says that if things cannot be judged, that is to our shame."

Cathy "And you know what? In the body of Christ, anybody is welcome. In the body of Christ, anybody is welcome to come into this house."

Liz "But the world is not the body of Christ, Cathy."

Cathy "God wants them to be though!

He loved us so much—He loved the world so much that He gave His only begotten Son, that whosoever believeth in Him, will not perish, but have everlasting life! And how will the world hear, but we tell them! May I ask you that?"

Huff "Is this going to be telling the world about Jesus Christ?"

Cathy "I Am not going to broadcast this to the world.

And if what you are saying, if it's for the Church's sake, that is exactly who it will be for. If you want the whole body to hear it, I don't have any problem with that at all."

Liz "I think you made every effort to be sure that everyone that's within this body, that you said God said should be here, is here."

Cathy "No, there are some other people I wish were here, but God is our witness and so it really doesn't matter."

Liz "Then why do we need the tape?"

Cathy "Because you've got something to hide.

And we don't have to have the tape...I don't want to get into an arguing match. And it doesn't matter."

AT THE START OF THIS MEETING I had truly hoped we would be able to work out our differences and that Mr. Huff would acknowledge and repent of the sin that the LORD had addressed during our last meeting on 28 February 1993, but regretfully that was not to be.

Instead, Mr. Huff asked my Husband if he had his permission to speak with me, something of which he had never done before in the past. Then he denied all the accusations that I had made against him.

However, when he realized that he was totally losing my support altogether, he changed his mind and admitted to everything that I had accused him of during the course of the evening. Then he proceeded to apologize to each person in the room, including me and my Husband.

My Husband asked him if he was sorry, then why the continued secrecy and lies. Under his breath, "Pastor" Huff made the statement: "I'm already dead."

About that time, Liz demanded for me to say whether or not the Holy Spirit resided in Pastor Huff. I said, "I won't make that kind of judgment—God knows the truth and that's all that matters."

Then Mr. Huff asks me, "Well, which *'god'* do you serve?" At that, I got really excited and I said, "By your own words you are condemned! If you have to ask me which 'god' I serve, you don't serve the same one that I do! You serve Satan!! And you are of the spirit of anti-Christ!" Strangely, neither Huff nor Liz denied these accusations.

At that point, my focus immediately turned to Wendell, and I started pleading with him that this was a battle for his very soul. However, because of everything that was revealed that night, he was just an emotional wreck and he could not even respond to me.

Cindy, on the other hand, seemed like she was in some kind of a trance. She was so different than I had ever seen her before; and she could hardly respond, except at the end when she just started repeating the statement, "If you can't forgive your brother, God can't forgive you."

As for Liz, except the initial dialogue at the start of our meeting, and her question about the Holy Spirit, she was unusually silent. At one point during the meeting, I got a little facetious with her and I said, "What's the matter, *cat* got your tongue?"

Needless to say, in light of all that was revealed, I could no longer support the leaders of La'el Ministries. I did not realize until later that everyone in the Bible study group would be rejecting me because of my stand against Satan; and even though I had sincerely grown to love these people, I could no longer have any associations with them as long as they were *Walking With The Enemy* of my God.

Philip, I want to thank you again for your thoughtfulness in contacting me to voice your support, and I would like to encourage you with this passage from the Holy Scriptures.

II Corinthians 10:4-6 "(For the weapons of our warfare are not carnal, but mighty through God to the pulling down of strong holds;)

Casting down imaginations, and every high thing that exalteth itself against the knowledge of God, and bringing into captivity every thought to the obedience of Christ; and having in a readiness to revenge all disobedience, when your obedience is fulfilled."

Thank you for taking the time to read this, and I do welcome any response that you might have. I pray that Almighty God will continue to bless you and your music ministry as you submit yourself to Him with your whole heart, soul, and mind. May He pour out His abundant love, mercy, and grace upon you as you serve Him in Truth.

Acknowledge the LORD God Almighty in all that you do, and He will direct your path into the Only Way that is worth going, into the real Truth that is worth knowing, and into the Everlasting Life that is worth having with God the Holy Father. And the only way to obtain it is through Jesus Christ His Son, the Eternal King!

BLESSING, AND HONOR, AND GLORY, AND POWER, AND MIGHT
BE UNTO HIM THAT SITTETH UPON THE THRONE, AND UNTO THE LAMB,
FOREVER AND EVER! AMEN!

Signed and sealed in the presence of a witness on the 13th Day of August in the year of the LORD, One Thousand Nine Hundred and Ninety-Three.

I NEVER HEARD BACK FROM PHILIP, so I really don't know what his response was, but I sincerely hope he believed my Testimony.

What prompted me to write the following letter is after I was questioned by Mr. Huff's wife as to why I was taking my children out of the public school—she being a teacher of that system.

Dear Becky, 17 August 1993

I feel very compelled to explain to you why my Husband and I have decided to start teaching our children at home again. I know when you came over yesterday you seemed to be very concerned about them not going to the public school this year, even to the degree that you felt they would be deprived of many opportunities they will need to be prepared for life in this world.

In this letter, I would like to calm your fears and alleviate the concerns you seem to be having about my family, and give you my perspective on the matter of training my own children.

My desire to teach them at home is in no way meant to condemn anyone else. It is a very personal decision, and I know I will give an account to God for what I have done with the children He has given me.

I have always taken that responsibility very seriously. Not that I have done it perfectly, but I thank the LORD God that He has been so kind and patient with me as I learn how to bring up my children in the way that they should go, so that when they are old they will not depart from the ways of Almighty God.

Considering all that is taking place in the public schools, I now understand why the LORD has led me to teach my children at home. (Please note this was written before all the school shootings.)

My greatest desire for my children is that they will truly love and serve the LORD God Almighty with their whole heart, soul, mind, and strength, and that they will love their neighbor as themselves.

And I Am sorry to say that the atmosphere and curriculum of public education does not promote the values and principles that I have tried so hard to instill in my children. In fact, it tears them down instead of building them up.

However, this is just a reflection of the society that we live in, not necessarily on the individual teachers or staff. It would be so different if our culture was based on Godly principles; and you know, as well as I do, that it is not.

Moreover, with the leadership that this country is under, and the apathy of those who could make a difference, it will only get worse.

It is very evident that Satan has a hand in every segment of our society, including the public schools. What is even more disheartening is that he has such a strong influence within many of the churches, "Christian" ministries, and religious organizations.

In light of the Times, I feel that one of the most important jobs I have as a mother is to prepare my children to be *in* this world, but not to be *a part* of this world, or unduly affected by it.

In order to equip them for this life, I feel that the wisdom of God is more important to obtain than the wisdom of man, or the wisdom of this world. My main objective is to influence my children to set their affections on the things above, rather than on the things of this earth.

I want my children to truly worship their Heavenly Father in Spirit and in Truth. I want them to know that they can trust and rely on the LORD Jesus Christ for all their needs, no matter how big or small, or how unimportant they may seem to be.

I Am not sure if I have ever discussed this with you or not, but it was due to the persuasive abilities of Liz and your husband as to why I quit teaching my children in the first place.

Due to this incredible control they had over me, they were able to influence my thoughts and decisions about every aspect of my life—even in regard to my beloved Husband and children.

They would always use the Scriptures to help establish their philosophies with me; and because of the experiences that I went through with them, I see how easy it is to be deceived if you are not truly grounded and established in the Truth of the word of God.

I believe in my heart that God expects me to protect and guard my children from the evils of this world until they can stand on their own. They are not yet mature enough, or strong enough in the LORD, to know and be able to recognize the many different ways that Satan attempts to get into their hearts and minds.

Moreover, the Devil is so subtle in many of his ways that *most* adults are not even aware of the influence that he has over them.

The night of 28 February 1993 was the beginning of the first day of my life as far as I Am concerned. The LORD called me out of Darkness into His glorious Light! And I Am able to see from such a different perspective than I have ever seen before in my life!

I truly hope my Testimony will help you to understand how I was able to be deceived by the Enemy so easily when I first came to your husband's Bible study group. You have stated to me that you were also very deceived by him, so I feel it is important for you to know what I went through, so maybe you can learn from my mistakes.

My concern for him began when he quit going to the Baptist Church. I felt like he was walking away from God, so I gave him the following letter. The original letter was sent to someone else but I liked it so much that I changed the salutation and started sending it to family, friends, and acquaintances who I really cared about.

To Whom it May Concern, *Fall of 1989*

I was just wanting to write a few of my thoughts about being a Christian. I know how hard it is with all the pressures of life, especially today. I would not be so worried about you if I knew God was the center of your life. It is so important to have Him in you.

It is quite a challenge to be a Christian in today's world because the Devil has such a strong influence in every sector of our society, but God is stronger! And it is so important to be on His side.

It has gotten to the point that riding the fence does not get it anymore. You have to make a stand one way or the other. And if you decide to live your life truly for God, that Devil will try to stand in your way every time. But you just have to pray for God to help you.

Just remember, that it is a very gradual process and quite a learning experience to become Christ-like.

You need to read the Bible to know what God wants you to do and how to live. He talks to you through His word—you just have to be open to receive what He is saying to you.

Don't worry that you are not able to understand everything in the Bible. That comes with time and wisdom. You also need to go to church...Look for a preacher that preaches from the Bible whether you want to hear what he is saying or not.

If he starts talking about things that make you think you ought to change something in your life, then he is probably speaking the truth. Just pray for God's guidance and He will help you in whatever endeavor you need to follow.

I hope you do not think I am preaching at you, but I guess I am. The only reason I am saying anything is because I love and care about you, and I want you to go to Heaven.

You can be a good person, but unless you make a stand for God, you will spend eternity in Hell.

I just want you to know that it is such a joy to be a true Christian, not just in name, but by example and attitude.

I will be praying for you. Take care and may God bless you and your family!

Cathy

When I wrote that letter I was very sincere, but I was totally unaware of the terribly self-righteous attitude that I had. It was that prideful arrogance that blinded my eyes. And it is only by the grace of God that I Am now able to see the Truth. Praise His Holy name!!

One thing I want to make very clear is that I Am not judging the intentions of their hearts. That is *only* for God to do. But because of what God did on the night of 28 February 1993, and the subsequent meeting we had on 2 March 1993, is why I Am now able to see the Truth.

Huff and Liz claim that everything they do is ordained of God, but I Am very certain that they are liars, even though they say otherwise. Not only are they *not* walking with the LORD Jesus Christ, but they are *Walking With The Enemy* of the LORD Jesus Christ!

My involvement with them was a very humbling experience, and looking back, I see the many ways where Satan is able to get a stronghold in people's lives in order to gain control over them.

Moreover, if we are not willing to deny our flesh, it too will have power over us, which will ultimately lead to our destruction.

I John 2:15-17 "Love not the world, neither the things that are in the world. If any man love the world, the love of the Father is not in him.

For all that is in the world, the lust of the flesh, and the lust of the eyes, and the pride of life, is not of the Father, but is of the world.

And the world passeth away, and the lust thereof: but he that doeth the will of God abideth forever."

What happened to me at La'el Ministries establishes even more in my heart the need to make sure that my children have the proper training while they are young. And I know that the LORD will enable me to accomplish whatever He calls me to do.

Nevertheless, I want to thank you for your concern. And I pray that the LORD'S peace and blessings will be with your family as you submit yourselves to Him in all that you do. I will continue to pray for you and your husband as the LORD directs me.

The greatest hope that I have for him, is that he will see the Truth and truly desire to walk in it. He will have to turn from all the lies and deceptions though. And I hope that he will *Heed the Call* very soon, because Time is running out!

Signed and sealed in the presence of a witness in the year of the LORD, One Thousand Nine Hundred and Ninety-Three.

HUFF

"These are spots in your feasts of charity,
when they feast with you, feeding themselves without fear:
clouds they are without water, carried about of winds;
trees whose fruit withereth, without fruit,
twice dead, plucked up by the roots;"
Jude 12

Huff, which means "fits of anger," is very characteristic of this man who claimed to follow the LORD Jesus Christ. Much of what I have learned about "Pastor" Huff could aptly apply to the late David Koresh. And even though the body and soul of Koresh was taken from this earth, his "spirit" still lives on in the hearts of some deceived and wicked men.

My Husband gave Mr. Huff the following letter while he was visiting his estranged wife when she still lived across the street from us.

Dear Pastor Huff, 24 August 1993

I have struggled with the idea of writing this letter to you, but the LORD has given me a sign that it is time, and I pray I will be very sensitive to His Spirit as to what He would have me say. And I know with certainty that only what God thinks is the most important thing to consider in this world *and* in the world to come.

One of the reasons why I Am writing this to you, is to hopefully convince you to turn from your sin, and turn back to the one, true, and only living God! And I would like to make an attempt in this letter to persuade you to choose Life instead of Death—Heaven instead of Hell.

However, you will have to turn from the Darkness and come to the Light so you can see why you are headed for ultimate destruction.

At this point, there is still a lot of pain and sorrow in my heart concerning you and those of La'el Ministries, of which I would think I could get over by now, but I still care about you.

It might seem by the outward appearance of things that I have completely rejected all of you, but because of what the LORD has revealed to me in the last six months, I have no choice but to continue to stand apart from you, unless you truly repent.

I believe I will always have hope, but if you die in your sin still pretending that what you do is ordained of God, and that you are a minister of the LORD Jesus Christ in righteousness, then when you stand before Him you will be so ashamed of yourself!

Reality will slap you in the face, and there will be no turning back then. Everything I have been trying to convince you of will become Truth for you, and you will no longer be able to hide behind your pride, or the deceit in your own heart.

I told your wife, in a letter, that my greatest hope for you is that you will see the Truth and really desire to walk in it. But you will have to acknowledge the lies and deceptions that you have been a part of, and turn from all your sins and do them no more.

It is the first step towards true repentance, and it is the most important step you could ever take. Please seriously consider what I Am saying because Time is running out!

I know because of everything that has transpired in your life, you must feel that there is no hope and no turning back—that you have just gone too far, and that God could never forgive you for all the things you have done against Him and other people.

But the LORD God is so merciful and forgiving, and His grace is so amazing, that if you were to truly experience His forgiveness for your many sins, your love for Him would be so great!

Luke 7:41-43 "There was a certain creditor which had two debtors: the one owed five hundred pence, and the other fifty. And when they had nothing to pay, he frankly forgave them both.

Tell me therefore, which of them will love him most? Simon answered and said, I suppose that he, to whom he forgave most. And He (Jesus) said unto him, Thou hast rightly judged."

I hope that you will read this letter with a humble heart that is willing to believe that I might conceivably be right. Please try and trust me just for this moment in Time, and give me the same benefit of the doubt that I gave you for the three years that I walked with you.

I really have no idea what I can say that will convince you to see the error of your ways, so I Am just going to trust the Holy Spirit to do that. He is One that fully understands what is going on in your heart and mind, and I sincerely pray that the LORD will lead me in this attempt to free you from the bondage of sin and Satan.

I Am going to assume that you are as deceived as I was and that you have sinned out of ignorance, instead of purposefully going against the commands of Almighty God and the LORD Jesus Christ.

I have first-hand knowledge of how easy it is to be deceived; and because of the sin that was in my own heart, I was blind to the truth of what was going on when I first came to your group.

I now understand why God constantly warns us throughout His word to obey Him and keep His commandments. It is not to deprive us of anything, but it is to protect us from the dangers of sin, and the evil influences of Satan and the world.

I will forever be grateful to the LORD God Almighty for giving me eyes that can truly see, and ears that can truly hear. Moreover, I desire that for anybody else who is genuinely seeking to love, serve, and worship God with all their heart, soul, mind, and strength.

I genuinely care about people who may also be ensnared in a trap by the Devil, and in this 'Little Book' I will show how I was blind to the Truth, held captive by the Enemy, brokenhearted by the hidden sin in my own heart, and bruised within the depths of my soul, all of which I believe is the condition of many of God's people.

Through my experiences, I have learned many of Satan's tactics, and I would like to share many of them with you, so you can see how you have become enslaved by the Devil, and need to be saved too.

I sincerely desire for you to be delivered from all that is evil, and I hope you believe that. In spite of all that has happened, there is still a great concern in my heart for those of La'el Ministries, but I will not stand with you and support you in your sin and iniquity.

God has called His people to stand apart from sin and rebuke all wickedness; and I will continue to do that.

My greatest desire for you and your wife, is that you live up to the commitment you made to her Twenty-Five years ago, and love her in the manner that God has ordained that a man love his own wife and children. If she was to ever accept you back, you would have to know that God definitely intervened on your behalf.

Whether or not she accepts you back, I hope you will truly humble yourself before the LORD God, and ask Him to forgive you, and then be willing to turn from all your sin. Only until you genuinely repent of the evil in your heart, will you ever experience forgiveness and the cleansing power of the LORD Jesus Christ.

Do you remember that passage of Scripture from Luke that I always used to think was for you? Strangely, I never even once applied it to myself while I was with La'el Ministries.

However, since I have been walking in the "True Light," the LORD has brought to my attention that He was indeed speaking to me. I was just not able to hear Him very clearly at that time in my life.

And I praise God for His mercy and His grace and for being so patient with me during my time of *Walking With The Enemy.*

Luke 22:31-32 "And the LORD said, Simon, Simon, behold, Satan hath desired to have you, that he may sift you as wheat: But I have prayed for thee, that thy faith fail not: and when thou art converted, strengthen thy brethren."

That scripture is the very essence of my Life in Christ. And due to what the LORD has revealed to me since our separation, I realize that my ultimate mission in this world is to share what I have learned about the Enemy, so as to help those who are walking in Darkness.

The Spirit of the LORD God Almighty is my guide, who I will follow with my whole heart, soul, and mind; and I will speak and do whatever He says regardless of the opposition that I Am sure will come.

It is only through God that I have the understanding that I have concerning His kingdom; and it is only through the LORD that I will continue to grow in that understanding. And I praise God that He has counted me worthy to know the mysteries of His kingdom!

So as to establish what was in my heart and mind while walking with you, the LORD has impressed upon me to use journal excerpts and various letters so you can see how I was deceived by Satan for the three years that I was involved with your ministry. And then maybe you will also be able to see how you have been misled too.

I feel it is important for you to be able to understand what kind of relationship my Husband and I had together prior to joining your Bible study group. These first two letters will show why I was so vulnerable to the tactics of Satan and his many deceptions.

I want you to realize that by me sharing this with you is in no way meant to condemn my Husband, or even imply that the sin that I walked in was his fault. However, I Am very certain that my unstable relationship with my Husband was a contributing factor as to why I was able to be led astray by the Enemy in such an Evil way.

To my Husband, *18 June 1989*

Today is Father's Day and since I can't talk to you, I guess I will write down my thoughts to you.

You not being here for the girls today goes along with the way things are the rest of the year.

I am not wanting to be negative, but I can't help how I feel about our relationship and the relationship you have with the girls.

I was watching a preacher from the First Baptist Church on TV today. He spoke about several different types of fathers and how important it is for the father to be the spiritual leader in the family—that a father needs to be there for quality and quantity time.

He told about a couple that went to a nice restaurant. The man ordered the best steak on the menu, but when he got his steak, it was just a tiny piece of meat, along with some nice-looking vegetables. He asked the waiter about such a small piece of meat and the waiter said it may be small, but the quality of that one piece of meat is the best you will find.

But you know, eating that made him want more. It is the same with the kids. If you give them bits of quality time too little and far between, it just leaves them feeling hungry and needing more.

He was also talking about the type of father that is at home a lot, but he might as well not even be there, because he does not ever really take time with anybody. He is just a fixture in the house.

I know you have other interests and obligations, but it would be nice if you made us feel like we are important too. You give your work 101% of your effort. You give the National Guard 101%. You would drop anything to go to your shooting matches, but I don't think you can honestly say you would do the same for your family.

You might tell yourself that you do those other things for us, but all they do is contribute to the financial support of our family, nothing else. Do you think that all a man is responsible to his family is to pay the bills? It isn't my expectation of a father, or a husband.

I just wish you would show as much enthusiasm to be around us as you do to go shooting or watching a war movie. You make me feel like being with us is the last place you want to be.

I know it is not as exciting as work and Guard, but the children do need you, and so do I. But you have gotten me where I don't really want to need you.

I did not finish that letter, and I don't know if he even read it, but I have given him similar ones that he has read. The next letter is more in line with the attitude that I feel God would desire that I have towards my Husband, but I do not want to imply that he will not be held accountable for what he does with what God gives him.

However, for my peace of mind and heart I really needed to start seeing things from a different perspective, instead of focusing on how discontent I was with our relationship.

I realize now that the only way to true peace is when you can look at this world from God's perspective. And I was going to be embarking on a journey that would teach me how to do just that.

As you know, it has been a very bittersweet journey. And I might add, it is not over yet.

My Dear Husband, *28 November 1989*

I just want you to know that I do love you, no matter what. And I really would not want to ever leave you. I guess I say that out of desperation or frustration.

I really need to be more grateful for what I have instead of getting upset about what I don't have. I guess your presence and your time is what I have been upset about not having.

I am really sorry about the way I make you feel sometimes, and I will try not to be so emotional about things.

I know you have other interests, and I will try to be more understanding about that. I just really wanted to let you know a few of my feelings. With God's help, I can become a better wife and mother. I love you.

Cathy

That letter was written only four months before I started coming to your Bible study group. My Husband and I were just completing a course in "MasterLife"[28] at the Baptist Church when I came to your group. *This* was to be the beginning of my journey into the "false light."

The first meeting I attended was on 29 March 1990, and I remember so clearly the astonished look on your faces when I showed up the following Thursday evening. It was as if you were so surprised that I even came back, but to your utter amazement I did, and hardly missed a night for the next three years.

Since Jesus is our example, we should expect to experience many things that He went through during His Time here on earth. Looking back, I consider the Time with La'el Ministries as a type of "wilderness" experience for me, where I was definitely tempted by the Devil.

Matthew 4:1 "Then was Jesus led up of the Spirit into the wilderness to be tempted of the Devil."

Since Jesus Christ is the Perfect One, He knew the Truth of the Holy Scriptures, and He was able to refute anything Satan had to tempt Him with. However, I was not even close to having a real knowledge and understanding of the LORD God and His word, but since I imagined that I did, that would be the cause of my fall.

My greatest desire is to worship God in Spirit and in Truth, and to really know the LORD Jesus Christ in a very personal way; howbeit He knew that my sin of pride and self-righteousness had to be dealt with.

In order to accomplish my desire, I would have to be broken in my spirit and humbled in my soul before I could ever receive the truth about Almighty God and His kingdom. I just thank God that He was with me when He led me by His Spirit through this time of temptation.

As He has said, *"I will never leave you or forsake you, I Am with you always, even to the end of the world."*

Due to my faith in God and His word, combined with the restraining hand of the LORD holding back the Enemy, is the only reason why I was even able to endure any of this. Praise the mighty name of my LORD Jesus Christ! Of whom I Am so very thankful.

This next letter will show how Satan was initially able to gain control over me, but only to the extent that God would allow. You may remember this. It is pertaining to the night when you "laid hands" on me and prayed for me to be filled with the "spirit."

Dearest Pastor Huff and Family, *20 April 1990*

I just felt compelled to write you a letter of some of my thoughts and feelings. I really would like to thank you for the gift of your friendship and trust.

I have been praying for a while now that I could truly know Jesus Christ and live my life centered around Him.

I do feel God led me to you all. And I know you have much more knowledge and wisdom than I do; and if I can learn from you how to truly come to know Christ in the Spirit, then my prayers have been answered.

I know what I saw in your eyes last night was the spirit of truth and love, and you passed some of it over to me through the grace of God; and I love you for that.

Please know you can depend on me for any help that I can give.

Yours truly through Christ,

Cathy

The following verse is extremely significant, and the LORD has since shown me exactly why. *I Timothy 5:22 "Lay hands suddenly on no man, neither be partaker of other men's sins: keep thyself pure."*

Due to my lack of knowledge, I allowed you to do something God specifically warns His people not to do. Had I not allowed you to "lay hands" on me, I would not have been deceived to the degree I was.

Keep in mind this was to be a learning experience that the LORD was leading me through. Of course, I did not realize I was about to fall, but praise God He did, and He would be there to pick me back up!

Romans 8:27-28 "And He that searcheth the hearts knoweth what is the mind of the Spirit, because He maketh intercession for the saints according to the will of God.

And we know that all things work together for good to them that love God, to them who are the called according to His purpose."

I want you to understand that I did not see the Truth of all this until God delivered me from the Power of Darkness. God's word has become so real for me, and the LORD Jesus Christ continues to prove Himself to me in so many wonderful ways.

And only by the grace of Almighty God am I now walking in the "True Light" and able to understand what was going on. You did not fill me with the "Spirit of Christ" as I assumed! What I saw in your eyes that night was not the Holy Spirit, but a demonic seducing spirit!

Because of my error, I allowed your sin to become a part of my life. I actually trusted and believed that what you did when you prayed for me was ordained of my God. But it is just like God warns us in His word: *"My people perish for lack of knowledge."*

And had I not truly loved the LORD God Almighty with all my heart and soul, I would be *Walking With The Enemy* even still!

This next excerpt is from my journal that was written exactly a month and a half after I joined your group.

My Dear LORD, *11 May 1990*

I have always addressed my words and thoughts to "My Little Book," but I am going to start addressing all my thoughts and words to "My Dear LORD."

I just want You to know what has been going on in my life lately. First of all, I have been blessed and filled with that wonderful Holy Spirit. I do not really know exactly how to describe the joy of it.

It is like I met up with someone that I have always been looking for and finally found Him.

There is a completeness in me that was not there before. My eyes see more clearly. I am starting to know what I have been sensing all along, but just did not know what it was.

I know dear LORD, that You have been watching over me. I can feel Your presence and Your love. And it is so beautiful!

I am so thankful for the people You have given me to learn from and be able to see You in them. I just figured out what draws me to them; and it is You LORD.

The love they have for You is just flowing out of them, and I just cannot help but to be attracted to it because I truly love You with my whole heart, soul, mind, and strength, and no man can take that away from me. I am starting to see the joy that Paul speaks of, and it is so wonderful!

I really want to know You fully! You are guiding my steps, and I will go wherever You lead me. Thank You for choosing me.

Cathy

I was very drawn to both you and Liz due to the seducing spirit that I received when you "laid hands" on me that evening. Nothing seemingly terrible happened, but due to the demonic influence, I had an unusual attraction to you, which I presumed was the love of Christ.

I did not understand the ramifications of what had taken place; thus, I would become more influenced by evil thoughts, rather than the word of God. It was so strange because I was willing to forget everything I had ever learned and fully trust you and Liz to the extent that only your opinions were all that mattered to me.

Do you remember the night that you and Liz had informed me that my youngest daughter was under a demonic attack? In retrospect, I realize that this was just a ploy by the Enemy to gain more control over me by increasing my dependence on you.

As a result of what transpired that night, I had a much greater respect for you due to your ability to fight off demons. In my eyes, you just *had* to be of God if you could cast out devils. You often referenced the following passage to give credence to your false claims.

Mark 16:15-18 "And He said unto them, Go ye into all the world, and preach the gospel to every creature. He that believeth and is baptized shall be saved; but he that believeth not shall be damned.

And these signs shall follow them that believe; In My name shall they cast out devils; they shall speak with new tongues; They shall take up serpents; and if they drink any deadly thing, it shall not hurt them; they shall lay hands on the sick, and they shall recover."

I wrote the following journal entry in regard to that very strange incident that took place in my home on that night.

My Dear LORD, *12 May 1990*

Last night sure was a night to remember! It was my first real confrontation with the other side. They were very persistent, but thank you Jesus for being who You are. I am so glad that I am on the winning side. This is really going to be a totally different kind of life. Living totally for the LORD Jesus and really knowing who He is, is really something!

This really puts new meaning and purpose in one's life. I am part of God's family now and I really feel like I understand what Paul went through. I have not experienced the kind of persecution as him of course, but I understand the spiritual side much more.

I really see things in a different light. I just pray that I will not ever let God down. I will try with all my strength to please Him.

Until later,
Cathy

I saw things in a different light all right! I was walking in Darkness and I did not know where I was going! Yet, by my words, you can see that I was convinced I was finally walking in the Truth.

In that letter, I did not go into what took place that night, so I will now. I Am not sure why you two were at my house, but I know I was glad because of what was going on with my youngest daughter.

Earlier that day I had rushed her to the doctor's office because she was having trouble breathing, which at the time I had no idea why. While they were taking x-rays of her chest, she suddenly coughed up pieces of a banana that had gotten stuck in her throat.

So, to my great relief, she was going to be fine. However, that night was a completely different story. Later that evening she began screaming as if she was in excruciating pain, and I started thinking that it was because of what took place earlier.

At Liz's prompting, I called the doctor at his home and he very impatiently told me that she should not be having any problems. Afterward, Liz informed me she knew that would be his response.

She went on to explain that it was not a physical problem, but that it was a demonic attack against my child. Liz proceeded to pray for her in other tongues while she held my screaming little daughter. She appeared to be casting out demons and demanding they leave my home.

My daughter eventually calmed down, but due to my ignorance, I trusted that what Liz was doing was approved of by God, but I now understand that you and Liz are under the power of demonic spirits, and that she was actually cursing my baby girl under the authority of Satan.

Moreover, I realize that just because someone is able to speak in other tongues does not mean that they are praying the will of God. Paul addressed this issue to the Corinthian Church, which I will quote.

I Corinthians 14:27-28 "If any man speak in an unknown *tongue,* let it be *by two, or at the most* by *three, and* that *by course; and let one interpret. But if there be no interpreter, let him keep silence in the church; and let him speak to himself, and to God."*

On 14 May 1990, God gave me the gift of speaking in other tongues and I Am certain it was of Him. I marked it on my calendar because I was so excited that I was finally able to pray in the Spirit.

Do you remember how frustrated you used to get when you would "lay hands" on me and pray that I receive the gift of tongues, but I would not be able to do it? In light of what I know now, I Am so thankful you were nowhere around when God gave me that gift.

The following excerpt from a letter that I wrote to some friends of mine will help shed some light on my condition then.

It was dated 15 May 1990.

"...Speaking of God, I have really been learning a lot about Him these days. He is so much more than churches claim Him to be. They put too many limits on His power and abilities.

I have really grown to love the LORD. I hope someday I can share some of my experiences with you. Of course, I will always be learning, but the more you learn, the closer you get to Him.

You know what? God does not really mind you drinking that beer of yours unless you make it an idol. The main thing you got to do is, read the Bible and ask God to help you to understand what He's saying, and ask Jesus Christ into your heart and go from there. Then learn how to listen to God.

I have been finding that a lot of what God has been telling me does not match up with what I have learned in all the churches. Just ask Him and He will lead you to the right church or group of people.

That neighbor I mentioned that stayed with the girls while I took my daughter to the doctor is a minister. But not your typical one.

He looks like the rest of us, and he even smokes occasionally, and drinks wine...And he is the godliest man I have ever met.

You might think I am crazy for saying this, but he acts like you would think Jesus was like when He was here. He is also very loving. Not in a lustful way, but very loving, and he makes you feel loved. But all of that is not because of him, but because of that Holy Spirit inside of him.

It's really neat to learn about the real truth of God, and I pray that you do if you haven't already."

The Devil was able to plant some very radical thoughts in my head about the love of God, but since being delivered, I now understand that it was through the use of seducing spirits, witchcraft, and twisting of the Scriptures that I was able to be deceived into believing many of the things that you and Liz told me.

Looking back it is so bizarre to think I actually believed that the adulterous relationship you had with Liz was ordained of God, despite the fact that both of you were married to different people.

Liz told me "God" revealed to her at the moment of conception, that she was pregnant with both of the children you had together as a sign that He approved of your unusual union.

And it still blows my mind how I could actually believe that God said you would be *like a husband to me*. You may remember the verse you used to help support this "revelation" you claimed was from the LORD.

Ephesians 5:24-27 "Therefore as the Church is subject unto Christ, so let the wives be to their own husbands in every thing.

Husbands, love your wives even as Christ also loved the Church, and gave Himself for it; That He might sanctify and cleanse it with the washing of water by the word, That He might present it to Himself a glorious Church, not having spot, or wrinkle, or any such thing; but that it should be Holy and without blemish."

I distinctly remember the night that we were sitting out by Liz's pool when we had the conversation concerning who my "own husband" was as established by God and His word.

Prior to this, you said that I needed to go and pray and ask God who you were to me as ordained by Him. So, I sincerely prayed about it as you had requested.

The night we discussed it you had asked me if the LORD revealed anything to me yet, and I remember telling you that He said, "You will learn a lot from this man." You agreed and said, "Yes, the Lord has appointed me as your teacher."

Apparently, it was not the answer you were looking for since you asked me, "What else did He say?" I was a little reluctant to tell you what else I heard because there was some confusion mixed with fear concerning the other things that were spoken to my heart.

After rationalizing what I thought God said to me, I stated, "He said you would be like a father to me." I believe you sensed my hesitancy and you stated, "No, that is not what He said."

I said, "Well, I did hear a little something else." And you said, "Well, what is it?" I said, "I think He told me that you would be like a husband to me." You quickly agreed that that's exactly what the Lord had said, and that He appointed you as my spiritual head, which meant that you would be *like* a husband to me.

I did not know what to do with this very unusual conversation, or understand what it actually meant, so I just put all of it in the back of my mind. I felt God would give me the understanding when it was time for me to know the true meaning behind this discussion.

I have discovered that Satan's tactics is to use the Scriptures to help establish his lies, and I might add he did it very effectively with me due to my lack of knowledge and true understanding of God.

As I reread that letter I wrote to my friends, I now see how blind I was to the real Truth. Due to the demonic control in my life, I actually attributed all my feelings for you as being from God, rather than from the lust within my own soul and the evil influence that I was under.

Please bear in mind that I Am just trying to establish the framework of what led up to some of the other outlandish lies and deceptions that Satan led me into believing was truth.

Moreover, due to my strong desire to be loved and to love, I allowed the deceptions of the Devil to become truth for me. James addresses this issue of which I will quote for you.

James 1:12-16 "Blessed is the man that endureth temptation: for when he is tried, he shall receive the crown of life, which the LORD hath promised to them that love Him.

Let no man say when he is tempted, I am tempted of God: for God cannot be tempted with evil, neither tempteth He any man: But every man is tempted, when he is drawn away of his own lust, and enticed.

Then when lust hath conceived, it bringeth forth sin: and sin, when it is finished, bringeth forth death. Do not err, my beloved brethren."

I hope you see this, because this is how it starts with all of us; and it gets progressively worse if we continue in our sin and not allow the LORD to reveal it to us. I now understand why the sin of pride and self-righteousness is so dangerous. It will keep you blind to the Truth and never allow you to acknowledge your own transgressions.

I John 1:8-10 "If we say that we have no sin, we deceive ourselves, and the Truth is not in us. If we confess our sins, He is faithful and just to forgive us our sins, and to cleanse us from all unrighteousness. If we say that we have not sinned, we make Him a liar, and His word is not in us."

Yet, on the other side of that, if we do not confess our sins, He will not be able to forgive us and cleanse us of the unrighteousness that sin has produced in our heart. Pride will keep us from ever confessing our sin, and the absolute end result will be DEATH! I just praise God that He is so long-suffering with us.

II Peter 3:9 "The LORD is not slack concerning His promise, as some men count slackness; but is long-suffering to us-ward, not willing that any should perish, but that all should come to repentance."

Since I was walking in Darkness unawares, it was reflected in my words and thoughts. Even though my intentions were sincere, I was still *Walking With The Enemy* and under his influence.

Because I was oblivious to your lies and deceptions, I even tried to get others to come to our Bible study group. I just praise God that He did not allow many people to be persuaded by my invitations.

One point I would like to make very clear, is if I had understood how to allow God's Spirit to teach me the Truth, instead of relying on the word a "man" I would never have fallen for the tactics of the Devil.

Since the LORD knew what it would take to break me of my pride and self-righteousness, He would be using what Satan intended for evil and turn it around for His will to be accomplished. All praise, honor, and glory to the LORD God Almighty!

The next journal entry will shed more light on the situation.

My Dear LORD, *18 May 1990*

I feel like You asked me to write some of my experiences down in the last month or so; and I will. First of all, Satan has really been trying hard to keep me from getting closer to God. He has tried a lot of different things to accomplish that, but he has not succeeded. At first he put an idea in my husband's head that I should not join Pastor Huff's Bible study group, but he let me go the next week.

Then Satan realizes I have really found something meaningful in this group of people, which is You LORD, so he steps up his attack. He makes our financial situation look worse and feel more pressure from that, so my Husband is ready to file bankruptcy. After about a week I am able to convince him that it is just not the way to go and he needs to put his faith in our dear LORD.

Then he really gets nasty! He attacks my beautiful daughter...That was a very rough night, but Pastor Huff and Alisha (Liz) were here and they really helped.

My Husband had gone on a shooting match...It was Mother's Day weekend, and even though all this was going on, Christ has put such an inner peace in me that is hard to put into words. I just know that He has His hand on me, and He has chosen me for a task that I am very willing to carry out.

I just want to please the LORD, and get closer to Him. I am really learning to listen to that wonderful Holy Spirit inside of me. It might not always seem logical, but I will do whatever is required of me. I am really starting to understand what Pastor Huff means when he says we must die to ourselves, and I am very willing to do that.

Until later,
Cathy

You know, one of the reasons why Satan was able to get such a strong hold in my heart and mind, is because he gave you the ability to speak some profound truths; and when the deception came, I did not recognize it, because I was already so trusting of you.

Truth mixed with lies! Just like in the Garden of Eden! Satan has not had to change his tactics because men are still so ignorant of the Truth. The following scripture would have been my salvation if I had only known how to accurately apply the word of God to my life.

I John 2:26-29 "These things have I written unto you concerning them that seduce you. But the anointing which ye have received of Him abideth in you, and ye need not that any man teach you:

But as the same anointing teacheth you of all things, and is Truth, and is no lie, and even as it hath taught you, ye shall abide in Him.

And now, little children, abide in Him; that, when He shall appear, we may have confidence, and not be ashamed before Him at His coming.

If ye know that He is righteous, ye know that every one that doeth righteousness is born of Him."

I know it is a very bold statement to make, and I Am sure you already know, but you have *never* been "born again" by the Spirit of God! And neither have a lot of other people who claim to be "born-again, spirit-filled" believers in the LORD Jesus Christ.

If you will be perfectly honest with yourself, and with God, you know that your conduct is an *abomination* before the LORD! And your actions certainly do not line up with the fruits of His Spirit!

Reread the scripture I just quoted: *"If ye know that He is righteous, ye know that every one that doeth righteousness is born of Him."*

Had I been walking in the "True Light," I would have been able to recognize all of this; thus, not putting myself in the position to be led into deception, and be a partaker of another man's sin. But I now realize that God has a plan that has not been completely revealed as of yet.

I also see that many "Christians" are under the false impression that just because they make an altar call or a profession of faith in Jesus Christ that they have somehow become a part of God's family. Yet, they fail to understand that only the LORD Almighty God has the authority to decide who will be a part of His Kingdom and who will not.

All of these lies have been a part of the grand scheme of Satan to mislead and deceive people into believing that they are "born again" by the Spirit of God, when in reality they are not.

Imagine the horror of finding out at the Gates of Heaven that you are denied entry because your faith was in a false-Christ, rather than in the true Christ! Regretfully, there will be *many* that find themselves in that condition on the Great Judgment Day.

I realize this could be a hard pill for you to swallow if you have been living your life under the presumption that you are going to Heaven just because *you* believe it, or someone else has said you are.

Keep in mind that the purpose of this letter is to show you that you need to be saved from your sin, not to condemn you. You are already condemned if you are not truly "born again" into God's Kingdom.

Jesus came to save sinners from death, and destroy the power that Satan has over us. Try to remember that as you read this, and do not allow pride to keep you from hearing what I Am saying. Listen with your heart and not your mind. The Truth of all this can truly set you free.

You will wish you had listened if you find yourself barred from the Holy City on the great and dreadful Day of the LORD.

These next journal entries will help explain what was going on in my heart and mind, as I was *Walking With The Enemy* in Darkness.

My Dear LORD, *22 May 1990*

Today I have been trying to get depressed and upset about the things I have been going through, and the changes that have been going on, and will continue to go on in my life.

First off, I have had a problem with the fact that so many people that I have learned about God from, and that I thought were such Godly people, really are not as close to God as I thought.

It is just hard for me to accept that all these people are wrong and only a few are right. But dear LORD, in Your wonderful way You led me to a passage that helped explain it to me.

I Peter 4:18 "And if the righteous scarcely be saved, where shall the ungodly and the sinner appear?"

I guess that means, just because you claim to be Godly, does not mean you are. And even if you aren't, but claim you are, God can use you to get to the people He knows will come to Him.

Concerning my Husband leaving...has me feeling lonely even though he has not even left yet.

I am learning to put my faith in God and what He has for me to do while I am here on earth, and I will try to not let the things and the cares of this world get to me.

I spoke with Alisha (Liz) a little while ago. It really helps to talk to her about things that go on. She can really help put it in perspective. I really care about Pastor Huff and Alisha. They are really very special people to me, and I am very thankful to God for the people He has led me to.

I will write you again soon.

Cathy

As you can tell from this letter it was really starting to bother me that we were supposedly the only people in town that were genuinely worshipping God in Spirit and in Truth.

Even though I actually believed everything that you told me, it was still disturbing for me. The good part about it was that it encouraged me to pray for the people of this town even more.

Another reason why I was so taken with you all is because of this inward desire to be accepted by a group of people I could call my friends. Since I grew up in the military, I never had the opportunity to establish lasting friendships, and Satan was aware of this, so he took advantage of that desire within me to lure me into being a part of your group.

I would especially like to note the statement that I made in that letter: *"Just because you claim to be Godly, it does not mean you are. And even if you aren't, but claim you are, God can use you to get to the people He knows will come to Him."*

Even though I was *Walking With The Enemy* in Darkness, the LORD was establishing His Truth inside my heart, because He knew that my desire was completely for Him and His word. And that desire has not diminished, it has only become stronger.

This next quote from my journal was in response to the book by Frank Peretti that you both had encouraged me to read.

My Dear LORD, *4 July 1990*

I feel compelled to write You. I just finished a book called "This Present Darkness" by Frank Peretti. It was a very enlightening book on the power of prayer and of the spiritual warfare going on around us.

I can now see and understand the many ways that Satan has control of people. I just pray that I can be a source of power in Christ Jesus to deter Satan's demons.

I love You LORD, and I just ask You to keep revealing things to me, and give me the strength and desire to carry out Your will. Thank You for all that You do, will do, and have done. Praise Your Holy and blessed name!

Cathy

In light of what I now know about La'el Ministries, I feel that the *only* accomplishment of that book was to prepare me for the demonic activity that followed you around. I praise God that He never allowed me to see the things that you said you saw, or be tormented by them the way Liz claimed that she was on several occasions.[29]

I do remember one experience back in January of 1991 that I will never forget though. You and Liz had gone out of town to meet up with your birth mother; and the Bible study group was gathered together at my home praying, when all of a sudden I heard this terrifying scream that seemed to be circling the outside of my house.

The first thought that came to my mind was that it was one of the children crying. Both Sue [30] and I clearly heard it, and we hurriedly ran upstairs only to find that every child was sound asleep.

Still, this eerie silence remained, and a brief fear came over me, but was immediately replaced with an excitement that our prayers to the LORD God were able to chase demons away screaming in terror!

I remember being so excited about it that I even called you and Liz to tell you about it. Do you remember? I used to wonder why that occurred in your absence, but I now understand that due to the demonic power given to you by the Devil, that when you and Liz left my home, the demonic spirits had no authority to stay either!

I could look at my experience of *Walking With The Enemy* as a time that God just gave me over to Satan, but since I truly desire to see things from His perspective, He has shown me how He was working to have His perfect will accomplished, in spite of what Satan intended.

Thus, I Am convinced that God is in complete control and Satan has no authority over anyone that is truly submitted to Him.

I know you have a lot of knowledge concerning what is in the Scriptures, and that you have been to seminary, and have been a pastor at many congregations—even in the military, but I hope that you will not allow all that to stop you from hearing the Truth.

You may also have somewhat of a problem since I Am a woman, but I really hope you have begun to see things from God's perspective instead of "man's" way of thinking. Notice what God says:

Galatians 3:27-28 "For as many of you as have been baptized into Christ have put on Christ.

There is neither Jew nor Greek, there is neither bond nor free, there is neither male nor female: for ye are all one in Christ Jesus."

On 28 February 1993, I was baptized into Christ! Praise His Holy name! You were a witness to it! And so was everyone else from La'el Ministries, but you and Liz continue to deny it for some reason.

God has truly anointed me to speak His word as He gives me the understanding, and that is all I Am doing. If you do not agree we me I hope that would encourage you to submit yourself to God through His word and by prayer, and allow His Spirit to reveal the Truth to you.

This next letter is from my heart to God's heart. One thing I want you to realize is that even though I was not yet able to see the complete Truth, my relationship with the LORD God Almighty was growing and becoming more beautiful every day, because He knew that I sincerely wanted to know the Truth, and to walk in it.

And the LORD God Almighty has been *so* faithful to fulfill my heart's desire! He is such a wonderful God, and I Am so thankful to Him for all that He has done. All praise, honor, and glory be unto Him!

My Dear LORD, *11 July 1990*

I would just like You to know that I truly love You and I pray that I can be worthy of the love You have for me. You are so wonderful and I praise Your Holy name—Jesus!

I really want to have the mind of Christ, and I hope and pray that I will attain it. I know the more I read Your word and pray I will one day. And by Your grace, I will fully know You, because I really want to know You as much as is possible while on this earth.

You are my life and without You I am nothing. Nothing on this earth can fulfill me without You. And I do thank You for leading me to the Truth and giving me Your Holy Spirit.

Until later,
Cathy

This next letter will help establish my feelings for you then.

Dearest Pastor Huff and Alisha, *16 July 1990*

I feel compelled to write you a letter today. The neat thing about it is I know God is prompting me to do it. I just want you to know that in the three and a half months since I have been coming to your Bible study, I have learned more about God than I would have in a lifetime of going to the traditional churches.

Ever since I accepted Christ into my heart, my desire has been to fully know Him, and to truly have wisdom, knowledge, and understanding of Him; and to know what His purpose is for me. I know He gave you to me to help me attain that, and I am so thankful. I do have my faith in Jesus Christ, and I do believe His word, and I know that He is all-powerful.

I guess my main problem is my confidence in myself to be able to carry out everything He asks me to do. I just never want to fall into the trap of Satan. I was reading II Peter 3:17 and II Peter 2:20-21 last night, and those verses makes one realize that it is quite possible for that to happen; and I pray that it will never happen to any of us.

I love the LORD, and I love you all. No matter where I am, I pray that I will always have that love in my heart.

I do want to have the mind of Christ, and when people look at me, I do not want them to be able to see Cathy—just Christ living in me and through me.

My prayer is that I will have the courage to stand up for my LORD and to do the will of the Father.

With Love in Christ,
Cathy

The following verses were referenced in the previous letter.

II Peter 2:20-21 "For if after they have escaped the pollution's of the world through the knowledge of the LORD and Saviour Jesus Christ, they are again entangled therein, and overcome, the latter end is worse with them than the beginning.

For it had been better for them not to have known the way of righteousness, than, after they have known it, to turn from the Holy commandment delivered unto them."

II Peter 3:17 "Ye therefore, beloved, seeing ye know these things before, beware lest ye also, being led away with the error of the wicked, fall from your own steadfastness."

My walk with the Enemy was so ironic! Here I Am praying that I will not ever fall into his trap and I Am already in his trap!

Do you remember when I first started coming to your Bible study group? I told you that as I was walking down my driveway over to your house, I heard a very still, small voice telling me to "turn around and never go back." For some reason I just attributed it to the Devil, but continued to have the nagging doubts as to whether or not you were truly of the LORD Jesus Christ as you claimed to be.

My worries and concerns were pretty much alleviated after I attended a seminar at the invitation of a friend. And if you recall I had asked you to come with me. I had wanted to see the minister's reaction to you, but since you said that you couldn't go, I went without you.

At the end of the meeting, they asked if anyone needed prayer or desired to be "filled" with the Holy Spirit. So, I decided to go up front. When the preacher came to me, he asked me what was my need, and I said that I wanted to be "filled" with the Holy Spirit.

Please note that you had already prayed for me to be filled with the "spirit," but keep in mind that the main reason why I went to this meeting was because I had been worried about what had taken place on the night of 19 April 1990, when you "laid hands" on me.

As the minister "laid hands" on me and proceeded to pray, his only response was, "You have already been filled with the spirit."

So, there was my confirmation! And since I felt that he was totally unbiased, I truly believed that I could finally trust you now. Therefore, I refused to entertain any more doubts that I had about you and Liz, or anyone else from the Bible Study group.

So, as far as the Devil was concerned, I was right where he wanted me to be. But I hope you are beginning to see and understand that I was also right where God wanted me to be too.

Here is another account of my experiences while walking with you and those of La'el Ministries.

My Dear L*ORD*, *30 July 1990*

I was just wanting to write down a few things that have happened in the last few days.

Last weekend we went to visit my mom and it was an interesting weekend. She did not come out and say it, but I feel she is a little skeptical about my Bible study group. If she fully understood, I do not think she would have any problems with it, but she is not really hearing from God, but I do pray that she will one day.

My Husband is getting a better understanding about God and how He works, and I pray he will become the man God intended for him to be.

Yesterday, several of us were baptized by Pastor Huff. I really felt led to be baptized again, and especially by him.

I really feel like he has some great things ahead that God will fulfill, and I am so glad to know him and be under his leadership. I just pray that I will live up to the things God plans for me and that I will fulfill His purpose for me.

I do love the L*ORD* *Jesus and I do believe Him. I just hope I will not allow the things of this world to get in the way. I know that the Devil will be trying all he can to make me not believe God, but with God's help, Jesus will overcome.*

Until later,
Cathy

This letter shows just how prideful and arrogant I had become. It was that very attitude, along with the demonic influences, that kept me blind to the truth of what was going on with my feelings and emotions.

I remember that I was so honored to know someone that loved Jesus the way you said you did, but I now understand that Satan's intent was to lure me in with the truth, and deceive me with the lies.

Colossians 2:4,8 "And this I say, lest any man should beguile (or deceive) you with enticing (or nice sounding) words...

Beware lest any man spoil you through philosophy and vain deceit, after the tradition of men, after the rudiments (or principles) of the world, and not after Christ."

Due to what I went through with La'el Ministries, I no longer under-estimate the power and abilities of the Devil. Furthermore, I know it is *only* by the grace of God as to why I Am able to understand any of this; and I will forever be indebted to my LORD Jesus Christ for delivering me from the power of Darkness!

Here is another letter that will further establish some of the feelings I was experiencing towards you at that time.

Dear Pastor Huff, *6 November 1990*

I would just like to express a few of my thoughts to you. Sometimes I can write them better than I can say them. Initially, I wanted to write a letter to my sister-in-law to straighten her out concerning you and my walk with the LORD.

The more I sought the LORD on it, He led me to scripture verses in II Corinthians 3:1-6. It was like He was telling me you do not need to write it down on paper, just let them see Jesus and His love in you; and if that is not enough, it is their decision to accept or reject Him.

It really bothers me sometimes when people speak of you and treat you in the manner in which they do. And I know that all these things have to be. It just does not make it any easier to watch what you go through.

I just wish I could do something to make them understand, and to know the truth about you and our LORD Jesus. I want you to know I understand and know the truth. I know Jesus lives in you, and His Spirit flows out of you like a river. I know you will follow your LORD no matter what this world says or thinks.

I just want to thank you for the things you have taught me about that beautiful LORD Jesus. And most of all to our Father for leading my steps to you.

Our bond is Jesus Christ, and because of Him, this tremendous love is flowing out of me. I know it is because of your desire to minister and teach the love of Christ that I have been able to understand the depth of His love. I do appreciate you and am ever thankful. I truly love you!

Your friend,
Cathy

The next Scripture reference is one you made a habit of quoting, especially in the beginning. I now understand that Satan prompted you to do so in order to cause me to feel sorry for you.

Philippians 3:10 "That I may know Him, and the power of His resurrection, and the fellowship of His sufferings, being made conformable unto His death;"

You used to tell me that your life was going to be one of terrible suffering and pain, and that eventually you would be put to death because of your stand for Jesus. Well, as I see it, you are a great deceiver, seducer, and a master at manipulating people emotionally, physically, and spiritually for your own personal gain.

And if you don't wake up, you will spend eternity in the unquenchable Lake of Fire with the one who has manipulated you into believing and carrying out his evil lies and deceptions!

Ephesians 5:11-16 "And have no fellowship with the unfruitful works of Darkness, but rather reprove them. For it is a shame even to speak of those things which are done of them in secret.

But all things that are reproved are made manifest by the Light: for whatsoever doth make manifest is Light. Wherefore he saith, Awake thou that sleepest, and arise from the dead, and Christ shall give thee Light. See then that ye walk circumspectly, not as fools, but as wise, redeeming the time, because the days are evil!"

I wrote this next letter prior to you and Liz taking that trip to visit your "birth mother" whom you had recently located. As I remember back, I was so happy that you were finally getting to see her for the first time due to the joy it seemed to bring you; and also because of the heartache you appeared to be having over Becky and the kids.

Dear Pastor Huff and Elisha, *15 January 1991*

I just wanted to let you know that you are very special people to me, and that I praise the LORD for your willingness to be used of Him to teach others about Him. I have learned some things about the love of God that just cannot be put into words.

He is my life, and I just want to please Him and to learn His ways and have His thoughts. And I am so thankful that He has given you to me to help teach me.

You will be very missed, but I am so glad that you have this time together. I pray that you will be strengthened in the LORD Jesus and be able to withstand whatever persecutions come your way.

I know the Enemy will try whatever means that he can to come between you. Just remember to keep the whole armor of God on. I love you both very much.

Cathy

As you can see from this letter, my love for both you and Liz was very genuine. I was so trusting of both of you even to the point that I was willing to believe that your relationship with Liz was truly ordained of God. I was very willing to stand by both of you regardless of what anyone else may have said about you.

As far as I was concerned, I was convinced you were of God, and that is all that mattered. It still amazes me how I could believe some of the outlandish things that you told me, especially since they were so against the very precepts of God's Holy word!

Moreover, it was due to your twisting and manipulation of the Holy Scriptures, that I was able to be enticed into believing your lies.

The statement, "I have also learned from His word that the only thing God considers sin is unbelief" is something you said quite often in your teachings, which I blindly accepted as Truth.

At one point, you said I should destroy all the letters I had ever written to you, and I did get rid of some of them, but the LORD led me to save the ones I did. I hope in sharing them with you again that you will see how we were both used by Satan as instruments of unrighteousness.

Regardless of all that happened, my heart was always to follow God no matter where that might lead or what I might lose in the process. And due to some of the very shameful things that occurred, I would become more humbled in my soul and broken in my spirit.

I wrote the following letter soon after my Husband left for military training. It is worth noting that the only way Satan could carry out his evil deeds was for me to be separated from my Husband.

Dear Pastor Huff, *Winter of 1991*

This is my attitude towards the LORD: That I want His will accomplished and not my own; and I know that some of the things He will lead me to do will mean forsaking the things I have acquired in this world in order to be able to put Him first.

I know I do not understand or perceive things the way He does, but it is my desire to be able to do that. I do know that He does desire that I be very sincere, and open and honest to those He has given to me; and I have tried to do that.

Concerning my relationship with you, I know the LORD has put you in my life for a very specific purpose. I know that doubts have come from every angle to mistrust that feeling in my heart towards you. The feelings that are there were not something I set out to have for you, they just kind of happened. I do not even know how.

It would be much easier for everyone concerned if those feelings were not there. But if they were established by God, they are not going to go away. A verse that always comes up is, ***"That what God has joined together let no man put asunder."***

I do want to learn to trust the LORD and have the same confidence that you have. The things that float around my heart and mind I want settled. And I know it does hinder my walk with Him because they are not.

There is still a fear in me concerning you, and I know it is because I have not matured in the knowledge of God's love and I do not fully understand how He thinks, and what His ways are.

But He knows I want to. I just have to purpose in my heart that I will trust Him to work in me, but sometimes I feel so inadequate, and I wonder who am I that He even bothers with me.

Sometimes I even feel that way about you. Why do you even bother with me? How come you care about me? I am not anybody—just some girl that used to live across the street from you. It is hard for me to understand why you put up with me, especially when I think about the ways I have treated you.

There are some things that come up in my mind that I am not really sure where they are from, and I am afraid to speak them, but you know, it doesn't really matter if they are true or not. I can wait until all things are revealed when the LORD comes back.

Concerning my relationship with the LORD, I just want to have the frame of mind that I will trust Him and live by faith in Him and His abilities; and no matter what I say and do, that it will be to give Him the glory, and not to appease my flesh or other people's.

One thing I am sure of is that I can learn from you and your example on how to trust Him.

Cathy

I was under a lot of condemnation by Liz, and she would always blame me for most everything that happened. Since I sincerely believed that God put you in my life to help teach me about His ways, at Liz's insistence, I was led to believe that *everything you did* was ordained of God for my benefit in order to reveal my sins and weaknesses.

This next letter expresses my feelings towards Liz (Elisha) at that time. I would like to mention that I pretty much trusted her right up until the night of 2 March 1993, when we had the major confrontation that resulted in our permanent separation.

My Dear Elisha, *15 April 1991*

I figure I should put this paper to use for a good reason. I just want to thank you for your thoughtfulness in giving me a baby shower. I want to thank you for being my friend. I also thank my LORD for bringing us together. Anything from Him is much more fulfilling and lasting than anything this world has to offer.

I just pray that we will not ever allow Satan to steal away what God has given us. I am very aware that he is out there to do just that, but because you are so sensitive to the Spirit, you bring things to light so that they are not able to get much of a stronghold.

I am very grateful for your words of encouragement and correction, especially in my ways of treating my baby girl.

One of my greatest desires is that all of my children follow after the LORD, and I want to do everything I can to encourage that.

I really don't mind if you bring it to my attention when I may be falling down in that area. I do love those children that God gave me. As it says in Psalms 127:3 "Lo, children are an heritage of the LORD: and the fruit of the womb is His reward."

When I realize what a big responsibility I have concerning those kids, and how my example will make a difference, I am able to consider them a blessing...

Elisha, I do love you, and I pray that I can be a source of encouragement and joy in your life. I do desire to have the spiritual insight that you have, so that one day I can be for you, what you are to me.

Thank you again.

Your friend in the LORD,
Cathy

My love for Liz was very genuine, but I never felt it was mutual during the whole time of walking with you. She had won my favor and respect, and I even let her tell me how to discipline my children, when I never really liked the way she treated her own.

Due to the strong demonic influence surrounding you and Liz, I submitted to many things contrary to the word of God. Had I actually been walking in the "True Light" I would have seen that I was not listening to the "Spirit of Truth" but the "spirit of error."

And even though I was *Walking With The Enemy,* I thank the LORD God Almighty that He has never forsaken me. Praise God!

The following message is one that I truly felt God gave me to write down for His body. I shared it with you privately and then during Bible study, and even though you seemed rather indifferent about it, you or Liz never denied it as being from the LORD.[31]

From the Lord *9 June 1991*

"If it bears witness with you, fine, do something about it. If it does not, do something about that too.

I have called all of you to be my body, but there are some parts missing because I have not added them yet. There is a very specific reason why I have not. In fact, I have even taken away that which you had. You may think it was the enemy and to some degree it was, but I allowed it.

You say that I am your Lord with your mouth, but your actions do not match up to what you confess.

Most of you only want me, and allow me to demonstrate myself in you, is when it is convenient for you, or when you feel like it.

Separately, you are planting seeds to some degree, but you would be much more effective if you work together like I intended for you to. Look at your daily lives and see how you treat one another.

I know you love me, but that was not my only commandment. You must love each other, and not just whomever you choose.

All of you are very spiritually perceptive, and you can be a mighty force for my kingdom, but only if you allow me to demonstrate my spirit in you. I want to add more to you, but you have not even used what I have given you in the manner that I have ordained for you to do.

You are my family, but I must be the head. If I am not, you will continue as you are: each of you doing your own thing individually, while in the midst of it I am still able to work.

I can be much more effective through you if you learn to deny yourself, take up your cross daily, and follow me. That is what you say you want to do, well then do it! You say you want people to see me in you? Well let me come out!"

Here is another letter that should help shed some light on the relationship I had with you and Liz. I wrote this to you when you got back in town after your visit with an old friend of Liz's.

Dear Pastor Huff, *28 July 1991*

I have been wanting to write to you a few of my thoughts, but I just could not put them down on paper. In fact, I sat down a week ago to write you, but I could not get past the first sentence.

I know you must think I am crazy because I write you so many letters, especially since I have the ability to speak to you. Most people write letters to those that live away from them, but I guess I am not most people—never really have been.

For some reason I can put my thoughts to you down on paper better than speaking face to face. In a way that kind of bothers me. I do not really understand why I get nervous around you at times. It is almost like my brain quits working. I would like to understand why I react that way, but I am sure God will reveal it to me in due time.

For the time being, I hope you do not get bored with my letter writing. I write these letters because I do want you to know what is going on, and I do feel led to share it with you.

I know you really care about everyone in our church, and our walk with the LORD Jesus, and it is because of your teachings that I have learned how to really get to know Him.

The verse that reminds me of you is in John 15:13, "Greater love hath no man than this, that a man lay down his life for his friends."

I know you have done that, and I do thank you. I am just sorry because I am so stubborn, and because I do not always see things, that you have to go to such extremes to get the point across to me. I am sorry for any pain I have caused you because of my unbelief. You have enough pain in your life, and I hate to be the cause of more.

I know you are a man of God, and that you will follow Jesus no matter what you are required to do, and no matter how much it might hurt.

It is because of your love for Jesus that I love and respect you so much. It is because of that attitude and your willingness to do that, that I have learned some very valuable lessons concerning my walk with the LORD God Almighty.

I have learned that my reliance and trust must be totally in the LORD and not men. I have learned that He can use all situations and turn them around for the good of those who love Him—and I do love Him.

And He uses those situations to show me where I need to work on my relationship with Him.

I know that my love for you is a spiritual one. I just know that the only thing that is fulfilling and produces life, His life inside of me, is what God gives by His Spirit. That is really all I seek. I so want His life to be a part of my life.

I know because of His word that He will continue to reveal Himself to me; and I will get to know Him more every day. I thank the LORD for all the people He has given me, and the love and friendships He has established between us.

For some reason, I am afraid to admit that I need other people, and that they might need me. All my life, whenever I have gotten close to someone, I have always had to say good-bye, and that was always very painful for me. That might be the reason I seem to close myself off to others.

I do have a desire in my heart to act in a godly way in all situations, circumstances, and relationships with people.

I know the LORD God will work that out in me, but my dependence is on Him to do it, and not myself, or other people...

I really do not feel like I am very mature in the word yet, but I truly desire to be. I know by your example and your willingness to teach and encourage us, that we will be. I thank the LORD that He has gone to such lengths to reveal Himself to me.

I thank you and Elisha for being the vessels He has used to show me things. I love you both very much. I pray that one day I will be a comfort to both of you like God said I should be.

Your friend,
Cathy

As I wrote that letter, I was extremely broken spiritually and emotionally. I was in a very confused state over our relationship, and the following verses will shed some light as to why this was so.

James 3:14-16 "But if ye have bitter envying and strife in your hearts, glory not, and lie not against the Truth. This wisdom descendeth not from above, but is earthly, sensual, devilish. For where envying and strife is, there is confusion and every evil work."

I Corinthians 14:33 "For God is not the author of confusion, but of peace, as in all churches of the saints."

Had I been walking in the Truth, I would have known that the strife and confusion in my heart was not of the LORD God, but of Satan; and he was battling for my soul! It is so important to live by God's word, because only the Truth will set us free from the lies of the Devil.

Dear Pastor Huff, *16 September 1991*

I wrote you a letter the other night, but I tore it up. After I read it a few times I felt like it wasn't what God would have me say to you. I really do want to have His thoughts and His ways. That is truly my desire. He has impressed upon me to give you some verses from His beautiful word.

Philippians 3:13-15 "Brethren, I count not myself to have apprehended: but this one thing I do, forgetting those things which are behind, and reaching forth unto those things which are before, I press toward the mark for the prize of the high calling of God in Christ Jesus. Let us therefore, as many as be perfect, be thus minded: and if any thing ye be otherwise minded, God shall reveal even this unto you."

Romans 10:11 "For the Scripture saith, Whosoever believeth on Him shall not be ashamed."

I love you! And it's not contingent upon anything you do or don't do. I know the feelings and emotions toward you that were put there by God will always be there, and anything else will fade away because He knows that my heart is for Him.

One of the hardest things that could happen to me in this life would be if I thought you no longer wanted me as a friend. I truly want to be called your friend. I am not ashamed in the least to be associated with you.

The feelings in my heart towards you and that beautiful wife of yours, is that I would, and will lay down my life for you. You two are the most special people I have ever been acquainted with in all my years of meeting people—and I have met plenty, but nobody like you.

I do pray that we will always walk together in like-mindedness, but if we do not, I will not worry because sooner or later God will reveal it to us.

Cathy

My emotions were being pulled in many different directions at this point in my walk with the Enemy. The only peace I could get was from God's word. If you recall I used to share the Scriptures with you hoping that it would give you as much comfort as it gave me.

I mentioned in that letter that one of the hardest things that could happen to me in this lifetime would be if I thought you no longer wanted me as a friend; but because you are an enemy of my God I can no longer befriend you, despite the feelings I *had* for you.

The following verses will show why this is true. Please seriously consider these words that God has brought to my heart.

I John 2:18-19 "Little children, it is the last time: and as ye have heard that anti-Christ shall come, even now are there many anti-Christs; whereby we know that it is the last time.

They went out from us, but they were not of us; for if they had been of us, they would no doubt *have continued with us: but* they went out, *that they might be made manifest that they were not all of us."*

I now realize that you are not a minister of the "Spirit" of Christ, but you are actually led by the "spirit" of anti-Christ! However, I did not even begin to comprehend any of this until the night of 2 March 1993.

Ezekiel 18:20-32 "The soul that sinneth, it shall die. The son shall not bear the iniquity of the father, neither shall the father bear the iniquity of the son: the righteousness of the righteous shall be upon him, and the wickedness of the wicked shall be upon him.

But if the wicked will turn from all his sins that he hath committed, and keep all My statutes, and do that which is lawful and right, he shall surely live, he shall not die. All his transgressions that he hath committed, they shall not be mentioned unto him: in his righteousness that he hath done he shall live.

Have I any pleasure at all that the wicked should die? saith the LORD God: and *not that he should return from his ways, and live?*

But when the righteous turneth away from his righteousness, and committeth iniquity, and *doeth according to all the abominations that the wicked* man *doeth, shall he live? All his righteousness that he hath done shall not be mentioned: in his trespass that he hath trespassed, and in his sin that he hath sinned, in them shall he die.*

Yet ye say, The way of the LORD is not equal (or fair). Hear now, O house of Israel; Is not My way equal? Are not your ways unequal (or unfair)? When a righteous man *turneth away from his righteousness, and committeth iniquity, and dieth in them; for his iniquity that he hath done shall he die.*

Again, when the wicked man turneth away from his wickedness that he hath committed, and doeth that which is lawful and right, he shall save his soul alive. Because he considereth, and turneth away from all his transgressions that he hath committed, he shall surely live, he shall not die.

Yet saith the house of Israel, The way of the LORD is not equal. O house of Israel, are not My ways equal? Are not your ways unequal?

Therefore I will judge you, O house of Israel, every one according to his ways, saith the LORD God.

Repent, and turn yourselves from all your transgressions; so iniquity shall not be your ruin. Cast away from you all your transgressions, whereby ye have transgressed; and make you a new heart and a new spirit: for why will ye die, O house of Israel? For I have no pleasure in the death of him that dieth, saith the LORD God: wherefore turn yourselves, and live ye!"

In case you have a problem with this passage because it's out of the Old Testament, I will reference passages from the New Testament in order to further establish the Truth. In so doing, I realize that this will refute the very popular theory "Once Saved Always Saved," which I have come to understand is a lie from the depths of Hell!

Romans 15:4 "For whatsoever things were written aforetime were written for our learning, that we through patience and comfort of the Scriptures might have hope."

Romans 16:25-26 "Now to Him that is of power to stablish you according to my gospel, and the preaching of Jesus Christ, according to the revelation of the mystery, which was kept secret since the world began,

But now is made manifest, and by the Scriptures of the prophets, according to the commandment of the everlasting God, made known to all nations for the obedience of faith:"

I Corinthians 10:9-12 "Neither let us tempt Christ, as some of them also tempted, and were destroyed of serpents. Neither murmur ye, as some of them also murmured, and were destroyed of the destroyer.

Now all these things happened unto them for ensamples: and they are written for our admonition, upon whom the ends of the world are come. Wherefore let him that thinketh he standeth take heed lest he fall."

Hebrews 3:12-14 "Take heed, brethren, lest there be in any of you an evil heart of unbelief, in departing from the living God.

But exhort (or urge) one another daily, while it is called To-day; lest any of you be hardened through the deceitfulness of sin. For we are made partakers of Christ, if we hold the beginning of our confidence steadfast unto the end;"

Hebrews 10:26-27 "For if we sin willfully after that we have received the knowledge of the Truth, there remaineth no more sacrifice for sins,

But a certain fearful looking for of judgment and fiery indignation, which shall devour the adversaries."

This next letter is the one I put in your Christmas card that year. I was rather reluctant to give it to you, but I got up the courage to go ahead even though it was quite a struggle to do so.

Dear Pastor Huff and Elisha, *21 December 1991*

I would like to address something that has been on my heart for a while now. If I am being presumptuous, or out of line, I certainly do not mind if you bring it up. For some reason, I am sure I will find out where I may have been led astray in my thinking. And my dear Elisha, I do thank the LORD for that.

You know at first when you are being corrected it is not so enjoyable, but later on, I do praise God for showing me the Truth. I desire to know the Truth and I know God will get it to me in whatever means I can receive it.

Oh well, back to the reason I am writing this letter. When I wrote up my Christmas cards, I contemplated whether I should address your card to both of you, or separately. It used to be that I would not question something like that. I would automatically figure what I said to one of you would apply to the other. I do think of you two as one, but for some reason I do not sense the unity or oneness that used to be there.

I remember when I first saw you and Elisha together. When I started coming to the Bible study, there was a very special bond between both of you that was very evident, but I do not see that anymore.

I know in the spirit you are one, as we all are one in Christ, but we certainly have an Enemy who would like to destroy that unity, or at least lie to us and make us think it is not there.

You two remind me of my Husband and me before I started putting my total expectations in the LORD Jesus. I used to have so many expectations of my Husband, and since I do not any longer, or at least I try not to—just in Jesus, he cannot let me down. Not that he doesn't sadden me and frustrate me at times, but he is not able to take my peace away because of what he does or doesn't do.

Now, I am not saying that Jesus isn't enough for you,[32] *but I hope you will examine your hearts, and see if there are any areas in your relationship with each other that doesn't line up with God's will for your lives. That has been a prayer of mine for you two—that you will be everything to each other that God has ordained for you to be according to the Truth of His word.*

I desire that all of us walk together in oneness, and I know the only way we can do that is if our total expectations are in Jesus and His word. If Jesus was not our bond, I really do not believe any of us would be together.

I love both you and Pastor Huff very much, but I feel almost afraid to show it at times. Elisha, I know you feel I favor him and that I love him more than I love you, but that is so untrue.

If you are one, you cannot be separated. So, if I love one of you, I have to love both of you. And I do! It was not put there by my desires; God has established the love I have for you.

I would like to close this letter with a verse from Philippians. This is a prayer that I pray for all of us, but especially for you two. You are our spiritual leaders, and I look up to and trust both of you.

I know Satan would love to get to you any way he can, but I pray you will stay on guard and keep trusting God in everything.

Philippians 1:9-11 "And this I pray, that your love may abound yet more and more in knowledge and in all judgment;

That ye may approve things that are excellent; that ye may be sincere and without offense till the Day of Christ;

Being filled with the fruits of righteousness, which are by Jesus Christ, unto the glory and praise of God."

Your friend in Christ,
Cathy

Even though I was intimidated by both you and Liz, I finally got up the courage to address your relationship. Cindy and I had discussed our concerns about the overly affectionate way you treated one another, but we were still willing to give you the benefit of the doubt. But when Liz started getting increasingly frustrated and discontent with you, it just gave room for more doubt.

This next message was one I believed the LORD had spoken to me. These words came to my heart at a time when I was extremely confused about many things, and due to my terribly distressed condition, I was ready to cut ties and just walk away from all of you.

I shared this with you and Liz, but you were not in agreement as to whether it was from the LORD, so that added to my confusion.

27 February 1992

"This is my word to you. All that you feel in your heart was put there by me to have my will accomplished.

Your love for him is genuine, it will always be there, and it will not fade away. He is my gift to you and you to him.

I told you long ago that you will be a comfort to him, and right now is the time my servant needs your comfort.

He is a very special, called, chosen, and set apart man with a very specific purpose I have called him to do on this earth. And all the feelings you have for him are put there by me.

You have submitted yourself to me with your whole heart and soul and thus I am able to use you.

Do not fight what you feel in your heart towards him, because if you do, it will affect how you feel about me.

Just remember, you only know in part, and you will prophesy in part, but on that day, you will fully understand all things. The truth will prevail!

Now quit being affected by what other people think, give no thought for tomorrow, and stand on my word to you. If you know with all certainty that I have called, chosen, and set you apart also, which I have, then you will never fall."[33]

At the time I heard this I actually believed that it was from God, and strangely, I never considered that it might be from the Evil One.

Since my heart's desire is to live by every word that proceeds from the mouth of God, my Enemy had to use the Scriptures to establish his lies within my heart and mind to persuade me it was from the LORD.

The following is scriptures that Satan had put in my mind at that time in an attempt to validate the message he gave me.

II Peter 1:10-12 "Wherefore the rather, brethren, give diligence to make your calling and election sure: for if ye do these things, ye shall never fall: For so an entrance shall be ministered unto you abundantly into the everlasting kingdom of our LORD and Saviour Jesus Christ.

Wherefore I will not be negligent to put you always in remembrance of these things, though ye know them, and be established in the present Truth."

Jude 24-25 "Now unto Him that is able to keep you from falling, and to present you faultless before the presence of His glory with exceeding joy, To the only wise God our Saviour, be glory and majesty, dominion and power, both now and ever. Amen!"

I wrote the following letter right after I received those words in an attempt to try and understand in my own heart what I felt God was saying to me. I was very compelled to share it with you privately, so I asked you to come over to my house. In retrospect, I Am certain it was due to the Devil's prompting, because it just gave you another chance to fill me with more lies and take advantage of my naïveté even further.

Dear Pastor Huff, *Winter 1992*

I am writing down my thoughts concerning that letter because sometimes when I am alone I can really see what is in my heart better, and I want you to know what's there concerning my relationship with you.

I do feel like those words came from my spirit instead of my mind. It was just very different from the regular junk that goes on. Regardless of all that, I tried to discern every line that I read to see if it would line up in the 'word,' based on my understanding on how to do that.

The questions that remain is, what is in my heart for you, and what really is God's idea of comfort? This is very hard to express, but I pray the LORD will give me the words to say.

There is this closeness and unity that I feel deep inside of me towards you that I know was put there because of our union with the LORD Jesus.

There is such a caring in my heart for what you go through. Whether it is good or bad it's almost like that doesn't matter—I just want to share it with you.

I really want to be a friend to you that you can really trust, and know that it doesn't matter what you do or don't do as to whether I am going to keep being your friend or not.

I just have such a desire in me to be involved in your life; not to where I am controlling your life, but being someone that God has given you to help you, and encourage, and comfort, and be with in the midst of this awful world we live in that really does hate us.

The encouragement and comfort I am talking about is that God would lead me by His Spirit to say and do what He would have me do, so that it would strengthen you in Him and push you closer to Him. I do know that He is the only reason worth living for.

I know if I did not have Jesus in my heart I would be so ugly and there would be nothing in me worth loving.

My desire is not to tear you down, but to build you up, so that you can endure the things that happen to you with confidence, patience, and assurance that you are doing what the LORD has called you to do; and you know with certainty that He has called you, chosen you, and set you apart to do a very special task.

I do know in my heart that you are a very special man to Him. You have been called to do something that is going to require His word to be so grounded, rooted, and established in your spirit that whenever you speak, it will only be the word of God, so that it will either kill people or give them life. I really feel that what you are going through with all of us is your training ground to get it established in your heart.

All these desires and feelings of comfort and encouragement I have inside of me for you, I also have for Elisha. Although, it is almost like she doesn't want it from me. I am not one she cares to be around—only when she really feels the LORD is leading her to talk to me, or a lot of times when she just wants to see what is going on in my head.

As you may know, I have this overwhelming love for her, and it feels the same way that I feel in my heart about you. The only difference is that you make me feel so loved and cared for. It is almost like she cannot receive anything from me.

You sometimes wonder whether I trust you or not, and the fact is that I do very much because my LORD said I can. It is me that I do not trust. And when I express doubt about things, it is because I know that I am not perfect and that I do have a sin nature that I really do not fully understand.

The thing about it is that I have told God that I want Him to change me and make me the way He wants me to be, and not the way the world or even I expect me to be.

I love you and Elisha so very much, and I know that because of our relationships together, the last few years have been some of the most painful to endure, but also the most joyful.

If because of all the things I have gone through with you produces godliness, then it has really been worth it.

My biggest fear concerning my relationship with you, is that because of my actions, I might encourage ungodliness instead of the thing I so desire—that all of us walk in perfect unity in love towards one another, and not allow the world, or even what people think of us to affect how we respond to each other.

I know the world will never understand us, and won't really ever desire to understand, unless they really want to know and understand our LORD and Savior. I will always pray for you.

Cathy

By the way, I Am still praying for you even though you were one of the instruments Satan used to try and drag me to Hell. And it is only because of God's love in my heart that I have no ill feelings for you or for any of the other members of La'el Ministries.

For your own good, I truly hope you did not purposefully seek to turn me away from my God. Here are some verses that will show what God thinks about the person who does that.

Proverbs 28:10 "Whoso causeth the righteous to go astray in an evil way, he shall fall himself into his own pit: but the upright shall have good things in possession."

Deuteronomy 13:1-11 "If there arise among you a prophet, or a dreamer of dreams, and giveth thee a sign or a wonder, And the sign or the wonder come to pass, whereof he spake unto thee, saying, Let us go after other gods, which thou hast not known, and let us serve them;

Thou shalt not hearken unto the words of that prophet, or that dreamer of dreams: for the LORD your God proveth you, to know whether ye love the LORD your God with all your heart and with all your soul.

Ye shall walk after the LORD your God, and fear Him, and keep His commandments, and obey His voice, and ye shall serve Him, and cleave unto Him. And that prophet or that dreamer of dreams, shall be put to death; because he hath spoken to turn you *away from the LORD your God, which brought you out of the land of Egypt, and redeemed you out of the house of bondage, to thrust thee out of the way which the LORD thy God commanded thee to walk in. So shalt thou put the evil away from the midst of thee.*

If thy brother, the son of thy mother, or thy son, or thy daughter, or the wife of thy bosom, or thy friend, which is *as thine own soul, entice thee secretly, saying, Let us go and serve other gods, which thou hast not known, thou, nor thy fathers;*

Namely, of the gods of the people which are *round about you, nigh unto thee, or far off from thee, from the* one *end of the earth even unto the* other *end of the earth; Thou shalt not consent unto him, nor hearken unto him;*

Neither shall thine eye pity him, neither shalt thou spare, neither shalt thou conceal him: But thou shalt surely kill him; thine hand shall be first upon him to put him to death, and afterwards the hand of all the people.

And thou shalt stone him with stones, that he die; because he hath sought to thrust thee away from the LORD thy God, which brought thee out of the land of Egypt, from the house of bondage. And all Israel shall hear, and fear, and shall do no more any such wickedness as this is among you."

I Am certain that your false teachings resulted in causing me to walk in ways that were quite contrary to the Scriptures. According to this passage, it seems that God expects me to be the first one to bring it to the attention of others so as to hinder this type of evil. And only by God's grace will I be able to carry out such a task.

I just praise the LORD God that He revealed my sin to me so that I could finally see the Truth; and I hope for your sake that you did not deliberately lead me into error and deception.

Although, I have serious reservations about Liz and her motives. She was always very subtle, and extremely hard to understand at times, but I truly believe her intention *was* to lead me away from *my* God!

I don't know if Liz ever mentioned it to you, but we had a very interesting conversation right before we broke-up that has caused me to realize that Satan has given her power to control demonic spirits through witchcraft and sorcery, which is why I seriously doubt her sincerity.

On the particular morning that this discussion took place, I had told her that I had a very strange dream about you, and she seemed to be quite intrigued and most eager to hear about it.

I said, "It was a pretty *weird* dream," but that just made her even more curious about it. Finally, she became really impatient with me and quite agitated and said, "Well, tell me about it!"

I told her that I dreamed you were fixing to bow your knee to Satan! And when I said that, she freaked out! She said you would let them skin you alive before you would *ever* do something like that!

I said, "Well, it seemed pretty real." Then I proceeded to tell her more about the dream, and right in the middle of my sentence my mind went completely blank—as if my thoughts had just been erased! I could not even remember what I was talking about.

After a long pause I finally said to her, "Liz, I really don't know where I am going with this." She then said, "Well, I guess not! I had to ask God to intervene!"

And I said, "You mean God can just take something right out of your mind like that?" She said, "Yeah, if He doesn't like what you are talking about."

I got so excited to think that God could actually stop me from talking about something I had no business saying. I even mentioned it to Cindy that night, but she didn't have much of a comment though.

I was *terribly* naive at that time in my life, but praise the LORD God Almighty I Am finally able to see the Truth!

In this next letter you will be able to see how you were still capable of manipulating me, which is what prompted this response, but praise God it would not be long before Satan's hold on me would be released and he would be running scared. Praise God!

Dear Pastor Huff, *22 May 1992*

Since you obviously do not want to speak to me, and I can understand why, I hope you will at least read this letter.

I just want you to know that what I did the other night was extremely hard for me to do. The last thing in the world that I would ever want to do, is humiliate you in front of other people. But I had to do it because I know the LORD said to do it that way.

But that did not mean it did not kill me inside to do it. I love you, and if you can believe it, I did it because I do love you. I want to know you in eternity with our Father in Heaven.

If I thought that I had a part in causing a man to walk away from the LORD, and what He has called him to do on this earth, I don't think I could bear that. Please don't do that to me, and more importantly don't do that to Elisha (Liz).

That woman is such a special person to me and I cannot really express in words how I feel about her. Her love for you is like no other love that I have ever seen for a woman to a man.

My greatest desires for us—and Jesus states it much better: "And the glory which thou gavest Me I have given them; that they may be one, even as We are one: I in them, and Thou in Me, that they may be made perfect in one; and that the world may know that Thou hast sent Me, and hast loved them, as Thou hast loved Me." John 17:22-23

My prayer for you is that you will let Jesus be your strength and your support, and accept the love of the people that He has placed around you.

Whether or not you ever speak to me again, I hope you always know deep down in your heart that my love for you is very genuine and it will always be there. Thank you for at least reading this.

Cathy

I wrote that letter after the meeting[34] we had over at your place in the presence of Cindy and Liz. I will never forget how nervous I was. It was obvious as the meeting progressed that I did not come in the boldness or strength of the LORD, even though I felt He had prompted me to confront you about this particular matter.

Because I was walking in Darkness and not completely free of the demonic influences in my life I was still very intimidated by both you and Liz. But praise the LORD God Almighty the stronghold that Satan had on me would soon be broken!

Do you remember the verse I quoted at the beginning of this letter? [24 August 1993 Letter] I would like to bring it up again, and especially notice Peter's response to the LORD.

Luke 22:31-34 "And the LORD said, Simon, Simon, behold, Satan hath desired to have you, that he may sift you as wheat: But I have prayed for thee, that thy faith fail not: and when thou art converted, strengthen thy brethren.

And he said unto him, LORD, I am ready to go with thee, both into prison, and to death. And He said, I tell thee, Peter, the cock shall not crow this day, before that thou shall thrice deny that thou knowest Me."

If someone had told me when I first started coming to your Bible study group that I would actually commit an act that would cause me to deny the LORD on three separate occasions, I would never have believed I could be capable of doing *anything* that would dishonor my God. But that is exactly what happened!

Due to my complete ignorance of the Devil's tactics, and my lack of knowledge of spiritual things, along with my self-righteous attitude, Satan was able to deceive me into believing the many lies that were put into my heart and mind by you, Liz, and the demonic voices that were sent to me—including the voice of the Devil himself!

However, on 17 June 1992, the day before my Husband came home, I finally came to terms with the guilt that was killing me inside, and I experienced God's forgiveness and His cleansing power.

Of course, it was Satan's plan from the start to lure me into sin. He especially wanted to lead me into the kind of sin that would keep me in Darkness and eventually kill me.

But the LORD knew everything that would happen between us from the very beginning, and He knew what would happen in the end. He also knew that I had to be completely crushed in order to break my prideful, self-righteous, and stubborn attitude.

And because of some of the very humbling and shameful things I experience while with you, I have more understanding and compassion for someone who has been manipulated by another person whose intent is to lure them away from God, and seduce them into a sin unto death.

And due to my "falling away" from the Truth of what I knew to be right, I Am much more aware of the extreme danger of this type of sin if it is allowed to take place, much less continue.

I certainly learned this lesson the hard way, but my hope is that others may learn from my mistakes and not have to go through what I went through. The problem Satan had with me, was that I could not keep quiet about what happened because of the disturbing effect it had on me emotionally, spiritually, and even physically.

You know, I never blamed you for my sin, and I still don't. I just see you as a deceiver, who is deceiving others, unto your own destruction. I just praise God that He saw fit to deliver me! And He will do the same for *all* who truly love Him and delight completely in His word, and are willing to take hold of the Tree of Life, and eat![35]

I realize that some people cannot even begin to understand how a true Christian can do such things, but this passage will help shed some light on the evil behind this kind of sin and deception.

Revelation 2:20-23 "Notwithstanding I have a few things against thee, because thou sufferest that woman Jezebel, which calleth herself a prophetess, to teach and to seduce my servants to commit fornication, and to eat things sacrificed unto idols.

And I gave her space to repent of her fornication; and she repented not. Behold, I will cast her into a bed, and them that commit adultery with her into great tribulation, except they repent of their deeds.

And I will kill her children with death; and all the churches shall know that I Am He which searcheth the reins and hearts: and I will give unto everyone of you according to your works."

Liz told me that she took great pleasure in seducing men into sexual sin, especially "Christian" men. Of course, she said this was *before* she started walking with the LORD and serving Him.

However, I have since found out that she has been lying from the very beginning, and the Truth is not in her! I have also come to understand that she is of the same "spirit" as that "Jezebel woman!"

When you let her read this letter, tell her to especially take heed to the scripture I just referenced. The LORD has put her on notice, and God has said to all who will listen: *"It is Time to repent, and turn from all your transgressions, so iniquity shall not be your ruin!"*

I don't know if you are aware of it, but the final straw came for me when Liz informed me about you and Kim, and how you seduced her into believing that you were her "spiritual" husband too.

When she told me, I just broke down and all the emotional pain, grief, and heartache that I went through came flooding back. I could not handle the thought of Kim going through what I had gone through, especially since she was so young and vulnerable.

I was under the mistaken impression that you repented and it had stopped with me, but based on what Liz told me, it had not! She realized she made an unfortunate mistake by mentioning this to me because at that point I was ready to throw you out of my house.

I told her I thought it was such an honor to have the Truth taught in my own home, but after this, any trust or respect I had for you was completely gone. She desperately tried to calm me down and convince me that I was wrong about you.

She insisted that you were our "pastor" as appointed by God, and that I really needed to respect His "anointed one."

However, at that point I said, "God never told *me* that you were my pastor, that's what *you* said!" The only thing I was sure that God had said to me is that, "I would learn a lot from that man."

She went on to say that this was an area you were weak in and that you just needed our prayers. She used to compare you with King Saul and she would reference the scripture where David would not kill him because he was "anointed" by God to be king.

And she said that since *you* were "God's anointed," I needed to let God handle all of this, otherwise I would be in sin.

She was finally able to persuade me after that statement. So, at that point, I handed all of my concerns about this to my Heavenly Father and I was just going to trust Him completely.

God knew how I felt and how I could not support you any longer after finding out that you had not repented of that detestable evil.

I had faith that God would deal with this in His way, and at the proper time, so I decided to just wait on Him.

And He handled it wonderfully! On 28 February 1993, He made His awesome presence known in such a mighty and supernatural way, that there is no doubt as to what He thought. Praise God!

Prophecy of 28 February 1993

"Many things you have been taught here has been done in secrecy and in Darkness. You have been taught truth mixed with lies, and the LORD says it will go on no longer!

And you, Mr. Huff, is the one who has taught the lies, and the LORD says it will go on no longer in this home. The LORD is giving you a chance to turn from your sin, and He is so forgiving that He will not hold your sin against you, if you repent. And if you do not, you will die!

He is my Husband, and I love Him with a love that cannot be broken. I love you too, but with a brotherly love. And I beg you to repent!

Everything you have learned here has been tainted with evil, and you cannot hold on to any of it. The only thing that you can hold on to is the fact that Jesus Christ died for you, and by His mighty power, God raised Him from the dead. If you believe that in your heart, and claim Him as LORD, He will put the same Spirit that raised Jesus from the dead inside of you, to lead you and guide you into the Truth!

Light will overshadow Darkness, and Darkness will not be able to stand in the presence of God!"

I sincerely hope that you will not deny your sin any longer, because if you do not ever face up to the Truth and truly repent, you will certainly die as the LORD God had revealed to us on that night.

Please do not disregard what the LORD God Almighty has spoken not only through His word, but by His Spirit. This could very well be your last chance to repent and turn from your iniquity.

I wrote the following letter soon after our separation, and even though I never finished it, I feel led to share what I have with you so that you can better understand my view after I left your group.

Dear Mr. Huff and Liz, *21 March 1993*

I Am not really sure why I Am even writing this letter, but I do feel compelled to write to you. It's not like you aren't use to it, but I Am sure you didn't really expect me to write you about anything ever again, especially in light of everything that has transpired in the last few weeks.

The whole time I have known you two—excuse me, the whole time I have walked with you would be much more accurate—I have written you letters which seems really foolish. And I Am sure you have gotten a good laugh at my stupidity.

From this side of it, I realize just how naive and ignorant I was. Oh well, I guess you live and learn.

You know, I had no idea things would ever turn out this way—that I would be the one standing up for the Truth, and all of you rejecting me. It still kind of blows my mind.

I Am sure this bit of information will give you great comfort to know, that you have been the cause of such great pain, sorrow, and grief in my heart, that I cannot really even put it into words how I feel.

Our whole walk together has been a most painful one, and I guess now I understand what the LORD meant when He said I would be a comfort to you. At the time, I did not realize you got your comfort out of destroying people's lives in whatever way you possibly could.

I know one thing that you must really hate about me, is my desire to know the Truth, and walk in it; and to be perfectly honest with all people. That desire has not changed at all, and I will continue to be that way.

Even though I have found out that your greatest desire was to drag me to Hell, I Am surprised that I do not have any real feelings of resentment and anger or hatred towards either of you.

Actually, the love I had for you two is still there, but it is almost like it is a futile effort. I just feel a lot of pain at the thought of someone I use to have such a deep respect and even honor for, and knowing that you are going to burn in Hell is really hard for me to grasp right at this moment.

I do not really desire that for you or anybody. And I know in my heart that in your present condition, that is exactly where you both will spend eternity—and whomever else you happen to grab a hold of will go with you.

I just thank my God that He intervened and revealed the Truth to me, and He will do the same for whoever else desires it.

Liz, you really had me fooled for the whole time. Not until Tuesday night (on the 2nd of March 1993), did I really realize just who you actually served. You are really a sly one. You are a real good hypocrite. You can pretend so very well...

But you know what Mr. Huff? For some reason I still feel like you have been ensnared in a trap, and you have just walked in such sin, and have transgressed God's laws for so long, that He has just given you over to a reprobate mind, and God has sent you a strong delusion to believe the lies.

Liz does have a lot of power over you. I don't really understand much about witchcraft, but I know she does not have power over me anymore because I have finally found out the truth about you two through the revelation of God Almighty! Thank God!!

The hardest of all of this to come to terms with, is the fact that we do not serve the same God; and all along I believed we did. But all you have to do is look at the fruits in your life—they are not of the Holy Spirit at all.

One thing I want you to know, which I Am sure you already know, is that my God is very upset with you two. And I happen to be His vessel, and I do not really question as to how He uses me.

Like for instance, the other day when you came to get the piano, I really didn't plan on that outburst of anger towards you, but for some reason when the Holy Spirit came over me, and started quoting that scripture, I just could not contain myself. It is based on Galatians 1:9 "If any man preach any other gospel besides the gospel of Jesus Christ, let him be accursed!"

Becky said she even heard me in her house all the way from across the street. My next-door neighbor and her whole family even came running outside to see what was going on. Pretty wild huh?[36]

That was the letter I couldn't complete because my Husband kept interrupting me to come to bed. However, I really don't feel that the LORD wanted me to finish it or even send you a letter at that time.

I was so upset before I started writing that letter because of a religious program that I had just watched on television. The preacher's sermon confirmed some things that the LORD God had spoken to me, and it was very significant because it was an answer to prayer.

God had been telling me that if any of you from La'el Ministries denied that what took place on 28 February 1993 was from the LORD, then you would be in danger of blasphemy against the Holy Spirit.

This was very troubling for me because I know it is the only unforgivable sin. I do not understand all the ramifications of this sin, but I know it is something you will carry with you forever. And the burden and weight of it is something you will sense for eternity.

I had asked the LORD to confirm that to me because I was very disturbed at the thought of any of you going to Hell, when just a few weeks before that I felt like I would know you forever.

God is so great! In less than a week He answered my prayer, and on national television! At the beginning of his sermon, he said that it was a very controversial subject, and that most ministers are very unwilling to preach on it. Moreover, he even quoted some of the very passages that God spoke to my heart days before this.

Matthew 12:32 "And whosoever speaketh a word against the Son of Man, it shall be forgiven him: but whosoever speaketh against the Holy Ghost, it shall not be forgiven him, neither in this world, neither in the world *to come."*

Hebrews 6:4-6 "For it is *impossible for those who were once enlightened, and have tasted of the Heavenly gift, and were made partakers of the Holy Ghost, and have tasted the good word of God, and the powers of the world to come, if they shall fall away, to renew them again unto repentance; seeing they crucify to themselves the Son of God afresh, and put* Him *to open shame."*

Hebrews 10:30-31 "For we know Him that hath said, Vengeance belongeth *unto Me, I will recompense, saith the LORD. And again, the LORD shall judge His people.* It is *a fearful thing to fall into the hands of the living God."*

I taped this program because I knew that it was a confirmation from God. Amazingly, I received the transcript of that program in the mail on the exact day I sent that "warning letter" to all the members of La'el Ministries and your families, so I included it in the mailing.

I would like to remind you that one of the reasons I Am writing this letter to you is to hopefully convince you to turn from your sin, and turn back to God, and serve only Him in all Truth and sincerity.

I would like to bring back to your memory the last page of the letter dated, 14 April 1993, that I had sent you and the other members of the group, along with the first page of the letter I sent to your families.

It was very fascinating to me that you received that "warning" right before David Koresh and his remaining followers were destroyed by the fire in Waco, Texas on 19 April 1993. It is especially significant for me because I feel that you and Koresh are one and the same man.[37]

Interestingly, 19 April 1990 is also the exact day you "laid hands" on me and attempted to pass on the "spirit" that is in you over to me, which by the way is the same "spirit" that Koresh was controlled by.

To Whom it May Concern, *14 April 1993*

Enclosed is a letter I sent to your child that I would like for you to read and be aware of. It is very important that they read and take heed to the words of that letter, because it is God's final word to them; and it may be their last chance to repent of their sin.

If you are truly a God-fearing person, I hope that you will pray for your child. It is a matter of eternal life and eternal death.

I had been involved with their Bible study group for over three years, and I Am no longer! They have not been allowed to speak, preach, teach, or anything else in my home since the LORD from above came down into my living room in a very mighty way, on the night of 28 February 1993, during Bible study to reveal the Truth. (By the way, that was the same day the Waco cult was revealed and exposed to the whole world.)

We had a subsequent confrontational meeting with a few of the other members on the evening of 2 March 1993 where more of the Truth was revealed; and I have been walking in the "True Light" ever since.

I do not stand in agreement with any of them; and ever since that night the whole group has rejected me. I actually love all of those people, and it hurts very deeply to think that they may spend eternity in Hell if they continue on their present course.

Many people have been deceived by them, and you may be one of them. I pray that you are not, but I do have confidence in the LORD that if you truly want the Truth, you will certainly find it.

Jesus is the door. Keep on seeking and you will find. Keep on knocking and the door will be opened up to you. Keep on asking and you will receive. He did it for me and He will do it for you!

I will pray for you and your child as the LORD directs me. And please mention the enclosed letter to them just in case they did not receive it or decided not to read it. This is a very important matter and I pray that you or they will not take it lightly and just dismiss it.

God has put them on notice and they may say they are suffering for Jesus' sake, but in actuality they are reaping what they have sown.

Sincerely,
A servant of the Most High God
C. Read

End of First page of "Warning Letter"

To Whom it May Concern, *14 April 1993*

The God of Abraham, Isaac, and Jacob says to you: This is your Final Warning! Repent and turn from your sin!

Your sin has darkened your eyes and you know not where you are going or where you have been.

You may think you are walking with the LORD God Almighty, but you have been deluded into believing a lie.

Your lives are based on lies! And we all know that Satan is the father of lies. Only Truth will set you free from the Power of Darkness!

I pray you will heed these words of "Warning" and humbly consider what the LORD God above is speaking to your heart. It is a matter of your Eternal Life or eternal death.

Whether you believe it or not I love you all very, very much, and so does the LORD. After all, He gave His Life for you so that you might live. He can forgive you of all your sin except blasphemy against His Holy Spirit. So please do not disregard what He did on the night of Twenty-Eight February Nineteen Hundred and Ninety-Three.

Also the following Sunday night when you came and got the piano was most certainly the Holy Spirit working through me, which I had no control over.

You know my stand with the LORD has always been, "Here I Am LORD, send me!" And He has done it! Praise the LORD God!

If you continue on your present course, the LORD will come upon you like a thief in the night. And when you stand before Him there will be no more excuses or justifications.

You cannot deceive the Perfect One! Blessing, and Glory, and Wisdom, and Thanksgiving, and Honor, and Power, and Might be unto my God! Forever, and ever! Amen.

"Let us hear the conclusion of the whole matter: Fear God, and keep His commandments: for this is the whole duty of man.

For God shall bring every work into judgment, with every secret thing, whether it be good, or whether it be evil." Ecclesiastes 12:13-14

End of Last Page of "Warning Letter"

Signed and sealed in the presence of a witness on the 22nd Day of September in the year of the LORD, One Thousand Nine Hundred and Ninety-Three.

End of letter to Huff dated 24 August 1993

THAT WARNING WAS GIVEN TO LA'EL MINISTRIES just days before the compound in Waco, Texas was engulfed in flames. All this proves to me that certain dates are *very* significant with the LORD, even though my Enemy would have me to believe otherwise. Mr. Huff or Liz has never admitted it to me, but I Am sure they are deeply disturbed at the fate of this "man" who claimed that he was "Christ."

The date of 14 April also has great historical significance. It was on that day in 1912 that the "warnings" were sent to the RMS Titanic! And had those in charge of this "once great" ocean liner realized the danger of ignoring the many "warnings" they could have spared the lives of so many innocent people from such a horrible and untimely death.[38]

The "sin" of pride is one of the reasons why they could not hear, and it's the same way in our day! Almighty God is warning His people, but they just will not listen to God and those whom He has sent.

It grieves the heart of God that the people He created do not even count His voice worthy of consideration; but they will greatly regret that decision one Day. And just as the many men, women, and children perished in the icy waters, on that early morning of 15 April 1912, so too will many be lost in the pits of Hell, because they did not take heed to the many "warnings" that Almighty God has sent to His people.

THE FOLLOWING MESSAGE was left by Mr. Huff on my answering machine on 12 September 1994. He made this phone call three days before Yom Kippur, the Holiest of all Jewish Holidays.[39]

"Hi Cathy. Ah, this is [Pastor Huff]. I would like to talk to you if it is at all possible. Oh, what did you say, Ten o'clock at night. And uh, I just would like to talk to you, if it is at all possible with you. My number is...and I just need to talk to you. I'd like to talk to you. Very much. Please pick up."

I was home when Mr. Huff left that message, but I did not have an inclination to pick up the phone and talk to him. However, I did sense that I would be calling him back at another time; and six days later the LORD impressed upon me to return his call.

The following transcript is a conversation I had with Mr. Huff over a year after I wrote him the letter dated 24 August 1993. Initially, I did not understand why God wanted me to tape our conversation, but afterwards I realized that He wanted me to include it in my Testimony.

I would like to note that both of us were extremely nervous about talking to one another, and so I left out some of the more obvious indications of our uneasiness, otherwise this recording is verbatim.

TAPED RECORDING BETWEEN MR. HUFF AND CATHY 18 SEPTEMBER 1994

Huff "...Hello?"

Cathy "Hello, Mr. Huff?"

Huff "Yes."

Cathy "This is Cathy..."

Huff "Hi. How are you doing?"

Cathy "Well, I Am okay. I got your message last week, and I was kind of waiting till I talked to [my Husband]...about calling you. And I guess I'm calling you."

Huff "Well, thank you. I'm glad you returned my call."

Cathy "Well, I think I— It's only the customary thing to do, I guess."

Huff "Okay."

Cathy "What did you need?"

Huff "I just wanted to talk to you for a few minutes. And you know, first of all, again, I wanted to apologize to you for all the things that have happened here."

Cathy "Wh–, why, why is that?"

Huff "Well, I mean, you know, Cathy, I found that my own heart is not what I would want it to be. And as I presented it before the Lord over the last few months and years, ya know, I've just allowed the Lord to, or hopefully allowed the Lord to do the work in my heart. And reveal areas of weakness, and sin, and Darkness that are there that stain our lives, or that stain my life, and cause me to be something that I don't want to be, or something that I don't choose to be. And ya know, the things that were there were not pleasing to me, and they are certainly not the things that I wanted to be.

So as I've looked at—had those things exposed, and will have them exposed in the future, by the Lord; as they come up and as they are brought to my attention, I go back and I try to rectify, and correct, and do what the Scriptures talk about doing, which is seeking forgiveness and forgiving those around me and—"

Cathy "Let me interrupt you just for a minute okay?"

Huff "Okay."

Cathy "I do want you to know that [my Husband is]...listening on the other end, and that's one of the main reasons why I waited to call you because he wasn't here last week.

And anything that I do I will go through Him before I even attempt to do it. So I hope you know that."

Huff "That's great."

Cathy "I really hope that what you're saying to me is genuine, but ya know, time will tell that too. Go ahead, I just wanted to let you know that."

Huff "Uh, well, you know, it's genuine to me, whether it is to anybody else or not."

Cathy "Well, it is between you and God. It's really—"

Huff "Ya know, I agree with what you said that night, that things were out of order; I do not agree with the spirit by which you said it, nor do I agree with the spirit by which you've operated since that time."

Cathy "Oh, you don't?"

Huff "No, because that's, that is, it's, ya know, that's a personal thing. You know, you got to do what you got to do. And I'm not here to judge it. I'm not here to condemn it either.

I'm just telling you that things were out of order. Things were out of order in my heart. Things were out of order in my life. I've not submitted some areas of my life to the Lord that He had been wanting to deal with. And ya know, that has caused me to walk in sin. And I'm calling you tonight, not so much to—ya know, I'm not trying to get you to do anything here."

Cathy "Oh, I don't take it as that."

Huff "Ya know, I think that perhaps things are—well, wherever they are, they are, but I am calling you, and one of the primary reasons that I am calling you is to ask you to very seriously and prayerfully consider being reconciled to both Liz and Cindy.

I want to tell you that neither one of them are opposed to you, and that they very much sincerely love you. And that they do not agree with me on what happened. That they're not standing around here supporting me.

And doing all kinds of things to, ya know, justify my position or anything else. Both of them have made it, and are still making it, very plain to me that those things were not right.

That neither the things that I taught, and many of the things that I believed, many of the things that I perceived as far as being from the Lord, that they were not.

And ya know, there is no reason in the world for you to feel like they're your enemies or that they're opposed to you.

And I guess if I had one primary purpose for calling you tonight, or calling you the other night, was to ask you to prayerfully consider re-establishing lines of communication and friendship with those two sisters in the Lord of yours.

And I'm not telling you to do that. I'm not begging you to do it. I'm just asking you to prayerfully consider a reconciliation with them.

And realizing that I'm not in the way here. I'm not asking you to be bosom buddies and to start something, or have anything, because I'm out of the picture."

Cathy "Do you not live with her anymore?"

Huff "No. I haven't lived with her in a long time."

Cathy "You haven't?"

Huff "No."

Cathy "How come?"

Huff "When Tom left, I left."

Cathy "How come? Tom's not staying there either?"

Huff "Tom and Liz are divorced."

Cathy "They are?"

Huff "Sure."

Cathy "When did they get divorced?"

Huff "Last November."

Cathy "Well, I know she has always wanted to."

Huff "I'm not sure she would have preferred that, but that's what happened."

Cathy "Oh, she didn't want to get divorced? I don't mean to get personal because I'm not—"

Huff "...You can talk to her about that, but it wasn't her that did it. No, Tom just left and he's now married to Sue."

Cathy "I had heard that, but I don't always listen to everything I hear. I guess you would know more than me. Somebody had asked me why don't I go up to the Chancery Clerk's Office and check for them. But I don't care to do that...

I do want you to know that I have been concerned about all of you. The love I had for any of you was not a pretense of any kind. But I do know—"

Huff "Well, I know that, and that's why I'm calling you now, because I really want, and I desire, and I really honestly believe that the Lord does, but I'm not putting that kind of pressure on you.

It was like I asked you before to prayerfully consider that matter of reconciliation with them.

Realizing that as far as, ya know, for the most part, Cathy, they agree with you. They agree with what you said. I don't know whether or not—

There may be differences of opinion—Just like there are differences of opinion with me concerning the methods that you used since that time, or even that night, but regardless—"

Cathy "What is it that you said, the spirit in which it was done? What do you mean by that? That you didn't agree with?"

Huff "Well, you know, the Bible is very clear isn't it? You know that you walk in love towards your brother."

Cathy "Well, wouldn't exposing their sin when they wouldn't hear it any other way? I mean, and I don't want to get in an argument with you about Biblical things."

Huff "I'm not going to argue with you."

Cathy "But that really wasn't me speaking that night. I attribute that completely to the Holy Spirit.

And I Am really concerned if you really think that that was a demonic spirit."

Huff "Cathy, I just know this. Okay, I just know this. I know that people that are led by the Spirit of the Lord—

Ya know, to—I can understand you coming against me. Okay? I can."

Cathy "Well, it's more against your sin, not necessarily you as a person."

Huff "No, I can understand you coming against me. I can understand you coming against the message; and false teachings, and erroneous doctrine, and sin in my life—"

Cathy "Well, you know what really got to me though? Was with Kim. When it happened to me—

When Liz told me about you and Kim—How you seduced her to make her think that you were her husband too. It's like when it happens to you, you can pretty much kind of overlook it, but when it happens to somebody else it was different."

Huff "Well, Cathy, I have taken all this before the Lord. These are the areas in my life that the Lord needed to deal with. And I've taken these areas before the Lord here.

And you know, the Lord is dealing with my heart, and dealing with my attitude, and dealing with my whole being about some of these things. And you know, I didn't—Ya know, I don't walk in justification for the things that I've done, whether they're right or whether they're wrong. If you believe sincerely, truthfully, and honestly in your own heart that you're led by the Spirit of the LORD—"

Cathy "Oh, I know I Am."

Huff "—to do those things that you've done, then you know, you stand on that. I'm not condemning you for that. And I'm not prejudging you for it. I'm just simply saying to you, Cathy, and to [your Husband], that I regret these things that have happened. It was my sin that caused it, not anybody else's. It was my attitude and the areas of my heart that I had refused to allow the Lord to deal with that led up to it. And that those areas are being dealt with very slowly, but very surely. And I called you tonight to, or last week—"

Cathy "Yeah, you're a little confused there, but—"

Huff "I'm talking to ya anyway tonight—to come to you and to say look, these two women do not support me."

Cathy "So, you don't preach over there anymore at all either?"

Huff "No. I don't preach anywhere at all anymore."

Cathy "Do you go to church anywhere?"

Huff "Oh yes, very much so.

Ya know, the thing here is, that these two women, Cindy and Liz, you know they love you. And you love them. And ya know, you may have differences of opinion.

One of the hardest things that's ever been in a church is for people who even have doctrinal differences, that you can walk with somebody even though you—You may have doctrinal differences, but you can still walk with them.

You can still love them. And you can still have a friendship with them. And you can still even be challenged by them, because nobody's arrived yet."

Cathy "Oh no, but I Am going. I can't wait... I Am getting there."

Huff "But I called you because I want you, Cathy.

You know, I don't have any visions that you're sitting over there all by yourself and locked away, and all this kind of stuff, but that's not what I'm talking about."

Cathy "What do you *mean*?"

Huff "I'm talking about two women who love you. And who care about you. And you who care about Liz and Cindy. And you know, being friends with them. And reconciling yourselves, all three of you, to a point where you are able to communicate, where you are able to share things again. Because you are all three sisters in the Lord. And there is no reason in the world for this thing that happened with me to be a guiding factor in the break-up of relationships and friendships between sisters in the Lord."

Cathy "Well, you know what? She does not agree with this, like you told me at the beginning here, that the spirit in which I've been operating in since I've left ya'll—she don't agree with that either. So, there's really no way that I could walk with somebody that thinks that I Am listening to the Devil instead of to God."

Huff "All of us do that, Cathy."

Cathy "Do what?"

Huff "Anybody who believes that they cannot be influenced and deceived by satanic voices or demonic influences—

You know anybody who believes that they can't be, has already become that way.

I don't say you are demonically possessed. I'm not trying to say anything like this.

Even if you have a difference of opinion, say between you and Liz have a difference of opinion about whether or not what you heard was from Jesus Christ, or what you heard was n— If she thinks it wasn't, then you know, that's still—The fact is that you profess Jesus Christ as your LORD and Savior. And the fact is that Liz and Cindy both profess Jesus Christ, *the same Jesus Christ,* as their Lord and Savior. That does say something.

That puts all three of you in one body. And you're not going to get to unity in the faith in Jesus Christ by remaining at odds, or saying I can't, or I won't, or anything else *that allows a continual valley to exist here. [Emphasis mine.]*

I'm trying to tell you that these two women do—They may have differences of opinion with you. You're going to have differences of opinions with them—"

Cathy "Oh, I have differences of opinions with a lot of people. You know, *that's* really not the issue."

Huff "Oh yes it is. Because you can have a difference of opinion and still walk with somebody and love them."

Cathy "Oh yeah, well, look at [my Husband]...I don't agree with him all the time. In fact—Well, I don't want to go into any details, but I still love him and I will not *ever* get rid of him.

But it is not quite the same. You know, with everything that was involved there...it would just be really hard to—

Ya know, once you have been really lied to, and lied about, that really puts like a bad taste in your mouth. And ya know, it's really hard to drink of that same cup again. And that is basically the situation here.

And not that I wouldn't forgive them. And if you are sincerely sorry for seducing me...I hope that that is the truth. I hope that you are really sorry. And I really hope that you did not intentionally pull me away from walking with God.

Because you know, when I first came to your group, that was my heart's desire, to walk in a deeper relationship with God. And you knew that. And God knew that. *[I became very emotional at this point.]*

And that sin that you seduced me into was about the worst thing that I could ever do in my life...

And that scripture that used to come up all the time—That *"Whatsoever God hath joined together, let no man put asunder."* That scripture didn't apply to you! It applied to...[my Husband]!

[I became extremely emotional at this point in our phone conversation.] And you were the "man" that was trying to take me away from my Husband! And that really bothers me. And it really hurts. And I hope you are sorry.

And you will have to answer to God for that. And if you are sorry, I know He will forgive you.

But I cannot come back to a group of people that sanctioned that. That agreed with it. You know, with their mouth, they say I do not agree, but I know with their actions they do. Because Liz stood by and watched it happen.

And I Am sorry I cannot be friends with her anymore, or Cindy. But I do hope—The only hope I have for all of you is that you will submit to God. Because He is the one who can put you into *Hell,* or allow you to come into His kingdom!

And that is my concern for you. That is the only reason why I've written you. That is the only reason why I have written anybody. Is because I do not want you to die in Hell. I really don't. And I hope you know that."

Huff "Yes, I know that. And I—"

Cathy "But *you* will be the one that places yourself there, based on your heart decisions.

That's really all I have to say there for a moment."

Huff "Well, let me just share this with you. Liz does not agree, neither does Cindy, nor did they stand by and let this happen. There was a battle, and there was a fight, and they lost. But they weren't the big losers here.

Ya know, I was the loser. And you were the loser. And ya know, I disgraced my father. I disgraced my Lord."

Cathy "So did I."

Huff "I disgraced them. And they did not stand there—and please do not believe that they did—and condone this, nor agree with it, nor pushed it to happen in any way. And there is absolutely no way in the world that Liz, nor Cindy, either one, ever, there was no time, there was no way that they agreed with it.

They were brokenhearted over it before. They were brokenhearted during it. And they have been brokenhearted afterward. Because of the destructive nature of it, and because of the sin, and the evil that was there in it. *[Emphasis mine.]*

And do not for a minute think that they stood there and supported me. They tried to love me through it as a brother in the Lord. They tried to help me to pick up the pieces.

But even with that, the destructive nature of that sin in my own heart, was so great that it destroyed a lot of things.

And it cost everybody. And don't think I don't know that. Don't think I don't know the price that you paid or the price that everybody else has paid that was involved with it.

So that's why I can come to you and say, look, they're not opposed to ya. They're not in disagreement with you *in that area.* They do not condone, nor tolerate, nor accept what I did. *[Emphasis mine.]*

And you can call it your sin all you want to Cathy, but the bottom line is that I am the one who is held accountable for it. I am the one who will be standing before the LORD giving Him account for it. Not you. Me. You are not the teacher. You are not the leader. You are not the one standing up professing yourself to be the spiritual leader. I was. And I will be the one who is held accountable for it.

And I know the hurt's there. And I know the pain is still there. But I assure you that one of the ways that you can reconcile that pain, and reconcile the hurt that's in there, is by being reconciled to your sisters here.

I'm being reconciled to you in the only area that I know how to do, and that's by coming to you, and speaking the truth to you, and telling you that I am sorry for it, and I regret it more than you will ever know.

I do not expect you to come back to any Bible study or teaching group or even accept anything here from me. In fact, all I wanted to do was have the opportunity to share this with you. And to say again to you the things that I have said.

But also to primarily say to you, yes, you can be reconciled to these two women. They are your sisters in the Lord. They love you. They do not agree with me. They do not stand beside me. They do not support me. Nor did they ever support me in the midst of all this. They tried to love me through it. They tried to help me through it. My own heart was hardened."

Cathy "Can I ask you a question?"

Huff "Uh-huh."

Cathy "...And you don't have to answer, but I just felt like asking. Did you ever have sex with Cindy?"

Huff "Nope."

Cathy "She wouldn't ever let you?"

Huff (After a long delay) "Never had sex with her."

Cathy "I know the other ladies, they used to tell me that you tried with them, and Cindy said you had tried with her; but she never did. And I was just wondering if that is true or not. I Am glad to hear that she wasn't lying to me.

...I Am glad I called you tonight. I Am glad to hear what you had to say. I will consider what you were saying. I had written Liz a letter, I think it was to Liz and Cindy, I don't know if they shared them with you or not—But did you share that letter that I wrote to you, with Liz? You know that one that I wrote a year ago?" [24 August 1993]

Huff "Oh yes."

Cathy "And it was real fascinating how it ended up. I had...[my Husband] give it to you and it was the Eve of Yom Kippur. And that was very fascinating to me. And ya know, I don't keep up with Jewish holidays, but that's like the final day to ask—"

Huff "It's the Day of Atonement."[40]

Cathy "Yeah, to ask the LORD to forgive you. And it was real neat that it ended up—And I don't know if you noticed that you called me during Rosh Hashanah. Did you notice that?"

Huff "Yeah, I knew what time of the year it was."

Cathy "You did?"

Huff "Yeah."

Cathy "To me it was just fascinating that it has kind of worked out that way. I do hope that you reconcile with God. That is the most important thing as far as I Am concerned. And I hope you realize that okay? And I guess I'll let you go."

Huff "I'm just trying to keep my heart before the Lord, Cathy. Let the Lord do the work here. And ya know, again, I didn't ask you, I didn't call you to do anything here except for you to prayerfully consider—"

Cathy "Oh, I was mentioning at the end of that letter that I wrote to Liz that if God ever impresses upon my heart that they have sincerely repented...and submitted themselves to Him, then I would consider.

But it would definitely have to be God confirming to me and letting me know."

Huff "Well, why don't you ask Him? And just prayerfully consider it and just see what He says. That's pretty much what I called to tell you and ask you to do, and I thank you for doing that. And if the Lord lays it on your heart to make contact with them, and have a line of communication with them, then please do that."

Cathy "Okay. Well, I've got to go."

Huff "Okay, goodnight."

Cathy "Okay, good-bye."

AS YOU CAN SEE, I Am not the one who initiated the contact between us. It was Mr. Huff who relentlessly tried to persuade me to re-establish a line of communication with Liz and Cindy, my former friends.

I had not spoken to Mr. Huff in over a year and a half since our separation, and he had never responded to any of my letters, so I was quite surprised that he would attempt to make direct contact with me.

I know that it took a lot of courage for him to break down and call me, and I could sense that he was extremely uneasy and even at times there was a desperation in his voice.

As I said during our conversation, I had hoped he was sincere, but deep down inside I really do not trust anything he said to me.

Just by what I perceive, I believe the only reason why he called me was as a last resort to try and persuade me to get back in with someone from the group, since nothing else has worked.

I feel like they know something is going on and they just don't know the details, and they were hoping to find out something. He should have discovered that I Am still trusting the LORD and I haven't, thus far, fallen into the traps set by my Enemy. Praise God!

I must say he was quite convincing, and I Am very certain that had I permitted pride and self-righteousness to become a part of my way of thinking again, I would have been blind to who they serve, and he could have succeeded in misleading me again.

Should that ever happen, I know it would be much worse the next time. I pray that I will never forget that it is *only* due to the LORD that I have "eyes to see" and "ears to hear." I just thank God that He has allowed me to discern the "spirit" behind their words; and it was certainly not the Spirit of Christ as he would have me believe.

Because of all that I have been through, I Am even more convinced of the importance to warn unsuspecting people of this sort of evil. Moreover, due to this conversation I had with Mr. Huff, I have no reservations whatsoever in allowing my Testimony to be made available for all to read if the LORD desires for that to happen.

I know that Satan must be displeased and very angry that they allowed me to get out from under their control in the first place. Furthermore, I feel they are probably being tormented even more by demonic spirits due to the mistakes that they have made in regard to me.

It really breaks my heart to think of what may befall these people that I had grown to love, but I Am much more concerned about innocent and unsuspecting souls that have been misled by the ministers of Satan.

I just thank Almighty God that He has revealed to me that I was *Walking With The Enemy;* and may He use this Testimony to uncover the Truth behind many of the deceptions of the Devil!

Luke 12:2-3 (Jesus spoke these words to His disciples) "For there is nothing covered, that shall not be revealed; neither hid, that shall not be known.

Therefore whatsoever ye have spoken in Darkness shall be heard in the Light; and that which ye have spoken in the ear in closets (or private rooms) shall be proclaimed upon the housetops."

EXPOSED

"For every one that doeth evil hateth the Light,
neither cometh to the Light, lest his deeds should be reproved.
But he that doeth Truth cometh to the Light,
that his deeds may be made manifest,
that they are wrought in God."
John 3:20-21

Due to the "True Light" finally coming into my life, I now know the reality of the Darkness. Thus, I Am better able to understand the nature of "man," the power of sin, and the subtlety of the Devil.

I did not realize the entire significance of the issues addressed in the following letters, but since the Wicked One has been exposed, I Am able to see the subtle ways in which Satan gets people to trust him.

Dear Deborah, 11 October 1993

I know you must be wondering why I have not written you or returned your phone calls.[41] It's not that I haven't wanted to, it just was not Time yet. However, God is now leading me to explain what my concerns are, and why it seems as though I have rejected you.

When I first spoke to you over the phone four months ago, I truly felt that you were a servant of the LORD, and based on what you have said to me it would seem that you are very devoted to God.

Moreover, you even stated some things that caused me to believe that you were of Him, but I have since come to understand that you are not walking with the LORD God Almighty in Truth, but you are indeed *Walking With The Enemy* of my God.

In this letter I would like to show you why I Am certain of this. My hope is that you truly love the LORD God, and are as genuinely deceived as I was, because then, there is still hope for you.

You know, in one respect, the easy way out for me would be to just forget about you and say nothing, but I just cannot do that with a clear conscience. I sincerely desire for you to walk in Truth and I would like to take this opportunity to let you know precisely why I have very serious doubts about you and those you seem to be following.

I don't know what you are feeling in your heart right now, but I pray you will let down your defenses just for a moment, and give me the benefit of the doubt. Please hear me out before you make any judgments, because what I Am addressing is so important for you to hear.

If you recall, back in July of 1993, you had recommended to me an organization called "Silent Unity." You said they have someone available to pray with you Twenty-Four hours a day, seven days a week. You stated to me that you could really sense the presence of God when they prayed with you, so I was really eager to call them.

I have since received some of their literature from the Unity School of Christianity in Unity Village, Missouri; the co-founders being Charles and Myrtle Fillmore.

I would like to share some of what I have learned about this organization that has been in existence for over one hundred years. As stated in one of their pamphlets, *"Unity does not have a dogmatic statement of faith with which it asks its followers to agree."*

But according to God's word, to be a true disciple of the LORD Jesus Christ, it is quite necessary to have a set of beliefs. The following is an essential doctrine which cannot be compromised; and this verse will prove that their policies are totally against Christ.

John 3:3 "Jesus answered and said unto him, Verily, verily, I say unto thee, Except a man be born again, he cannot see the kingdom of God."

They also believe there is good in every religion, and we should keep our minds "open" so we may find good when the opportunity presents itself. Mr. Fillmore has also stated, *"One might describe Unity as a religious philosophy with an 'open end,' seeking to find God's truth in all of life, wherever it may be."*

That is so contrary to the words of Jesus when He said:

John 10:1,9-10,14-18 "Verily, verily, I say unto you, He that entereth not by the door into the sheepfold, but climbeth up some other way, the same is a thief and a robber...

I Am the door: by Me if any man enter in, he shall be saved, and shall go in and out, and find pasture. The thief cometh not, but for to steal, and to kill, and to destroy: I Am come that they might have life, and that they might have it more abundantly...

I Am the good Shepherd, and know My sheep, and am known of Mine. As the Father knoweth Me, even so know I the Father: and I lay down My life for the sheep. And other sheep I have, which are not of this fold: them also I must bring, and they shall hear My voice; and there shall be one fold, and one Shepherd.

Therefore doth My Father love Me, because I lay down My life, that I might take it again. No man taketh it from Me, but I lay it down of Myself. I have power to lay it down, and I have power to take it again. This commandment have I received of My Father..."

John 14:6-7 "Jesus saith unto him, I Am the Way, the Truth, and the Life: no man cometh unto the Father, but by Me. If ye had known Me, ye should have known My Father also: and from henceforth ye know Him, and have seen Him."

All of these statements are absolute and they leave no room for any other opinion. Jesus came to reveal the Truth, and it is our great privilege to receive it, and to live it out in our daily lives.

The literature of "Silent Unity" proves that they do not require their members to abide in the doctrine of Christ, and these verses will show what the LORD God Almighty thinks of a different doctrine.

II John 9-11 "Whosoever transgresseth, and abideth not in the doctrine of Christ, hath not God. He that abideth in the doctrine of Christ, he hath both the Father and the Son.

If there come any unto you, and bring not this doctrine, receive him not into your house, neither bid him God speed: For he that biddeth him God speed is partaker of his evil deeds."

Galatians 1:6-9 "I marvel that ye are so soon removed from Him that called you into the grace of Christ unto another gospel: Which is not another; but there be some that trouble you, and would pervert the gospel of Christ.

But though we, or an angel from Heaven, preach any other gospel unto you than that which we have preached unto you, let him be accursed. As we said before, so say I now again, If any man preach any other gospel unto you than that ye have received, let him be accursed."

Romans 16:17-18 "Now I beseech you, brethren, mark them which cause divisions and offenses contrary to the doctrine which ye have learned; and avoid them. For they that are such serve not our LORD Jesus Christ, but their own belly; and by good words and fair speeches deceive the hearts of the simple."

Mr. Fillmore states in his booklet *The Adventure Called Unity* that *"Collectively, people have built up false beliefs about sin, sickness, and death, causing us to lose sight of the true meaning of life, which is that we are all children of God. As such, it is our privilege, in fact, our very mission, to be heirs to God's kingdom."*

This is most certainly a false statement and the following scriptures will prove that not all "men" truly belong to God.

II Peter 2:1-3 "But there were false prophets also among the people, even as there shall be false teachers among you, who privily (or in secret) shall bring in damnable heresies (or wrong teachings), even denying the LORD that bought them, and bring upon themselves swift destruction.

And many shall follow their pernicious (or evil) ways; by reason of whom the way of Truth shall be evil spoken of.

And through covetousness (or greed) shall they with feigned (or false) words make merchandise of you: whose judgment now of a long time lingereth not, and their damnation slumbereth not."

I John 3:8-10 "He that committeth sin is of the Devil; for the Devil sinneth from the beginning. For this purpose the Son of God was manifested, that He might destroy the works of the Devil.

Whosoever is born of God doth not commit sin; for His seed remaineth in Him: and He cannot sin, because He is born of God.

In this the children of God are manifest, and the children of the Devil: whosoever doeth not righteousness is not of God, neither he that loveth not his brother."

II John 7 "For many deceivers are entered into the world, who confess not that Jesus Christ is come in the flesh. This is a deceiver and an anti-Christ." [Emphasis mine.]

Matthew 13:36-43 "Then Jesus sent the multitude away, and went into the house: and His disciples came unto Him, saying, Declare unto us the parable of the tares of the field.

He answered and said unto them, He that soweth the good seed is the Son of man; the field is the world; the good seed are the children of the kingdom; but the tares are the children of the wicked one; the Enemy that sowed them is the Devil; the harvest is the end of the world; and the reapers are the angels.

As therefore the tares are gathered and burned in the fire; so shall it be in the end of this world. The Son of man shall send forth His angels, and they shall gather out of His kingdom all things that offend, and them which do iniquity; and shall cast them into a furnace of fire:

There shall be wailing and gnashing of teeth. Then shall the righteous shine forth as the Sun in the kingdom of their Father. Who hath ears to hear, let him hear."

Not only do the children of the Devil really exist, but they are *very prevalent* within the churches and "Christian" ministries. And even more so, due to the Times in which we are now living.

II Corinthians 11:13-15 "For such are false apostles, deceitful workers, transforming themselves into the apostles of Christ. And no marvel; for Satan himself is transformed into an angel of light.

Therefore it is no great thing if his ministers also be transformed as the ministers of righteousness; whose end shall be according to their works."

Mr. Fillmore also states that it does not matter to God the seriousness or the number of our mistakes. He says that God holds no grudges and has no account book.

He states that there is no depth to which we can sink, and that God is ready to help us if we sincerely wish to be lifted up. That view is most certainly contrary to the word of God in every respect and here are several passages of the Scriptures that will refute those statements.

Revelation 20:11-15 "And I saw a great white throne, and Him that sat on it, from whose face the earth and the Heaven fled away; and there was found no place for them.

And I saw the dead, small and great, stand before God; and the books were opened: and another book was opened, which is the Book of Life: and the dead were judged out of those things which were written in the books, according to their works.

And the sea gave up the dead which were in it; and Death and Hell delivered up the dead which were in them: and they were judged every man according to their works.

And Death and Hell were cast into the Lake of Fire. This is the second death. And whosoever was not found written in the Book of Life was cast into the Lake of Fire."

I John 5:16-20 "If any man see his brother sin a sin which is not unto death, he shall ask, and He shall give him life for them that sin not unto death.

There is a sin unto death: I do not say that he shall pray for it. All unrighteousness is sin: and there is a sin not unto death.

We know that whosoever is born of God sinneth not; but he that is begotten of God keepeth himself, and that wicked one toucheth him not.

And we know that we are of God, and the whole world lieth in wickedness. And we know that the Son of God is come, and hath given us an understanding, that we may know Him that is true,

And we are in Him that is true, even in His Son Jesus Christ. This is the true God, and eternal life."

God will certainly keep a record of all that people say and do, especially concerning His word, and we will be judged accordingly. Every idle word that we speak is taken into account by the LORD.

The following scripture will prove that God will reward all of us according to our works in Light of the Holy Scriptures.

I Corinthians 3:11-15 "For other foundation can no man lay than that is laid, which is Jesus Christ.

Now if any man build upon this foundation gold, silver, precious stones, wood, hay, stubble; Every man's work shall be made manifest: for the day shall declare it, because it shall be revealed by fire; and the fire shall try every man's work of what sort it is.

If any man's work abide which he hath built thereupon, he shall receive a reward. If any man's work shall be burned, he shall suffer loss: but he himself shall be saved; yet so as by fire."

All sin is wrong, but the many ways in which we are able to disobey God has different consequences. The longer we walk in sin, the more power it can have over us, and eventually enslave us completely.

To say that Almighty God is not concerned with the seriousness or number of our sins is just not true; and it will most certainly affect our relationship with Him, which is why we *must* resist sin at all cost!

Romans 6:16-18 "Know ye not, that to whom ye yield yourselves servants to obey, his servants ye are to whom ye obey; whether of sin unto death, or of obedience unto righteousness?

But God be thanked, that ye were the servants of sin, but ye have obeyed from the heart that form of doctrine which was delivered you. Being then made free from sin, ye became the servants of righteousness."

Galatians 6:7-8 "Be not deceived; God is not mocked: for whatsoever a man soweth, that shall he also reap. For he that soweth to his flesh shall of the flesh reap corruption; but he that soweth to the Spirit shall of the Spirit reap life everlasting."

Luke 12:8-10 "Also I say unto you, Whosoever shall confess Me before men, him shall the Son of Man also confess before the angels of God: But he that denieth Me before men shall be denied before the angels of God.

And whosoever shall speak a word against the Son of Man, it shall be forgiven him: but unto him that blasphemeth against the Holy Ghost it shall not be forgiven."

I Corinthians 6:18-19 "Flee fornication. Every sin that a man doeth is without the body; but he that committeth fornication sinneth against his own body. What? Know ye not that your body is the temple of the Holy Ghost which is in you, which ye have of God, and ye are not your own?"

I believe adultery and fornication are among the worst sins a person could ever commit due to the ramifications of these particular transgressions, and also because they can adversely affect so many lives.

Not only does it open the door to many other sins, but if it is allowed to continue without repentance it may lead to the very depths of Satan himself, which could ultimately lead to blasphemy against the Holy Spirit of God, *which is the only unforgivable sin!*

Satan's desire is to kill, steal, and destroy whomsoever he is able, and he is willing to go to any length possible to accomplish that goal. He has done a good job of deceiving many people, even the chosen of God!

The Wicked One has been exposed, and the LORD God will continue to bring to Light the many lies and deceptions of the Devil!

The following is the prayer that a member of "Silent Unity" prayed for me on the night that I had called them. Hopefully, you will be able to see exactly why I Am certain that they do not serve the same God that I serve. I made this call on 10 October 1993.

PRAYER OF "SILENT UNITY"

"All right dear, let's go to God in prayer, Cathy. Silent Unity begins praying with you now. Knowing and giving thanks that with God all things are possible. Know that God is with you. That he is bringing you peace and harmony.

We see you centered in the one infinite life and light and power. You are confident in the knowledge that God is where he is needed. A loving, active, strengthening partner in your life.

You are God's child filled with his light and love and power. You are in command of your life and affairs.

God's light guides you. God's love strengthens you. God's power makes the way easier for you.

You are with God. And as you pray in faith, God reveals right answers and leads you to your highest good.

And these blessings we pray for you in the name and through the power of Jesus Christ. Amen."

First, I would like to say that the minister of "Silent Unity" never spoke about my relationship with the LORD Jesus Christ. She did not even ask me whether I had ever truly repented before God, or if He had forgiven me of my sins and cleansed me of the unrighteousness.

Furthermore, she never said I must believe the Testimony of Jesus Christ with all my heart, and confess Him as LORD of my life in order to even have the opportunity to be a part of His Kingdom.

She never mentioned that to be saved from the wrath of God that is to come upon all the children of disobedience, that I must obey the Truth and keep the Commandments of Almighty God.

She never mentioned that for me to be a true disciple of the LORD Jesus Christ, I must deny myself completely, take up my cross daily, and follow Him wherever He may lead me.

She never mentioned that if I truly loved God, I would seek to obey Him with all my heart because of my earnest desire to please Him; and that it would be such an honor and privilege to be called one of His, regardless of the opposition that would come.

To further establish their ideology, consider these statements from their writings: "*When you are aware of the presence of God, the Christ power to claim and decree good is yours...During your prayer period, do not let your mind wander from Truth. If it should, bring it back by saying, Be still, and know that I am God.*"

If you notice, they imply that we are as powerful as Christ, and that we can take control of our lives. They even teach meditation and relaxation techniques as a way of becoming closer to God. But the question that remains: "Which 'god' are *they* praying to?" Based on the evidence, my answer has to be Satan—the *god* of this world!

There is only one, true, and living God, but through their methods of prayer, they lead you to imagine that *you* are "god." I contend that if people continually repeat their suggested statement, "*Be still and know that I am God,*" they could actually start believing it unto their own destruction; which is *exactly* what Satan intends.

I hope this will prove to you that this organization is not serving the LORD Jesus Christ who has come in the flesh, but obviously their allegiance belongs to someone other than Almighty God!

I John 4:1-6 "Beloved, believe not every spirit, but try the spirits whether they are of God: because many false prophets are gone out into the world. Hereby know ye the Spirit of God: Every spirit that confesseth that Jesus Christ is come in the flesh is of God: And every spirit that confesseth not that Jesus Christ is come in the flesh is not of God:

And this is that spirit of anti-Christ, whereof ye have heard that it should come; and even now already is it in the world.

Ye are of God, little children, and have overcome them: because greater is He that is in you, than he that is in the world.

They are of the world: therefore speak they of the world, and the world heareth them. We are of God: he that knoweth God heareth us; he that is not of God heareth not us.

Hereby know we the Spirit of Truth, and the spirit of error."

I would like to emphasize that John said to "try the spirits." The ministers of "Silent Unity" profess to be followers of Jesus Christ, but because God has allowed me to discern what spirit is behind their words I know that they are not of the Spirit of Christ as they claim to be, but they are most certainly of the spirit of anti-Christ!

Furthermore, it is only because of the LORD God that I Am able to see and hear the Truth of all this; and I attribute it completely to Him. I totally depend on my Heavenly Father and the LORD Jesus Christ to give me the ability to perceive when the Devil is seeking to deceive me.

If you sincerely love the LORD God Almighty I pray that you will truly bow before Him and allow the LORD Jesus Christ to reveal to you what sin is keeping you from seeing the Truth.

God has been in the process of shining His "True Light" on the Darkness, and only those who love the LORD God Almighty and His Truth will be saved from the Wicked One. As *He is* the only one that can deliver you from the power of sin, and death, and Satan.

I Peter 5:6-11 "Humble yourselves therefore under the mighty hand of God, that He may exalt you in due time: Casting all your care upon Him; for He careth for you.

Be sober, be vigilant; because your adversary the Devil, as a roaring lion, walketh about, seeking whom he may devour: Whom resist steadfast in the faith, knowing that the same afflictions are accomplished in your brethren that are in the world.

But the God of all grace, who hath called us unto His eternal glory by Christ Jesus, after that ye have suffered a while, make you perfect, stablish, strengthen, settle you. To Him be glory and dominion for ever and ever. Amen."

I Corinthians 1:9-10 "God is faithful, by whom ye were called unto the fellowship of His Son Jesus Christ our LORD.

Now I beseech you, brethren, by the name of our LORD Jesus Christ, that ye all speak the same thing, and that there be no divisions among you; but that ye be perfectly joined together in the same mind and in the same judgment."

I Am sorry if I seem presumptuous or boastful in any way, but I hope you realize that the only reason why I Am confronting you with any of this is because I sincerely love God's people.

And it is really not my love, but the love that God has put in my heart towards those who belong to Him.

Signed and sealed in the presence of a witness on the 19th Day of October in the year of the LORD, One Thousand Nine Hundred and Ninety-Three.

I HAD TOLD MY HUSBAND that "Silent Unity" would be praying for us for a month, and we needed to be on guard. Three days later he had a serious car accident where he totaled his car. The officials said he should have been dead considering the condition of the vehicle, but he walked away with a few scratches, but nothing serious. I just praise God for His protection and comfort, despite what the Enemy would have wanted.

This next letter was sent to a girl who was with La'el Ministries while I was. She was staying with Katie, Cindy's half-sister, at the time, but the last I heard she was still with the group, despite the warnings.

You can tell people the Truth, but it is their choice whether to believe it. I Am certain that she will greatly regret her decision one Day, *but she has been warned!* Apparently, Satan has a very stronghold on her, and she takes more pleasure in unrighteousness, than in the Truth.

That is a dangerous place to be, especially in these Final Days! God *is* holding people accountable to the choices they have made in their lives and the LORD God Almighty will reward us accordingly.

Revelation 22:12 "And, behold, I come quickly; and My reward is with Me, to give every man according as his work shall be."

Dear Kim, 28 October 1993

It has been exactly eight months since the LORD revealed the Truth about La'el Ministries, and you were a witness! But there still seems to be a lot of confusion in your heart and mind as to whether or not it was truly the Holy Spirit speaking through me that night.

When Katie called last Sunday evening to tell me that you had left Cindy, and was staying with her, I was somewhat skeptical; but I was also excited at the thought of you finally seeing the Truth.

Even though I was thrilled to get the chance to speak to you, I was quite reluctant due to the fact that I really don't trust you; but I went ahead and asked Katie if I could speak with you anyway.

Our conversation felt so strange to me, and there was such a desperation about me because I felt like it was going to be my last chance to try and convince you to see the error of your ways.

I remember that I was just trying to think of anything I could say that would make you understand how serious this is. But after I got off the phone with you, I got the impression that you have no idea of the danger that you are involved in.

I perceive I did not get through to you at all. But I hope I will impress upon you the urgency of the situation, and also help you realize what could happen should you continue to be a part of their fellowship.

My prayer is that I will be very sensitive to what the LORD would have me say to you, so that I might clear up any doubts and confusion that you may have. After all, Almighty God is the only one who truly knows all things; and only His Truth will pierce your heart so as to reveal your true thoughts and intentions.

To refresh your memory I would like to repeat the words that were spoken on that wonderful night, which was to be the last time that La'el Ministries would ever be gathering together in my home for a Bible study or prayer group. Praise the LORD God Almighty!

Prophecy of 28 February 1993

"Many things you have been taught here has been done in secrecy and in Darkness. You have been taught truth mixed with lies, and the LORD says it will go on no longer!

And you, Mr. Huff, is the one who has taught the lies, and the LORD says it will go on no longer in this home. The LORD is giving you a chance to turn from your sin, and He is so forgiving that He will not hold your sin against you, if you repent. And if you do not, you will die!

He is my Husband, and I love Him with a love that cannot be broken. I love you too, but with a brotherly love. And I beg you to repent!

Everything you have learned here has been tainted with evil, and you cannot hold on to any of it. The only thing that you can hold on to is the fact that Jesus Christ died for you, and by His mighty power, God raised Him from the dead. If you believe that in your heart, and claim Him as LORD, He will put the same Spirit that raised Jesus from the dead inside of you, to lead you and guide you into the Truth!

Light will overshadow Darkness, and Darkness will not be able to stand in the presence of God!"

You need to keep in mind that this is a battle for your very soul, so please realize this is a very serious matter that will affect your Eternal Life or Death forever. The most important decision you have before you, is whether you are going to continue in the lies or embrace the Truth.

God has given all men the ability to know right from wrong, but it is your choice as to what you will or will not believe. However, I must proclaim that there is only one Truth, and only One God who gave it!

Do you remember that statement about La'el Ministries that you shared with me a while back? It was scribbled on some paper that you left lying around my house. There was not a date on it, but it was written while you were in high school—before you ran away from your mother.

Kim's Statement: "Those of you that have been lying to yourselves are going to get your tongues turned around.

You're going to get exactly what you've been confessing, which is a lie. God's going to build a church of truth here.

Warning from the Lord: If you choose to walk in a lie, you will not walk in the truth."

You really do have the truth written in your heart, just as God's word says, but Satan is stealing it from you. By the same token, your own personal sin is blinding your eyes to the reality of what is going on; which is why disobedience of any kind is so dangerous.

If sin goes unacknowledged and without repentance, it will only grow and become stronger and have more control and power over us. But Jesus Christ won the victory over sin and death and came to set us free from all that is evil, if we would only trust and believe His word, unto complete obedience of the Truth.

The LORD is giving you another chance to walk with Him and I happen to be the one He is using to direct your way back to Him. I Am nothing! He is everything! And I will only speak to you what I hear my Father say, so please seriously consider what I Am saying to you now.

During the incident in Waco, Texas the people were given the chance to leave before David Koresh and his remaining followers were destroyed by the fire on 19 April 1993. Likewise, I believe Almighty God will spare all those who sincerely love and belong to Him before He will completely destroy this earth as foretold in the Holy Scriptures.

God will make a way out of every temptation if we are only willing to take it, but realize you must be prepared to follow the Truth and everything that is right and just without compromise.

There are many passages in the Holy Bible that I could bring to your attention that would refute all of the lies that the Devil has spoken to you, but I really don't feel like now is the time for that.

I believe it is more important for you to know what it truly means to have Eternal Life. Please reflect on these passages of the Holy Scriptures so that the LORD can speak to your heart.

Genesis 3:22-24 "And the LORD God said, Behold, the man is become as one of Us, to know good and evil: and now, lest he put forth his hand, and take also of the Tree of Life, and eat, and live forever:

Therefore the LORD God sent him forth from the garden of Eden, to till the ground from whence he was taken. So He drove out the man; and He placed at the east of the garden of Eden Cherubim's, and a flaming sword which turned every way, to keep the way of the Tree of Life."

Psalm 119:92-93 "Unless Thy law had been my delights, I should then have perished in mine affliction. I will never forget Thy precepts: for with them Thou hast quickened me."

John 1:1,14 "In the beginning was the Word, and the Word was with God, and the Word was God...And the Word was made flesh, and dwelt among us, (and we beheld His glory, the glory as of the only begotten of the Father,) full of grace and Truth..."

John 14:6 "Jesus saith unto him, I Am the way, the Truth, and the life: no man cometh unto the Father, but by Me."

I Corinthians 2:14 "But the natural man receiveth not the things of the Spirit of God: for they are foolishness unto him: neither can he know them, because they are spiritually discerned."

Matthew 13:18-23 "Hear ye therefore the parable of the sower. When any one heareth the word of the kingdom, and understandeth it not, then cometh the wicked one, and catcheth away that which was sown in his heart. This is he which received seed by the way side.

But he that received the seed into stony places, the same is he that heareth the word, and anon with joy receiveth it; Yet hath he not root in himself, but dureth for a while: for when tribulation or persecution ariseth because of the word, by and by he is offended.

He also that received seed among the thorns is he that heareth the word; and the care of this world, and the deceitfulness of riches, choke the word, and he becometh unfruitful.

But he that received seed into the good ground is he that heareth the word, and understandeth it; which also beareth fruit, and bringeth forth, some an hundredfold, some sixty, some thirty."

While I was with Mr. Huff, I did not realize that Satan could steal the truth right out of my heart. And due to my ignorance of the tactics of the Devil, I put my complete trust in the word of a "man."

It is *only* because of the LORD God Almighty that I Am now walking in the "True Light." It is *only* because of Him that I have access to the Way of the Tree of Life. And *He is* the only One who deserves all the glory, as *He is* the One who gave His life so we might live.

I Am not asking you to believe me! I Am asking you to put your faith, hope, and trust in the LORD and fully depend on Him. Only through God can you truly get understanding. Men can deceive you, sometimes knowingly, and sometimes very innocently, which is why we desperately need the LORD to show us the Truth.

I sincerely desire that you and all God's people be saved; especially all who are under the delusion that they are walking with the LORD Jesus Christ, when in reality they are *Walking With The Enemy* in Darkness, and are a partaker of his evil deeds.

As a result of my experience with La'el Ministries, I Am much more cautious than I have ever been. I have found that just because someone may claim to love and serve the LORD, does not mean they do.

It is so important to be in union with the LORD God Almighty, by His Spirit, so that He can reveal the Truth to us. Otherwise, we are at the mercy of the Devil; and his objective is to destroy us any way he can. These next verses will help establish what I Am saying.

II Corinthians 11:13-15 "For such are false apostles, deceitful workers, transforming themselves into the apostles of Christ. And no marvel; for Satan himself is transformed into an angel of light.

Therefore it is no great thing if his ministers also be transformed as the ministers of righteousness; whose end shall be according to their works."

I John 2:26-29 "These things have I written unto you concerning them that seduce you. But the anointing which ye have received of Him abideth in you, and ye need not that any man teach you:

But as the same anointing teacheth you of all things, and is Truth, and is no lie, and even as it hath taught you, ye shall abide in Him.

And now, little children, abide in Him; that, when He shall appear, we may have confidence, and not be ashamed before Him at His coming. If ye know that He is righteous, ye know that every one that doeth righteousness is born of Him."

If you have truly been anointed by God's Spirit then what John is saying here applies to you; but if you have never truly committed your heart, soul, mind, and body to the LORD then it is past time that you did.

Moreover, if you sincerely love God and belong to Him, I believe He will allow you the privilege of living with Him forever.

Not only did Jesus speak the Truth, *He is the Truth!* And He lived out the Truth on this earth as an example for all men to follow. God greatly loves the people of this world, and He proved it at the cross!

These passages of Scripture will affirm that His willingness to give up His very life was due to this tremendous love in His heart—a love that can only come through the Spirit of the Living God.

Romans 5:6-11 "For when we were yet without strength, in due time Christ died for the ungodly. For scarcely for a righteous man will one die: yet peradventure for a good man some would even dare to die.

But God commendeth His love toward us, in that, while we were yet sinners, Christ died for us. Much more then, being now justified by His blood, we shall be saved from wrath through Him.

For if, when we were enemies, we were reconciled to God by the death of His Son, much more, being reconciled, we shall be saved by His life. And not only so, but we also joy in God through our LORD Jesus Christ, by whom we have now received the atonement."

Ephesians 2:1-10 "And you hath He quickened (or gave life), who were dead in trespasses and sins; Wherein in time past ye walked according to the course of this world, according to the prince of the power of the air, the spirit that now worketh in the children of disobedience:

Among whom also we all had our conversation in times past in the lust of our flesh, fulfilling the desires of the flesh and of the mind; and were by nature the children of wrath, even as others.

But God, who is rich in mercy, for His great love wherewith He loved us, Even when we were dead in our sins, hath quickened us together with Christ, (by grace are ye saved;)

And hath raised us up *together, and made* us *sit together in Heavenly* places *in Christ Jesus: That in the ages to come He might shew the exceeding riches of His grace in* His *kindness toward us through Christ Jesus. For by grace are ye saved through faith; and that not of yourselves:* It is *the gift of God: Not of works, lest any man should boast.*

For we are His workmanship, created in Christ Jesus unto good works, which God hath before ordained that we should walk in them."

Romans 10:1-4 "Brethren, my heart's desire and prayer to God for Israel is, that they might be saved. For I bear them record that they have a zeal of God, but not according to knowledge.

For they being ignorant of God's righteousness, and going about to establish their own righteousness, have not submitted themselves unto the righteousness of God. For Christ is *the end of the law for righteousness to every one that believeth."*

Romans 10:9-13 "That if thou shalt confess with thy mouth the LORD Jesus, and shalt believe in thine heart that God hath raised Him from the dead, thou shalt be saved. For with the heart man believeth unto righteousness; and with the mouth confession is made unto salvation.

For the Scripture saith, Whosoever believeth on Him shall not be ashamed. For there is no difference between the Jew and the Greek: for the same LORD over all is rich unto all that call upon Him. For whosoever shall call upon the name of the LORD shall be saved."

Salvation is a Gift from God that has been so misunderstood. God freely gives Life to those who willingly receive it, but He only gives it to those who humbly bow before Him, and worship only Him.

If you have truly received His perfect gift, as given by His only begotten Son, the LORD Jesus Christ, His seed is planted in your heart.

However, because of the sin of pride, and our lack of knowledge, we fall into the traps set by Satan, which keep us from fully experiencing the awesome gift that we have received by faith in Jesus Christ.

That is why it is so important to study the Bible so we can grow in the true knowledge of God; but if you have never met the True Christ, you are still in your sin, and the wrath of God remains upon you.

I Corinthians 15:1-4 "Moreover, brethren, I declare unto you the gospel which I preached unto you, which also ye have received, and wherein ye stand; by which also ye are saved, if ye keep in memory what I preached unto you, unless ye have believed in vain.

For I delivered unto you first of all that which I also received, how that Christ died for our sins according to the Scriptures; And that He was buried, and that He rose again the third day according to the Scriptures:"

It is so important to read the written word of God so that we can come to know the One who lived and died for us—The glorious One who was raised from the dead so as to give us eternal life!

Thus, through the *true* knowledge of the LORD Jesus Christ, God can grant us the understanding and wisdom we need in order to refute all the lies and deceptions of the Wicked One!

And contrary to what you and I learned from Mr. Huff and Liz, the Old Testament is *just* as relevant as the New Testament.

Romans 15:4 "For whatsoever things were written aforetime were written for our learning, that we through patience and comfort of the Scriptures might have hope."

II Peter 1:21 "For the prophecy came not in old time by the will of man: but Holy men of God spake as they were moved by the Holy Ghost."

II Peter 3:2 "That ye may be mindful of the words which were spoken before by the Holy prophets, and of the commandment of us the apostles of the LORD and Saviour:"

You may think I Am being very presumptuous for claiming that God actually speaks through me; and I admit that I can understand why it could disturb some people, but I know what God has spoken to me; and I will do whatever He says, whether anyone agrees with me or not.

My allegiance is to Almighty God, and Him alone. If others want to stand with me, that is wonderful! If not, then I will stand alone. But in essence, I will never be alone since my LORD is always with me.

I want to share a very personal journal entry so perhaps you can understand why I Am so committed to the LORD God, and why I have such a strong desire to please Him in all that I say and do.

Dearest LORD God Almighty, *Wednesday 12 May 1993*

I found out from Steven (Cindy's ex-husband) yesterday that he got a court date. I Am so excited at the thought of having the opportunity to stand before people and speak Your word.

I know that last time when the Bible study group was called before that court room[42] I was a nervous wreck.

I bet Liz must have been going nuts inside hoping that I would contain myself. She seemed so calm and cool, along with Cindy.

I really had a very hard time that day. That was the first time I had ever snapped at Liz or Cindy, and I ran out of the room crying. They came back to my room to comfort me, and they were able to calm me down.

But I know the reason I was so crazy was because I knew in my heart that there were many things in my life that I would be so ashamed of if I had to speak of them in public.

But LORD, those same things are in my past, and You have cleansed me of the unrighteousness that I was walking in, and now I can speak without being ashamed before You.

I still feel a sense of shame at what I allowed myself to be a partaker of, and I have reaped what I have sown, but I see the Truth now; where before, I was Walking With The Enemy in deception.

I praise You, and I Am ever thankful to You for coming down by Your mighty power to show the Truth. And You did it during Bible study on the night of 28 February 1993.

That date is a Day I will never ever forget! You released the chains that bound me! You gave sight to my eyes! You unstopped my ears! You released the power that Darkness had over me!

Praise the Mighty Name of my LORD and my Savior Jesus Christ the Anointed One!!!

And now I can walk around with an ability, because of You, to see exactly what is in front of me. I will take each day as it comes, and not be concerned about what is up ahead, because I trust You completely! You are a Light unto my path!

Thank You for the understanding that You have given me, and the wisdom to apply what I know about You.

I Am still trying to learn how to be quick to listen and slow to speak. I truly want to guard what comes out of my mouth.

I now understand the verse that says "Don't cast your pearls before swine because they will trample them under their feet and turn around and tear you to pieces."[43] Praise God You are able to heal my wounds. They most certainly did exactly what You said in Your word that they would do, but the thing I was mistaken about was, I thought they served You. I thought they loved You. I thought they loved me.

But You shed Your glorious Light on the situation because of Your love for me, and the whole world. I say the world, because I do realize the calling You have placed on my life from birth.

And Father God, I accept that calling with no reservations whatsoever. I will forsake all to follow You and You alone.

I know there are many people that will not understand. There are many people that will say bad things about me. There are many people that will hate me, and lie about me, and even give false testimony about me.

But you know what? Even if they try to imprison me for doing nothing wrong, I will count it a joy to suffer shame and disgrace for the mighty name of Jesus my LORD!

I fully accept the Commission that You have called me to.

Signed on this Day of 12 May 1993.[44]

A servant of the Most High God,
and the Jesus who came and died for me, that I might have Life
forever with the Father, Creator of all things! Amen!

In case there is any doubt in your heart as to whom I truly serve, I will close with this last excerpt from a letter that I wrote to Cindy. I never finished that letter, so if you ever share this with her, I hope you will impress upon her that there is still time to come to the LORD, but please tell her to come quickly, before They close the door.

Proclamation of 8 May 1993

At this time, I would like to clarify who My LORD and My God is to whom I serve. He is the LORD God Almighty! Maker of Heaven and earth and everything that is made.

He is All-Powerful! He is the Most High God! He has all authority! And He loved the world so much that He sent His only begotten Son to die for us so that we might live to serve and worship Him in Spirit and in Truth.

And to prove to Satan, that only the LORD God Jehovah is All-Powerful; He raised Jesus from the dead. And death had no more power over Him.

To all that believe in their heart that God was able by His Mighty Power to do that, and confess Him as LORD, will be saved from the wrath that is to come on all the children of disobedience.

Jesus Christ won the Victory! And He is my Master! And He is my LORD! And because I have been obedient to Him and to the Testimony of Jesus Christ, He has anointed me with His Holy Spirit. Praise the Holy Name of Jesus!

I would also like to clarify who my God's adversary is: He's that Old Serpent, who is the Devil, and Satan who hates my God and His saints.

He is a very powerful foe! He is the second highest power! He has much authority here on earth. He can kill! He can steal! He can destroy people's lives! And that is his primary objective.

His target is God's people! And you may not be able to see him, but he works in the children of disobedience.

So don't under-estimate his abilities. And don't think for a minute that he won't try any way he can to get to you. He is very sly, wily, crafty, and cunning. And he uses underhanded and calculated methods to secretly introduce his lies and deceptions. And he can only operate in Darkness!

For the most part people do not give Satan credit for many of the things that he does. And he prefers it that way. He masquerades as a Christian. He pretends he loves the LORD Jesus. He pretends he serves the LORD Jesus. He claims he would die for the LORD Jesus.

And he uses unholy men to make these proclamations through the spirit of anti-Christ! And he has deceived many people.

He is working very hard these days because he knows his time is coming to a close very soon. You will know that is true because the world will get more and more wicked as you see the Day approaching.

Most people don't acknowledge God or give Him credit for what He does either. You may not be able to see Him, but He works in the children of obedience. So don't under-estimate His Power and abilities either. And don't think for a minute that He won't save those that truly love and belong to Him.

He is very loving, kind, gentle, compassionate, merciful, and so forgiving. He is truly an awesome God! He uses honesty, sincerity, and Truth to present Himself to us. And there is only One Way that He can come into your life. That Doorway is Yeshua HaMashiach! Jesus, The Christ!

And He can only operate in the Light!

End of Excerpt

Kim, I hope you know that my love has always been true!

Signed in the presence of a witness on the 1st Day of November in the year of the LORD, One Thousand Nine Hundred and Ninety-Three.

I WOULD LIKE TO MENTION that the 7th of May 1993 was the day the LORD brought back to my memory the very words that He spoke to me on that remarkable evening of 28 February 1993.

I truly believe the LORD Jesus came back on that awesome night, in fulfillment of the Scriptures, and I Am so humbled that He would reveal Himself to me, even though I was in the presence of my enemies!

Moreover, Liz wrote me many letters after I left La'el Ministries in order to win back her trust and friendship. I did not always respond to her, but I did acknowledge the letters that the LORD led me to.

I wrote the following letter just as I had finished a three-day fast, by direction of the LORD; and it is so amazing how much more clearly I can hear God when He leads me to abstain from eating.

Dear Liz, 4 December 1993

I received your October letter, which I have responded to, but the LORD said you wouldn't receive it, so instead He told me to start a new letter after I was finished reading through the Scriptures.[45] I have done that, so in this letter I will speak only what I feel the LORD would have me say to you.

I hope that I will not allow my feelings to get in the way of what He would have me put down on paper. All I desire to proceed from my mouth is the Truth of the word of God, and I have come to understand in a more intimate way exactly why it is so important to seek only His wisdom; and to live it out in our lives every day.

A very significant factor I have come to realize, is exactly how and why I came to be so deceived into believing that I was walking in the Truth during my time with you. And after reading through the word of God that fact has been even more established.

Your recent letter confirms this even further, and I would like to refresh your memory as to what you said to show you why I see your letter as a continuation of the lies and deceptions.

Dear Cathy, 18 October 1993

I won't get bogged down in a lengthy or wordy letter. I know you have mentioned in a couple of your letters if we ever think of you or reread your letters, so I wanted to take a brief moment to tell you that I have been thinking of you lately.

Even though our paths have taken different courses, I do still praise the Lord for the time we had together. Those months and years were precious to me—they always will be.

The love in my heart for you will never fade away or be tarnished by situations or circumstances!

I have learned so much since I counseled you. Cathy, the Lord showed me specifically in my relationship with you that I strived so mightily in my own strength to convince you of so many things that God specifically set forth in His word.

It wasn't just you I did this with, it was everyone. What I failed to realize for so very long was the truth of the Holy Spirit's job and responsibility. I kept thinking I had to somehow break through and convince people of the truth!

The Lord is so gracious and good! He has shown me that only the Holy Spirit can shine the light of the gospel in the hearts of believers and non-believers alike.

That's His job—not mine! The burden of responsibility that I have carried for so long has been lifted by the knowledge of truth.

The need to set others straight at all times has been re-delegated to the one in authority to reveal truth—the Spirit of the one true and living God!

I need only point out or speak when directed by the Lord. My job is to continually ask the Lord to allow His light of truth to shine in another's heart by the Holy Spirit—until it does—no amount of human convincing will actually convince.

I grieve that this lesson was learned only after our separation Cathy, but I know God orders our steps and I trust His ways!

I do love and miss you terribly!

Liz

On the surface there isn't really anything seemingly wrong or out of order with anything you said. Actually it was a very kindly worded letter that I would love to be the Truth.

However, I Am now able to see that it's just another attempt to manipulate my emotions in order to cause doubt, and to make me think you have had a change of heart and finally realized the Truth.

Furthermore, everything you stated in that letter is the exact position I presumed you held while I was with you, so I really don't understand what new truth you are referring to.

Since I perceive you are trying to persuade me that I Am the one who is *Walking With The Enemy* and listening to him, I Am going to disregard what you spoke in that letter, and just confront you with what I feel in my heart to be the Truth behind your words.

The LORD God has given me an obligation to bring these things to your attention, and whether you receive what I Am saying or not is ultimately between you and the LORD.

I contend that I Am a child of the LORD God Almighty, and have been from the very beginning! On the other hand, I contend you are a child of the Devil, and have been from the very beginning!

Further, I will explain precisely why I believe you are not of the Spirit of Christ as you claim, but are of the spirit of anti-Christ!

To help you to understand why I have come to this conclusion I feel it's necessary to bring up some things that I Am aware of through my own personal relationship with you, and also through my interaction with some of the other members of the Bible study group.

And the following will substantiate why we are so contrary to one another, and why I could never be a part of La'el Ministries again.

The most outrageous thing you have ever told me about your past was when you used to pursue men with the intent of seducing them into a sexual encounter whether they were married or not.

I recall you saying that you preferred Christian married men because they were so much more of a challenge.

You stated that it was like a game with you, and you would tease and flirt with them until you were sure that you had won them over completely. Then after you were able to achieve the desired objective you would just cut all ties without any concern for the spiritual and emotional damage you had just inflicted on these men.

As you told me about this, I just imagined you laughing in their faces as if you took considerable pleasure and satisfaction in their pain. I remember asking if you were even concerned about the hurt this must have caused them, and you said, "No, it was their problem—they should have known better."

The following sworn statement transcribed by a court reporter on 25 March 1993, in regard to the custody case between Cindy and her former husband, will also help shed some light on your true character.

RECORDED STATEMENT BETWEEN CATHY AND AN ATTORNEY

Q. "I think this may be the easiest way to get into it. You mentioned earlier in your statement that you left the group recently, in early March, due to the fact that there was some allegations made to Mr. Huff of which he did not repent?"

A. "He didn't deny the allegations. He pretty much just sat there."

Q. "Did he admit them?"

A. "The sexual allegations, yes, he did."

Q. "Now, let's just take the sexual allegations first. And what were those allegations? And, again, I'll caution you that it's really not necessary at this point in time for you to use names, but just, if you can, describe the situations."

A. "He pursued the ladies in the group in a sexual way if they would have it. You know, I mean, it wasn't—It is really weird to try to explain it. Basically, he would lead you to believe that he was your spiritual husband and pretty much seduce you into having a relationship with him."

Q. "Now, of your own personal knowledge, are you aware, and remember you're under oath, of any actual sexual relations that he had with any members of the group?"

A. "That I'm actually aware of?"

Q. "Yes."

A. "Yeah."

Q. "And how many?"

A. "Where I actually saw or just knew from them telling me?"

Q. "Let's say where you actually witnessed."

A. "Two."

Q. "Now, what I really want to know, first of all, is the sexual acts that you witnessed."

A. "Two, actually."

Q. "Were those sexual acts in a group situation?"

A. "No, they were not, at all."

Q. "Was Mr. Huff and the other individual who was having sex aware of your presence?"

A. "Very much."

Q. "And would you describe, without names, how that occurred?"

A. "Well, it was after a Bible study meeting."

Q. "At your home?"

A. "This was when it was at Liz's."

Q. "Across the street?"

A. "No...We were just sitting there talking."

Q. "Who's "we?" Mr. Huff and the other person and you? Is that correct?"

A. "Yes. And we were just—I was sitting in front of the couch and they were in their chairs. They were sitting there and all of a sudden they just started taking off their clothes and having sex right there on the floor in front of me. And that was basically it. And I was pretty shocked at it. It's a weird thing."

Q. "Now let me ask you this. The three of you were sitting after a meeting. Who else was present in the house at the time this occurred?"

A. "The children were in the back..."

Q. "Rebecca (Cindy and Steven's child) was not present?"

A. "No."

Q. "Cindy was not present?"

A. "No."

Q. "And were ya'll in a locked room?"

A. "No. We were in the living room where the front door was still unlocked or, actually, the...carport door."

Q. "Did the children have access?"

A. "Sure, very much."

Q. "Now, the way you described it was that they just commenced to do this?"

A. "No warning at all."

Q. "Did they ask you to leave?"

A. "No. They took pleasure in me being right there."

Q. "What did they say?"

A. "Nothing."

Q. "I mean, the meeting was over, ya'll were talking and they—"

A. "I asked them why they did that and they said God told them to, and that was about it."

Q. "And when you said they had sex, did they actually complete the sexual act? They completely disrobed?"

A. "Oh yeah."

Q. "And how long did this take? I mean, was this—"

A. "It wasn't real long. Thank God."

Q. "Did they invite you to participate?"

A. "No, they didn't..."

Q. "Why did they tell you that God told them to do it?"

A. "Because I was such a self-righteous Christian. God wanted to do shocking things to me. Because they used to cuss in front of me and say such disgusting things in front of me.

And then they did that, and said it was to get me out of the mode of being self-righteous and being able to accept shocking things. Because when you go out in the world to witness, you're going to need to not be affected by what you see on the outside and be able to look at people on the inside.

That was mainly—It was like shock treatment for me, and it was very shocking, actually."

Q. "Did Mr. Huff admit this allegation in front of other people that this occurred?"

A. "No. This has never been brought out."

Q. "Now, how many others? You said there was one other occasion you witnessed. Was that in the presence of anyone else?"

A. "No."

Q. "Is anyone else aware that that occurred?"

A. "Yes."

Q. "Is the group aware that that occurred?"

A. "At present, yes. Well, not actually the whole group, it was at our confrontation."

Q. "Members of the group are aware?"

A. "Yes."

Q. "Did that occur at one of the meetings that is taped?"

A. "No. It was after hours."

Q. "...was there more than one occasion that you witnessed this?"

A. "Three."

Q. "On these three occasions, were there any other people in the house?"

A. "Children."

Q. "And did the children have access to the area where this took place?"

A. "Uh-huh."

Q. "Did any of the children witness any of this occurring?"

A. "No. I am so thankful."

Q. "Was Rebecca one of those children?"

A. "I don't think she was there then. It's quite possible she was for the first time. I believe she was in the back room, yes, because that's when they were living with me. So it's very likely she was there. I can't say yes, exactly that I remember her being there, but it's very likely she was because Cindy and Liz had just left for a moment, just for fifteen or twenty minutes."

Q. "Now, what other allegations were made—sexual allegations have been made against him?"

A. "This isn't an allegation, but it's an actual personal experience that I saw him do during a meeting and it was when he was ministering...And he was praying for him, laid hands on him, and then he started French kissing him."

Q. "By French—"

A. "...Just a real sexual kiss."

Q. "What was the reaction of the group when this occurred?"

A. "I was kind of shocked myself, but I don't really—Nobody spoke about it. It was not something we talked about."

Q. "What was the purpose of the kiss?"

A. "I'm assuming this—because I didn't discuss it with Mr. Huff...[He] used to say that the reason—And he would kiss me that way when I initially came to the group; and he said that it was because he had the love of Jesus inside of him and that is how God had him demonstrate the love of Jesus."

Q. "Did he kiss other people in the group the same way?"

A. "Yes."

Q. "Did he kiss any of the children that way?"

A. "Not that I know of. I'm sure—Is a seventeen-year-old a child?"

Q. "That's correct."

A. "Yes, he did kiss her that way. She's the other allegation that was made that Tuesday night that we had the confrontation. He actually had sex with her."

Q. "And did he admit that?"

A. "He admitted that, and the adoptive mother was present, Cindy... she admitted it. And Liz is actually the one that told me about it..."

Q. "And how did this incident occur with the minor?"

A. "I don't know if he's gone into the details with you, but this is when the court was trying to get Kim to come back to her home. It's when she was seventeen. I even have a letter that she wrote me while she was away. It's when she just—This is based on what they told me after the fact... Mr. Huff was supposedly to have gone up there and seduced her, and told her that she was his wife. And they—"

Q. "Had sex?"

A. "Yes."

Q. "On one occasion?"

A. "Just from my knowledge of what they told me it only happened once."

Q. "In the presence of any other person?"

A. "I don't think so. I think it was just her and him..."

Q. "Does Cindy approve of the actions of Mr. Huff having these relations with these women? French kissing the man? French kissing the women?"

A. "No, she doesn't."

Q. "She does not approve that?"

A. "She stated to me that she doesn't."

Q. "Has she attempted to stop Mr. Huff from doing that?"

A. "No. Well, when he pursues her she stops it, so she says."

Q. "Has she left the group?"

A. "No."

Q. "She continues?"

A. "She condones it by being a part of the group now."

Q. "It's wide open now and she continues to be a part of the group?"

A. "Sunday night not everything was divulged, but Tuesday night I went through everything that had ever taken place with me in the presence of Wendell...Cindy, Mr. Huff, Liz, and my Husband, and made those allegations. And so all of them are completely aware of everything that has transpired as far as that goes. And she's still part of the group. She condones that behavior, yes."

End of Transcript

After my appearance in the courtroom on 17 May 1993, it is very interesting that even though I never spoke a single word to the Judge or to Cindy's lawyer, that she decided to relinquish all rights and let her former husband have full custody of their daughter.

Could it be that you are afraid of the Truth being brought out into the Light of Day? I would like to remind you that the LORD has said that there is nothing covered that shall not be revealed; and nothing hidden that shall not be made known. Praise God!

Since you have continued in the lies and deceptions along with condoning the sin of others, your error will be exposed by the LORD God for all the world to see on that dreadful Day. But had you acknowledged your sin and truly repented, it never would have come to this.

I take no great pleasure in any of this, but the LORD will not allow you to blaspheme His Holy name much longer! His anger is certainly being kindled against all who commit sin and wickedness; and in His perfect justice He will bring down all workers of iniquity!

The following indicates how the LORD God feels about evil and what He plans to do about it at the *Appointed Time*. And if you are in this state at His return, you will be utterly cast down too!

Psalm 5:4-6 "For Thou art not a God that hath pleasure in wickedness: neither shall evil dwell with Thee. The foolish shall not stand in Thy sight: Thou hatest all workers of iniquity.

Thou shalt destroy them that speak leasing (or falsehood): the LORD will abhor the bloody and deceitful man."

Psalm 145:20 "The LORD preserveth all them that love Him: but all the wicked will He destroy."

Psalm 21:8-11 "Thine hand shall find out all Thine enemies: Thy right hand shall find out those that hate Thee. Thou shalt make them as a fiery oven in the time of Thine anger: the LORD shall swallow them up in His wrath, and the fire shall devour them.

Their fruit shalt thou destroy from the earth, and their seed from among the children of men. For they intended evil against Thee: they imagined a mischievous device, which they are not able to perform."

Based on God's Word, those who do evil will not prosper and will eventually be destroyed. For you to say you are Jewish and a prophet of God, when in reality you are *Walking With The Enemy* in Darkness, and luring others into believing your lies and deceptions is totally inexcusable and an abomination before God and man!

The following scripture will illustrate that Paul encountered a very similar situation that we find ourselves in, and I would like you to especially note his response. Please read this very carefully.

Acts 13:6-11 "And when they had gone through the isle unto Paphos, they found a certain sorcerer, a false prophet, a Jew, whose name was Bar-jesus: Which was with the deputy of the country, Sergius Paulus, a prudent man; who called for Barnabas and Saul, and desired to hear the word of God.

But Elymas the sorcerer (for so is his name by interpretation) withstood them, seeking to turn away the deputy from the faith.

Then Saul, (who also is called Paul,) filled with the Holy Ghost, set his eyes on him, and said, O full of all subtlety and all mischief, thou child of the Devil, thou enemy of all righteousness, wilt thou not cease to pervert the right ways of the LORD?

And now, behold, the hand of the LORD is upon thee, and thou shalt be blind, not seeing the sun for a season. And immediately there fell on him a mist and a Darkness; and he went about seeking some to lead him by the hand."

Your sin will find you out and be your ruin! You will reap corruption because you've sown to your flesh and listened to the Devil. And due to your total disregard for the Laws of God, He will not allow you or any other workers of iniquity to go unhindered any longer!

Proverbs 5:21-23 "For the ways of man are before the eyes of the LORD, and He pondereth all his goings. His own iniquities shall take the wicked himself, and he shall be holden with the cords of his sins. He shall die without instruction; and in the greatness of his folly he shall go astray."

You may have it worked out that all is well with your soul, but that is a lie too! The "deceiver" has been very successful if you believe that everything you do is truly ordained of God.

Based on the fruits of your life, it is apparent that you follow that which is evil and wicked. I now understand why demonic spirits have the authority to torment you—It's because you *belong* to them!

Even though you say you are a servant of the LORD Jesus I know without a doubt, that you are *not* of the same Spirit that I Am.

I John 4:1-6 "Beloved, believe not every spirit, but try the spirits whether they are of God: because many false prophets are gone out into the world. Hereby know ye the Spirit of God:

Every spirit that confesseth that Jesus Christ is come in the flesh is of God: And every spirit that confesseth not that Jesus Christ is come in the flesh is not of God: and this is that spirit of anti-Christ, whereof ye have heard that it should come; and even now already is it in the world.

Ye are of God, little children, and have overcome them: because greater is He that is in you, than he that is in the world. They are of the world: therefore speak they of the world, and the world heareth them.

We are of God: he that knoweth God heareth us; he that is not of God heareth not us. Hereby know we the Spirit of Truth, and the spirit of error."

Because of my very humbling experiences in connection with La'el Ministries I have come to a greater dependence on the LORD God instead of relying on myself or other people.

I have gained valuable insight into the fact that I *must* rely upon the Holy Spirit of Almighty God to show me who truly belongs to Him, and what "spirit" a person is actually controlled by.

I know when we first met, you were under the mistaken impression that I had not been a Christian very long, but had you been aware of the Truth, you would have known that I Am very committed to the LORD God and had been for over ten years at that time.

Not only did you not know me, but I did not know you; which is the reason why Satan was able to deceive me from the very beginning.

Had I known that I would be enticed away from my church and family and become committed to a false prophet, you would never have known me!

Had I known that the Devil would attempt to seduce me away from my God by the use of witchcraft and sorcery, you would never have known me!

Had I known that you bow your knee to Satan while claiming your allegiance to the one, true, and living God, you would never have known me!

But my God had different plans. He knew all these things and He could have stopped me from ever meeting you, but He wanted me to know you! And in His infinite wisdom He used this extremely naive and unsuspecting person to expose the deceptions of the Devil himself!

Had I taken pleasure in sin, I would be with you even still. Had I been that newborn Christian as you all assumed that I was when I first started coming to your group, I probably would have been another one of those statistics of broken individuals that you leave in your path.

Don't get me wrong, I was very adversely affected by my association with those of La'el Ministries, and it is only by the grace of God that I Am still standing! And only through Him will I continue to stand until He is ready to take me home to be with Him!

The following verses will show you exactly why I Am certain that you are of the "synagogue of Satan," and that his purpose and plan is to steal, to kill, and to destroy God's people. And he uses disobedient, unholy men to carry out his evil deeds and deceptions.

II Peter 2:17-22 "These are wells without water, clouds that are carried with a tempest; to whom the mist of Darkness is reserved for ever.

For when they speak great swelling words *of vanity, they allure through the lust of the flesh,* through much *wantonness, those that were clean escaped from them who live in error. While they promise them liberty, they themselves are the servants of corruption: for of whom a man is overcome, of the same is he brought in bondage.*

For if after they have escaped the pollutions of the world through the knowledge of the LORD and Saviour Jesus Christ, they are again entangled therein, and overcome, the latter end is worse with them than the beginning.

For it had been better for them not to have known the way of righteousness, than, after they have known it, *to turn from the Holy Commandment delivered unto them. But it is happened unto them according to the true proverb, The dog* is *turned to his own vomit again; and the sow that was washed to her wallowing in the mire."*

Matthew 13:24-30 "Another parable put He forth unto them, saying, The kingdom of Heaven is likened unto a man which sowed good seed in his field: But while men slept, his enemy came and sowed tares among the wheat, and went his way. But when the blade was sprung up, and brought forth fruit, then appeared the tares also.

So the servants of the householder came and said unto him, Sir, didst not thou sow good seed in thy field? from whence then hath it tares? He said unto them, An enemy hath done this.

The servants said unto him, Wilt thou then that we go and gather them up? But he said, Nay; lest while ye gather up the tares, ye root up also the wheat with them.

Let both grow together until the harvest: and in the time of harvest I will say to the reapers, Gather ye together first the tares, and bind them in bundles to burn them: but gather the wheat into my barn."

Matthew 13:36-43 "Then Jesus sent the multitude away, and went into the house: and His disciples came unto Him, saying, Declare unto us the parable of the tares of the field.

He answered and said unto them, He that soweth the good seed is the Son of Man; The field is the world; the good seed are the children of the kingdom; but the tares are the children of the wicked one;

The Enemy that sowed them is the Devil; the harvest is the end of the world; and the reapers are the angels.

As therefore the tares are gathered and burned in the fire; so shall it be in the end of this world. The Son of Man shall send forth His angels, and they shall gather out of His kingdom all things that offend, and them which do iniquity; And shall cast them into a furnace of fire: there shall be wailing and gnashing of teeth. Then shall the righteous shine forth as the Sun in the kingdom of their Father. Who hath ears to hear, let him hear."

You are probably sorry that you ever met me and just wish that I would go away, but because you contend that you have done no evil, God in His perfect justice cannot allow the wickedness to continue without exposing you and the lies that you have taught in His name.

If you haven't noticed, Darkness is being exposed all over the world, and only those who have "eyes to see and ears to hear" will be able to see and understand what is going on in these final days.

I sincerely loved you and there was never any pretense or hypocrisy on my part. And because I was so trusting of you and Mr. Huff is why you were able to take advantage of me to the degree that you did.

But the LORD has such a wonderful way of comforting me. He has shown me in His word that King David was also betrayed by someone that he thought was his friend, which is why the word of God is such a great source of strength and encouragement for me.

Psalm 41:9-13 "Yea, mine own familiar friend, in whom I trusted, which did eat of my bread, hath lifted up his heel against me. But Thou, O LORD, be merciful unto me, and raise me up, that I may requite them.

By this I know that Thou favourest me, because my enemy doth not triumph over me. And as for me, Thou upholdest me in mine integrity, and settest me before Thy face forever. Blessed be the LORD God of Israel from everlasting, and to everlasting. Amen, and Amen."

These scriptures will explain why you are not able to truly understand why I have come to the conclusions that I have and why evil men will never have the ability to comprehend true judgment.

Proverbs 28:4-5 "They that forsake the law praise the wicked: but such as keep the law contend with them. Evil men understand not judgment: but they that seek the LORD understand all things."

Proverbs 4:14-19 "Enter not into the path of the wicked, and go not in the way of evil men. Avoid it, pass not by it, turn from it, and pass away. For they sleep not, except they have done mischief; and their sleep is taken away, unless they cause some to fall.

For they eat the bread of wickedness, and drink the wine of violence. But the path of the just is as the shining Light, and that shineth more and more unto the perfect Day. The way of the wicked is as Darkness: they know not at what they stumble."

God's word is *so* true when He says that the fearful, the unbelieving, the abominable, the murderers, the whoremongers, the sorcerers, the idolaters, and all liars shall have their part in the lake which burneth with fire and brimstone: Which is the Second Death!

Blessing, and Honor, and Glory, and Power, and Might be unto the Holy One who sits upon the Heavenly Throne, and unto the Lamb of God forever and ever! Amen.

Sincerely,
A servant of the Most High God
C. Read

PS. I would like to familiarize you with the first letter that I had initially written, so you can have the opportunity to compare the two and see the benefits of prayer, fasting, and the word of God!

Dear Liz, 3 November 1993

Thank you for your letter. I hope you know that I Am still very concerned about you and what might happen to you. Contrary to what you may think I still love you very much and I hope the best for you.

The day I received your letter was so neat because earlier that morning you had really been on my heart, and I had actually thought about writing you a letter.

I had been thanking the LORD because everything I learned about Him during my wilderness experience with La'el Ministries caused me to have more of a deeper love, respect, and dependence upon Him than I have ever had before in my life.

Not only did I learn so very much about God, but I also learned so many things about the Enemy of my God. If I had never known you, I would not have had the opportunity to have my senses exercised to discern both good and evil.

I Am very thankful that the LORD did not allow me to walk with the Enemy long enough to experience the very depths of Satan, but just long enough for me to know and understand how dangerous it is to walk in self-righteousness, pride, and sin of any kind.

I appreciate your letter because it has given me a glimpse of what is going on in your life right now. I can see that you still feel that I Am wrong and that you are right. You are still calling sweet for bitter and bitter for sweet. In essence, you are still professing to be in the Light when in reality you are walking in Darkness.

I sincerely desire for you to walk in Truth and I know Satan would much rather that I write you off and forget all about you, but I cannot until I know you are aware of what you are involved with.

And in this letter, I would like to establish what the purpose of God's word is in relation to those who desire to serve Him with their whole heart, and contrast that with those who are against Him.

That way you can determine in your own heart and mind exactly what category you find yourself in.

But before man can be equipped to do God's will, we must study the Scriptures so we will know what is written. Knowledge in itself is not enough. The LORD must also give us wisdom and understanding

II Timothy 3:16-17 "All Scripture is given by inspiration of God, and is profitable for doctrine, for reproof, for correction, for instruction in righteousness: That the man of God may be perfect, throughly furnished unto all good works."

II Peter 1:20-21 "Knowing this first, that no prophecy of the Scripture is of any private interpretation. For the prophecy came not in old time by the will of man: but Holy men of God spake as they were moved by the Holy Ghost."

Proverbs 2:6-7 "For the LORD giveth wisdom: out of His mouth cometh knowledge and understanding. He layeth up sound wisdom for the righteous: He is a buckler to them that walk uprightly."

That passage implies that there are different types of wisdom. Please note what the LORD has brought to my attention concerning this.

James 3:13-18 "Who is a wise man and endued with knowledge among you? Let him shew out of a good conversation his works with meekness of wisdom. But if ye have bitter envying and strife in your hearts, glory not, and lie not against the Truth.

This wisdom descendeth not from above, but is earthly, sensual, devilish. For where envying and strife is, there is confusion and every evil work.

But the wisdom that is from above is first pure, then peaceable, gentle, and easy to be entreated, full of mercy and good fruits, without partiality, and without hypocrisy. And the fruit of righteousness is sown in peace of them that make peace."

I Corinthians 2:4-5 "And my speech and my preaching was not with enticing words of man's wisdom, but in demonstration of the Spirit and of power: That your faith should not stand in the wisdom of men, but in the power of God."

I Corinthians 3:18-20 "Let no man deceive himself. If any man among you seemeth to be wise in this world, let him become a fool, that he may be wise. For the wisdom of this world is foolishness with God. For it is written, He taketh the wise in their own craftiness. And again, the LORD knoweth the thoughts of the wise, that they are vain."

Based on these words it establishes that there is wisdom from God, wisdom from the Devil, wisdom from man, and wisdom of the world. Please consider the following scriptures:

Proverbs 1:7 "The fear of the LORD is the beginning of knowledge: but fools despise wisdom and instruction."

Proverbs 2:1-5 "My son, if thou wilt receive My words, and hide My commandments with thee; So that thou incline thine ear unto wisdom, and apply thine heart to understanding; Yea, if thou criest after knowledge, and liftest up thy voice for understanding; If thou seekest her as silver, and searchest for her as for hid treasures; Then shalt thou understand the fear of the LORD, and find the knowledge of God."

Proverbs 8:13 "The fear of the LORD is to hate evil: pride, and arrogancy, and the evil way, and the froward mouth, do I hate."

I know you are very familiar with the Scriptures, but these ones will help you determine whether your perspective is from the wisdom of the world, your own wisdom, or even worse, the wisdom of Satan.

However, I know with all certainty that your wisdom is not from the LORD God Almighty; because if it was, you would hear and understand everything I have been trying to say to you since the night of 28 February 1993. The following scripture will confirm this.

I John 4:6 "We are of God: he that knoweth God heareth us; he that is not of God heareth not us. Hereby know we the Spirit of Truth, and the spirit of error."

I know you are in error, and all I Am trying to do is convince you of that before it's too late. Had you truly been on the side of the LORD, you would not have come against me on the night of our confrontation.

Here is a scripture that the LORD brought to my attention soon after we broke-up which will show exactly why I Am certain that you are not of the one, true, and living God as you claim to be.

I John 2:18-19 "Little children, it is the last time: and as ye have heard that anti-Christ shall come, even now are there many anti-Christs; whereby we know that it is the last time. They went out from us, but they were not of us; for if they had been of us, they would no doubt have continued with us: but they went out, that they might be made manifest that they were not all of us."

In case you have a problem with me trying to persuade you, I would like to note that Paul tried to convince men to see it his way too.

II Corinthians 5:10-11 "For we must all appear before the judgment seat of Christ; that every one may receive the things done in his body, according to that he hath done, whether it be good or bad.

Knowing therefore the terror of the LORD, we persuade men; but we are made manifest unto God; and I trust also are made manifest in your consciences."

I know it would be very humbling for you to admit that you have been wrong all along, but please don't let your pride send you to Hell. God is so merciful and He is giving you a chance to repent and turn from the error of your ways. Please do not pass up this opportunity.

Last Sunday at the Baptist Church, one of your sisters came up and hugged me, and I thought that was so kind of her. It was like her way of saying that she has not rejected me too. Afterward, I thought how wonderful it would be if that could have been you.

You might feel like I totally despise you, but my love for you has always been true. I know when I was with you I never really felt like there was a real unity between me and you, but I had always wanted there to be. And because I still do love you, I will try to help you realize what you have been walking in all of these years.

Proverbs 27:5-6 "Open rebuke is better than secret love. Faithful are the wounds of a friend; but the kisses of an enemy are deceitful."

You stated in your letter dated 24 June 1993, that Paul never exposed evil or spoke against those who opposed him. I would like to refute that ideology. Here is your statement regarding this.

Liz's statement: "I reasoned to the Lord: Father, Cathy isn't persecuting us because she thinks we are godly!!! She is stating just the opposite, actually. This community doesn't persecute us because THEY think we are GODLY, they do so because they profess we are ungodly and a breed of the worst sort! The answer that God gave me at that moment was so comforting that I doubt that anything except those words could have soothed my pain and anguish. He said, 'Child, when have I commanded my children to persecute anyone EVEN THE UNGODLY?

I have given instruction to point out sin when it is present within that local church body. I have instructed people to go personally to each other. But where have I ever instructed a believer to harass, pursue, expose to the world, talk about, discuss, and otherwise make a mockery of the gospel to point out something?'

Paul had MANY who tried to discredit him. He had them go behind him and try to seduce his churches, yet he never attacked them and made them his life mission to expose. He walked in love, teaching of Jesus that they might perhaps see the true nature of Jesus Christ in him, that they might be won to Christ as he completed, in his own body, the sufferings of the Messiah."

The following scriptures will prove why your statements are completely unfounded and not based on the Truth of God's word.

II Timothy 2:14-18 "Of these things put them in remembrance, charging them before the LORD that they strive not about words to no profit, but to the subverting of the hearers.

Study to shew thyself approved unto God, a workman that needeth not to be ashamed, rightly dividing the word of Truth. But shun profane and vain babblings: for they will increase unto more ungodliness. And their word will eat as doth a canker: of whom is Hymenaeus and Philetus; Who concerning the Truth have erred, saying that the resurrection is past already; and overthrow the faith of some."

Did you notice that Paul specifically named the two people who had erred from the truth, along with the particular ways that they were causing others to fall away? Also consider the warning that Paul has for Timothy in this next passage of Scripture.

II Timothy 4:10a,14-15 "For Demas hath forsaken me, having loved this present world, and is departed unto Thessalonica...

Alexander the coppersmith did me much evil: the LORD reward him according to his works: Of whom be thou ware also; for he hath greatly withstood our words."

Not only did Paul make a point of mentioning their names, but also their exact whereabouts in certain instances.

To establish my point further, I would like to reference the words of one of the disciples that had a very personal and intimate relationship with the LORD Jesus while He lived here on earth.

III John 9-11 "I wrote unto the Church: but Diotrephes, who loveth to have the preeminence among them, receiveth us not.

Wherefore, if I come, I will remember his deeds which he doeth, prating against us with malicious words: and not content therewith, neither doth he himself receive the brethren, and forbiddeth them that would, and casteth them out of the Church.

Beloved, follow not that which is evil, but that which is good. He that doeth good is of God: but he that doeth evil hath not seen God."

Apparently, the ungodly can be in positions of leadership within the churches, of which the Apostle John is writing about.

This next passage will show an extreme case of what Paul did concerning those who have chosen to continue to walk in sin, even to the point where they have begun to blaspheme God.

I Timothy 1:19-20 "Holding faith, and a good conscience; which some having put away concerning faith have made shipwreck: Of whom is Hymenaeus and Alexander; whom I have delivered unto Satan, that they may learn not to blaspheme."

I hope you are beginning to see and understand that the voice you are listening to is not the voice of God, especially since it completely contradicts the very precepts of His Holy word.

You say when people walk away from you and Mr. Huff, that they are rejecting Jesus and bad things come upon them because of their disobedience to God, but I say that their misfortune is not only due to walking apart from God and His word, but also because they were tainted with the evil that surrounds you and your ministry.

We are certainly affected by what we come in contact with, and all throughout the Bible God warns and instructs His people about what we allow into our homes and who we associate with.

II Corinthians 6:14-7:1 "Be ye not unequally yoked together with unbelievers: for what fellowship hath righteousness with unrighteousness? And what communion hath Light with Darkness?

And what concord hath Christ with Belial? Or what part hath he that believeth with an infidel? And what agreement hath the temple of God with idols?

For ye are the temple of the living God; as God hath said, I will dwell in them, and walk in them; and I will be their God, and they shall be My people.

Wherefore come out from among them, and be ye separate, saith the LORD, and touch not the unclean thing; and I will receive you,

And will be a Father unto you, And ye shall be My sons and daughters, saith the LORD Almighty.

Having therefore these promises, dearly beloved, let us cleanse ourselves from all filthiness of the flesh and spirit, perfecting holiness in the fear of God."

You contend that I Am the one who is not able to discern God's word accurately, and when I was with you that certainly was very true. But thank the LORD God Almighty I Am not the same as I was before! I see with different eyes! I hear with different ears! And I perceive from a completely different perspective! Praise God!!

Based on your letters it appears that you do not believe that what transpired on the evening of 28 February 1993, was of God's Spirit; but that is understandable considering who *you* are walking with.

The Devil has to keep you believing the lies, otherwise you would be forced to look at your own life. I cannot emphasize to you enough that you are walking on shaky ground because of your contention that what took place on that unforgettable night was of demonic spirits, instead of the Holy Spirit of the living God.

Nevertheless, it reinforces the conviction in my heart that you and your followers are most certainly *Walking With The Enemy* of my God. And as long as you say I Am speaking by the power of Satan, rather than by the LORD, I will continue to be against you; along with all those who stand in support of you and your teachings.

I have come to the realization that I Am absolutely nothing without God working in my life. It is only by His grace that I Am able to share any of this with you. And it is all due to the fact that God has translated me from Darkness into His glorious Light!

The reason why I have chosen to stand apart from you and those of La'el Ministries is not only because of what took place on that night, but due to everything that led up to that night; and more importantly because of what has transpired *since* that night.

Please humble yourself before the LORD and allow Him to speak to your heart. I just pray that you will listen to His word as if your eternal life depended on it, because it does!

I Corinthians 5:1-13 "It is reported commonly that there is fornication among you, and such fornication as is not so much as named among the Gentiles, that one should have his father's wife. And ye are puffed up, and have not rather mourned, that he that hath done this deed might be taken away from among you.

For I verily, as absent in body, but present in spirit, have judged already, as though I were present, concerning him that hath so done this deed, In the name of our LORD Jesus Christ, when ye are gathered together, and my spirit, with the power of our LORD Jesus Christ, To deliver such an one unto Satan for the destruction of the flesh, that the spirit may be saved in the day of the LORD Jesus.

Your glorying is not good. Know ye not that a little leaven leaveneth the whole lump? Purge out therefore the old leaven, that ye may be a new lump, as ye are unleavened.

For even Christ our Passover is sacrificed for us: Therefore let us keep the feast, not with old leaven, neither with the leaven of malice and wickedness; but with the unleavened bread of sincerity and Truth.

I wrote unto you in an epistle not to company with fornicators: Yet not altogether with the fornicators of this world, or with the covetous, or extortioners, or with idolaters; for then must ye needs go out of the world.

But now I have written unto you not to keep company, if any man that is called a brother be a fornicator, or covetous, or an idolater, or a railer, or a drunkard, or an extortioner; with such an one no not to eat. For what have I to do to judge them also that are without? Do not ye judge them that are within? But them that are without God judgeth. Therefore put away from among yourselves that wicked person."

These excerpts from a lesson you wrote up will show how the words you speak are so inconsistent with your actions.

Liz's Statement: "Among you (within your body—among the parts of the body,) there should be no mention of each other committing sexual sins of any kind.

The outside world will persecute us, they will speak all manner of evil against us, but within our body, there should be no mention of misconduct. If the body will respond to each other in a godly manner, no one could even misunderstand something that looked to be misconduct—nothing would look ungodly!"

Liz, in light of these statements that you made, how can you support a man that seduces women into believing that he is their spiritual husband as ordained by Almighty God and His word?

More personally, how can you condone your own adulterous relationship with him? You were always ready to condemn me, but for some reason, you never applied the word of God to yourself.

You say that your relationship with him is ordained of God, including your illegitimate children, but if you were honest with yourself and more importantly with the LORD, you would have to admit that you have always had lingering doubts concerning all of it. God will never allow you to have peace in that relationship because it's of the Devil!

If you keep rejecting the Truth, you will continue in the lies and lead others into it as well. Please do not allow Satan to deceive you any longer! I hope and pray that you will take hold of the Truth and live.

But you will never be able to see and understand the Truth until you genuinely acknowledge the LORD God and submit yourself to Him with all your heart. Then as you repent of your own sin, you will be able to see the sin of others so as to truly help them.

But since you are still *Walking With The Enemy* he will continue to control how you think, what you do, and even influence how you perceive God's word, regardless of how much you read it.

If you have a sincere love for Almighty God, you will have to turn from all the lies and deceptions that you have been walking in, and bow before the LORD God and seek His forgiveness.

I realize Satan has a much stronger hold on you than he had on me, but Jesus Christ won the victory over sin, death, and Satan. And He *will* deliver all those who truly love and belong to Him.

You stated that Cindy thought *she* was right for the eight months that she walked away from La'el Ministries, but death was still at work in her body. While all of that was very true, the reason why she did not see the Truth is because when she left you, she was still blinded by her sin, and thus she continued *Walking With The Enemy*.[46]

It doesn't matter where you are, you can walk with the Enemy anywhere. If you will not give up your sin and embrace the True Light, then the Power of Darkness will continue to have control over your life, regardless of where you are walking, or who you are walking with.

You have been used as a vessel unto dishonor and shame! You have been used as an instrument of unrighteousness unto sin! You are *Walking With The Enemy* in Darkness and it will only get darker!

Depending on what your motives really are, will determine to what degree God will allow Satan to affect your life. Nevertheless, I sincerely hope you will be one that overcomes.

Revelation 21:7-8 "He that overcometh shall inherit all things; and I will be his God, and he shall be My son. But the fearful, and unbelieving, and the abominable, and murderers, and whoremongers, and sorcerers, and idolaters, and all liars, shall have their part in the lake which burneth with fire and brimstone: Which is the second death."

I know how committed you can be, and what a wonderful thing it would be if we were truly on the same side! That has been my hope ever since our separation; and only you and God knows for certain whether you will ever come to Him; or remain in the Darkness forever.

II Timothy 2:19-26 "Nevertheless the foundation of God standeth sure, having this seal, the LORD knoweth them that are His. And, let every one that nameth the name of Christ depart from iniquity.

But in a great house there are not only vessels of gold and of silver, but also of wood and of earth; and some to honour, and some to dishonour.

If a man therefore purge himself from these, he shall be a vessel unto honour, sanctified, and meet for the Master's use, and prepared unto every good work. Flee also youthful lusts: but follow righteousness, faith, charity, peace, with them that call on the LORD out of a pure heart. But foolish and unlearned questions avoid, knowing that they do gender strifes.

And the servant of the LORD must not strive; but be gentle unto all men, apt to teach, patient, In meekness instructing those that oppose themselves; if God peradventure will give them repentance to the acknowledging of the Truth; And that they may recover themselves out of the snare of the Devil, who are taken captive by him at his will."

Revelation 22:13-15 "I Am Alpha and Omega, the beginning and the end, the first and the last. Blessed are they that do His commandments, that they may have right to the Tree of Life, and may enter in through the gates into the city. For without are dogs, and sorcerers, and whoremongers, and murderers, and idolaters, and whosoever loveth and maketh a lie."

I know it is hard for you to believe that someone like me can actually be inspired by the Holy Spirit, especially since you always considered me the weakest one. At times, it even overwhelms me, but I know what the LORD has spoken to my heart.

I just praise God that He allowed me to see the Truth! And I believe He brought about my release from the power of Darkness because of my sincere desire to please Him and walk in His ways. Read this next scripture very carefully regarding God's wisdom.

Proverbs 8:33-36 "Hear instruction, and be wise, and refuse it not. Blessed is the man that heareth Me, watching daily at My gates, waiting at the posts of My doors.

For whoso findeth Me findeth life, and shall obtain favour of the LORD. But he that sinneth against Me wrongeth his own soul: all they that hate Me love death."

Liz, I have not judged your heart motives in any of this, and I won't. That is only for the LORD God Almighty to do. But He has instructed that we look at each other and judge whether our actions are the fruits of His Holy Spirit or the fruits of our sinful flesh.

Galatians 5:19-21 "Now the works of the flesh are manifest, which are these; Adultery, fornication, uncleanness, lasciviousness, idolatry, witchcraft, hatred, variance, emulations, wrath, strife, seditions, heresies,

Envyings, murders, drunkenness, revellings, and such like: of the which I tell you before, as I have also told you in time past, that they which do such things shall not inherit the kingdom of God."

If you will be completely honest, you know that you fit into almost every category that Paul has stated here. I do not bring this to your attention to condemn you, but so that you might be saved.

God has so wonderfully allowed us to see that all of us were walking in lies and deception, but if you continue to reject the Truth, you will die in your sin and iniquity.

I know in my heart that God desires for all men to be saved, but I have sadly come to the realization that some people love the Darkness more than they do the Light. Only God knows if you are one of these people; and if you are, God has said in His word that your sin will be exposed on that great and dreadful Day of the LORD, if not before.

I Timothy 5:24-25 "Some men's sins are open beforehand, going before to judgment; and some men they follow after.

Likewise also the good works of some are manifest beforehand; and they that are otherwise cannot be hid."

Galatians 6:7-8 "Be not deceived; God is not mocked: for whatsoever a man soweth, that shall he also reap.

For he that soweth to his flesh shall of the flesh reap corruption; but he that soweth to the Spirit shall of the Spirit reap life everlasting."

My sincere hope is that you truly desire the wisdom of God, because if you do, He is faithful to His word. You will have to turn from all the wickedness and lies that you have been walking in, and earnestly plead for God's mercy and forgiveness, so that maybe He will allow you the great privilege of walking with Him in Truth, instead of the disgrace of *Walking With The Enemy* in deception.

Signed and sealed in the presence of a witness on the 14th Day of December in the year of the LORD, One Thousand Nine Hundred and Ninety-Three.

AFTER I FINISHED THESE LETTERS, the LORD told me not to send them to her because they would only provoke her to anger. Thus, the only way she will be able to read these words is if she receives a copy of my published Testimony of "Walking With The Enemy."

This next letter is addressed to two members of La'el Ministries that were a part of the group when I was. They have been told the Truth, but apparently, they have rejected it.

As far as I know they are still *Walking With The Enemy*, and I just hope they will come to the True Light, before God pours out His wrath and indignation upon the children of disobedience.

There is Still Time

"But of that Day and that hour knoweth no man,
no, not the angels which are in Heaven, neither the Son, but the Father.
Take ye heed, watch and pray: for ye know not when the Time is."
Mark 13:32-33

The following letter is one that I had written to some of the remaining members of La'el Ministries with the hope that it would show them that they are going the wrong way. The LORD never led me to send it to them, however He has directed me to publish it in this book.

Dear Wendell and Cindy, 29 December 1993

The reason why I Am addressing this letter to the both of you, is because my message to you is the same, and anyone else that is walking in Darkness, yet knows not where they are going.

You may say that I Am the one who is *Walking With The Enemy,* but if you believe that, then you have been deluded into believing lies, because you do not have a genuine love for the Truth.

I still have hope for you though, and I would like to make a final attempt to persuade you to see the Truth about La'el Ministries. You may feel that I Am being extremely presumptuous, but I Am actually very concerned about you, and all of God's people for that matter.

My primary reason for writing this is because God said to, and since *He is* the one who has directed that I bring these issues to Light, what you do with them is of the utmost importance.

I hope that you will take the time to read what I have written, and take it into serious consideration. May God show you how this applies to you, and how your decisions will determine your destiny.

Because you have remained with Pastor Huff and Liz, I can only assume that you are still supporting their teachings and their beliefs. Since you have stood by them, even after the warnings, indicates to me that you have entrusted them with your very life! Your eternal life!

There is still time to get out, and in this letter I will show you why it is imperative that you hurry before the opportunity passes you by. Additionally, I will prove beyond a shadow of a doubt that those with whom you are walking, do not serve the LORD God Almighty.

Cindy, you have expressed doubts and concerns about Huff's behavior and even his teachings, but you have always trusted Liz, just as I had. That is, up until the night of 2 March 1993.

I Am going to share with you parts of a transcript from a Bible study that Liz conducted right before the LORD intervened, which will show that her teachings and beliefs are also truth mixed with lies.

Read this for informational purposes only. It's important for you to read it so you can see for yourself the error of her teachings, but I hope that you will keep in mind that she is the Enemy of God.

TRANSCRIPT OF BIBLE STUDY MEETING WITH LA'EL MINISTRIES
4 FEBRUARY 1993 THURSDAY NIGHT

Huff "Liz is going to share some things with you tonight."

Liz "Well, first of all, I'm going to tell you right off the bat, that I'm going to do something that I swore I would never ever do. And I criticized other people tremendously for doing. And just in doing that, I want to say the Lord has certainly dealt with my heart about some things. And He's shown me some things.

And one thing more than any other thing, that I rejoice in the Lord in, is that His word is true, and He very vividly promises us that anyone who diligently seeks Him, that He'll reveal Himself to them. And if we continue to seek Him out, and to search for His truth, that He will be faithful to accomplish the good work He started in us.

And that is really not dependent on us. The only dependence on us is that we continue to seek Him. And as long as we do, no matter what, God is faithful to His word. And He will go forth and accomplish that which He has said that He would.

And, um, as I was studying today, the Lord specifically impressed upon me the need to read this book that I got. And quite honestly, I had a different purpose in mind, and intent in mind when I started reading this book today. And I thought the reason why the Lord wanted me to read it was for another reason. And it wasn't until I began to get into it that I realized that was not the reason at all.

And as we have continued to seek the Lord and ask the Lord to reveal anything here that's not of Him, that anything that's been twisted or distorted, any teachings that might have gone forth that were not His heart—any areas that we may have been, um, out of order in—that He would reveal that to us.

And today as I was studying again, when I get to the point where I finally think that I am beginning to get a handle on it—

I'm finally beginning to see clearly, *it's like God jerks the rug right out from under me.* And I find out that all the ground that I've gained was not gained ground at all, and yet it was because I had to go through all that to see the truth. *[Emphasis mine.]*

The reason that, um, I'm going to share this with you tonight rather than [Pastor Huff] sharing this; and he hasn't heard this yet, so this is going to be, um, for him, just like for you; the first time that he's heard it. But I prayed about it because there is a spiritual authority, and there is a manner God has ordained that we do things.

And the reason the Lord impressed upon me that I need to come and do this is because it has been through some of the things that I've taught, both publicly, and you know, with the children's ministry, and privately in ministering to some of you all that *I have twisted God's word in certain areas.* I've done so out of stupidity and like Paul out of total ignorance. But the Lord said I was to come and present this tonight, so that, you know, no one that had received the things that I had said would be sitting here going, ah, that's not right. I'm—We've got this settled. *[Emphasis mine.]*

So, as I bring this tonight I want you all to know that I have humbled myself before the Lord, that I have asked God's forgiveness, and also ask you to forgive me; and anything that I said apart from God's word was done in total ignorance. Not in rebelliousness or disobedience to God.

I'm going to read to—I'm going to read to you out of this book. And it is about four pages, but this is a very—This man is Watchman Nee. It's called *A Spiritual Man*.[47] He wrote this in 1927 and 1928. He was a China-man. He was Chinese. This has been transferred from Chinese into—translated into English. He actually requested that his work was not to ever be translated, but they did. So people did translate simply because the Lord instructed them to do so.

And I'm going to, rather than try to discuss in my own words, I'm going to read to you what God has shown me today; because these words are truly words of the Holy Spirit, and there is no way, even listening a hundred percent to the Holy Spirit, I feel, that I could even begin under the same anointing to state what this man has stated so beautifully.

And I'm going to read slowly because there—almost every word is so compact, that you have to go through this slowly. And today I've read like seventy pages, and I'm a very fast reader; but you can't read this fast because *it's just like the word of God.*

Everything, every sentence means something very important that is so packed full of God's word and His truth, that it's the same manner. This particular section is on salvation; and I'm going to start here." *[Emphasis mine.]*

Nee "If one believes in the death of the Lord Jesus as his substitute he already has been united with the Lord Jesus in His death..."

Liz "Now again, he's saying that to believe—if you believe that Jesus was a substitute for our sin; then Jesus has been punished in our place. He has taken our punishment. The penalty of my sin is death."

Nee "There can be no salvation otherwise."

Liz "And that's exactly what happened. Jesus suffered death. He suffered the penalty of death that was paid. The penalty of sin was death. And Jesus suffered that penalty. He paid that penalty on the cross. And because of that, if we believe and receive His substitution—Him being the substitution for our sins, then we have died in Him. That's the whole point of salvation. That's what the born again experience is all about.

...If you believe it you have eternal life. It's that simple.

...One of the things with me that has been such a deceptive force in my life, and in my walk with the Lord, has been over this one thing, because I've never been able to understand how you could separate someone who is concerned with the penalty for sin, yet not concerned with the effects of sin, or the power of sin within the born again Christian.

And yet, it doesn't matter whether that person is concerned merely with the penalty of sin, or the power of sin. The whole point is that him being united with the Messiah is the common possession that he shares with all who are united with the body of Christ. The point is, if he is in union with the Messiah, he is—he is part of God's body, of Christ's body. Okay?"

Nee "He who is not united with the Lord has not yet believed, and therefore, has no part in Him."

Liz "That's very self-explanatory. If you've not yet believed, this is not for you, don't worry about it."

Nee "In believing, one is united with the Lord. To be united with Him means to experience everything He has experienced."

Liz "And that's very true. If we are united with Him, *we can't experience everything that He's experienced;* we don't have to. But it's available to us to be able to. That again is a matter of choice. But nonetheless, whether you choose to appropriate the things of God or not, the fact remains, that they've been poured out on you." *[Emphasis mine.]*

Nee "...We should beware lest we insist that a man is not born anew unless he has experienced death and resurrection with the Lord. The scriptures deem anyone who believes in the Lord Jesus as already regenerated."

Liz "There again, this is something I have always struggled with within my own life, and I know that all of us do, because I've talked with each of you at length. It's very easy for us to look at other people and judge, and think that because someone has not experienced certain things in their walk with Jesus, that they've not been made new.

But that is not true. We should beware lest we insist that a man is not...already regenerated. When you believed, you were already regenerated. You are not going to be regenerated later. Even though it is a continuing process, you are regenerated at the time that you believed.

...Again, it's easy to look at someone and if we don't see the regenerated, resurrected power of God working in someone's life, it's easy for us to say they are not born again, they are not walking with God. But the fact is those that call upon the name of the Lord shall be saved.

Those who believe that Jesus was their substitution for sin have been raised again to sit in Christ Jesus in heavenly places. Regardless of whether they have experienced these things or not. Whether they've experienced anything in their Christian walk or not.

God's word is truth, and whether we like the way He does it or not, whether we like the way our brother or sister walks or not, His word is truth. And us not liking it does not change the reality or the truth of His word."

Nee “Do not confuse, then, position with experience. At the time one believes in the Lord Jesus he may be most weak and ignorant; he is nonetheless placed by God in the perfect position of being considered dead, raised and ascended with the Lord.”

Liz “And most of us do. Except those of us who have been in churches all of our lives. Most of us come to the Lord Jesus very weak and ignorant. We don’t know anything. And yet, simply by believing in the substitution that Jesus paid, confessing that before God, we immediately came to be considered by God dead, raised, and ascended with the Lord.”

Nee “He who is accepted in Christ is as acceptable as Christ Himself.”

Liz “And many times we have stated here that after we have been cleansed with the blood of Jesus—After Jesus paid the penalty for us, when God looks at us, He does not see us, He sees Christ, He sees Jesus. *That* stands in front of us.

And no matter where we’ve been or what has happened to us—*No matter what we’re not able to get in control of in our life,* the prerequisite is that we have received— *[Emphasis mine.]*

We have believed and received what God has given in the form of His son. And when we have, we’ve been accepted in Christ, and we are as acceptable to God as Christ.”

Nee “*...No life relationship existed at all between Adam and God.* His being called "the son of God" is similar to the angels being so called, for he was created directly by God. We who believe in the Lord Jesus, however, are "born of God" (John 1:12-13).” *[Emphasis mine.]*

Liz “And I want to stop there. He’s commenting on a comment he made earlier in the book and quite honestly, since I do not fully understand that, I’m going to let that go till the Lord gives me a more clearer understanding of it. And I don’t even want to touch it. I don’t know. Okay?”

Nee “Accordingly, there is a life relationship. A child born inherits his father’s life; we are born of God. Therefore, we have His life (2 Peter 1.4). Had Adam received the life which God offered in the tree of life, he immediately would have obtained the eternal uncreated life of God. His spirit came from God, and so it is everlasting. How this everlasting spirit shall live depends upon how one regards God’s order and upon what choice he makes.”

Liz "Now, we're talking about the person who has been born of God, who has been born again, and this is something that I want everybody to understand.

We are an everlasting spirit born again to God at this point, if we're believers. How our born again everlasting spirit will live, depends upon how you and I regard God's order, and upon what choice we make. It does not change the fact that we're born again, but it certainly will depend on how our lives will be lived and on the choices we make, and how we view God and what God says."

Nee "The life we Christians obtain in regeneration is the same which Adam could have had but never had: God's life. Regeneration not only retrieves out of chaotic darkness the order of man's spirit and soul; it additionally affords man the supernatural life of God. Man's darkened and fallen spirit is made alive through being strengthened by the Holy Spirit into accepting God's life. This is new birth."

Liz "We certainly know that it is through the Holy Spirit that we are led into accepting the life that God offers."

Nee "The basis upon which the Holy Spirit can regenerate man is the cross (John 3.14-15)."

Liz "And we know that the penalty that Jesus paid was on the cross, therefore the basis which the Holy Spirit can regenerate is through the cross. There is no other way except for the cross."

Nee "...A life relationship is established with God in new birth. It resembles the old birth of the flesh in that it is once and for all. *Once a man is born of God he can never be treated by God as not having been so born of Him." [Emphasis mine.]*

Liz "It says the life relationship is established with God in new birth. It resembles the old birth of the flesh in that it is once and for all. When we're born in the flesh, we're only born once—that's it. If we die we're not going to get born again in the flesh. What he's saying here is the new life, the new birth that we experience through the life of God is the same way; once we are reborn we cannot be reborn again.

That is it. That is the birth. It's forever. *Once a man is born of God, he can never be treated by God as not having been born of Him." [Emphasis mine.]*

Nee "However endless eternity may be, *this relationship and this position cannot be annulled.* This is because what a believer receives at *new birth is not contingent upon a progressive, spiritual and holy pursuit* after he believes, but is the pure gift of God." *[Emphasis mine.]*

Liz "God's word plainly tells us that salvation is a gift from God, that no man may boast. No man may obtain it by works. And our new birth, our eternal life we receive from Him, is not dependent upon a progressive walk with Him or a holy spiritual and holy pursuit after what the believer believes God wants even. It is given as a free gift. It is accepted as a free gift.

If there was any way we could obtain it through holiness or purity or anything else, *God could have given us the standards by which to walk* and we could therefore have walked by them. *[Emphasis mine!]*

It would have been absolutely pointless for Jesus to have died, because we could have done it. And having Jesus die on the cross, it is still beyond a shadow of a doubt, nonessential for us to do anything. Even after we are born again.

If we can do anything that would save us, the gift would not be free. It would still be based on works.

(I had a question but the recorder did not pick it up.)

...I'll cover that later, just don't be confused there."

Nee "What God bestows is eternal life. *No possibility exists for this life and position to be abrogated.* Receiving God's life in new birth is the starting point of a Christian walk, the minimum for a believer." *[Emphasis mine.]*

Liz "And I want to stop and share something here. I shared this earlier with Cathy today because at the time I did not realize that the Lord would have me share this tonight. And when I got to this point Cathy goes, wait a minute, what about what God said in Revelation that, that—What was the question?"

Cathy "What if your name is blotted out of the Book of Life?"

Liz "Yeah, what about that verse that says ya know, to be careful or your name will be blotted out of the Book of Life. Well, you know, I gave her some real lame excuse about we could make—*We could twist the word of God and make it say anything we wanted to. [Emphasis mine.]*

And you know—And it didn't satisfy either one of us. But both of us were willing at least to see God's point here and we went on. And I went on down, and after I read the next sentences, 'Receiving God's new life in the new birth is the starting point of the Christian walk, the very minimum for a believer,' the Lord spoke to my heart, and He explained that verse to me. And I want to explain because that is a question. If we can never lose our salvation, why does God's word say that we could possibly have our names blotted out? *And the Lord told me that everybody's name is written in the Book of Life.* It was never God's intention that anybody died. *[Emphasis mine.]*

His word is very plain. He does not desire that any man perish, but all should come to know Him. It was not His desire that any man should be lost. He sent His son so that all mankind might be saved. *All men were born alive to God, all mankind had their names written in the Book of Life.* The only way your name can be blotted out of the Book of Life is if you receive—if you refuse to receive the sacrifice—the substitute of Jesus. Then your name will be blotted out of the Book of Life." *[Emphasis mine.]*

Cindy "Is that great or wow!!"

Liz "Correct?" *[Mr. Huff just nodded in agreement.]*

Cindy "Ah! So-o-o neat!"

Liz "And, Cathy and—I mean that just blew me away. I just began to cry at that point because I just realized that the Lord loves us so much, and He wants us to know the truth so much, that even when we have questions. Because He wants us to see the truth, He gave us revelation knowledge of something I didn't even know, so that there couldn't be any ground for the enemy to come and say what about that? What about that? That's not true because if it was true it would all be true.

So, God immediately gave me revelation knowledge on exactly what that meant, so the enemy wouldn't have any ground; so the enemy wouldn't be able to come in and pick like the little foxes at the base of the vine.

And it blessed my heart so much that God immediately gave this revelation on that so we could know what He said here is true. That our salvation is—What? *(I made a comment.)* That's right, Hell was not made for man.

And it's God's heart that we all be saved. And it is God's heart that we do know the truth. And He will go to any length for those who truly want to know the truth. He will go to any length to reveal that.

...No matter how religious, moral, learned, or zealous a person may be, if they have not yet believed on the death of the Lord Jesus and received supernatural life, this is not believing with your mind—I believe it. The devils believe. Believing with your spirit. Supernaturally allowing the Holy Spirit to recreate us and change us. It doesn't matter. *We're still dead if we haven't done that. [Emphasis mine—Do you see the obvious contradictions?]*

...God has poured out on us at the time that we honestly believe in our heart and ask Him. He gives us everything completely. It is complete and it is perfect. But that which He has given us remains inside of our human spirit, until such time that the Holy Spirit begins to work in conjunction with our soul.

Because the soul is the mind, will, and emotions that wait in perfection inside of us, in the inner man, until such time as the soul co-operates with the Holy Spirit, so that maturity can begin. The maturing process—Jesus grew in grace and wisdom. The same happens with us with the born again renewed spirit.

...At the beginning of the new birth, life is not full grown. A baby does not come here fully-grown. When we are born, we are not full grown. Even though as [Pastor Huff] has said numerous times, all the potential for a full grown adult is there, everything they need is there, but it comes through maturity.

...I have just a couple more paragraphs here, and I'd like to mention that this is the thing that—This is the one thing that has caused me to stumble more, and to begin to go back and doubt, and disbelieve that you could lose your salvation. That you could really mess up and just blow it out the window. So I want everyone to pay really close attention to this because everyone in this room fits in one of these categories."

Nee "Two kinds of Christians: The apostle in I Corinthians 3.1 divides all Christians into two classifications. They are the spiritual and the carnal. A spiritual Christian is one in whom the Holy Spirit dwells in his spirit and controls his entire being."

Liz "His soul consisting of his mind, will, and emotions. And his body."

Nee "What is meant, then, by being carnal? The Bible employs the word "flesh" to describe the life and value of an unregenerated man."

Liz "That's the flesh. It's made up of everything which issues from his sinful body and his soul.

...Instead of allowing his soul in conjunction with the Holy Spirit to mature that which is already perfect within him, and complete within him, he continues to allow his flesh to rule. He continues to be overcome by his flesh.

...The carnal Christian is one whose spirit has been made alive, but who still follows his soul, which consist of the mind, will, and the emotions and body, into sin.

One of the things that he has pointed out before we got to this point is that the soul is in the middle. The soul is the one who is comprised of the mind, will, and the emotions. The soul makes all the calls.

The spirit does not over-ride the soul. The soul makes the choice because God put within it the will. And God made us a free will. And for the spirit to over-ride the soul, even a spirit that is alive to God, would be to remove from us the very thing that God gave us to make us people who have choices. So, it is the soul who makes choices. But the soul is the one that makes the calls.

And after we are born again, it is the soul, not the body, but it is the soul that makes the choice on whether or not it will submit itself to the leadership and guidance of the Holy Spirit, or whether it will continue to operate in the flesh or the soul of man.

...It doesn't do away from the fact that he is born again. But if he continues to remain carnal without allowing the soul to be under the influence of the Holy Spirit, and to take its suggestions from the spirit, rather than the soul—Or the soul will either work in connection with the spirit who's born again to God, which works in connection with the Holy Spirit to produce God's life, to conform us and transform us.

Or it will be dominated by its own desires, by the emotions, by the intellect of man, and his reasoning capabilities. Or either he will allow the body to begin to do things outwardly and when the body—the flesh, begins to do things outwardly, that almost immediately begins to control the soul.

Because *the soul will almost never be able to override what the flesh wants*, because *what the flesh wants is so strong.* It rises up within us. We want that piece of chocolate cake. We want it, we want it, *eventually we're going to give in* and have it. *[Emphasis mine.]*

Certainly we do, sometimes, exert that will power, but most of the time, *once we come under the power of the flesh, the soul usually gives in and goes with whatever the flesh wants because the flesh does exert so much power.* The flesh—Then he will remain in that carnal position. And *this carnal position will actually hinder God.* It will hinder us from receiving what God has poured out on us. God has poured it out. They are there. They are available to us, but if we continue to walk in sin, if we continue to allow our flesh to rule, then we will not experience the full potential of our salvation. *[Emphasis mine.]*

We will not walk in all the things that God has promised. We will not receive from God all the things He has poured out. They are available to us if we would simply receive them. Even though they are there, even though they are inside of us, even though they are perfect in nature within us. As long as we remain carnal, and as long as we remain controlled by the soul and the spirit, we won't receive those things. Those things will not be matured inside of us.

...One thing [Pastor Huff] has said to me many times in the past, I guess, year or so, that's really hacked me off; where I just wanted to *rip his throat out* is when he's told me that, um, 'probably, my worst problem is that I try to make people conform to my standards of where I am.'

And as I read this today, and as the Lord really bore witness in my heart by His Holy Spirit that this word is truth. *This has been the same truth that has been in my heart ever since I have known Him. (Referring to the words of Watchman Nee.)*

A lot of things have swayed that. Actually my soulish man with the intellect and reasoning abilities said one and one is two. And yet those principles don't work in the spiritual kingdom. *They work here, but God has defied all logic.* He has used things that absolutely do not make sense. *He's used the foolishness of the cross to save us.* And the wisdom of this world is foolishness to Him. *[Emphasis mine.]*

And while it is very, very true that many and most of the things that God has been showing me for the last two years, have been for a deeper walk with Him, and a deeper commitment with Him, because those have stemmed out of a heart that truly desires to be committed to Him.

It's also been very easy to say, 'Well, if this is true for me, then it must mean that if everybody else is not doing it this way, that they're out of order with God, and God can't work with them. And God wants them to get their act straightened up, and God wants them to submit to Him.'

And while all of those things are true, it is very true God does want us to submit to Him; He wants us to submit everything. But the whole point is, the only thing He asks you to do is to believe in His son, to accept the sacrifice that He made for your sins. And if you do, He will meet you right there. And will take the spirit inside of you that's dead to Him, and you will become born again, and you will receive eternal life; which means exactly what it says, eternal life. And you will live forever with Him.

And that begins the process of your walk with Jesus. It can be the beginning of the end. You don't have to go no farther. If you don't, then you have salvation forever and forever and ever...in the presence of God in His kingdom.

There is so much more that God desires for us to have. He has poured out everything in His kingdom. Not for later, but for now. He says we can have it now. If we will submit ourselves to Him and let Him do His work in our heart and He will change us from the inside out.

But it is not for the Christian who is submitted unto the Lord— *It is not their place to go and look and say, but they're not doing that—They're out of order.* You're not really walking—You're not really—

Only each individual person can make the decision of what they want and what they're really willing to receive from God. And I can tell you that we're much more critical of one another than God is of us. *[Emphasis mine.]*

As we were singing tonight God reminded me of that. I don't know if it was my own ears or God just wanting to..."

End of transcript ~ The tape ran out.

I hope you were able to see that her lesson on Watchman Nee's book was truth mixed with lies. And I would like to take this time to refute a few of her statements with the use of the Scriptures, to show that her beliefs are quite contrary to God's Holy word.

Liz's statement: "No matter how religious, moral, learned, or zealous a person may be, if they have not yet believed on the death of the Lord Jesus and received supernatural life—This is not believing with your mind—I believe it. The devils believe.

Believing with your spirit. Supernaturally allowing the Holy Spirit to recreate us and change us. It doesn't matter, we're still dead if we haven't done that."

Just because you say you believe in the death of Jesus is not that unusual—men *die* every day. But if you were to actually believe in your heart that God raised His Son from the dead, *that* would be something!

Romans 10:9-13 "That if thou shalt confess with thy mouth the LORD Jesus, and shalt believe in thine heart that God hath raised Him from the dead, thou shalt be saved.

For with the heart man believeth unto righteousness; and with the mouth confession is made unto salvation. For the Scripture saith, Whosoever believeth on Him shall not be ashamed.

For there is no difference between the Jew and the Greek: for the same LORD over all is rich unto all that call upon Him. For whosoever shall call upon the name of the LORD shall be saved."

James 2:17-20 "Even so faith, if it hath not works, is dead, being alone. Yea, a man may say, Thou hast faith, and I have works: shew me thy faith without thy works, and I will shew thee my faith by my works.

Thou believest that there is one God; thou doest well: the devils also believe, and tremble. But wilt thou know, O vain man, that faith without works is dead?"

In order to be saved from sin and death you must believe with all your heart that God was able to raise Jesus Christ from the dead, and also be willing to confess Him as the LORD of your life.

If God has given you the faith to truly believe that He brought His Son back to life, then you will have no trouble believing all of the other wonderful works of God. And if Jesus Christ is truly your LORD you will most certainly want to please Him.

Her lesson is filled with such contradictions and half-truths! On the one hand, she says all men are born alive to God, but then she turns around and says all men are dead until they believe in the death of Jesus.

She says your actions really make no difference with God—that there is no standard to go by, and that living by the flesh or carnal nature is permissible with God, but these verses will prove her wrong.

Romans 12:1-2 "I beseech you therefore, brethren, by the mercies of God, that ye present your bodies a living sacrifice, holy, acceptable unto God, which is your reasonable service.

And be not conformed to this world: but be ye transformed by the renewing of your mind, that ye may prove what is that good, and acceptable, and perfect, will of God."

It all starts with what you believe. So if you are taught lies, you will believe lies; and you will have faith in lies. However, if you are taught the Truth, you will believe the Truth, and you will have faith in the Truth. And it is so important to walk in Truth, because only the Truth will set you free from the lies of the Devil!

II Corinthians 11:3 "But I fear, lest by any means, as the serpent beguiled Eve through his subtlety, so your minds should be corrupted from the simplicity that is in Christ."

Satan's whole purpose is to try and destroy what the LORD God Almighty has planned, and what better way to accomplish that objective than to convince people that they are "born again" into the kingdom of Almighty God when in reality they are not.

After contemplating her lesson the LORD brought the following Scripture verses to my attention concerning the "born again" experience.

John 6:44 Jesus said, "No man can come to Me, except the Father which hath sent Me draw him: and I will raise him up at the last day."

John 1:12-13 "But as many as received Him, to them gave He power to become the Sons of God, even to them that believe on His name: Which were born, not of blood, nor of the will of the flesh, nor of the will of man, but of God."

John 3:5 "Jesus answered, Verily, verily, I say unto thee, Except a man be born of water and of the Spirit, he cannot enter into the kingdom of God."

Based on those scriptures, it should be absolutely clear that God is in complete control, and *He is* the one who decides who will be born into His kingdom and who will not. Yes, He has given all men the opportunity to be a part of His kingdom, but not all will be called the sons of God, and not all will rule and reign with Him.

The overriding tone of this lesson by Liz is that we are ultimately in control of our own destiny, and that we are the ones who decide what we will receive from God, and what we will not accept. It is as if she thinks she can tell God what to do!

She acts like we can do whatever we want and still be acceptable in the sight of God, as long as we believe in the death of Jesus as our substitute. But I contend that these opinions are all lies!

A person who is truly seeking God, and desiring a personal relationship with Him, will most certainly allow His word to take effect in their life. God offers His gift freely and He will never force it upon you, but you must come to Him willingly, and *on His terms*.

A person who is truly born of the LORD God above will seek to keep His commandments and pursue a life of holiness and purity with all sincerity, which I might add is quite contrary to the beliefs and teachings that Liz expressed during her Bible study lesson.

Ephesians 5:1-7 "Be ye therefore followers of God, as dear children; And walk in love, as Christ also hath loved us, and hath given Himself for us an offering and a sacrifice to God for a sweet-smelling savour.

But fornication, and all uncleanness, or covetousness, let it not be once named among you, as becometh saints; Neither filthiness, nor foolish talking, nor jesting, which are not convenient: but rather giving of thanks.

For this ye know, that no whoremonger, nor unclean person, nor covetous man, who is an idolater, hath any inheritance in the kingdom of Christ and of God. Let no man deceive you with vain words: for because of these things cometh the wrath of God upon the children of disobedience. Be not ye therefore partakers with them."

John 3:16-21 "For God so loved the world, that He gave His only begotten Son, that whosoever believeth in Him should not perish, but have everlasting life. For God sent not His Son into the world to condemn the world; but that the world through Him might be saved. He that believeth on Him is not condemned: but he that believeth not is condemned already, because he hath not believed in the name of the only begotten Son of God.

And this is the condemnation, that Light is come into the world, and men loved Darkness rather than Light, because their deeds were evil. For every one that doeth evil hateth the Light, neither cometh to the Light, lest his deeds should be reproved.

But he that doeth Truth cometh to the Light, that his deeds may be made manifest, that they are wrought in God."

Titus 2:11-15 "For the grace of God that bringeth salvation hath appeared to all men, Teaching us that, denying ungodliness and worldly lusts, we should live soberly, righteously, and Godly, in this present world; Looking for that blessed hope, and the glorious appearing of the great God and our Saviour Jesus Christ;

Who gave Himself for us, that He might redeem us from all iniquity, and purify unto Himself a peculiar people, zealous of good works.

These things speak, and exhort, and rebuke with all authority. Let no man despise thee."

Based on these scriptures, it is very clear that God expects us to turn from our sins and submit to Him so that He can purify us.

Moreover, He also instructs those who are led by the Spirit of Christ to expose the false teachers in order to warn unsuspecting souls of the dangers that lie behind the words of deceptive men.

As long as the LORD God Almighty leads me to warn others about the evil workers of iniquity, especially within the churches, I will strive to obey God regardless of what other "men" may think.

Titus 3:8-11 "This is a faithful saying, and these things I will that thou affirm constantly, that they which have believed in God might be careful to maintain good works.

These things are good and profitable unto men. But avoid foolish questions, and genealogies, and contentions, and strivings about the law; for they are unprofitable and vain.

A man that is an heretic, (which is a person who holds controversial opinions or doctrines at variance with established religious beliefs) after the first and second admonition (or warning) reject; Knowing that he that is such is subverted, and sinneth, being condemned of himself."

The word of God will prove why those who claim to be born into God's Kingdom, yet carelessly disobey His Commandments and teach others to do so, are liars and the Truth is not in them.

Almighty God *will* bring every work into judgment, with every secret thing, and hold all men accountable as to what they do in their bodies, whether it be good or whether it be evil!

Luke 8:17-18 "For nothing is secret, that shall not be made manifest; neither any thing hid, that shall not be known and come abroad.

Take heed therefore how ye hear: for whosoever hath, to him shall be given; and whosoever hath not, from him shall be taken even that which he seemeth to have."

I John 5:2-4 "By this we know that we love the children of God, when we love God, and keep His commandments. For this is the love of God, that we keep His commandments: And His commandments are not grievous.

For whatsoever is born of God overcometh the world: and this is the victory that overcometh the world, even our faith."

I John 5:18-21 "We know that whosoever is born of God sinneth not; but He that is begotten of God keepeth Himself, and that wicked one toucheth Him not. And we know that we are of God, and the whole world lieth in wickedness.

And we know that the Son of God is come, and hath given us an understanding, that we may know Him that is true, and we are in Him that is true, even in His Son Jesus Christ. This is the true God, and eternal life. Little children, keep yourself from idols. Amen."

One very important factor to always keep in mind is that God *is* in control, and He is the One who decides who He will share His Heavenly gifts with, and who He will withhold them from.

According to the Scriptures, before God will even seal you with His Spirit you must believe the Testimony He gave of His Son; but due to wrong teachings many are under the mistaken impression that they have been born of His Spirit, when in reality they have not.

As you read the following verses keep in mind that the Apostle Paul is speaking to a body of believers that have a strong abiding faith in the gospel of the LORD Jesus Christ.

Ephesians 1:4-14 "According as He hath chosen us in Him before the foundation of the world, that we should be Holy and without blame before Him in love: Having predestinated us unto the adoption of children by Jesus Christ to Himself, according to the good pleasure of His will, To the praise of the glory of His grace,

Wherein He hath made us accepted in the beloved. In whom we have redemption through His blood, the forgiveness of sins, according to the riches of His grace; Wherein He hath abounded toward us in all wisdom and prudence; Having made known unto us the mystery of His will, according to His good pleasure which He hath purposed in Himself:

That in the dispensation of the fullness of times He might gather together in one all things in Christ, both which are in Heaven, and which are on earth; even in Him:

In whom also we have obtained an inheritance, being predestined according to the purpose of Him who worketh all things after the counsel of His own will: That we should be to the praise of His glory, who first trusted in Christ. In whom ye also trusted, after that ye heard the word of Truth, the gospel of your salvation:

In whom also after that ye believed, ye were sealed with that Holy Spirit of promise, Which is the earnest of our inheritance until the redemption of the purchased possession, unto the praise of His glory."

To be born of the Holy Spirit is exclusively the work of God and for Him to do as *He wills*. When you truly become One with God, and He becomes One with you, a special union takes place that is not of this world. No amount of human effort can ever make it happen! It is *totally* in the hands of Almighty God. *This* is the New Birth!

And once He has granted you the great privilege to become one of His sons or daughters you are a new creation and you will see things from a completely different perspective.

As a child of God, He will give us authority over our sinful flesh nature with the same power that He used to raise Jesus Christ from the dead. And as we grow in Him, and experience His word growing in us, we will come to better understand what took place during the death, burial, and resurrection of the LORD Jesus Christ.

However, in order for us to even begin to comprehend this great mystery and partake of this awesome gift, we must repent of our sins, and fully submit to Almighty God by keeping His commandments.

In so doing, God will show us the many ways in which Satan has so twisted and distorted the word of God in an attempt to keep us from worshipping our Heavenly Father in Spirit and in Truth as He so deserves and greatly desires of His creation.

Moreover, as we become more knowledgeable of the tactics of the Enemy of God and pursue godliness instead of the things of this world, we can actually get to the point in our walk with the LORD that we will not sin against our Creator.

I realize this could be hard for you to believe, but based on God's word it is quite attainable. Christ is looking for a glorious Church! One without spot, or wrinkle, or any such thing! One that is Holy and set apart by Him, and for Him; in order to rule and reign with Him!

I Peter 4:1-2,7-8 "Forasmuch then as Christ hath suffered for us in the flesh, arm yourself likewise with the same mind: for he that hath suffered in the flesh hath ceased from sin; That he no longer should live the rest of his time in the flesh to the lusts of men, but to the will of God...

But the end of all things is at hand: be ye therefore sober, and watch unto prayer. And above all things have fervent charity among yourselves: for charity shall cover the multitude of sins."

I John 3:1-6,10 "Behold, what manner of love the Father hath bestowed upon us, that we should be called the sons of God: therefore the world knoweth us not, because it knew Him not.

Beloved, now are we the sons of God, and it doth not yet appear what we shall be:

But we know that, when He shall appear, we shall be like Him; for we shall see Him as He is. And every man that hath this hope in Him purifieth himself, even as He is pure. Whosoever committeth sin transgresseth also the law: for sin is transgression of the law.

And ye know that He was manifested to take away our sins; and in Him is no sin. Whosoever abideth in Him sinneth not: whosoever sinneth hath not seen Him, neither known Him...In this the children of God are manifest, and the children of the Devil: whosoever doeth not righteousness is not of God, neither he that loveth not his brother."

The main question to ask yourself: Is your heart's desire to do the will of the LORD God Almighty? Or is it more important to satisfy your own will or the will of another?

Please note the following verses which will show what God requires of His disciples and those who belong to Him.

I Thessalonians 4:3-8 "For this is the will of God, even your sanctification, that ye should abstain from fornication: that every one of you should know how to possess his vessel in sanctification and honour; not in the lust of concupiscence (personal desire), even as the Gentiles which know not God:

That no man go beyond and defraud his brother in any matter: because that the LORD is the avenger of all such, as we also have forewarned you and testified. For God hath not called us unto uncleanness, but unto holiness. He therefore that despiseth (or will not listen), despiseth not man, but God, who hath also given unto us His Holy Spirit."

Liz shows very little regard for the commands and laws of Almighty God. Moreover, her Bible study lesson was completely based on her own opinions and that of another man. And if the opinions you have chosen to believe are not firmly established in God's word and derived from His Truth, then they are not from His Holy Spirit.

The following is the verses she referenced in the "revelation" she said she received from God. You should be very familiar with it because it was the "warning" I had sent you via the postal service that you should have received on the first day of the summer of Ninety-Three.

Revelation 3:1-6 "And unto the angel of the Church in Sardis write; These things saith He that hath the seven Spirits of God, and the seven stars; I know thy works, that thou hast a name that thou livest, and art dead.

Be watchful, and strengthen the things which remain, that are ready to die: for I have not found thy works perfect before God.

Remember therefore how thou hast received and heard, and hold fast, and repent.

If therefore thou shalt not watch, I will come on thee as a thief, and thou shalt not know what hour I will come upon thee.

Thou hast a few names even in Sardis which have not defiled their garments; and they shall walk with Me in white: for they are worthy.

He that overcometh, the same shall be clothed in white raiment; and I will not blot out his name out of the Book of Life, but I will confess his name before My Father, and before His angels.

He that hath an ear, let him hear what the Spirit saith unto the churches."

Since this was written to the churches, it is evident that God was speaking to those who had professed to believe in the LORD; otherwise they should not have been a part of the Church.

Some of them had fallen away from the faith, and there may have been some who had never truly committed their lives to the LORD. Nevertheless, it was very obvious that God was greatly displeased with this church and was warning them to repent or face punishment.

This completely refutes Liz's opinion on the Book of Life, and I would like to repeat exactly what she stated so that you can have an opportunity to see the obvious contradictions, and also some of the subtle errors mixed throughout her teachings.

Liz's statement: "All men were born alive to God, all mankind had their names written in the Book of Life. The only way your name can be blotted out of the Book of Life is if you receive—if you refuse to receive the sacrifice—the substitute of Jesus, then your name will be blotted out of the Book of Life."

She almost slipped up and said the actual way to have your name blotted out of the Book of Life. Anyone that worships the Devil and receives his "spirit" will not even be written in the "Book of Life," and the following scriptures will completely refute her contention that "all mankind had their names written in the Book of Life."

Revelation 13:4-9 "And they worshipped the dragon which gave power unto the beast: and they worshipped the beast, saying, Who is like unto the beast? Who is able to make war with him?

And there was given unto him a mouth speaking great things and blasphemies; and power was given unto him to continue forty and *two months. And he opened his mouth in blasphemy against God, to blaspheme His name, and His tabernacle, and them that dwell in Heaven.*

And it was given unto him to make war with the saints, and to overcome them: and power was given him over all kindreds, and tongues, and nations.

And all that dwell upon the earth shall worship him, ***whose names are not written in the Book of Life of the Lamb slain from the foundation of the world.*** *If any man have an ear, let him hear."*

Revelation 17:6-8 "And I saw the woman drunken with the blood of the saints, and with the blood of the martyrs of Jesus: and when I saw her, I wondered with great admiration.

And the angel said unto me, Wherefore didst thou marvel? I will tell thee the mystery of the woman, and of the beast that carrieth her, which hath the seven heads and ten horns.

The beast that thou sawest was, and is not; and shall ascend out of the bottomless pit, and go into perdition:

And they that dwell on the earth shall wonder, ***whose names were not written in the Book of Life from the foundation of the world,*** *when they behold the beast that was, and is not, and yet is."*

Revelation 20:11-15 "And I saw a great white throne, and Him that sat on it, from whose face the earth and the Heaven fled away; and there was found no place for them.

And I saw the dead, small and great, stand before God; and the books were opened: and another Book was opened, which is the Book of Life: and the dead were judged out of those things which were written in the books, according to their works.

And the sea gave up the dead which were in it; and death and Hell delivered up the dead which were in them: and they were judged every man according to their works.

And death and Hell were cast into the Lake of Fire. This is the second death. ***And whosoever was not found written in the Book of Life was cast into the Lake of Fire."***

If you have an unsettling fear of dying, especially after reading those verses from the book of Revelation, I hope you will seriously consider who you are walking with. It is Time to pay attention as to what direction you are headed in, before it is too late!

If you are truly repentant and desire to be saved from eternal death, you must turn from all that is evil and submit yourself to the LORD God above with your whole heart, soul, and mind; and put all your faith, hope, and trust in the LORD Jesus Christ and His word.

There is still time to come to the LORD for those who have not bowed their knee to Satan, or worshipped the image of the beast, or received his mark; and *only* God knows how much time is left.

Based on God's word, once the doors are closed there is no way to gain entry into the Holy City. If you reject the word of the LORD you will wish you had listened when you stand before Him on that Great Judgment Day. But if you wait till then, it will be too late.

Note the following definitions which should help give you a clearer understanding of what it actually means to put your faith, trust, and belief in a person or ideology.

THE "AMERICAN HERITAGE DICTIONARY"

- Belief: 1-The mental act, condition, or habit of placing trust or confidence in a person or thing; faith. 2-mental acceptance or conviction in the truth or actuality of something. 3-Something believed or accepted as true; especially a particular tenet, or a body of tenets, accepted by a group of persons. (Tenet is an opinion, doctrine, principle, or dogma held by a person or, more especially, an organization.)
- Trust: 1-Firm reliance on the integrity, ability, or character of a person or thing; confident belief or faith. 2-The person or thing in which confidence is placed. 3-Custody or care. 4-Something committed into the care of another; a charge.
- Faith: 1-A confident belief in the truth, value, or trustworthiness of a person, idea, or thing. 2-Belief that does not rest on logical proof or material evidence: faith in miracles. 3-Loyalty to a person or thing; allegiance: keeping faith with one's supporters. 4-Belief and trust in God and in the doctrines expressed in the Scriptures or other sacred works; religious conviction. (Conviction: A fixed or strong belief.)

I must warn you if you continue to put your faith and trust in the likes of Huff and Liz, you will no longer be able to justify yourself or your actions before God, by giving the excuse that you did not know. In fact, ever since 28 February 1993, God has been in the process of exposing the evil agenda of the Devil in a major way.

By virtue of the fact that you are still with La'el Ministries, even though the Truth has been exposed, indicates that you really do trust them and have faith in their doctrines and philosophies.

I hope after reading the evidence presented here against them, that you will see that you are indeed *Walking With The Enemy*. Moreover, you really need to seriously consider what your end will be should you continue despite all the warnings you have been given.

This next statement by Liz is very revealing, and I truly hope that you will have "ears to hear and eyes to see" her true character; however, that *too* is totally in the hands of Almighty God.

Liz's statement: "One thing [Pastor Huff] has said to me many times in the past, I guess, year or so that's really hacked me off; where I just wanted to rip his throat out, is when he's told me that, um—'Probably my worst problem is that I try to make people conform to my standards of where I am.'

And as I read this today and as the Lord really bore witness in my heart by His Holy Spirit that this word is truth. This has been the same truth that has been in my heart ever since I have known Him. [Referring to the words of Watchman Nee.]

A lot of things have swayed that. Actually, my soulish man with the intellect and reasoning abilities said one and one is two. And yet those principles do not work in the spiritual kingdom.

They work here, but God has defied all logic. He has used the things that absolutely do not make sense.

He's used the foolishness of the cross to save us. And the wisdom of this world is foolishness to Him."

I would especially like to draw your attention to the following statement when Liz said, *"He's used the foolishness of the cross to save us."*

Keep those words in mind as you read the following verses and compare it with what God's word says regarding a person who thinks that the work on the cross is foolishness.

I Corinthians 1:17-18 "For Christ sent me not to baptize, but to preach the gospel: not with wisdom of words, lest the cross of Christ should be made of none effect.

For the preaching of the cross is to them that perish foolishness; but unto us which are saved it is the power of God."

I Corinthians 1:21,27-29 "For after that in the wisdom of God the world by wisdom knew not God, it pleased God by the foolishness of preaching to save them that believe...

But God hath chosen the foolish things of the world to confound the wise; and God hath chosen the weak things of the world to confound the things which are mighty; And base things of the world, and things which are despised, hath God chosen, yea, and things which are not, to bring to nought things that are: That no flesh should glory in His presence."

Just because Liz may claim to serve the one, true and living God, I Am certain that she does not! Based on her own words and her hateful attitude, the only conclusion I can come to is that her "god" is the Devil!

Moreover, the Spirit of Christ within me bears witness that she *is* indeed of the spirit of anti-Christ! The one who rules the Darkness! The one who will be cursed forever! Amen.

If this does not persuade you that you are going in the wrong direction, nothing will! You will just perish along with all the others who continue to believe the lies and perversions of the Devil.

I just praise God that He has given me the opportunity to warn others who are trapped by the Enemy and have no way out, but truly want out. To them I must proclaim: *The Truth will set you free indeed!* But they must be willing to repent of their sin and come to God.

Her teachings are truth mixed with lies, but unless you are walking in the "True Light" you will not be able to fully discern truth from error. Furthermore, the wrath of God will ultimately come down upon all who pretend to be walking in the Truth, but in reality are serving Satan and causing others to be ensnared by him.

Romans 1:18-19 "For the wrath of God is revealed from Heaven against all ungodliness and unrighteousness of men, who hold the Truth in unrighteousness; Because that which may be known of God is manifest in them; for God hath shewed it *unto them."*

The most important decision "man" has to make is whether or not he will obey the Commandments of God, and believe the Testimony that God gave of His beloved Son Jesus Christ.

The attitude and actions of a person will determine what choice they have truly made in their heart, and if you decide to obey God and His Truth, you will have the great joy of spending eternity with Him. But if you choose to disobey God and reject His Truth, you will have the disgrace of being separated from Him forever.

I hope that you will no longer contend that I Am the one who is *Walking With The Enemy*. If you do, it will only prove to me that your enemy is Almighty God, and that your "god" is the god of this world, who is Satan, the father of all lies!

Romans 6:16,23 "Know ye not, that to whom ye yield yourselves servants to obey, his servants ye are to whom ye obey; whether of sin unto death, or of obedience unto righteousness?...For the wages of sin is *death; but the gift of God* is *eternal life through Jesus Christ our LORD."*

If you are seeing the Truth about Huff for the very first time, I know that it could be extremely disheartening for you; and I understand what you may be going through right now. It is a hard thing to accept when you find out that you have been deceived by someone that you sincerely love and trust, especially someone that claims to serve God.

It is also very hard to realize that you have been wrong all along while claiming to be right, and have actually been an enemy to the cross of Christ, instead of a defender of the most Holy faith.

Please do not allow pride or humiliation prevent you from receiving the Truth of all that the LORD God Almighty has revealed in His word, by His Spirit, and through His beloved Son.

Just humble yourself before God, and sincerely ask for His mercy and forgiveness. If you really mean it, He can be so gracious. And once you have truly been forgiven for your sin, just continue to put your trust in the LORD Jesus Christ, and He will help in your time of need.

Isaiah 40:31 "But they that wait upon the LORD shall renew their strength; they shall mount up with wings as eagles; they shall run, and not be weary; and they shall walk, and not faint."

I would like to share a Bible study I did with my children not long ago. It was at my oldest daughter's suggestion that we tape it. I had no idea I would be sharing this with others, but it just proves to me even more that God has been using all of us in some form or fashion so as to have His will accomplished, whether we have been aware of it or not.

By now I hope you are able to see and understand that this is a battle for your very soul! And only the "True Light" will dispel the Darkness that is within your own heart and mind!

Please be willing to come to the Light of God's word so you can see the wickedness of the sin that you have been involved with.

As you read what I have written, I hope you will seriously consider this next passage of the Scriptures. It should help you to determine whether what you see and hear is from Almighty God, or whether it is from the "Enemy" of Almighty God.

James 3:13-18 "Who is a wise man and endued with knowledge among you? Let him shew out of a good conversation his works with meekness of wisdom.

But if ye have bitter envying and strife in your hearts, glory not, and lie not against the Truth. This wisdom descendeth not from above, but is earthly, sensual, devilish. For where envying and strife is, there is confusion and every evil work.

But the wisdom that is from above is first pure, then peaceable, gentle, and easy to be entreated, full of mercy and good fruits, without partiality, and without hypocrisy. And the fruit of righteousness is sown in peace of them that make peace."

PROVERBS CHAPTER 15
Based on a Bible Study Lesson with our Family

My oldest Daughter: Today is October 16, 1993. And this is our morning Bible study.

Mommy: All right, we are in Proverbs and I want you to listen with your heart and allow the LORD to establish His Truth inside of you.

Proverbs 15:1-3 "A soft answer turneth away wrath: but grievous words stir up anger. The tongue of the wise useth knowledge aright: but the mouth of fools poureth out foolishness. The eyes of the LORD are in every place, beholding the evil and the good."

Do you hear that? God is watching us. He watches everything that goes on with all of us. And He watches what goes on with evil people too. He doesn't necessarily listen to their prayers, but He sees what they are doing.

Proverbs 15:4-5 "A wholesome tongue is a tree of life: but perverseness therein is a breach in the spirit. A fool despiseth his father's instruction: but he that regardeth reproof is prudent."

[Speaking to my second child] Today when I came to your room to see what was going on with you, you were receptive to me. Especially since I came in a loving spirit, instead of an angry one.

I showed you the error and you listened. You were very wise in that. Your attitude showed that you really do want to listen.

See a foolish person despises instruction, but you weren't being foolish. And after you received what I said to you, see how good it made you feel inside?

Proverbs 15:6-8 "In the house of the righteous is much treasure: but in the revenues of the wicked is trouble. The lips of the wise disperse knowledge: but the heart of the foolish doeth not so.

The sacrifice of the wicked is an abomination to the LORD: but the prayer of the upright is His delight."

First of all, to be in the house of the righteous you must be a disciple of Christ. And in order to be one of His, you must be chosen by God. Then to be a faithful follower it's not just saying I believe—that's only the beginning. Jesus said to be a true disciple, "You must deny yourself, take up your cross daily, and follow Me."

He also says, "If you put your hand to the plow and if you turn back again, you are not worthy to be My disciple." That means if you make a commitment to walk with the LORD and start walking in the world again, you do not deserve to be a part of His kingdom.

To be able to endure, you must set your course on the right path and keep going forward. And always be aware that the Enemy will be right there to try and get you off course.

Satan tries to get you thinking and doing other things so as to divert your attention away from what God would have you to do. And many times we give into his tactics, but praise the LORD God He has shown us the Truth!! And our duty is to obey what is written in His books so we can grow in grace and wisdom; and ultimately carry out the good, and acceptable, and perfect will of God.

Proverbs 15:9-10 "The way of the wicked is an abomination unto the LORD: but He loveth him that followeth after righteousness.

Correction is grievous unto him that forsaketh the way: and he that hateth reproof shall die."

If you don't like to be corrected, you despise it, and if you won't allow it, God says you are going to die. This is where our will comes in, and we can either reject or accept what God says.

Likewise, if we let pride be a part of our life, it will stand in the way of our receiving the Truth. Thus, we will be in danger of being separated from our Creator if we continue in sin.

Proverbs 15:11-12 "Hell and destruction are before the LORD: how much more then the hearts of the children of men? A scorner loveth not one that reproveth him: neither will he go unto the wise."

You hear that? Somebody that doesn't want to listen to God, and doesn't care for anyone to correct him, or show him where he is wrong, certainly won't go to those that are wise.

As a result of that hardened heart condition, his end will be destruction!

Proverbs 15:13-16 "A merry heart maketh a cheerful countenance: but by sorrow of the heart the spirit is broken.

The heart of him that hath understanding seeketh knowledge: but the mouth of fools feedeth on foolishness.

All the days of the afflicted are evil: but he that is of a merry heart hath a continual feast. Better is little with the fear of the LORD than great treasure and trouble therewith."

The one that has understanding in his heart; the one that truly understands what's going on in this world; why we are here, who God is, who Satan is, knowledge of the Holy One, knowledge of what Jesus Christ through His Holy Spirit can give us—The one who has this kind of knowledge and understanding is going to earnestly seek after the things of God.

And as we obtain the knowledge of His word, it grows up inside our hearts, and then one day we somehow understand more than we did before. It will set us free from the lies and the deceptions of this present evil world system so that we can truly worship God the Holy Father in Spirit and in Truth.

But you know what? If you don't ever put His word inside your heart, inside a heart that really wants to know the Truth, you won't ever know it, and your faith won't ever grow.

We need to trust that what God says is true. We need to know it and live like we actually believe it. There will come a day when you will really need the love, faith, and hope that only His word can produce inside your heart.

Proverbs 15:17 "Better is a dinner of herbs where love is, than a stalled ox and hatred therewith."

That is a good one! It is better to have vegetables with love, instead of a nice piece of steak with hate. Godliness with contentment is of great gain. It is a wonderful thing to have! And only the LORD God Almighty can give it to you.

Proverbs 15:18 "A wrathful man stirreth up strife: but he that is slow to anger appeaseth strife."

If there is some problem going on and someone comes along and they are really angry, and they exhibit their anger, it gets the problem even more stirred up.

Child: Mama, what's anger? *[This was a question from my youngest daughter who was four years old at that time.]*

Mommy: You know when I get angry with you, don't ya? A wrathful man causes strife and anger, but the opposite of that is someone that is very calm and relaxed.

If truthful words are spoken that go to the heart of the matter so as to determine the cause of the anger; and it is received in a good heart, the results can be peace, joy, and love; instead of strife, anger, and hate.

Just with the example of me and your sister, she got up in a nasty mood and she had such an attitude, so I sent her to her room.

And when the LORD prompted me to go, I went to her in a loving way and I just asked her, "What's the problem here? Why are you being this way?"

I was able to talk with her and let her know that her flesh nature was rising up. That she was allowing it to control her behavior instead of the Spirit of the LORD. And when you see that happen, what you need to do right then is go before God in prayer and see what the problem is.

If there is sin in your life, He will bring it up to you, and you will have the opportunity to repent of it and ask God to forgive you. And He is so merciful to forgive us and cleanse us of the unrighteousness in our heart if we are genuinely sorry.

Just as I was talking to your sister about it, she recognized that she had sinned and then I told her the Truth about it—that it had no more power over her.

Sin really does not have any power over those who truly submit themselves to the LORD. And just as we were speaking, it melted away. And my sweet little girl was back. Instead of a mean ole nasty one.

My youngest daughter: Which one? Satan?

Mommy: He was trying to get control over her, but praise God we belong to Jesus Christ and He has won the victory over sin and death and Satan! He no longer has control over those that have Jesus Christ as their LORD and Savior! Because as the word of God says, "Greater is He, who is in me, than he that is in the world."

Proverbs 15:19-21 "The way of the slothful man is as an hedge of thorns: but the way of the righteous is made plain.

A wise son maketh a glad father: but a foolish man despiseth his mother. Folly is joy to him that is destitute of wisdom: but a man of understanding walketh uprightly."

Even some of the junk that these foolish folks get into they enjoy it. They like it! They like all the contention and strife that goes on around them. It's like they take pleasure when they are causing trouble in their own life and in the lives of those around them.

Proverbs 15:22-23 "Without counsel purposes are disappointed: but in the multitude of counselors they are established. A man hath joy by the answer of his mouth: and a word spoken in due season, how good is it!"

All these interruptions that you children are doing; that's not going to get it! You need to show a little more respect when we are reading the word of God, and not allow your fleshly impulses to get you distracted from what you are supposed to be doing.

That is exactly Satan's intent? He is right there to throw things in our path to get us off what God wants us to do. He is laying out traps and if we are not listening to God and watching as to what is going on around us we may fall into those traps set by the Enemy.

God wants us focused on Him and His word, and what He asks us to do. If you are listening to the Holy Spirit and line up what you hear with the word of God, then He will be able to lead and guide you, and tell of things to come, so as to prepare you for what is up ahead.

The LORD Jesus Christ is the only way to the Truth, and if we follow Him then He will give Light to our path. And if we allow His word to dwell richly in a heart that really wants to know Him, then we will continue on the narrow way that leads to eternal life.

One lesson that I have learned very well, is that God will not speak to you anything apart from His word or His ways. That's why we have the word of God—Because it's a more sure word of prophecy since it is written down for us to see and understand, and it has been confirmed by many witnesses.

Since Jesus only spoke what His Father revealed to Him, then it would seem to me that those who profess to be disciples of the LORD Jesus Christ should do the same.

Anyone that attempts to teach others about God's Kingdom should be very certain that the LORD is the one from whom they are listening. If not, they may be found guilty of mixing truth with lies.

Consider those who wrote the Holy Scriptures. They didn't necessarily write down everything they thought or felt, but as they were inspired by the Holy Spirit they wrote what God the Father would have them put down on paper.

I Am certain they were very careful to only present the Truth. Now it's not to say that these men were not experiencing everything that they spoke of. The sorrow that was in their heart, the pain, the joys, the happiness, all the different emotions that these men and women were going through was very real. But their heart was to write from God's perspective so that others could learn about Him and His ways based on their experiences.

So I want you to understand that we have an Enemy that wants to trip us up, which is why it is so important to listen to God's word and apply His principles and precepts to our everyday life. God wants to protect us, but many times we walk out from under His protection due to unwise counsel and our wrong decisions.

Just like if I tell you to do something, and tell you that it's wrong, and that I don't want you to do it, and if you completely ignore what I say, you could get hurt. Couldn't you?

For example, if I tell you not to go out into the road, but you decide for whatever reason that it's okay and you go out there anyway, depending on the situation, you could get really hurt if you don't listen to what I had told you.

It is the same with God's word. He has shown us exactly what He expects of us, but if we do not obey His commands we are putting ourselves in a position to get hurt.

Depending on the circumstances, it could be very minor or extremely serious. Although, if we do fall, we learn how dangerous sin really is. God's word is so true! We reap what we sow! And many times God lets us go through certain things just so we can truly understand Him and His ways in a more real way.

It is not God's heart that we be disobedient and rebellious, and He would really like for you to learn through the experience of the Scriptures, and through what the Holy Spirit can teach us; but depending on our heart motives, and our attitude towards the LORD, He will protect us even in our ignorance if we are under the mistaken impression that we are doing a work for Him.

Many times God will allow the consequences of your sin to affect you to a certain point, but He will have a mighty protection around those who truly love Him. And when we fall, God can keep us from being utterly cast down. Praise the Name of Jesus!

That is one of the purposes behind His mercy and grace, something of which Almighty God has poured out in abundance on Christ Jesus our LORD, the perfect Lamb of God!

And the Grace of God comes to those who humbly bow before our Creator God, and truly believe in the atoning sacrifice of the Son of God who came to take away the sin of the world.

Proverbs 15:24-26 "The way of life is above to the wise, that he may depart from Hell beneath. The LORD will destroy the house of the proud: but He will establish the border of the widow.

The thoughts of the wicked are an abomination to the LORD: but the words of the pure are pleasant words."

An evil person's thoughts are detestable in God's sight. But the words of the pure in heart is pleasing to Him. God says, "That which proceeds from the mouth is of the abundance of the heart." When we speak the Truth He delights in our prayers and our thoughts.

Our God is so wonderful and precious! He is such a great God to serve! It is truly a privilege to serve such a loving, compassionate, considerate, kind and merciful God; instead of one that is mean, angry, and hateful—one that knocks you down every chance he gets.

But that is exactly how Satan is. People that serve him live in fear and torment. They are always angry. They have strife and worry in their hearts. They argue with one another a lot. They cannot walk outside and really feel good about themselves because of the shame and guilt, but all the while they pretend to themselves and to others that they live in peace. What a terrible way to live!

Proverbs 15:27 "He that is greedy of gain troubleth his own house; but he that hateth gifts shall live."

A bribe is when someone says, "I will give you this, if you do this for me. I'll cheat for you, if you will cheat for me." It is usually used to either manipulate or to entice somebody to do something wrong. But one day they will be found out. Every secret thing will be revealed!

Proverbs 15:28 "The heart of the righteous studieth to answer: but the mouth of the wicked poureth out evil things."

A righteous person does not just automatically offer an opinion. He stops and listens to what is going on in his heart to see if he even needs to speak. That is something all of us need to be careful to do. To be slow to speak and quick to listen to the LORD and what He may be impressing upon our hearts.

God says that by your words you will be justified, and by your words you will be condemned. By this, it is obvious to see that the LORD considers our words of very high importance.

All men will be held accountable for everything they say, most especially concerning the Word of God! Teachers and preachers will be held to an even higher degree of accountability.

If God has allowed them to be in a position to teach and influence others, and if they don't weigh their thoughts and words very carefully, God will be extremely displeased if their teachings are not based on the Truth of His word.

Proverbs 15:29 "The LORD is far from the wicked: but He heareth the prayer of the righteous."

There are a lot of people doing some good things these days, but many have the wrong motives. They do it to get. They do it so they look good. They do it to build up their own pride and ego to satisfy something from within. And at times even to alleviate guilt.

Still, your goodness accounts for nothing unless it is done as unto the LORD. The only good in man that has eternal significance, is what God can put in that man. And only what God has established will make a lasting difference in the lives of others.

That is why God says to set your heart on the things above, because where your heart is, your treasures will be there also. And the things of Heaven will become even more purified at His coming.

The Son of God, is coming back one Day in all His glory! And when He shines upon this earth, it is just going to melt away. If your heart is set upon the things of this world instead of the things of God, then when this world is over you will have nothing to show for your life.

I realize that it can be hard to understand that the things of God are real possessions that we can have for our very own while here on this earth; but the knowledge I have of God, the understanding He has put inside my heart, and the relationship I have with His dear Son, I would never trade for anything this world has to offer.

He is so much more important to me than anything I could ever acquire in this world—Anything! Jesus says, "Seek Me first and the kingdom of Heaven and all these things will be added unto you."

I know that God will not let me go hungry. I know that He will always make sure that I have clothes on my back. I know He will always provide a place for me to sleep and rest in peace. I know, because I Am His. And you are His. He will take care of us.

But when the things of this world become more important to us than He is, our relationship with Him will be compromised. He is an extremely jealous God. He wants to be first in our lives; and He rightly deserves to be! If He is not, you will never experience the ultimate love, joy, and peace that only He can give.

I know how enticing the world can be and how it can even seem more real than the things of God; but in actuality the kingdom of Heaven is more real than this world.

If you could look at this world as if it were a mirage, you would see and understand that it is going to pass away one day. Many people think that this is all there is, but if they could only look beyond what they see here, they would realize that there is so much more ahead for those who truly trust and obey the LORD.

We need to learn to look at this world from God's perspective. Not with our limited mind and abilities, but with God's view as to how things really are. And the only way to know the thoughts and ways of God is to earnestly seek Him, diligently study His word, and fervently pray to Him in all Truth and sincerity, and be willing to obey Him.

And in so doing you will find that because of the sacrifice of the LORD Jesus Christ on the cross at Calvary, He made the way for us to come unto the Father by His Spirit.

But unless you are truly in union with His Son Jesus Christ, you will never have a genuine relationship with the one, true, and only living God; the Creator of all things!

Proverbs 15:30-32 "The Light of the eyes rejoiceth the heart: and a good report maketh the bones fat. The ear that heareth the reproof of life abideth among the wise. He that refuseth instruction despiseth his own soul: but he that heareth reproof getteth understanding."

[Speaking to my second daughter] Since you were willing to hear the Truth, you got understanding. Because you understood what was going on with your sin nature, you asked the LORD to help, and He did. And it is because you listened to my instructions.

And because I listened to the LORD, I came to you in a kind, gentle, and loving manner instead of being angry and demanding.

Now Satan would have loved for me to come in there with that kind of attitude, but I didn't, and I thank God for that.

Proverbs 15:33 "The fear of the LORD is the instruction of wisdom; and before honour is humility."

God says in His word that we must humble ourselves before Him and submit to His leadership in all of our ways.

We need to come before God with a heart that says, "LORD I know nothing of myself, but I submit my whole heart, soul, mind, and body to You, for Your will to be accomplished in whatever manner You may choose." We need to be willing to lay down our lives before God so that He can raise us up again one day.

You also need to be very, very careful how you hear. There are so many different "voices" in this world, and you must be able to discern what "spirit" you are hearing before you can truly depend on the thoughts that come to your heart and mind. That comes by experience as you trust God in your life.

Nevertheless, only the Holy Spirit will bear witness to God's word—the other voices will tell you many things that sound very similar to the Truth, but unless you have a genuine relationship with the LORD, along with the knowledge and the understanding of Him and His word, you can be very limited in your ability to know whether what you are hearing is from God, or whether it is from the Devil.

TRUTH MIXED WITH LIES EQUALS LIES!
TRUTH MIXED WITH TRUTH EQUALS TRUTH!

And only the Truth will set you Free!
Praise the Mighty Name of Jesus Christ of Nazareth!
The One who came to set us free indeed!

End of Bible study lesson on Proverbs 15

Are you able to discern which Bible study lesson was of God and which one was of Satan? Can you see which was of the Spirit of Christ, and which was of the spirit of anti-Christ? I truly hope so.

If you are starting to realize that you have been believing lies all along, I hope you will seriously consider what the LORD may be speaking to your heart, and be willing to turn from your sin.

The following is a "prophecy" that "Pastor" Huff gave to a former member of the group during a private meeting prior to her leaving La'el Ministries. I Am so thankful that she got out of here when she did, and I praise God that the Enemy was not able to succeed in breaking up her family as he had obviously intended to do.

Keep in mind that this "man," who *set himself up* to be a pastor over a group of people, claimed to be a prophet of God. And even though his lies have been completely exposed, he still claims to be a follower of the LORD Jesus Christ.

PROPHECY AS GIVEN BY MR. HUFF ON 18 NOVEMBER 1992

"Okay, Evelyn. I want you to come sit right here. Right here on the floor before me. The Lord has instructed me to share some things with you. And I am putting them on tape for you so you can take them home with you. Okay?

I want you to sit here. And I want you to receive these things. And the Lord wants you to receive these things from Him. So I want you to just shut everything else out. Close your eyes. Look down in your own spirit. Don't hang on to your hands. And turn your palms face up to the Lord. Just like you are receiving something." [There was a delay before he spoke again.]

"My daughter, I come, to speak, today,
and these are the words, that I have to say.
The words that I speak are for your heart ,
so that you might be strengthened,
and established, and whole, and not apart.
For you've thought many things, and you've seen many days,
when you've even wanted to turn and run away.
And your mind told you that you really couldn't hear,
and it's even told you that I didn't even hold you very dear.
You've watched others seek me, and say that they see;
and you've judged your own walk by the things that you see.
You've let the things of the world be your guide,
but behind it all have been my holy eyes.
So I come to you now to bring some things out.
And darlin, one day, you're going to give a shout.
For what I have for you, you've never imagined;
but it's all been my plan just for you in my heavens.

CONTINUING WITH HUFF PROPHECY

So listen to me, and listen well, and heed what I say and that I tell.
You've thought in the past that yours was a hard lot,
and there's things inside that have just said stop!
You don't understand why you feel like you do,
and many times the ways you act, or even what you want to.
The confusion abounds, and runs rampant inside;
and feels like a flood in a never-ending tide.
And your stomach's all torn up and tied up in knots;
and you think, my God, is this what I get for being your child, and your tot!
Listen Evelyn, my dear daughter, the apple of my eye, my joy and delight;
I tell you this, the things that have happened were by my plan,
you didn't cause them to happen.
You think people don't like you because of how you look,
and I tell you I made you exactly like I wanted ya to look.
You think you can't control some of the things that occur,
but if you could see in the spirit realm,
you'd know that I'm the one that stirs,
and molds and shapes your steps as you walk;
and gives you the words as you speak and you talk.
And you think that you are left alone because of you,
but I tell you, I had a hand in that too.
For if you knew the depths of my love,
you'd know how I protected you and kept you from harm.
You know that I've ordered your steps to this place,
and I've set you here so that you might taste,
the goodness of my word, and the joy of my life.
For believe it or not, you are my wife!
And I've placed you in the body of the bride of my son,
and made provisions upon provisions, and darlin, you've won.
Now I speak to your heart and tell you this,
if you really want to enjoy my bliss; let go of the anger and rage inside,
and open your heart and get it real wide.
Cuz I've got a lot to give you and pour into you,
and darlin believe that I will give it too.
The rage and the anger are confusing enough;
and the road seems like it's gotten too tough.
But those feelings and emotions are not aimed at others;
you take the blame for the faults of others.
I don't ask you to hate them, and I don't ask ya to reject them.
I simply ask ya to see the truth of what I've done.

Now listen, and listen, and listen well,
the faith walk is a life that spells out every word that I've ever said,
and opens the doors that seem closed instead.
I will guide you and lead every step,
but I want ya to trust me and depend on my help.
I don't ask great things that you do not know.
I simply tell you that I've made your way so.
If you will trust me and walk in my word,
I'll give to you everything that you've heard.
And as you take my word into your heart,
you'll find that you've got a brand new start.
Now receive my joy and my blessings as they abound,
and Evelyn you no longer have to run around,
hoping and wishing that I'll answer your prayer;
for my daughter, you've always been in my care.
Trust me, and receive from me, that which I've given,
and open your heart to receive what I've given.
Do not think you're less or the least;
because Evelyn, you sit at my heavenly feast."

END OF HUFF'S PROPHECY

Do those words truly bear witness in your heart as being from a man that is inspired by the Holy Spirit? Would you trust this man with your eternal destiny? I must say you are doing exactly that because of your decision to continue to be a part of La'el Ministries.

Cindy, this next transcript is from a meeting I arranged with your family right after we broke up. If you are still holding Steven responsible for taking your daughter, I hope to dissuade you since he was only responding as any loving and concerned parent would.

I would like to mention that when I transcribed this tape it was the first time I had actually listened to it; and even though I Am the one who spoke these words, much of what had been brought out during this meeting was like I never even heard it before. And I Am sure Satan would love for me to forget everything I once knew.

I understand very clearly now that those who are "born again" of the Spirit of God once knew the Truth from the very beginning, but Satan wants to prevent God's people from seeing the Truth by way of the Darkness and deception, in order to stop them from putting forth their hand, and taking of the Tree of Life, so they can eat, and live forever.

But I must proclaim: The Appointed Time is closer than it has ever been! Praise His mighty and Holy name!

TRANSCRIPT OF TAPED MEETING WITH CINDY'S FAMILY[48]
6 MARCH 1993

Cathy "Just for the benefit of whatever reason this tape will be used for, my name is Cathy... I have been involved in a Bible study group for the last three years. Huff is the leader...So-called pastor of the Bible study group. Liz is like the co-pastor. [She also goes by] Elisha... Another name that [he] goes by is Patrick...

...My Husband...pretty much hasn't been involved in it... He was gone for a year and a half in these last three years, so he was not a real part of it.

I do want to state that my LORD and Savior is Jesus Christ. I serve the God of Heaven. All through this that's who I served. When God and "enemy" was spoken in this Bible study group, we weren't talking about the same god. I was talking about the God in Heaven, and they were talking about the god, the prince of the power of the air, who is Satan. The "god of this world" is Satan. That's who they were talking about. Their enemy was my God. But at the time, of course, I didn't know this. And this is part of their deception...

I have no secrets. My heart is completely open to every person in this room. Completely open to the LORD. I have nothing to hide, and they do. And I would like...for you to play this tape. This was a tape when we had a major confrontation last Tuesday night. It was like a showdown! It was beautiful! It was like Light against Darkness! And you could see it! It was so beautiful! I wish the world could see it. And it will. But go ahead and play this tape."

TRANSCRIPT OF 2 MARCH 1993

Cathy "I know when I first came to this group that I was crying out to the LORD to relieve me of some of the burdens that were in my heart.

And I know I gave you a letter—" [Speaking to Mr. Huff.]

Liz "I would like to stop you here."

H... "Let her talk please." [Please note: H... is my Husband.]

Cathy "Could you at least—"

Liz "No, I'd like to stop here, cause I have an objection to the taping."

H... "Why?"

Cathy “Why? Is there anything you have to hide Elisha (Liz), as to the reason why you don’t want anything on this tape?”

Liz “No, there is not, but everyone in our church is here.”

H... “No, they are not.”

Cathy “Not everybody. I wish everybody was here, but they’re not. And I wish you had addressed this issue Sunday night, but you didn’t. And that’s because you do have something to hide.”

Liz “No, I don’t.”

Cathy “Then let’s tape it.”

Liz “No, I’m not in agreement with the taping.”

Cathy “Could you state why?”

Liz “Yes, because unless this is for this church which is present here—”

Cathy “Why the secrecy? Why can’t the Church know exactly—You told me that—”

Liz “The church *is* here, Cathy.”

Cathy “No, you told me—”

Liz “God’s word is specific here.”

Cathy “No, you told me that anything that you say to me, anything you say to her, (referring to Cindy) could be preached on the house, uh, mountaintops!”

Liz “Yes, it can.”

Cathy “So then, what’s the problem?”

Liz “Because the only reason you are making this tape is not for this church, but for members outside of this church.”

Cathy “That’s a lie!”

Liz “And God—”

Cathy “I Am not! I Am not that type of person! And you have known me for three years...”

Liz “Church affairs out of the church...” (Both of us were talking at the same time.)

Cathy “That’s crazy! You are lying! I Am sorry. That is not what I—How can you judge the intents of my heart?”

Liz “I’m not judging the intents of your heart.”

Cathy "You are saying this is for outside purposes. If there is anything that happened, why would you care? You said the mountaintops! The mountaintops is everywhere!"

Liz "Well, what does God's word say, Cathy?"

Cathy "It says that anything—That any secret thing will be revealed! *Every* secret thing! Thank God!!!"

Liz "It says that things will be taken care of in the church. *That's* what it says."

Cathy "All right."

Liz "It says we're not a part of the world."

Cathy "Thank the LORD I Am not a part of this world!"

Liz "And it says that if things cannot be judged, that is to our shame."

Cathy "And you know what? In the body of Christ, anybody is welcome. In the body of Christ, anybody is welcome to come into this house."

Liz "But the world is not the body of Christ, Cathy."

Cathy "God wants them to be though!

He loved us so much—He loved the world so much that He gave His only begotten Son, that whosoever believeth in Him, will not perish, but have everlasting life! And how will the world hear, but we tell them! May I ask you that?"

Huff "Is this going to be telling the world about Jesus Christ?"

Cathy "I Am not going to broadcast this to the world.

And if what you're saying, if it's for the Church's sake, that's exactly who it will be for. If you want the whole body to hear it, I don't have any problem with that at all."

Liz "I think you made every effort to be sure that everyone that's within this body, that you said God said should be here, is here."

Cathy "No, there are some other people I wish were here, but God is our witness and so it really doesn't matter."

Liz "Then why do we need the tape?"

Cathy "Because you've got something to hide.

And we don't have to have the tape...I don't want to get into an arguing match. And it doesn't matter."

End of 2 March 1993 Transcript

Cathy "...You see the resistance against me speaking and having evidence against them...Not that that was my intent when we first had this meeting. God just laid it on my heart to have the tape player ready so that we could tape. I felt in my heart that we were not going to get to tape it, but since the LORD told me to still have the tape player ready; I had it ready. And that's what we got to hear is the resistance against the taping of anything.

...They had to have the appearance of godliness around me because that was my whole purpose behind even being in that group...At that point in my life, I was crying out to the LORD. I had been studying His word and really desiring a relationship with God. The one they talk about how you can have the peace that passes understanding. And I read His word, and I tried to do what His word said, but the peace wasn't there. It just wasn't.

...[My Husband] wasn't seeking after the LORD. He was still after the world and doing his own thing. He...didn't have the same goal as me. So, I was almost at the point of leaving him. And then I met these people.

He lived across the street from me. His wife still does. He no longer lives there...He lives with Liz and Tom...[Huff] and Liz sleep together. Tom has a room to himself...

And how they did this and why they did it I have no idea, but I saw those two actually have sex together...They live over there, he claims to be a pastor, a godly man, he's a Christian, but it's all lies. And to understand how I got sucked into it is through such deception and lying...

And this is the scripture I want to read pertaining to the pastor of [the]...Baptist Church. When I first got into this group he came to me and [my Husband]...and tried to warn me...

He gave me this particular scripture. And of course, when you are in the clutches of people who are working for Satan, they like sneak in, and this scripture will explain what they did.

It is almost like you're in a hold by them, and it's a real weird thing. They got a lot of different things that go on that *they* know about, but me being a very naive person, I didn't know about.

II Timothy 3:1-5 "This know also, that in the last days perilous times shall come. For men shall be lovers of their own selves, covetous, boasters, proud, blasphemers, disobedient to parents, unthankful, unholy, Without natural affection, trucebreakers, false accusers, incontinent, fierce, despisers of those that are good, Traitors, heady, high-minded, lovers of pleasures more than lovers of God; having a form of godliness, but denying the power thereof: from such turn away."

Everything that is written about these kinds of men...Huff is this man. He is this man! From those turn away completely! You get away from them! They will taint you! Their evil will get on you and it will get you!

II Timothy 3:6-7 "For of this sort are they which creep into houses, and lead captive silly women laden with sins, led away with divers lust, Ever learning, and never able to come to the knowledge of the Truth."

That was me at the point that I came to these people. I was learning. I was reading. I was trying to get the Truth. But it was like I was never able to really come to the Truth. And God wanted me to know the Truth. And that's the thing about the whole deal. *He* wanted me to know the Truth.

II Timothy 3:8-9 "Now as Jannes and Jambres withstood Moses, so do these also resist the Truth: men of corrupt minds, reprobate concerning the faith. But they shall proceed no further: for their folly shall be manifest unto all men, *as theirs also was."*

Okay, that's what's going on right now. God has ordained and actually anointed me to go out and speak about these people because I was right there walking with them for three years. And this is something He has revealed to me recently.

The thing I want you to realize, I was always serving the LORD God Jehovah! The whole way...The reason you can be so sucked in, because when they say God you're assuming they're meaning your God. But they weren't."

Lynn "Did you all use the Holy Bible as your reference?"

Cathy "Yeah."

Lynn "How could you use the Holy Bible?"

Cathy "Because they will state things in the Scriptures. See if you're not really knowing the Truth you're at the mercy of man. If you really don't know the Truth—If you put yourself in the position to receive from men—

Not that there aren't very good teachers out there, there is, but if you put your sole commitment to a man, that man can deceive you. That man can be deceived by the Deceiver. So you have to rely on what God's word says to you; and what He says to your heart."

Katie "It was going around town that [Mr.] Huff was writing his own Bible. Is that true?"

Cathy "I don't know. Who knows? I wasn't privy to a lot of their stuff. They had secret meetings that I was not a part of. See, they had to appear godly in front of me because I was serving God. I was walking with God, but they did not want me to serve my God.

God knew where I was; and Satan knew where I was. And I'll read a prophecy that God gave me not long ago that will explain a lot of everything that's been going on. They did not want me to really catch a hold of the Truth; because if I did, I'd find out who they were.

And because God was leading me, I found out who they were. He let me go through a lot of the things to be able to know the manipulative, deceptive, lying, secretive tactics of the Enemy, so I could come tell other people... God does ordain certain people to do certain things...I Am not any more important to God.

You are just as important to God as I Am, but I have been through an experience that God has shown me that the sole purpose of these two people are to drag as many people to Hell with them as possible—through deception, through lies, through manipulation, through very, very, subtle tactics.

And if people can really learn what Satan's up to they won't get hooked into it. And...what I Am here to do; is first to expose these things, so that hopefully we can get Cindy out of there. And get Rebecca and Kim...

They are not *actually* worshipping Satan. They're still under the guise or thought that they are serving God. Almighty God! And that's how the deception is.

They're walking along thinking—And it's very hard to try and... completely understand with your natural mind. That's why I want you to listen with your heart...

Your mind will come to you and say this is crazy. Forget it! No! Don't believe this...woman. She's been walking with these people all this time, why believe her now. She's probably one of them, and she's just trying to get into your heart...

If you accepted Jesus Christ in your heart...You got the Spirit of God...You got the same Spirit that raised Jesus Christ from the dead inside of you! Satan don't want you to know it.

That's why he's leading silly women laden with sins away, so they won't know the power of God inside your heart. They don't want you to know about it..."

Break

Cathy "They alienated me from my [Husband's]...family. If you could understand the deception and subtlety that goes on; they don't want you to have contact with other people. And it's not something you consciously decide.

It's part of the teaching and indoctrination that teaches you that everybody without doesn't want to serve God; they're just walking in their flesh; walking in the world. They don't really serve God. We are the only ones that truly want to have a real relationship with God..."

(Break / Phone call from Cindy)

Cathy "And I don't want to try and justify my behavior or what was going on, because I had the Holy Spirit inside of me, but God pointed out to me just recently that—

And I used to ask Liz about this particular scripture and she didn't ever want to let me know what she knew on it. It's like certain scriptures that I brought up to her she wouldn't tell me about them because I was getting too close to the Truth.

God was starting to open my eyes up to the Truth and certain scriptures were coming up that she didn't want me to know about. She would always act like and say, 'Well, God hasn't given me revelation knowledge on that, and when it's time for you to know, you'll know.' That was her excuse to Scripture that she couldn't explain to me.

Matthew 4:1 "Then was Jesus led up of the Spirit into the wilderness to be tempted of the Devil."

I don't know if you've ever read the temptations of Jesus, but...there were three temptations: the lust of the flesh, the lust of the eyes, and the pride of life. Those are the three temptations that this pertains to.

And those are the three things that if a believer can actually get under control in their life, Satan will have nothing to tempt you with. Satan is the tempter. You are drawn off by your own lust. Your *own* lust! And when that's conceived, it brings forth sin, and when sin is fully grown, it brings forth death! So, what I Am saying to you, is that God actually led me into this Bible study group...

At the point that I came to this Bible study group I didn't sin as far as obvious sin. *[At least from my perspective.]* I didn't commit adultery; I didn't lie, cheat; I didn't steal; I didn't do anything against the Ten Commandments.

I didn't do anything against the laws of God...but there was still sin in me that I didn't know about...

It's not obvious sin in your body that you are committing. It's sins that through the knowledge of God you find out about. Through the true knowledge of walking with the LORD you find out about it.

And those are the sins Satan can come to you and tempt you with. And one thing [Mr. Huff] used to tell me in our Bible study group, and he always said this; 'God will meet you where you're at.' His "god" will meet you where you're at. Not *my* God!

My God wants to bring you up and sit you in Heavenly places in Christ Jesus! That's where my God wants you. And that's where you are if you follow Him. But the tempter comes out to tempt you away from where God has wanted to put you, and puts these things in front of you to entice you through sins that you don't know.

So, Satan will meet you, if you are walking in your flesh, he will meet you right there. He does not even have to bother with you.

With me, and I Am not trying to think highly of myself, but I was getting to a point where I truly wanted to worship God in Spirit and Truth.

I knew there was more to God...I knew there was more to God than just the Ten Commandments.

And so, Satan himself, a man led by Satan himself, had to come to me and tempt me. That's what God said happened in this situation. He led me there, and He knew that I would endure that temptation.

And after I got out of it He knew I would be strengthened. And I would be able to come and tell people like you about what happened. So, what I Am saying to you right now...Satan's very real, very alive right now. He is wanting to—

Cindy, she is very, very committed to God; the Holy God. She thinks she's serving the Holy God, but she is not! She has been captured alive by the Enemy...I do not want to take her daughter from her. I don't desire that for any mother, but if she is walking with Satan...

If she continues there is fear for Rebecca, for any little children in that group...If Cindy was to turn from this and get out of there, then there would be no need for taking her. She'd be in a loving home. A home that would be very safe. But right now she's not because she's walking with Satan, but she don't know it."

Lynn "When you all are meeting, where are the kids?"

Cathy "For a time...they had their own Bible study."

Lynn "Did they use a Jewish Bible?"

Cathy "Most of the time, yes."

Lynn "Who teaches them?"

Cathy "For quite a long time Liz did. Then Cindy did. And Liz would go back to it. And recently we have switched from the kids only having Bible study on one night.

See, we'd meet three nights a week; Wednesday, Thursday, and Sunday. And the kids lately have only been meeting one night, and the rest of the time they've been down there with us.

This is done in my house. I don't know if I've stated that. First it was done at Becky and [Mr. Huff's] when he lived there, and finally she got fed up with the junk...

Most people don't stay long enough to get into it. It's like the Holy Spirit...is warning them. Get away! Get out! Don't come!

But the kids were meeting with us most of the time... During prayer night they'd go lay down. My kids would go to bed...We'd have a Bible study for the children; we'd have praise and worship where we sang and he'd play the guitar and Liz played a keyboard. The kids would be involved in that, but then they'd go to bed."

Lynn "Was it like they didn't want anyone to see what was going on?"

Cathy "No. There was nothing they could see that would be damaging to the children. It's the thoughts, and it's the teaching that would have been very damaging."

Lynn "The reason I'm asking, because you said Rebecca's in danger. Because we love her and if she's in danger we want to protect her."

Cathy "I'll tell you that the thing right now that's very serious is...I was going to read that scripture to explain to you where Cindy is and what we can do to get her out of that. And it's not what we can do, *but what God can do.*

II Timothy 2:24-26 "And the servant of the LORD must not strive; but be gentle unto all men, apt to teach, patient, In meekness instructing those that oppose themselves; (Right now Cindy is very much in opposition to me.) *If God peradventure will give them repentance to the acknowledging of the Truth; And that they may recover themselves out of the snare of the Devil, who are taken captive by him at his will."*

That's where Cindy is right now. She does not have the Truth. God's the only one who can intervene right here.

She has been taken captive by Satan. By people that work with Satan. That worship Satan. That bow their knee to Satan.

And I do not know any of their junk that they do in secret. And I couldn't even from experience tell you what they're doing because I was never involved in any of that.

And I Am so thankful to God that I didn't get that deep into it...And that's the danger here."

Break

Cathy	"What finally broke me—See, there were a lot of things that happened to me; sexual advances...But it was alluring, deceptive ways of getting me to do that..."
Lynn	"Was this during the services?"
Cathy	"No. Not at all. See, during the services they'd have to appear godly. This is when he had come over one time. Cindy, Liz, and him had come over to watch a movie. This was after my Husband left...[for military training.] And to understand how I could get to that point of doing something like that with a man, which is about the worst thing I could ever do against my Husband. But [Mr. Huff] came to me...Just with these deceptive tactics. Everything I did, I thought I was doing in the name of God. I actually thought this 'man' was my Husband...!"
Lynn	"Did he do that way with all the women?"
Cathy	"Yes. He wants them to think that he is their husband. He lies. He brings Scripture to prove his point...If a woman won't get into the sexual thing with [Mr. Huff] they'll try another avenue. That's where Satan is very, very sneaky...With me, a problem that I had just in my growing up years—If a man pursued me...it was like I was open prey. It was like I couldn't resist."
Lynn	"He preys on, in other words, whatever your weakness is?"
Cathy	"That's exactly right."
Lynn	"Does he do this to all of them?"
Cathy	"Satan will meet you right where you're at. Wherever you're weak he's going to come in and try to sneak in that door."
Lynn	"Do you know if Cindy or Rebecca or Kim or any of them have ever been involved in any of this?"
Cathy	"Okay, from personal experience and seeing things—Cindy used to tell me that [Mr. Huff] tried it with her, but he didn't ever do it..."
Katie	"Not with Cindy. What I am saying is, she's good about doing stuff and then turning around telling somebody she didn't do it."
Cathy	"Oh she is? She's good at lying?"
Katie	"Yeah."

Cathy "Okay, well, that's just part of this. And with the subtle tactics, the indoctrination—

You have to understand how wicked when you're dealing with people that deal with Satan. They speak something... Send a spirit to you and put stuff in your mind.

And they'd come back to you and say, 'Well, what'd God tell you?' And they knew exactly what spirit they sent to put stuff in your mind, and you're thinking God told you...

And see, then you're confused about how to hear the Holy Spirit versus the junk..."

Lynn "Did he actually tell you that he was your husband?"

Cathy "Well, see, the first thing that he said to me when I first started coming there—'I want you to go pray and ask God who you are to me.' "

Lynn "Who you are to him? To [Mr. Huff]?"

Cathy "Yeah...Or who he was to me. That was the question. And I said, 'Okay.' See when you first come to this Bible study group, this man speaks some real profound truths..."

Katie "It's stuff you want to hear at the time?"

Cathy "Well, no. It's really deep truths about God."

Katie "It's what you're looking for?"

Cathy "Yes. I was wanting the real deep truths of God. So he would say these things, just like Eve in the garden. The serpent came to her and gave her some really profound truth, but mixed lies in it...The truth is what caught me. But I couldn't discern the lies because of the curses they were putting on me...

When I read the Bible I couldn't truly interpret it because they were sending spirits to me, they were putting curses on me to keep me from really seeing the Truth. That's what is so wicked and deceiving about this kind of stuff.

So the question—When I went to God and asked Him, 'Who is this man to me?' I went to my God and prayed, and the main thing that was real clear...was that I would learn a lot from this man...That's what I felt *my* God said.

But also these other things came that he was my husband, and my mind couldn't handle that...since I was married I couldn't accept husband.

So I went back to him, and told him what God said. I said, 'God told me that I'd really learn a lot from you.' And he said, 'Yes, I will be your teacher. What else did God say?' And I said, 'Well—' and I was very confused at that point...so I said, 'He said you'd be like a father to me.'

And I was very honest with these people, and you know, that is where Satan can get you...God wants you to be very wary and don't be deceived, but I got deceived. Very deceived! And so he said, 'No, that's not what God said. He said husband to you.' "

Lynn "[Mr. Huff] actually said this to you?!"

Cathy "Yes."

Lynn "He was to be your husband?"

Cathy "Yes."

Lynn "And you're already married?"

Cathy "Yes. The reason why he could go with that, and the way he could substantiate that in my logical thinking—Not in my heart, my heart had major question marks.

But...he would bring Scripture up to me and said, 'But there is a spiritual mate. One man for every woman, and regardless of who you're married to in this lifetime there's still one man for every woman...'

When you're hooked into this deception they contradict all the time, but you don't see the contradictions."

Katie "With Rebecca and Kim—Is there a chance that [Mr. Huff] is going to tell them that he's their husband?"

Cathy "Yeah. He tried that with Kim...I got to the point that I saw the wrong of it...Liz was trying to side with me, to act like she knows [Mr. Huff] is wrong, but he's just a little deceived *in this area*." *[Emphasis mine.]*

Lynn "With what?"

Cathy "With trying to approach me..."

Ronald "Let me ask you a question. Is Cindy, I mean Rebecca in physical danger or spiritual danger?"

Cathy "Both."

Ronald "How is she? That's what we want to hear."

Cathy "Okay, we just got to establish that it's a very deceptive thing."

Lynn "And he feels like he's to be their husband? It's like the women that come in—He's to be their husband?"

Cathy "He tries that with every woman that comes there."

Lynn "And so it's like when Rebecca comes of age it could be the same thing. Kim's already of age so he's already approached her?"

Cathy "Yes."

Katie "He's already had sex with her if what we've heard is right."

Cathy "That was the accusations that was made to them Tuesday night and he—"

Lynn "He acknowledged it?"

Cathy "Yes. He did."

Lynn "He acknowledged it? He acknowledged having sex with Kim?"

Cathy "Yes. And that's what got to me...I had these things happen to me and I forgave [Mr. Huff] because Liz is right there to try and appease me—Trying to tell me how...'He's deceived in areas, but you know, God's working with him—You have to hear the truth that he's preaching. He couldn't speak the truth like that except God be with him. He's God's anointed...'

But the thing that got to me is—Liz, through ignorance, or stupidity, or just wanting to crush me even more, told me about Kim. About how [Mr. Huff] went to Kim..."

Katie "Let me ask you this. Did Rebecca watch [Mr. Huff] have sex with Kim?"

Cathy "I don't know. No, no, because after she ran away—"

Katie "This is *before* she ran away."

Cathy "Okay, well, I don't know nothing about that."

Katie "Well, we were told that she—That [Mr. Huff] had sex with Kim, and Rebecca walked in on them."

Cathy "That's quite possible, but I don't know. I couldn't say."

Katie "This happened at Cindy's house before Kim ever ran away."

Cathy "The thing about Kim—Liz told me about it over the phone and I pretty much broke down, and I couldn't handle this man coming after a little baby Christian.

And I said, 'Liz, when are the lies going to stop?! I can't handle this!' And she goes, 'You are just going to have to trust God.' "

Lynn "What did she tell you?"

Cathy "That...when Kim had run away from her parents, she went to [an old friend of Liz's who lived several hours away]. ...She stayed there. And [Mr. Huff] went up there when she was there by herself...and told her that she was his wife..."

Lynn "He told Kim she was his wife?"

Cathy "That's right."

Steven "Did all ya'll know where Kim was when this court took place?"

Cathy "No. No. They would not—I had speculations, but they did not share this stuff with me. Purposely. [Mr. Huff] knew. Liz knew. And Cindy knew. They knew."

Katie "And Rebecca knew? Rebecca *did* know."

Cathy "I don't know if Rebecca knew or not. Probably not. They wouldn't want a child to maybe slip. I am sure they didn't tell Rebecca..."

Lynn "Okay, so he went up there to her?"

Cathy "Yes."

Lynn "Had sex with her?"

Cathy "That's from what Liz told me. I did not experience it. I did not see it...That was the breaking point for me...And I went to my Father in Heaven and said, 'LORD I see what's going on. I Am starting to see the Truth. I Am starting to see the lies. I Am starting to see the deceptions. I can't handle untruth being spoken in my house. I can't handle this anymore. And I Am giving it to You.' "

Steven "So what you're saying is that as long as they associate with [Mr. Huff] and Liz, as long as they're staying there, they're in danger mentally and physically?"

Cathy "Yes. That's right."

Lynn "And spiritually."

Cathy "Oh yes! Very much spiritually! That's my concern."

Lynn "Physically what happened to Kim, can happen to Rebecca?"

Cathy "Sure. Very much. I saw Rebecca yesterday at the school. She's like she is in a little trance. And that's how they will keep her because they don't want her to know. They don't want the Truth to get to her...

See, I gave this to the LORD and He intervened Sunday night...

One night during prayer time—I could hardly pray around these people. And they intimidated me.

They made me feel very inferior because I couldn't pray out loud in front of these people. Near the end I started being able to pray out loud as I got past the intimidation, but now I understand why I couldn't pray..."

Lynn "So instead you'd have these prayer meetings, and it was more of a condemnation?"

Cathy "At the beginning it was...How we are just living in the world, we walk in our flesh, we don't go out and preach the gospel...condemnation like that...But see near the end those tactics didn't get to me because I knew I was walking with God.

I knew I was starting to see the Truth. I knew that I was actually seeing what God's word was saying to my heart. God was strengthening me at the end."

Lynn "Did Cindy see this?"

Cathy "No. She doesn't. She's very, very blind to it. And let me tell you—"

Bob "What he knew in making himself important was making everyone depend on him?"

Cathy "That's right."

Bob "Is that right?"

Cathy "That's exactly right!"

Lynn "He makes them dependent on him?"

Cathy "Yes. But all the while, he's telling you that you got to depend on Jesus.

But in his subtle tactics and his lies and his deceptions, it's really—You need to depend on him and Liz.

Liz is the more powerful one in this thing. For Scripture sake he is the head and she is the one who has to submit to him for appearance sake..."

Katie "I wondered about that."

Cathy "She is."

Lynn "In these Bible studies does she—Liz and him both—What do they do?"

Cathy "He's just out there preaching."

Lynn "He and she both?"

Cathy "Sometimes. He for the most part. For a long time she used to teach the children and all the adults that wanted to be there, were there. And I was usually there."

Lynn "Okay, she taught the kids? And she felt like she was his wife also, and she lives with him? And he lives in her house and sleeps with him?"

Cathy "Yes."

Lynn "You know that for a fact?"

Cathy "Yes, I do. I even saw them have a sexual—Uh this was really weird and I don't know why they did it...but they did, and it's for their own demise, because they did it in front of me."

Lynn "They had sex in front of you?"

Cathy "Yeah!"

Steven "What about the kids?"

Cathy "Now I don't know about any of that."

Steven "You don't know if they were there?"

Cathy "They weren't there at this particular time. It was after a Bible study meeting and everyone had left and I was just sitting there.

They were wanting to talk to me about something and then all of a sudden they got up and started kissing, and carrying on, and taking off their clothes. And I'm sitting here saying, *(to myself)* 'What...are they doing?!' "

Bob "The whole thing was intimidation?"

Cathy "Yes."

Lynn "Where was her husband at this time?"

Cathy "Tom—He is, and I don't know the full story about him. I feel like—And this is certainly speculation. One time during a prayer meeting [Huff] used to pray for people. Lay hands on them and—"

Lynn "He actually lays hands on you?"

Katie "That's a weird experience because I saw them do it to Cindy. When that happened I liked to have freaked out. I went back to her bedroom and stayed back there in the corner."

Lynn "When he lays hands on you, what happens?"

Cathy "I don't know, just from my own of what God's revealed to me, he's passing stronger demons through you."

Lynn "Does she prophesy or what happens? Whenever he lays hands on you, what do they do?"

Cathy "They just kind of sit there and look into his eyes."

Lynn "Like in a trance?"

Cathy "They like sit there in a little circle."

Lynn "Sort of like Rebecca...say for Brownies, right?"

Break

Cathy "Okay...where were we?"

Lynn "You were talking about Tom? Tom was there when they had sex?"

Cathy "No. No, he wasn't there. It was just me."

Lynn "Oh, just you?"

Cathy "It was just me...And I just kind of freaked about it."

Lynn "And they're saying this is part of the worship services? That this is spiritual?"

Cathy "No. No, it wasn't part of the worship. It was just part of the subtle tactics—

That is what is so bad with pornography. See when people look at books like that, and see those bad movies, that is a deceptive tactic of Satan himself to get people.

It's like it turns on the enmity of God that's inside each one of us. It's like it turns it on. Makes it alive. Turns on the lust there, and it is like you want to do it. You got to be around it...When you start looking at it, pretty soon if you look at it long enough, you are going to start doing it yourself.

That's why we've got murderers and killers out there. But all this started with a little tiny seed that Satan planted. Then it's sin that goes unchecked, unconfessed, and then it gets a little worse sin, and then finally you're getting into really bad sin.

Finally, way down the line you're raping, killing, cutting up people, and doing all kinds of wicked evil stuff that Satan wants. So that is what's so evil about all this.

So if they stay in it a long time, if they keep in this without getting out, they will eventually—

And this is something God has impressed upon my heart, why it is so important.

Right now, they are running scared because I Am speaking against them. They know something is going on. That's why they keep calling. They had Rebecca call first. Cindy called. They know something's going on. They want to know where you all are at. They're afraid I Am talking to you right now. And by the spirit they know I Am...

The reason why I Am fearful for Cindy, is I Am afraid she's in so deep that they're going to take her to one of their meetings, and through fear force her to bow her knee to Satan.

And if she does that she'll be condemned to Hell. She will eternally live in Hell the rest of her life. I know that."

Lynn "So this is sort of like a cult?"

Cathy "Whatever a cult is, I really don't know."

Katie "How much contact does [Mr. Huff] have with Rebecca?"

Cathy "I don't know. Cindy and Rebecca and Kim go over to their house a lot. I was never invited over there a lot. The only time that I was ever invited was if they were trying another tactic..."

Lynn "Well, you know, Cindy and Rebecca lived with them for a long time?"

Cathy "Yes."

Lynn "And [Mr. Huff] lived in that house. And Liz lived in that house?"

Cathy "I do not think [Mr. Huff] lived there during that time."

Steven "He was there all the time."

Cathy "He came a lot, but he didn't live there then. He did not move out until two years ago...If this all goes to a situation where you are going to try and get—"

Steven "We're definitely going to court."

Lynn "Was Rebecca and Kim ever left...with [Mr. Huff]?"

Cathy "I don't know."

Lynn "Baby-sit? You know, a lot of times Rebecca—We would take her home maybe on Sunday evenings and there would be some guy—I can't remember who it was. She would say his name, he's going to take care of us. It was one of the guys—"

Steven "That was Wendell."

Lynn "Okay. Wendell was to take care of them. Everyone else was going to be gone...Wendell was going to watch after them."

Cathy "Now those were things I didn't know about."

Steven "Wendell, I know Wendell. I've been knowing Wendell since I was fourteen years old."

Katie "Now Wendell, I don't really have a problem with."

Cathy "No, he's a helpless victim right now. He was invited to our confrontation last Tuesday night and he just sat there in a little heap, wondering what's going on. 'Here's this girl I really care about saying all these things against those people.'

And here they're sitting there dumbfounded and not saying a word about the accusations I made...

I told you the reason I Am fearful for Rebecca...because if Cindy ever bows her knee to Satan there's no hope for her. Once you do that—"

Lynn "If Cindy bows her knee and goes along with what [Mr. Huff] is saying, then she will allow him to have access to Rebecca? Whatever he wants to do?"

Cathy "That's exactly right."

Lynn "That's what you're saying?"

Cathy "That's what I Am saying. If Cindy actually, willingly... Scripture pertaining to that, Hebrews—"

Lynn "In this thing that you're saying with this prophecy, is it something that they had?"

Cathy "No. It's something that God—And when I read it in the church I was so nervous, I could hardly even speak it."

Lynn "You read this in their church?"

Cathy "At our church meeting."

Lynn "Will you read that so the tape could pick it up?"

Cathy "Yes, very much. I sure will."

Lynn "Where did this come from?"

Cathy "God gave it to me."

Lynn "When you're saying God—"

Cathy "My God. My God gave it to me."

Lynn "And what was their reaction when you read this?"

Cathy "[Mr. Huff] denied it. He said, 'No, that's not from God...'"

Lynn "Okay. Would you read—"

Cathy "Okay. This is the prophecy. This will give you the reason why there's still hope for all of them right now at this point. This is a prophecy God gave me. I was praying in the Spirit..."

Break (Second Tape)

Cathy "This is a continuation from the...first tape. The date, I don't think we stated the date. What's today's date?"

Steven "Saturday the sixth."

Lynn "Saturday March 6, 1993."

Cathy "Okay...continuing in the seriousness of the ramifications of this situation. Tuesday night this week, I accused him—These are the accusations that I made to...Liz...and [Mr.] Huff. I stated to them that they are workers of Satan.

I stated to them—through their prompting. It wasn't that I just came out with this. At first they tried to ask me if I believed if they had the Holy Spirit inside of them? And I said, 'I'm not going to make that judgment. That's not for me to judge. God's your judge.'

They started saying something to the effect of—You know, they were pretty disgusted with me, cuz all I could speak was the Truth to them; and they couldn't say nothing hardly. And that's how Satan is. If Truth is spoken without doubt, Satan cannot stand that. So they were pretty silent that night.

But the reason they weren't vicious...is because Wendell was sitting there...See, they couldn't let their true colors out, because there were two souls they're still fighting for. Souls that they're wanting to drag to Hell with them!

That's the only reason why they were not as vicious...I can't remember the sequence and it would be wonderful to have it on tape, but we don't, so we'll have to just go by what me and [my Husband]... experienced.

[Mr. Huff] has a real snide remark like, 'Which *god* do you serve?' And at that point I said, 'By the words of your own mouth, you are condemned yourself! If you can even ask me what *god* I serve, I know you don't serve the one I serve. You serve Satan! You walk with him! You work with him!'

And that's when I pointed to Wendell and started speaking very strongly to him, that these people were out to get his soul and drag him to Hell with them. Their words actually condemned them, and it even says in the Scriptures that that's what'll happen.

And so, I accused this man of being a false prophet. I accused him of being—And at that time Liz stops me and says, 'What spirit is he?' And I looked her straight in the eyes and said, 'The spirit of anti-Christ!' And all these accusations were made, and they did not deny one single one of them. They could not deny them, because I was speaking them through the power of God. And I was speaking the Truth."

Lynn "Did they ask you to leave at any time?"

Cathy "No, they were at my house."

Lynn "They didn't get up and leave?"

Cathy "They didn't want to leave because they still wanted Wendell. See, he's sitting here, a little heap of a man. He had a lot of confidence in these people; he had a lot of confidence in me; and here I Am accusing this man that he has been sitting under his teachings. And I Am accusing him of being anti-Christ. I Am accusing him of being a false prophet. I Am accusing him of lying and deceiving, and luring people in. I Am accusing him of unstable souls, wanting to drag them to Hell. I Am accusing these people of this, of being workers together for Satan.

And Wendell is just sitting here, he couldn't say anything. I said, 'So Wendell, what do you got to say about this? What do you think?' "

Lynn "Well, what is Cindy doing?"

Cathy "She's in a trance. She is in like some kind of weird junk over there. She could not say nothing. All she tried to do—And one thing—

See, what happened Sunday night, the Spirit of God fell on me. His anger and wrath was being poured out of me.

It was a wild, wild event! I have never ever experienced anything like this in my life.

But see, the prayer I had to God at this point was...'I have given this over to You. I see the lies. I see the deception, but I don't know what to do.' It was almost like I was powerless to do anything—To get out of it. And I said to God, 'You got to intervene.' And He did! He poured out His Spirit inside of me...

[My Husband]...had just made a major commitment to the LORD to follow Him; and I felt like something was going to happen that night, but I thought it'd be through him."

Lynn "Did you make a commitment with these people?"

Cathy "No, he made it to God. God alone."

H... "No, this was something separate."

Lynn "You had gotten away from them?"

Cathy "[My Husband] has been gone... So he hasn't been involved in it—Not like me..."

H... "And I was there. Did you tell them about—"

Cathy "And when he was there, they would put spells on him to make him sleep. He would sleep the whole time...And they would substantiate to me that he's just not interested. The world's more important to him. He don't want to hear any of this. And in all actuality, they had a spell on him so he couldn't hear it."

Lynn "Well, see, most courts, or judges, or whatever—You know, I believe that, because I am a Christian, but most courts, they're just going to dismiss that."

H... "Right."

Cathy "That's why I Am saying to you, this is in God's hands. God intervened. And don't try to rationalize this up here.

God's intervening, and He's not going to allow this to happen. And let me read this to you and you'll understand exactly why.

Twenty-Seven August is when this prophecy came to me. I was praying by myself. Not with these people.

And God spoke to me and said, 'Write these words down.' It's like this scripture is coming true for my life—

God said in His last days He's going to pour out His Spirit on all mankind. People will prophesy. Men will dream dreams. And I actually—God allowed me to prophesy His words."

Break

Cathy " *'The words I speak to you are Spirit and Life. I Am calling My people, those whom the Father has given Me, unto Myself...'*

And I want you all to realize the way God...had me write it down. It was like God was speaking through me. This wasn't Cathy... saying these things.

This was God speaking through me to write these words down...So I'll start over again..."

Prophecy of 27 August 1992

"The Words I speak to you are Spirit and Life. I Am calling My people, those whom the Father has given Me, unto Myself. All men through all Ages has had an opportunity to come unto Me; and they will continue to have that opportunity, but this Age is soon to come to an end.

I have a special task for certain people at this time. I Am, and have been preparing people for a work that I have called them to do. I have impressed upon the hearts of those to whom I have called, and none of this will come as a surprise to them. But they will still have a choice in the matter as to whether they will allow Me to shape and mold them.

There are some very hard struggles going on with certain people, and they know who they are. Your works are being tried by Fire. The only ones that I will place the Special Anointing on, is the ones who can pass through that Fire.

I Am training many people all over the world for this task, and this is one place where that training process is going on. Why do you think that it's such a stronghold for the Enemy?

Satan does know who you are. And he will try every means possible to destroy what I have planned. That's why it is so important for you to depend on Me and My Word.

As you noticed My Anointing does not come as you will it, but as I will it. But there will come a time when everything you say will be My Words. And I will give you the boldness you will need to speak those Words. And you will have much opposition to the Words you speak, just as you are encountering now.

Like I said, this is a training period for you, and all soldiers must be prepared for battle. If you thought you were in the battle zone before, you have not even gotten into the Real War yet.

You have been behind the lines, but very soon I Am going to be sending some of you across the lines to claim those that are Mine.

Their hearts and minds have been blinded up to this point, but because of My Words, that you will speak, the blinders will be removed, and they will have an opportunity to receive Life or Death. And if they choose death it's because they actually hate Me in their hearts, so don't have sympathy for them.

Whoever is against Me, is not for Me. And don't be surprised when you find more against Me than you do for Me. As you noticed, most people don't want to live by every word that proceeds from the mouth of God.

A true Jew is not by descent, but by circumcision of the heart. And whether you are adopted in makes no difference to Me; because you will rule and reign with Me whether or not you are from the Bloodline of David. The Spirit gives Life; the flesh conveys no benefit whatever.

There's been talk of a large church in the making, but that is not in My plan for you. As the time gets closer, I will reveal to you more of the events of the future. But for now, all I ask of you is to continue to learn of Me, worship the Father in Spirit and in Truth, and pray for My people.

And remember, I will equip you with the amount of Faith you will need to do anything I call you to do.

I AM your strength. Just keep on learning how to deny yourself, take up your cross, and follow Me. I AM THE WAY, and I have some people that I would like for you to direct their way to Me.

You are My servants because you chose to be. So if I ask you to do some hard things, realize I know the outcome, and trust Me completely.

After all, I AM THE LORD!"

Cathy "This is the prophecy He gave me in August of last year. And I did not really completely understand it. And I went before the church and—And I hate to call it the Church—There were some people that were part of the Church of Jesus Christ, but there were people that were part of the Church of Satan.

So when I got before that meeting I tried to read this, and I could hardly read it. [Huff] was very opposed to it. He tried to make me think it was not from God—That it was not true.

When the Spirit fell on me Sunday they tried to come to me and tell me...that it just was not true.

...It was *not* of their "god." It *was* of my God! The Great Jehovah! The Almighty God is the one that gave me these words. And He is the one that just poured His Spirit inside of me to anoint me to be able to come and to speak...

So what He says to me, which is very important right now; is to pray for them, to listen to Him, and do what He says in how to proceed with this whole thing.

And the thing that I perceive right now that we can do, and God will work it out. He will! He is wanting them out of there. He wants them. He knows their heart intent. He knows whether they want out. He knows whether they are serving Him, but in actuality being used by the Enemy. And just in my heart I feel—

I read this prophecy to Cindy privately—First I read it to Liz over the phone. She used to call me a lot...to make sure she knew what God was telling me; because she knew I got to the point that I was listening to God and talking to Him, and that He was talking to me.

But I was not hearing Him as clearly as I could because I had not learned how to really, actually, purge myself from all the different ways of sin that you just don't recognize as sin. And since God has taught me how to do that, He is talking to me very clearly...

And I did not completely understand this at the time, but when I read it to Cindy she just broke down crying and she knew...

I had no idea of the meaning of this prophecy when God gave it to me, but I understand it now. I did not realize that I would actually be, because of God leading me, to help get people out from under Satan's control...

And that is why I Am talking to you here. And the main thing that I feel in my heart that we can do for Cindy is...get her away from there and out from under their influence..."

Katie "That's the key. Mama has invited her to dinner at her house, and rather than come she'll say that Liz and them have something planned that is more important."

Cathy "That is their indoctrination. They want to keep it that way. And it worked with me. But let me tell you, if God's working here, He will work something out..."

Lynn "I want to ask you—Rebecca used to cry when we would take her to your house or to Liz's. If her mother wasn't there she would just go to pieces."

Cathy "And I didn't ever understand that."

Lynn "Do you know why?"

Cathy "Yeah they used to say bad things happened at your house... They would tell me that Steven was a bad influence—You know, just speak evil of you...See there's so many things that are said and done, that if I had my eyes completely open I couldn't have stood for any of that.

The indoctrination is that...we are here for one another to point out sin to one another. So that person, if they are still sinning—God just has not been able to deal with them...

[Mr. Huff] would still have this spirit of lust on him because it is something he has not addressed with God, hadn't confessed it. 'But we still need to pray for our brother. We don't need to reject our brother...'

And since I Am not spiritual, I didn't have the right to go to him. In Galatians it talks about those that are spiritual...But since I wasn't spiritual in their eyes...I didn't have the right to go to my brother...But I still did at certain times."

Lynn "Well, she does not really talk to us. She did at first."

Cathy "She can't because of the spell she is in."

Lynn "She talked to Steven's mother on Sunday afternoon and Steven's sister in-law... And I was there, but she cried and cried. She said, 'Mama never spends time with Kim and I. She's never here.' Where does she go? We don't understand."

Cathy "Well, either she is on the phone, or Liz is there talking to her. Or she is down at Liz's doing something. They did not invite me to a lot of their meetings, so I don't know what they did."

Lynn "Was she not there with Rebecca? Did she just leave Rebecca?"

Cathy "I couldn't really say."

Lynn "Did she leave her a lot with you?"

Cathy "Well, she used to live with me. And I have been like the baby-sitter amongst all this. See they would go out and do things and leave all the kids with me."

Lynn "Well, was this done a lot?"

Cathy "Yeah. Pretty good bit."

H... "See, part of the indoctrination too is—With our case, and specifically in Cindy's case, she lives two or three houses up from...[Liz and Mr. Huff]...right across from [Liz's] mother's house. She knows who she is seeing. That is part of the manipulation and control, is who you are in contact with. Explain all the times she'd call you and want to pick your mind."

Cathy "Oh yeah, she would do that all the time."

H... "She does that—It is part of the psychological control of your thinking, and who you should be seeing. It's a control thing...It's a very subtle process. And once you are in, you don't really see that you are in it."

Katie "I think Liz and [Mr. Huff] put Cindy up in trying to get me to come. She would come and see me and want me to go somewhere; and then the whole time she was preaching all this stuff."

Lynn "We would like to hear how you got brought into it, and what you saw that you think might have harmed Rebecca or Cindy; since you were sort of an outsider and then came in. And how they got you in and everything."

H... "In my case—"

Cathy "State your name."

H... "I Am...Cathy's Husband.

Well, basically, first Cathy had gone through her scenario in her search for the LORD. And we had gone through a discipleship program called MasterLife...I went through the program, but I was not really committed.

Of course, Cathy was very committed, searching for the LORD and—"

Lynn "This wasn't their church. Right?"

H... "No, this was the Baptist...Church...The program was over, and somehow or other [Mr. Huff] had told us about...the Bible study group.

And Cathy was interested in going. I did not like it. For some reason I did not like the idea of it. And she wanted to go and I said, 'No.' And then she didn't go.

And that went on for about three weeks. And we were kind of at a very unstable point in our relationship...She became very insistent about going...And I had the idea in my head that if I didn't let her go, that she was going to be gone. And that's a fact!

...So she started going. They met a couple times across the street, and then they started meeting at...[Liz's] house... And I would stay with the kids and Cathy would go. And it was like driving me nuts, her going over there...And it was not a jealousy thing or anything like that. It was a concern."

Ronald "Curiosity?"

H... "No, not curious. I was not curious at all at that point. I was fearful for Cathy...For whatever reason, I was. I really didn't know why. Like I said, I really wasn't searching for the LORD at that time.

A lot of things were going on inside that I didn't really understand. I could not stand it. I told Cathy, 'If you are going to go, I am going to go with you.' ...Of course that really upset [Mr. Huff]...at the fact that I started going."

Lynn "They didn't want you to come with her?"

H... "Oh no."

Lynn "Did they tell you that?"

H... "No."

Lynn "Did they tell you?"

Cathy "No, of course not."

Lynn "It was just their general—The way they acted?"

Cathy "And if you could really understand—"

H... "See, they want to work on one spouse—"

Cathy "...They want to act godly, but see since they're involved with Satanic type junk, which I Am not real knowledgeable on, and just from my experience I know it's true, because of...the different things God is showing me is going on, now that I Am not with them anymore.

They say one thing with their mouth, that would appear scriptural; but they would send spirits that would come and plant thoughts in your mind to make you think something else.

And even come and act like they are prophesying to you as to what God told you. And it would make you even more convinced that these people were of God."

Lynn "Why would they not want him to come and be a part of that?"

H... "Because, see, they want to separate you. That keeps you weaker to start with...What they want to do is, they want to split the relationship up...They want dissension... They prefer one spouse is out of the picture, that way they got control over half."

Cathy "Then they'll lure the other one in later. After one is caught, then they get the other one. And then you end up in a situation...

But I did...see [Mr. Huff] French kiss (him) at one time during a meeting. He was *actually* kissing him...

Because once you introduce sex into it, you don't sin just against God; you sin against your own body. You actually become one with that individual that you've joined yourself to.

So there's much more of a deeper tie that Satan has on you if you've actually indulged in a sexual relationship with either somebody of the same sex, or the opposite sex, or children being involved.

Two weeks ago Cindy called me on the phone and said Rebecca finally got "born again." That she finally accepted the LORD...I was so happy because I thought she meant Jesus...I was so excited...that she actually got "born again" by God's Spirit. And I went over there that night...

Rebecca was so accepting of me then. And she said, 'Oh I love you, Ms. Cathy. I just always have.' And she was so different.

Before it was a fight because she didn't want to be there. It was like she couldn't stand it.

But after that point...she was accepting of me and finally said she loved Ms. Liz, when she used to talk about her all the time."

Katie "She's never liked Liz."

Cathy "You'll find if you come across her now, she'll have a different attitude towards Liz. She won't have a different attitude towards me because I Am out of the group now."

Katie "But she had a different attitude towards you the whole time anyway...She didn't talk about you like she talked about Liz."

Break

H... "Basically I went into the group with a lot of reservations. I was having a lot of personal checks inside, but once you are in there you become numb to those checks.

I'd have reservations about something...like a scriptural thing. They would interpret one thing, say, interpret fornication and adultery. And [Mr. Huff] would come back and say the Bible says that, but let's go to the Greek translation and see what it says. The Greek reads it and says adultery and fornication are idolatry.

So he discounts fornication and adultery in the Bible, and says it really means idolatry—You are worshipping other idols. And that fornication and adultery are okay, basically."

Lynn "He says that they're okay?"

H... "Right."

Lynn "Did he come out and say this?"

H... "No. No it's a real subtle thing in that area..."

Break

H... "...As far as immoral? No, because...for the most part, they did not want me to see anything like that. They did not want me to witness anything.

The only things that I really saw, and it would not really do a lot of good, but the things are that [Mr. Huff] is a master at psychology. He is very well trained. Very well versed...

[He] is a very emotionally sick person, but you'd never know that...Up front to me he never revealed that."

Cathy "I got a little tiny glimpse of it every now and then."

H... "He's very unstable. Like I said, but I never saw it. I am not really privy to his instability, but like Cathy said, she's seen it on a couple of occasions."

Katie "His daughter can't stand it. I went to school with his daughter in college. [She] cannot stand the ground he walks on because of what she watched....He's crazy like a fox."

H... "Yes. He has deception, manipulation, lies—He has all that very well under control.

He has got the right answers for any question. We were there as a Bible study group. And the real sad part, and the part that really does upset me, is the fact that my family gave them credibility...

Here we've been going to the Baptist Church...Trying to serve the LORD and all this. And then comes [Mr. Huff] along, and more or less enticed Cathy into the group."

Cathy "I want to state to you right now, and like I said, I don't want to think more highly of myself, but I know, just looking back, that God led me through there.

And with this prophecy, it substantiates some things. Right now the only thing we can do...

I know you want to take this to court—The only thing I feel inside that you could do right now is—What's a temporary injunction?"

Steven "Temporary custody?"

Cathy "Do you happen to know a judge you could take that...so you could get temporary custody of her?"

Steven "Well, I'll have to go find a lawyer."

Lynn "We don't even know that we have enough there...We need to get as much as we can on this tape."

H... "Yeah. Let me just get back to [Mr. Huff]. [He] is very good at psychological control. And that is the part with the children that I know. First hand, as far as the children, there is the psychological abuse that...the children are nothing. They are always subjugated; set apart. Not allowed to interact with the group itself. They're always pushed aside."

Steven "If Rebecca's under a spell or whatever, how can we break it?"

H... "Get her out from their control."

Cathy "No. Remember when I read this prophecy?...If you get like a temporary injunction to get her away."

Break

Cathy "But that is hearsay...Just by what I perceive in my heart, that whoever listens to this that is a Christian, they will understand and it will bear witness.

That the sexual aspect is what holds people.

Cindy had told me that [Mr. Huff] never had sex with her. He tried and even tried to say that she was his wife, but he could not get through that door.

...Liz used to talk to me about a problem she had. And I think it was when she was in the military. That was one of her hang-ups. And I think Cindy had a hang-up with that... That is what I feel like and perceive in my heart is the hold they have on Cindy. That it is keeping her so tight in with them.

See the thing with me, whenever I had a relationship with [Mr. Huff]...I couldn't handle it. I knew it was sin in my heart. I went to the LORD and asked repentance and He cleansed me of it. And I was okay for a while.

And Liz would come right back and justify what had happened, and try to take the blame off [Mr. Huff] and put all the condemnation on me, saying that I was a stumbling block. I was the one that instigated it...

I said, 'What do I do that's ungodly?...I sure don't want to encourage this. What can I do to stop him from pursuing me? I don't want to be a stumbling block.'

But I always took the responsibility of it...I kept going to God and saying, 'I see that this is sin, and I am sorry for it, and please cleanse me of it.' And He would...But he'd come back after I was at a real weak moment."

Lynn "[Mr. Huff] would come back to your house?"

Cathy "Yes...the first time was just like...I didn't even know it happened hardly. I was so confused. It was just a weird thing. Then the second time was when I was just fed up with everything, and I just could not handle it. And I didn't know what the problem was.

Why I couldn't handle it was...the guilt feelings. What I did to my Husband. What I did to Liz. Because they were, at that time, apparently married. I mean, not married in the natural. They were spiritually married. And they *are* spiritually married!"

Lynn "[Mr. Huff] and?"

Cathy "And Liz. But it's in *Satan's* kingdom! Satan has joined them together. Not *God!"*

Mandy "Do you think any of the women might be abusing the kids?"

Cathy "Not that I know of. I know that I did not. And I do not think that Cindy did.

One thing that I want you to know right here...as far as Cindy getting out—If she truly loves God with her whole heart, soul, and mind...

When I speak, I don't know what I Am going to say to her. Just like when I came to you all, I did not know exactly what I was going to say to you.

I just know that my heart's been open, and I Am very honest and willing to state to you anything that has taken place...And that has been my statement to people.

Then when God has me speak to Cindy...she will have the opportunity—When God anoints me to speak to her—She will have the opportunity to receive life or death.

If she chooses death, it's because she hates God in her heart, so don't have sympathy for her.

And realize that God is still going to take care of your little daughter. You pray for her. And every Christian in this room, pray for her. That is what God said to do. He will rescue that little girl out.

If Cindy—And she decides—If she hears the Truth, and it breaks her free of it, she will come out of it. She will drag her daughter with her. She will not let anything happen to her daughter.

She will be as turned on to the LORD as I Am. She will be released from the chains that are binding her. She will be free! The Truth will set her free!

And when those people left my house Tuesday night, they took their junk with them. You will not ever experience the freedom I felt inside my heart!

I felt like I had my house back. I felt like I was truly married to that man and had him back. He had me.

It was almost like I could feel the chains gone. Everything was gone that was binding me up."

Mandy "Well, do you think it would help any if we just go to Cindy's and get all her stuff and take it back down to the country?"

Cathy "No. You can't do nothing. *God* can do everything. You can't do a single thing. I can't do nothing.

It's *only* through the power of God..."

Lynn "The only way that any of them is ever going to change is to get away from their influence. In other words, is what you're saying, their influence is making them do things, and see things that happen?"

Cathy "And act like they're okay. Act like they're okay with God. It's part of the deception."

Lynn "Like the sexual encounters that are happening?"

Cathy "And it is not *a lot* of sexual encounters. That's the thing. See it happened to me the second time when I was so guilt ridden and broken that I couldn't handle it anymore."

Lynn "But he's supposed to be your pastor? Right?"

Cathy "Yes."

Lynn "And he is saying he is your husband and doing this? And he is her pastor also?"

Cathy "When I presented Scripture to him—"

H... "Yes."

Lynn "This is her pastor and she is saying that what he says and what he does is right? This is what I am going to follow? This is what I believe?"

Cathy "No. No, see when I got Scripture to back up why the adultery was wrong, they had to go through another angle and say, 'Okay it was wrong. [Mr. Huff] repented of it. He is not going to do that anymore. God's dealt with him *in that area,* so you don't have to worry about that anymore. God's dealt with him. So, you forgive your brother. Do what God's word says. If you can't forgive your brother, God can't forgive you.' *[Emphasis mine.]*

See they use all kinds of Scripture."

Lynn "Did Cindy ever know any of this went on between you and him?"

Cathy "Yes. I went to [them] with it—[Mr. Huff] and Liz—The first time—I just could not handle it. I had to confront them with this...[He] was freaked that I really admitted it."

Lynn "Was Cindy—What did you do?"

Cathy "Cindy was not there. Okay, after the second time...This is something I was very ashamed of. This is not something I was really willing to talk about.

It was a real struggle to even go to these people—to confront these people with this. I did not even want to discuss it with Cindy. I did not want to discuss it with nobody...

If you committed adultery with a man you wouldn't go telling people about it. It's a shame..."

Steven "But did you tell her?"

Lynn "She was aware?"

Cathy "She confronted me. Well, no, let me tell you what happened. And I'll tell you why God even let me go by Scripture to—Do you know where it talks about if your brother has something against you?"

Break

Lynn "...[Mr. Huff] was used by God?"

Cathy "They would say [Mr. Huff] was used by God in such a way to point out people's failures, their sin, the things that they were weak in. So that he would actually be used by God to show people their faults.

See he was led by God to do these things, but I was weak in this area and it was just showing how I fell into adultery. That was *my* weakness. So because of the experience I went through, Liz's comment would be, 'Look at all the things God was able to show you.'

And that is true. Scripture is true where it says God can use all things for the good of those that love the LORD and are called according to His purposes. That was a true Scripture, but they perverted it.

He was saying the truth when he was saying "god" used him to show people their weaknesses. *Satan* used him to show people their weaknesses, and he tried to pull people in because of their weaknesses!

See the thing with me and with Cindy...I feel her heart is to follow the LORD. She is deceived into thinking that these people are following the same God as her.

And so when these sexual encounters happened with me, I went to them first. Based on this scripture:

Matthew 18:15-16 "Moreover if thy brother shall trespass against thee, go and tell him his fault between thee and him alone: if he shall hear thee, thou hast gained thy brother. But if he will not hear thee, then take with thee one or two more, that in the mouth of two or three witnesses every word may be established."

And that's what I did...After it happened to me the second time, and that was right before I was fixing to get out of that group...I was so beaten down; I couldn't handle it anymore and he came to my house that night...

I remember that night very clearly; how upset I was. It was like my heart was ripped out of me. I mean it was just a real hard time, but thank God, He is a healer. He does heal those kind of things. But...we had an encounter that night that hooked me back in..."

Lynn "This is when the two or three witnesses came in?"

Cathy "No, when we had the encounter nobody was there."

Lynn "No, I mean afterwards."

Cathy "Okay, then finally I got to the point where I saw [Mr. Huff] was not going to wake up. He is definitely having problems... And Liz all along is appearing to be on my side with all this...She is my friend. She is my confidant.

She speaks about [Mr. Huff] and says how wrong he is, but we'll pray for him..."

Lynn "Okay, you said then, Liz and Cindy, you took them with you?"

Cathy "I took them and made the accusations to [Mr. Huff]."

Lynn "Was it just Liz and Cindy?"

Cathy "Yes."

Steven "Was Wendell aware?"

Cathy "Wendell didn't find out about all this until Tuesday night..." *(2 March 1993)*

Lynn "He found out about the encounters—Wendell did?"

Cathy "Yes. Tuesday night he did. I went through everything that had happened."

Lynn "...Tuesday night you brought all this stuff up?"

Cathy "Yes."

Lynn "And what caused all the ruckus?"

Cathy "Yes. Well, Sunday, was the beginning of God intervening when He—"

Lynn "Well, what did Cindy say about this, when ya'll went forward?"

Cathy "...She didn't agree with the sexual encounters, she just agreed that...there was sin that people needed to repent of and that's why she was willing to go with me that night."

Lynn "And forgive him?"

Cathy "Yes. To forgive him. But if you only knew, he has already committed the unforgivable sin!

He has blasphemed the Holy Spirit! He has turned the grace of our LORD God into lasciviousness and despicable acts! He is *not* going to be forgiven!

He is going to Hell! He does not have a chance to repent!! He has gone through his chances of repentance! He will go to Hell!! And he wants to take anybody that will be willing to go with him! Through deception! Through lies! Through any means!

That is what is going on here. And that is why *only God* can stop this. I know you are very concerned—"

Lynn "Cindy does not see this?"

Cathy "No she don't! She does not see this yet...She is going to have a chance to hear the words God wants her to hear. The blinders will be removed at that point.

God, like His word has said, that My disciples will have the authority to bind and loose things—Things that are bound in Heaven and things that are...loosed in Heaven. They have that authority...

The thing about God's word, if you doubt it, it's not going to help you...I Am at the point where I have been through so many things, that I don't doubt God's word.

He has strengthened me in this because I went through all these temptations...

It's not to say that I Am anybody more important, but God will anoint me to speak to her; and the blinders will be removed for her to see the Truth.

It will be able to go into her heart, and she will hear the Truth and she will either accept it or reject it. And if she rejects it, she's going to go to Hell with them!"

Lynn "The thing right now that we're so concerned with—Right now we have got to get to the point—"

Cathy "Yes, so you take this tape—"

Lynn "Just in case it didn't copy earlier for some reason, just say again that you feel like why...they are in danger."

Cathy "The reason why I feel, and I sense in my heart—And this is things that I have not ever experienced, so this is pretty much just feelings that I feel that God has told me."

Lynn "And things that have happened to you."

Cathy "Well, just the sexual encounters are things that have happened to me, the sexual encounters I have seen other people in. Those are the only things that I can actually say that I have seen.

Now I do know, just because of the spell that I know that they had on me, because of the ways that they were able to take...something right out of my mind when I was talking...I know that they can cast spells on you. I know that because it happened to me. I know they can put thoughts in your head.

So people that do that kind of junk...When you are really heavy into worshipping Satan, you start doing all these things..."

Lynn "So you are saying, if Rebecca really stays in this, that they are being exposed to this?"

Cathy "They are in danger of—See right now I have not come in contact with these people since Tuesday night, since I kicked them out of my house. And I did!"

Lynn "You asked them to leave?"

Cathy "I told them they will not—"

(My Husband made a comment, but I did not get his response.)

Lynn "And what did they say when you told them this?"

Cathy "They were trying to—"

H... "Want to know what they could do to convince her, convince us that they had changed..."

Cathy "It was empty words."

H...	"Yeah. What they could do to get back in our graces...He started out—She went through the whole thing, all the accusations. [Mr. Huff] denied everything that she was accusing him...I forget the question exactly..."
Cathy	"Oh yeah. I think I asked him if he denied any of this."
H...	"Right. That's it...He was sitting down. He gets up. He is nervous. He's pacing around. And then he sits down and he's like, he's fixin to say no. And he goes, 'Yes. You know, yes. Everything you said is true.' "
Lynn	"He admitted everything was true? That you accused him of?"
H...	"Yeah. Right."
Cathy	"The sexual things, even with Kim."
H...	"Right."
Lynn	"And he admitted to the sexual things with Kim?"
H...	"Yes. And then he looks at Cathy, and goes, 'Cathy, I'm sorry for all the things I've done to you...' Then he looks at me and says, 'I'm sorry for—' What'd he say?"
Cathy	"I think defraud you."
H...	"...And [he] says, 'Cindy, I'm sorry for all the things I've done to you and your family.' "
Cathy	"Then she jumps up and says, 'I forgive you.' I didn't say a word."
Lynn	"So she forgave him of all...that he's done?"
Cathy	"And she brought up the scripture to me; she says, 'Cathy, if you cannot forgive your brother, God cannot forgive you...' That's a perverting of the Scriptures!"
H...	"[Mr. Huff]...turned to Liz and asked forgiveness of her, and of course she said that, 'You have not defrauded me.' "
Cathy	"...That wasn't the story yesterday! She always used to say how disgusted she was with [Mr. Huff]..."
H...	"Right. So [Mr. Huff] admitted to everything Cathy had accused him of."
Lynn	"But ya'll did not actually get this on tape?"
H...	"No...what you heard is all that we had on tape."

Cathy "And Liz, in the beginning...said that we are going to use this for the world, and I Am not using it for the world. I Am using it for God's people. I want them to know the Truth. I want them to hear it, so that they can be aware."

Lynn "Well, see we are not aware that these things really are going on. We know that they go on, but you don't think that it is going to affect your family or your loved ones."

H... "No. Not at all."

Cathy "It can though. That's what is so serious about it. And it has happened with you."

Lynn "I guess what concerns me is, he up and says it's okay; and then he denies it. And now he turns back and acknowledges it, like when he thinks he's lost ya'll."

H... "Once confronted...it seems like from what she had told me, when she would go to him...he denied everything, but Liz came back to her at a later date and admitted that [Mr. Huff] had admitted to her that it had happened. Of course, he would never admit to Cathy that it happened. It was always that it didn't happen when he was confronted.

Of course even there Tuesday night, he was denying it until he realized that after Cathy said, 'We are not like-minded in this. I do not agree. We are not in agreement. You people are going to have to go. Take your stuff and no more.' And that's when he came across and said, 'What can I—' And went into the thing about admitting to everything."

Lynn "When you say admitted, will you say what he admitted to?"

Cathy "All he admitted to was the sexual encounters with me. Sexual encounters with Kim. He just said, 'Whatever I've done to you, Cindy, I'm sorry. Liz, the way I've defrauded you.' And Liz was so adamant and said, 'You haven't defrauded me.' "

Lynn "He said Cindy and family. Right?"

H... "Right."

Lynn "Whatever he's done, he's done to the family also?"

H... "Right."

Cathy "Yeah."

Mandy "Well, is there any way we could find out what he's done to Rebecca?"

(Everybody was talking at once.)

Cathy "If you could get her away—"

H... "I don't know if there is anything there, but I do know that she had a change a couple of weeks ago."

Cathy "It's possible that if you get her away, I could talk to her."

Lynn "But you all did see an actual change in her life after Cindy let—"

Mandy "Do you think it was sexual or spiritual?"

H... "I would love to think it was spiritual..."

Lynn "The change in Rebecca, do you think it was sexual or spiritual?"

Cathy "...Probably both. But the spiritual is what truly matters here."

Ronald "I think the best thing to do is get Rebecca and let Katie get her off, cuz she'll talk to Katie more than you. A lot more."

Mandy "She'll talk to me too."

Katie "It's going to have to be either me or Mandy."

Cathy "Not with the spells she's in right now."

Lynn "We cannot talk to anybody right now."

Cathy "No, you can't. They don't need to know that I have come to you today. They don't need to know that you know as much as you do."

Lynn "She's a child. She's having to live in this house."

Cathy "There is nothing that's going to break that—

Like I said, if you go *the way* God has said to go, you will get that little girl out of there. This has been a very painful situation for everyone concerned, but if you can be a little patient and long-suffering—Just rest and relax and *know* that God is in charge.

You know, even through all this, looking back, here I Am walking with this man. And you know, this is when I Am looking back...sitting in my living room; imagining him sitting there on my fireplace hearth, thinking I have actually had a man that was serving Satan sitting in my house. And then I think about...."

End of the Tape

AT THE TIME THIS TESTIMONY WAS GIVEN, I had no idea that the LORD would have me publish it in a book to be sent out to others, but I Am very certain that God knew exactly what was up ahead.

God also knew how people would respond to what He would be leading me to do, and I Am so thankful He prepared me for the rejection, anger, and apathy that I have experienced from others.

But the thing that has been the most disheartening for me is that most of the rejection has come from those who profess to be Christians. I would expect it out of non-believers, but not from God's people.

Yet, I realize that due to Satan's subtle control and influence over people's lives, they are not able to truly discern right from wrong. And if we are dependant upon our own wisdom, or that of another man, we are extremely limited in our ability to discern Truth from error.

In my walk with the Enemy, I have learned that we can never accurately determine whether someone is of God or of Satan, unless the LORD God shows us the Truth by His Holy Spirit.

And it is so important to be found standing on the side of Truth at the return of the Messiah, but so many people will be ashamed on the Day of the LORD when we all give an account of ourselves before God.

There is Still Time to call upon the name of the LORD; but please hurry while He still may be found. I believe that it is the most important call that you could ever make in this life, and in the Life to come!

"While ye have Light, believe in the Light, that ye may be the children of Light. These things spake Jesus, and departed, and did hide Himself from them."
John 12:36

SHINING LIGHT ON THE DARKNESS

"Then Jesus said unto them,
Yet a little while the Light is with you.
Walk while ye have the Light, lest Darkness come upon you..."
John 12:35a

The LORD had me personally deliver this letter to Cindy at her place of employment so I could be certain that she did indeed receive it. I have hoped that one day the remaining members of La'el Ministries would finally wake up and see the Truth, but as of this writing it would seem that they are still *Walking With The Enemy,* and the Devil is still able to control and influence their lives.

Dear Liz and Cindy, 21 February 1994

It has been almost a year since the night we broke-up, and I feel the LORD is leading me to write one final letter to you. I have written both of you a separate letter that I have not mailed as of yet, but I will have them sent to you, if and when the LORD directs me.

After Mr. Huff's "little book," I Am sure you are not eager to get another letter from me, especially since it was so long. I consider my time with La'el Ministries as a type of "wilderness" experience, and for that reason it was very significant for me that the original letter I sent to him inadvertently ended up being forty pages long.

I don't know if you realized it, but the LORD arranged for him to receive that letter on 24 September 1993, the Eve of Yom Kippur. Since you both claim to be Jewish, you must know the great importance of this very special day for God and His chosen people.

At the time, I did not realize that this 'Day of Atonement' is the holiest of all Jewish holidays, which gives "men" the final opportunity to repent and ask God for forgiveness of their sins.

It was very fitting that he would receive it on that exact date, especially since the purpose of my letter was to help him see the error of his ways, and to persuade him to repent before it's too late.

And I attribute it completely to Almighty God! In fact, every letter or card that I have written to any of you, since our separation, has been under the inspiration and direction of the LORD.

And I do not make that statement lightly. Actually, it is quite an awesome responsibility, plus a tremendous honor and privilege to be entrusted with the word of Almighty God.

Ever since the LORD has given me more of an understanding concerning how Satan works, I know that you may not even realize that you are the ones that are actually *Walking With The Enemy*.

Based on God's word, if you do not have a sincere love for Truth and righteousness, God can and will, send a strong delusion to believe the lies. Please seriously consider these verses.

II Thessalonians 2:8-12 "And then shall that Wicked be revealed, whom the LORD shall consume with the Spirit of His mouth, and shall destroy with the brightness of His coming:

Even Him, whose coming is after the working of Satan with all power and signs and lying wonders,

And with all deceivableness of unrighteousness in them that perish; because they received not the love of the Truth, that they might be saved.

And for this cause God shall send them strong delusion, that they should believe a lie: That they all might be damned who believed not the Truth, but had pleasure in unrighteousness."

It is so important to walk in the Truth, and God is certainly no respecter of persons. Regardless of who you are, what your profession is, or what power and authority you may have on earth, you will be held accountable as to what you do with His word.

The only way to the Truth is through the LORD Jesus Christ, the "Anointed One" that God sent to reveal that Truth. And because He was obedient to the will of His Father, all "men" will be without excuse when they stand before Almighty God on that Day.

In these verses, Peter had just healed a man in the name of Jesus Christ of Nazareth; and due to his Testimony many believed in God, which is truly my hope for all who read this Testimony.

Acts 3:13-26 "The God of Abraham, and of Isaac, and of Jacob, the God of our fathers, hath glorified His Son Jesus; whom ye delivered up and denied Him in the presence of Pilate, when he was determined to let Him go.

But ye denied the Holy One and the Just, and desired a murderer to be granted unto you; and killed the Prince of Life, whom God hath raised from the dead; whereof we are witnesses.

And His name through faith in His name hath made this man strong, whom ye see and know: yea, the faith which is by Him hath given him this perfect soundness in the presence of you all. And now, brethren, I wot (or know) that through ignorance ye did it, as did also your rulers.

But those things, which God before had shewed by the mouth of all His prophets, that Christ should suffer, He hath so fulfilled.

Repent ye therefore, and be converted, that your sins may be blotted out, when the times of refreshing shall come from the presence of the LORD;

And He shall send Jesus Christ, which before was preached unto you: Whom the Heaven must receive until the times of restitution of all things, which God hath spoken by the mouth of all His Holy prophets since the world began.

For Moses truly said unto the fathers, A prophet shall the LORD your God raise up unto you of your brethren, like unto me; Him shall ye hear in all things whatsoever He shall say unto you.

And it shall come to pass, that every soul, which will not hear that Prophet, shall be destroyed from among the people.

Yea, and all the prophets from Samuel and those that follow after, as many as have spoken, have likewise foretold of these days.

Ye are the children of the prophets, and of the covenant which God made with our fathers, saying unto Abraham, And in thy seed shall all the kindred's of the earth be blessed.

Unto you first God, having raised up His Son Jesus, sent Him to bless you, in turning away every one of you from his iniquities."

I know the LORD God has been leading me in my efforts to expose the lies of the Wicked One; and I just pray that those of you who are headed for destruction will see the Truth; and be willing to repent of all your sins, so that you may be saved from eternal Death.

I don't know what is going on in your personal lives, but by the outward appearance of things, it would seem that you are no longer recognized as a viable church in regard to the local paper, since they no longer allow La'el Ministries to be listed on the "Devotional Page" section of their newspaper. [As of this date.]

Moreover, it seems that many who used to support you are no longer standing with you; and I would think that would cause you to look at your ministry and question your beliefs; especially in Light of what God had spoken to us on the night of 28 February 1993.

I still have hope though, and I realize it is quite possible that God could have blinded all of our eyes for a time, so as to have His will accomplished through us; especially since that is what He did with the nation of Israel regarding Jesus Christ being the Messiah.

Romans 10:21-11:36 "But to Israel He saith, All day long I have stretched forth My hands unto a disobedient and gainsaying people. I say then, Hath God cast away His people? God forbid.

For I also am an Israelite, of the seed of Abraham, of the tribe of Benjamin. God hath not cast away His people which He foreknew.

Wot ye not what the Scripture saith of Elias? How he maketh intercession to God against Israel, saying, LORD, they have killed Thy prophets, and digged down Thine altars; and I Am left alone, and they seek my life.

But what saith the answer of God unto him? I have reserved to Myself seven thousand men, who have not bowed the knee to the image of *Ba'al.*

Even so then at this present time also there is a remnant according to the election of grace. And if by grace, then is it *no more of works: otherwise grace is no more grace. But if* it be *of works, then is it no more grace: otherwise work is no more work.*

What then? Israel hath not obtained that which he seeketh for; but the election hath obtained it, and the rest were blinded. (According as it is written, God hath given them the spirit of slumber, eyes that they should not see, and ears that they should not hear;) unto this day.

And David saith, Let their table be made a snare, and a trap, and a stumbling block, and a recompense unto them: Let their eyes be darkened that they may not see, and bow down their back alway.

I say then, Have they stumbled that they should fall? God forbid: but rather *through their fall salvation* is come *unto the Gentiles, for to provoke them to jealousy. Now if the fall of them* be *the riches of the world, and the diminishing of them the riches of the Gentiles; how much more their fullness?*

For I speak to you Gentiles, inasmuch as I Am the apostle of the Gentiles, I magnify mine office: If by any means I may provoke to emulation them which are *my flesh, and might save some of them.*

For if the casting away of them be *the reconciling of the world, what* shall *the receiving* of them be, *but life from the dead? For if the first fruit* be *holy, the lump* is *also* holy: *and if the root* be *holy, so* are *the branches.*

And if some of the branches be broken off, and thou, being a wild olive tree, wert grafted in among them, and with them partakest of the root and fatness of the olive tree; boast not against the branches. But if thou boast, thou bearest not the root, but the root thee.

Thou wilt say then, the branches were broken off, that I might be grafted in. Well; because of unbelief they were broken off, and thou standest by faith. Be not high-minded, but fear:

For if God spared not the natural branches, take heed *lest He also spare not thee. Behold therefore the goodness and severity of God: on them which fell, severity; but toward thee, goodness, if thou continue in* His *goodness: otherwise thou also shalt be cut off.*

And they also, if they abide not still in unbelief, shall be grafted in: for God is able to graft them in again.

For if thou wert cut out of the olive tree which is wild by nature, and wert grafted contrary to nature into a good olive tree: how much more shall these, which be the natural branches, be grafted into their own olive tree?

For I would not, brethren, that ye should be ignorant of this mystery, lest ye should be wise in your own conceits; that blindness in part is happened to Israel, until the fullness of the Gentiles be come in.

And so all Israel shall be saved: as it is written, There shall come out of Sion the Deliverer, and shall turn away ungodliness from Jacob: For this is My covenant unto them, when I shall take away their sins.

As concerning the gospel, they are enemies for your sakes: but as touching the election, they are beloved for the Fathers' sakes. For the gifts and calling of God are without repentance.

For as ye in times past have not believed God, yet have now obtained mercy through their unbelief: Even so have these also now not believed, that through your mercy they also may obtain mercy. For God hath concluded them all in unbelief, that He might have mercy upon all. O the depth of the riches both of the wisdom and knowledge of God! How unsearchable are His judgments, and His ways past finding out!

For who hath known the mind of the LORD? Or who hath been His counselor? Or who hath first given to Him, and it shall be recompensed unto Him again? For of Him, and through Him, and to Him, are all things: to whom be glory forever. Amen!"

Throughout the ages men have attempted to mix the Holy with the profane, even unto this day; and in the following passage you will see that due to men's misunderstanding and misuse of God and His power, many were destroyed. Keep in mind that God's people did not do this, but they were completely responsible for what happened.

I Samuel 5:1-6 "And the Philistines took the Ark of God, and brought it from Ebenezer unto Ashdod. When the Philistines took the Ark of God, they brought it into the house of Dagon, and set it by Dagon.

And when they of Ashdod arose early on the morrow, behold, Dagon was fallen upon his face to the earth before the Ark of the LORD. And they took Dagon, and set him in his place again.

And when they arose early on the morrow morning, behold, Dagon was fallen upon his face to the ground before the Ark of the LORD; and the head of Dagon and both the palms of his hands were cut off upon the threshold; only the stump of Dagon was left to him.

Therefore neither the priests of Dagon, nor any that come into Dagon's house, tread on the threshold of Dagon in Ashdod unto this day. But the hand of the LORD was heavy upon them of Ashdod, and He destroyed them, and smote them with emerods, even Ashdod and the coast thereof."

According to that scripture, it seems that this particular "god" was still worshipped by the people, but God made it very clear that He is All-Powerful and that no other "god" can stand in His presence.

God said that one Day He will bring to an end all other "gods," but until then it so important to be found standing on the side of the Most High God and the LORD Jesus Christ.

This world is under the Judgment of God because men worship the work of their own hands, rather than Almighty God; and only those who truly love God will be spared from the wrath that is to come.

God has been *Shining Light on the Darkness*, and the following articles will show how far America has gone in compromising the word of God by acknowledging and accepting the worship of other "gods."

ARTICLE FROM "THE HORNBLOWER" DATED NOVEMBER 1993

"Girl Scouts Broaden Spiritual Base

At Girl Scouts' National Council Session / 46th Convention which was held October 22-25 in Minneapolis, Minnesota, a vote by approximately 2,000 delegates kept the word 'God' in the Girl Scout Promise and allowed individual members to substitute wording appropriate to their own spiritual beliefs for the word 'God' if they chose to do so.

Contrary to some misinformation that has been found in local newspapers and radio and television broadcasts, the proposal does not change the Promise. The official Promise will still read '...to serve God and my country...'

The motivating force in Girl Scouting is a spiritual one and we recognize that some religious and cultural groups believe in a motivating spiritual force, but use words other than 'God' to express that spiritual force, according to Girl Scout National Executive Director Mary Rose Main.

The proposal simply allows Girl Scouting to continue with its commitment to serving the increasingly diverse religious, cultural, racial, and ethnic populations in the United States.

The Congressional Charter of Girl Scouts of the USA clearly states that we are a non-sectarian organization. The motivating force in Girl Scouting is, and always has been, a spiritual one.

However, GSUSA makes no attempt to interpret or define the word 'God' for its members, allowing each member to establish for herself the nature of her belief.

The belief in a spiritual principle is fundamental to Girl Scouting, but religious instruction is the responsibility of parents and religious leaders. The policy simply allows girls the flexibility to use their own terms for this spiritual being. Girls are encouraged and helped through the Girl Scout program to become better members of their own religious group.

Since the organization's inception in 1912, Girl Scout founder Juliette Gordon Low wanted Girl Scouting to extend to all girls from diverse backgrounds. Over the organization's 81 years, that diversity has expanded. Through this policy, Girl Scouting will continue meeting the needs of all girls from all walks of life."

46TH SESSION OF THE NATIONAL COUNCIL SUMMARY OF ACTIONS

The National Council of Girl Scouts of the USA, in meeting assembled in Minneapolis, Minnesota, October 22-25, 1993, took the following actions:
Proposal # 3: *Flexibility in working for spiritual beliefs in the Girl Scout Promise.*
Motion: *That, since the Girl Scout organization makes no attempt to interpret or define the word "God" but encourages members to establish for themselves the nature of their spiritual beliefs, it be the policy of GSUSA that individuals when making the Girl Scout Promise may substitute wording appropriate to their own spiritual beliefs for the word "God."*
Action: *Proposal #3 adopted.*
Proposal #4: *Review of the wording of the Girl Scout Promise and Law.*
Motion: *That the National Board of Directors appoint a task group of council and GSUSA representatives to review the wording of the Girl Scout Promise and Law and related elements of our basic documents within the next triennium to ensure that the language is contemporary and meaningful to our increasingly diverse, pluralistic society while continuing to reflect the fundamental principles of the Girl Scout Movement.*
Action: *Proposal #4 adopted.*

It was hard for me to believe that the Girl Scouts of the United States of America would actually endorse the worship of other gods, but it is becoming even more apparent that the subtle tactics of the Enemy are hard at work in every facet of our society.

For Girl Scouts to pledge they will serve "God and Country" while acknowledging the worship of other gods is a contradiction in terms, and no nation on earth will stand if this practice is permitted!

The question before us all is: Are we going to serve our Creator with our whole heart, soul, and mind; or will we allow other "gods," idols, and any other evil to be a part of our life?

Based on our own personal decisions will determine what kind of relationship we will have with the LORD God Almighty, which in turn will ultimately affect our eternal destiny.

My hope is that you will truly come to understand how turning away from the one, true, and only living God can enable this sort of evil to become very prevalent in our society even though this nation claims to be "One Nation under God."

The following passage gives a great example of the character and nature of the only true God who is worthy of all praise and honor. I have included the entire Psalm so you can get the full picture.

Psalm 106 "Praise ye the LORD. O give thanks unto the LORD; for He is good: for His mercy endureth forever. Who can utter the mighty acts of the LORD? Who can shew forth all His praise? Blessed are they that keep judgment, and he that doeth righteousness at all times.

Remember me, O LORD, with the favour that thou bearest unto Thy people: O visit me with Thy salvation; That I may see the good of Thy chosen, that I may rejoice in the gladness of Thy nation, that I may glory with Thine inheritance.

We have sinned with our fathers, we have committed iniquity, we have done wickedly. Our fathers understood not Thy wonders in Egypt; they remembered not the multitude of Thy mercies; but provoked Him at the sea, even at the Red Sea.

Nevertheless He saved them for His name's sake, that He might make His mighty power to be known.

He rebuked the Red Sea also, and it was dried up: so He led them through the depths, as through the wilderness. And He saved them from the hand of him that hated them, and redeemed them from the hand of the Enemy. And the waters covered their enemies: there was not one of them left. Then believed they His words; they sang His praise.

They soon forgat His works; they waited not for His counsel: But lusted exceedingly in the wilderness, and tempted God in the desert.

And He gave them their request; but sent leanness into their soul. They envied Moses also in the camp, and Aaron the saint of the LORD. The earth opened and swallowed up Dathan, and covered the company of Abiram. And a fire was kindled in their company; the flame burned up the wicked.

They made a calf in Horeb, and worshipped the molten image. Thus they changed their glory into the similitude of an ox that eateth grass. They forgat God their Saviour, which had done great things in Egypt; Wondrous works in the land of Ham, and terrible things by the Red Sea.

Therefore He said that He would destroy them, had not Moses His chosen stood before Him in the breach, to turn away His wrath, lest He should destroy them.

Yea, they despised the pleasant land, they believed not His word: But murmured in their tents, and *hearkened not unto the voice of the LORD.*

Therefore He lifted up His hand against them, to overthrow them in the wilderness: To overthrow their seed also among the nations, and to scatter them in the lands. They joined themselves also unto Ba'al-pe'or, and ate the sacrifices of the dead. Thus they provoked Him *to anger with their inventions: and the plague brake in upon them.*

Then stood up Phinehas and executed judgment: and so *the plague was stayed. And that was counted unto him for righteousness unto all generations for evermore.*

They angered Him *also at the waters of strife, so that it went ill with Moses for their sakes: Because they provoked his spirit, so that he spake unadvisedly with his lips.*

They did not destroy the nations, concerning whom the LORD commanded them: But were mingled among the heathen, and learned their works. And they served their idols: which were a snare unto them.

Yea, they sacrificed their sons and their daughters unto devils, and shed innocent blood, even *the blood of their sons and of their daughters, whom they sacrificed unto the idols of Canaan: and the land was polluted with blood.*

Thus were they defiled with their own works, and went awhoring with their own inventions.

Therefore the wrath of the LORD kindled against His people, insomuch that He abhorred His own inheritance. And He gave them into the hand of the heathen; and they that hated them ruled over them.

Their enemies also oppressed them, and they were brought into subjection under their hand. Many times did He deliver them; but they provoked Him *with their counsel, and were brought low for their iniquity.*

Nevertheless, He regarded their affliction, when He heard their cry: And He remembered for them His covenant, and repented according to the multitude of His mercies. He made them also to be pitied of all those that carried them captives.

Save us, O LORD our God, and gather us from among the heathen, to give thanks unto Thy Holy name, and *to triumph in Thy praise.*

Blessed be *the LORD God of Israel from everlasting to everlasting: and let all the people say Amen. Praise ye the LORD."*

This aptly characterizes God's people in our day; and just as He heard the cries of His people at that time, I hope He will hear the cries of His people Today! It is time for true Christians to earnestly pray to God for His mercy, grace, and forgiveness for the many sins of the nations.

It should be very obvious that the LORD has handed America over to the Enemy; and it will only be through Him that wickedness will be brought to an end. I do see a time when evil will be no more, but until then, my hope is that those who truly love and belong to Almighty God will come to the "True Light" before it's too late!

Malachi 3:11-4:3 "And I will rebuke the devourer for your sakes, and he shall not destroy the fruits of your ground; neither shall your vine cast her fruit before the time in the field, saith the LORD of hosts. And all nations shall call you blessed: for ye shall be a delightsome land, saith the LORD of hosts.

Your words have been stout against Me, saith the LORD. Yet ye say, What have we spoken so much *against Thee? Ye have said, It* is *vain to serve God: and what profit* is it *that we have kept His ordinance, and that we walked mournfully before the LORD of hosts?*

And now we call the proud happy; yea, they that work wickedness are set up; yea, they that *tempt God are even delivered.*

Then they that feared the LORD spake often one to another: and the LORD hearkened, and heard it, *and a Book of Remembrance was written before Him for them that feared the LORD, and that thought upon His name.*

And they shall be Mine, saith the LORD of hosts, in that day when I make up My jewels; and I will spare them, as a man spareth his own son that serveth him.

Then shall ye return, and discern between the righteous and the wicked, between him that serveth God and him that serveth Him not.

For, behold, the day cometh, that shall burn as an oven; and all the proud, yea, and all that do wickedly, shall be stubble: and the day that cometh shall burn them up, saith the LORD of hosts, that it shall leave them neither root nor branch.

But unto you that fear My name shall the Sun of righteousness arise with healing in His wings; and ye shall go forth, and grow up as calves of the stall. And ye shall tread down the wicked; for they shall be ashes under the soles of your feet in the Day that I shall do this, *saith the LORD of hosts."*

I can say with all certainty, of which I think you would agree, that one Day every "man" will bow their knee before Almighty God, and acknowledge that Jesus Christ is LORD, all to the glory of God!

I look forward to the day when Truth, Justice, and Mercy will prevail among the people of this world. In the meantime, I pray that the grace of God will be poured out on all those who desire for His kingdom to come, and for His will to be done on earth, as it is in Heaven.

One Day the LORD will deliver His people from all the Evil that has become so prevalent among us. In fact, God has been showing me where He is shining His Light on so many of the lies and deceptions of the Wicked One—even at the Highest level!

I would like to share with you excerpts from the radio interview whereby I became aware of this particular matter. The topic they spoke about was very fascinating, considering all that God has been revealing.

This issue has enabled US Congressmen to be very secretive and deceptive about what they actually support, but in public stand for something completely different. In other words, hypocrisy has been officially upheld by the Congress of these United States.

This transcript is from a program I heard on WWAR. The date is extremely significant to me because it is the one-year anniversary date of a very enlightening Prophecy as given by the LORD on 27 August 1992.

GUEST SPEAKER: CONGRESSMAN FROM OKLAHOMA
27 AUGUST 1993

Host “Cathy...joins us...thanks for calling.”

Cathy “Well, thank you. I'm kind of nervous...”

Host “That's all right, don't be nervous. It's just the four of us.”

Cathy “Well, I just want to make a comment, and then a question. When I heard you talking about this, this morning, such an excitement came over me because it's so important to walk in Truth; and that's one thing I've come to realize.

And I really see the LORD starting to open things where Darkness is no longer able...to operate without being exposed; and I see this Bill as doing that.”

Host “Shining Light on the Darkness. You are exactly right!”

Cathy “And I just want to encourage you to not back off because this is something that is so important, and it'll hold people accountable for the decisions they make in their lives that affect us and our country. And I'd like to ask you Congressman, what is it that the voters can actually do that will really make an impact on their representatives...?”

Guest "That's the whole reason for being on these talk shows. I mentioned, Cathy, that this is my 45th one in two weeks.

What you can do is the list...Those individuals that signed discharge petition # Two, they all know which one it is.

You don't have to identify it to thank him for having the courage to stand up against the elitist leadership of Congress. It took courage to do it...

Those who have not signed, if you just let them know your feelings. Maybe they haven't heard from their constituents and I think they should.

We have got our 218th signature, but I know for a fact that the leadership is working on these guys, and some of them are going to go up there on the 8th of September and pull their name off.

Specifically, what you can do, Cathy, and all the rest of the listeners, is call the people that are not on this discharge petition and encourage them to get on. Go out and get the 17th of August *Wall Street Journal* if you need to have this down in writing, so you will know what the issue is and who the names are."

Host "I think you believe in prayer, don't you, Congressman?"

Guest "I think your listeners might be happy to know that there are two strong Christian groups in Congress—One is the House Prayer Breakfast, which is a very large group. We have a prayer breakfast every Thursday morning and I am the President elect of that group."

Host "Good!"

Guest "The other group is the Christian Embassy which is an offshoot of Bill Bright's operation. And we have a Bible study at One o'clock in the Chapel in the Rotunda of the Capitol every Thursday. So there is, uh, Christ is in Washington despite what some people might think."

Co-Host "There are probably some things happening that the LORD is doing that we will some day know about."

If you are wondering why I have shared all of this with you, suffice it to say, if you are truly on God's side, you should be very concerned about the many injustices taking place. But if you are totally unconcerned, it's Time to consider who you are walking with.

I Corinthians 6:2-3 "Do ye not know that the saints shall judge the world? And if the world shall be judged by you, are ye unworthy to judge the smallest matters? Know ye not that we shall judge the angels? How much more things that pertain to this life?"

Jesus Christ won the victory! And it is Time for the true body of Christ to stand up in the power and might of the Holy Spirit and denounce the hidden things of Darkness! Truth will prevail! And it will be so important to be found standing on the side of LORD on that Day.

Zechariah 3:7-10 "Thus saith the LORD of hosts; If thou wilt walk in My ways, and if thou wilt keep My charge, then thou shalt also judge My house, and shalt also keep My courts, and I will give thee place to walk among these that stand by.

Hear now, O Joshua the High Priest, thou, and thy fellows that sit before thee: for they are men wondered at: for, behold, I will bring forth My servant the BRANCH.

For behold the stone that I have laid before Joshua; upon one stone shall be seven eyes: behold, I will engrave the graving thereof, saith the LORD of hosts, and I will remove the iniquity of the land in one day.

In that day, saith the LORD of hosts, shall ye call every man his neighbour under the vine and under the fig tree."

I really take no pleasure in the thought of you or any other man burning in Hell; and I believe the hardest thing for me to accept, is how could you choose Death over Life. It still saddens me at the way things have turned out between us. I felt like we would be friends forever.

If God ever reveals to me that you have come to Him with a repentant heart, and you have turned from the wickedness that you have been apart of, and have truly decided to follow Him with all your heart, then you will always have a friend in me, if you ever need one.

Signed and sealed in the presence of a witness on the 28th Day of February in the year of our LORD, One Thousand Nine Hundred and Ninety-Four.

I WOULD LIKE TO MENTION that I did send a letter to each of the representatives from our state. I received a reply from most of them, but in some cases the initial response was not consistent with their final vote.

I have learned that what a person says, will not necessarily match up with what they do, which is why it is so important to pay close attention to not only what a person speaks, but to their actions as well.

Moreover, due to the policy of the Girl Scouts in regard to the worship of other "gods" as being an acceptable practice, my Husband and I revoked our daughter's membership from this organization. And I praise God that she was in agreement with our decision.

Although, I Am disheartened by the response of the Churches. Many have chosen to remain silent on this issue or continue to be a part of this organization, despite all that has recently been revealed about it.

I have since addressed some very important issues with many prominent religious and political leaders, but it would seem that my thoughts and opinions are not worthy of serious consideration.

I Am so disappointed with many of the things that are allowed in this country—a country that claims to be "One Nation Under God." And one day God *will* hold the men accountable who are responsible for the very shameful and unjust laws that have passed the U. S. Congress.

I just praise God that my faith and confidence is not in men—Only in Him! If I was only able to see this world from the perspective of men, it would be an utterly hopeless situation, with great reason to fear; but I thank God that I Am able to see many things from His view.

Many injustices and despicable evils are taking place in our day, and it is only getting worse, just like the LORD God said it would. But the thing that I Am most concerned about, is that many organizations, and even "Christian" ministries, are using God's name for personal gain.

They do not follow God and His word in their methods; their focus is not on Truth and justice; and all they seem to care about is their own agenda as it relates to political, social, and economic advantages.

God is shaking things up these days, and if you are a part of a church, ministry, or organization that is not truly of Him, yet claim to be, when they come crashing down, you will be greatly affected too.

Thus sayeth the LORD, "Woe, woe be unto them who are guilty of taking His name in vain!" For God will not hold them guiltless!

God will judge each one of us according to our works, in Light of the Commandments of God, and depending upon our own heart motives will truly determine our destiny. It is either Heaven or Hell! There is no middle ground in this war between God and the Devil!

There has been such a departure away from the Truth among those who profess to be followers of the LORD Jesus Christ, and when I look at the condition of the Churches I truly believe that we are in the great "apostasy" as spoken of by Paul in the Holy Scriptures!

The future of this nation, the world, and the souls of men are at stake! We are no match against the Devil, and unless the LORD God is truly on our side, we don't have a chance against the Wicked One!

The Enemy has been very instrumental in the process of writing this book, but none of this would have been possible without God working among so many others to have His will accomplished.

I Am beginning to understand why Satan has such a stronghold over the Churches and God's people, and it will only get worse as long as His people are willing to compromise the Truth of God's Word.

I foresee such great pain, suffering, and heartache ahead for so many people, and I just hope they will finally get to the point where they are willing to repentant of all that is evil, and seek God's forgiveness.

I will continue to pray for God's people as the LORD leads me. I just hope and pray that the "Sleeping Giant" will soon wake up; before the Nations of this world reach the point of no return.

God is *Shining Light on the Darkness,* and He will use the Truth to expose the lies of the Devil. It would seem that those who are against Christ are winning, but not for much longer. Praise God!

And I must proclaim to every nation, and kindred, and tongue, and people that the hour of His Judgment is come! All praise be to the Holy One of Israel! Amen!

Isaiah 42:1-9 "Behold My servant, whom I uphold; Mine elect, in whom My soul delighteth; I have put My Spirit upon Him: He shall bring forth judgment to the Gentiles. He shall not cry, nor lift up, nor cause His voice to be heard in the street.

A bruised reed shall He not break, and the smoking flax shall He not quench: He shall bring forth judgment unto Truth.

He shall not fail nor be discouraged, till He have set judgment in the earth: and the isles shall wait for His law.

Thus saith God the LORD, He that created the Heavens, and stretched them out; He that spread forth the earth, and that giveth breath unto the people upon it, and spirit to them that walk therein:

I the LORD have called thee in righteousness, and will hold thine hand, and will keep thee, and give thee for a covenant of the people, for a Light of the Gentiles; to open the blind eyes, to bring out the prisoners from the prison, and them that sit in Darkness out of the prison house.

I Am the LORD: that is My name: and My glory will I not give to another, neither My praise to graven images.

Behold, the former things are come to pass, and new things do I declare: before they spring forth I tell you of them."

THEN IT WILL BE TOO LATE

*"And Death and Hell were cast into the Lake of Fire.
This is the second Death. And whosoever was not found written
in the Book of Life was cast into the Lake of Fire."
Revelation 20:14-15*

The following letter will further prove that Almighty God is able to use what the Devil intends for evil, and turn it around for the good of "All God's People." And may the Majesty on High receive all the glory, honor, and praise for anything that He leads me to do!

Dear Liz, 8 March 1994

After receiving an article in the mail without a return address on it I will assume that it is from you, especially since it's in line with your teachings. You did not include any comments, so I can only conclude, based on the subject matter, that you are still contending that I Am the one being controlled by demonic spirits.

In a way, I Am delighted that you would think that of me, especially since they also used to accuse the LORD Jesus Christ of the same thing. But I Am equally disappointed, because it shows me that you are still *Walking With The Enemy* and totally under his control.

It seems like I should be able to just put you out of my mind and not be concerned about any of you from La'el Ministries, but God has not allowed me to do that. Actually, I Am very thankful for my time with you because it's given me the chance to understand how Satan works.

Please note that I will only be addressing the issues that you highlighted in the article that was sent to me.

EXCERPT FROM: HOLY SPIRIT VERSUS DEMON SPIRIT GUIDES

"Christians who have never been involved in the occult need to know how demon spirits act as spirit guides. Why? Because the sad truth is that many Christians today are accepting a demon spirit guide thinking it is the Holy Spirit. Most of these errors could be avoided if Christians had a good basic understanding of how scripture describes the functions of the Holy Spirit in our lives."

I Am sure you will never admit that La'el Ministries is a cult, but I know different. And even though I was with you for three years I thank God that He did not allow me to gain knowledge of the very depths of Satan—but just enough to know many of his deceptive tactics.

To help substantiate my claims I would like to reference the following definitions which will prove that La'el Ministries does indeed fulfill the requirements of cultic practices.

AMERICAN HERITAGE DICTIONARY

- *Cult: 1-A system or community of religious worship and ritual, especially one focusing upon a single deity or spirit. 2-Obsessive devotion or veneration for a person, principle, or ideal. 3-An exclusive group of persons sharing an esoteric interest. (Esoteric: Intended for or understood by only a small group.)*

- *Oc.cult: 1-Of, pertaining to, dealing with, or knowledgeable in supernatural influences, agencies, or phenomena. 2-Beyond the realm of human comprehension; mysterious... 3-Available only to the initiate; not divulged; secret: occult lore. 4-Rare. Hidden from view; concealed.*

Even though you were very secretive about many things, I was always very open and honest with you about everything. Of course, you led me to believe that I was your trusted friend, but now it seems that your sole purpose was to obtain personal information from me with the intent of using my words against me any way you possibly could.

After I joined La'el Ministries I was led to the following passage, but Satan was always one step ahead of me to dissuade me from holding onto the Truth. I praise the LORD Jesus Christ that His Truth has prevailed in my life; and only by the grace of Almighty God will I continue to walk in the "True Light."

II Corinthians 11:3-4 "But I fear, lest by any means, as the serpent beguiled Eve through his subtlety, so your minds should be corrupted from the simplicity that is in Christ.

For if he that cometh preacheth another Jesus, whom we have not preached, or if ye receive another spirit, which ye have not received, or another gospel, which ye have not accepted, ye might well bear with him."

Because of my misunderstanding and lack of knowledge, I did not realize that a man could claim to be an anointed prophet of God that said he was sent to proclaim the Truth, yet preach another gospel while using the Holy Scriptures to distort and pervert the word of God.

Because of my misunderstanding and lack of knowledge, I did not realize that just because a man claims that Jesus Christ is his LORD and Savior, and that he would lay down his life for Him, does not mean he is referring to the only begotten Son of God.

Because of my misunderstanding and lack of knowledge, I did not realize or understand what it meant to receive another spirit; but due to my affiliation with La'el Ministries, I was exposed to many spirits that were in direct opposition to the Spirit of God.

The shroud of secrecy and deception has been removed, and I now understand exactly why many things occurred as they did. I found out that we do not serve the *same* Jesus, and there is no way our relationship could have remained the same after the Truth was revealed during our meetings on 28 February 1993, and 2 March 1993. And had I stayed with you after that divine intervention, I would have forfeited my relationship with the one, true, and only living God.

The LORD has been revealing to me some of the numerous ways that the Devil has control over people without them being aware of it, along with the methods that he uses to introduce his demonic spirits.

One such way is through the medium of television and movies. Some seemingly very innocent and presumably wholesome programs and motion pictures are tainted with evil, which in turn will acquaint children and adults alike with demonic spirits.

To give an example of what I Am talking about, this past weekend I watched a movie with my children called "Free Willy." By all outward appearances, it was a nice little movie about a whale called Willy. Certainly nothing to be alarmed about, or so I thought.

I should have known something was wrong due to the unusual fascination my children had for this particular movie; but I just dismissed it and I bought the movie for them anyway.

When I later found out that one of my girls had lied to me so as to persuade me to buy the movie for them in the first place, that should have alerted me that something was definitely wrong, but I just dismissed that too, and I let them watch it anyway.

As they were watching the movie, I discovered that a very undesirable music video was at the beginning, and I assumed that was why I had a problem with it; so I had them fast-forward that part.

But not until I sat down watched the entire movie with them did I finally realize and understand exactly why I continued to have the nagging doubts, which I believe was the LORD trying to warn me.

The scene that I was most concerned about is where the little orphan boy has learned how to repeat an incantation that he hopes will give the whale supernatural power to jump over the wall to freedom. Of course the chant worked, and "Willy" was set free!

Regretfully, most people do not see this as something to be very concerned about. And since their minds have been conditioned by the "world" and the Devil to be accepting of this seemingly innocent chanting, they unwisely regard it as harmless.

The LORD has been giving me such an insight to know that this subtle tactic of the Enemy will enable Satan to control people's thoughts and actions by the use of demon spirit guides.

And I contend that the Devil is the one that is behind this cultic practice that demonstrates to the unsuspecting viewers how to conjure up demonic spirits; which in turn prepares them to be very accepting of this outside evil influence over their lives.

Moreover, it is vitally important for people to recognize the evil of chanting. Not only do they curse God when repeating these chants, but it gives power to evil spirits so they can carry out their wicked deeds.

The Devil is behind it all, and we should be extremely guarded against any of it, but since this practice is so prevalent in every aspect of our society, we have been reaping the effects of this sin in our land.

Something is terribly wrong, and it can no longer be ignored! If it is not acknowledged and rejected as an acceptable practice, people will continue to be plagued with this evil and will reap its destructive nature.

It is so distressing when you hear about someone, whether it be a child or an adult, committing a despicable act of violence. You can be very certain that demonic spirits were involved.

Part of the problem is that the perpetrator, who is controlled by the demon spirits, may not even realize what they are doing at the time, or they may have no recollection of what happened. And if they do, they may not understand how they could have done such a horrible deed.

God's people need to wake up before it's too late! The scripture that says, *"My people perish for lack of knowledge,"* is so true. But thanks be to God, He is exposing the many evils of Satan in order to give His people the opportunity to stand apart from the wickedness of sin in their lives before it completely destroys them.

In fact, the main purpose behind this letter, or any other letters that I have written since the LORD God Almighty delivered me from the power of Darkness, is to share the Truth of what God has revealed to me concerning my walk with the Enemy. I sincerely hope to be able to warn others about the very subtle schemes of the Devil, but they must believe the Truth of what I Am saying, otherwise it will not help them.

If people receive the Truth, and believe the Truth, it will truly set them free them from the bondage of sin, Satan, and Darkness. And then God's people can truly worship Him in the manner He so deserves.

Since you still seem to be trying to convince me that I Am wrong and hopefully sway me to your way of thinking, I will take this opportunity, with the guidance of the Holy Spirit, to show you why I perceive the article that you sent me to be Satan's attempt to create a false impression, with the intent of distracting me from the Truth.

It would bring Satan such great pleasure if you could cause me to doubt and disbelieve what the LORD God Almighty has spoken to me. But I Am finally standing on the Rock of Christ, and it is *only* due to Him that *I Am* still standing. And only by God will I continue to stand.

EXCERPT FROM: HOLY SPIRIT VERSUS DEMON SPIRIT GUIDES

"The Holy Spirit values our individuality. He does not try to usurp our individual personality in any way.

Demons hate human beings! They try to usurp the individual's personality and replace it with their own. The Holy Spirit wants us to be in control and responsible for our own actions. He works in us to 'will to do God's will.' (Phil. 2:13)

Demons want total control. They will frequently knock the person unconscious and then use them in any way they want. The Holy Spirit is gentle. When he comes into a person, he is so gentle that when you look inside yourself, you can't tell what is the Holy Spirit and what is you. The Holy Spirit is holy and pure. He brings purity into our lives. He gives us power to overcome sin."

The main thing that comes to my heart as I read some of these statements is that of my conversion experience. When I gave my life to the LORD over fourteen years ago there was definitely a change in me. When the Holy Spirit was given to me I knew it!

There was an obvious change in my thoughts and actions, and there was no doubt in my heart that the Spirit of the Most High God was with me. Since then, the LORD has been continually changing my old personality to be more like unto the nature of His dear Son.

I agree, the Holy Spirit is very gentle, but because I have asked my Heavenly Father to purify my heart, it has been an extremely painful and difficult process of realizing the sin that I have walked in.

When my old selfish nature rises up, the Holy Spirit is right there to lovingly remind me of it. Of course, it is my choice as to whether I will submit to the LORD Jesus Christ and His word, or will I allow myself to give into the desires of my old flesh nature.

And since I have decided to submit my whole heart, soul, and mind to the LORD God above, He will give me the ability and power to resist sin. And for that I will always be so grateful to Him!

Moreover, God has never knocked me out so He could work through me. I Am quite aware of what God does inside my heart, although it was mixed with fear and confusion while I was with you.

The night of 28 February 1993 was a different matter altogether. It was very evident that we were in the presence of the Holy Spirit of Almighty God; and I had the opportunity to either repeat what the LORD Jesus Christ was speaking to my heart, or I could have allowed fear and intimidation to stop me. Obviously, that was not to be. Praise God!

On that evening, there was a supernatural strength about me that was completely unlike my normal personality. Like you said, of which I will agree, there was no stopping me. You have to admit, that was such an extraordinary event for everyone involved.

I believe this attempt to persuade me that I Am wrong, to be a form of subterfuge on the part of my Enemy, and this article that you sent me is also truth mixed with lies, just like the LORD warned us about!

EXCERPT FROM: HOLY SPIRIT VERSUS DEMON SPIRIT GUIDES

"Demons hate Jesus! They glorify the person in whom they dwell, always drawing attention to the person himself instead of toward Jesus. Pride is the hallmark of demons and the people they inhabit. The Holy Spirit never blanks out our minds...Demons frequently blank out a person's mind. They function best when the person passively lets them take over...

They always encourage periods of mental passivity. The Holy Spirit will never give us any communication that contradicts God's word. Demons will twist and turn God's word and take it out of context to justify sin. We can never control the Holy Spirit...

The Holy Spirit demands that we walk in faith—Not by sight or emotions. Therefore, he does not frequently or routinely give us visions or emotions. The Holy Spirit does not satisfy carnal desires for emotional rewards. Because we must walk by faith and not by sight, the Holy Spirit rarely lets us see the spirit world, and certainly not on a routine basis, or when we want to.

Demons love to manipulate human emotions. They control many by giving them emotional 'highs' or rewards. The Holy Spirit never goes against our free will. God doesn't want puppets or robots. The Holy Spirit helps us to understand the scriptures. (John 14:26) Demons bring confusion. They block a person from understanding the scriptures. "God is not the author of confusion." (I Cor. 14:33)

Far too many Christians make the fatal error of thinking the Holy Spirit will come and 'take control of them' so that they do not know what they are doing...Only demons do this.

One of the most common deceptions of demon spirit guides is to give the person many false 'words of knowledge' which is really simple divination. Demons also give many individual 'prophecies' which is really fortune telling. Prophecy in the scripture is usually for the whole body of Christ, rarely for individuals, and certainly not on a frequent basis."

Liz, I do not even want to imply that I know everything there is to know about God and how He works, but I know He is in complete control! And He is working to have His perfect will carried out no matter what Satan and his ministers may try to do.

From my own personal experiences, I know for certain that God has been watching over me whether I was aware of it or not. And not until I really started acknowledging Him, was I able to see and understand all the many wonderful ways He has been working to have His will accomplished in my life.

Based on the premise that some of the statements in that article that you presumably sent me are true, you have no choice but to agree that the conduct of you and Mr. Huff, in many instances, places both of you in the category of those led by demon spirit guides.

In your quest to prove me wrong, you have helped expose the evils of the ministry that you are a part of; and because that article was also truth mixed with lies, its "author" cannot be trusted.

Proverbs 5:21-23 "For the ways of man are before the eyes of the LORD, and He pondereth all his goings. His own iniquities shall take the wicked himself, and he shall be holden with the cords of his sins. He shall die without instruction; and in the greatness of his folly he shall go astray."

I realize if you are not able to discredit me, you will be forced to admit that you have been wrong all along, and have wronged many others in the process. If you ever come to this realization, and are truly repentant, it could be an extremely hard thing to bear. But consider the alternative should you stand before God condemned.

Hebrews 10:31 "It is a fearful thing to fall into the hands of the Living God!"

I Am committed to my LORD Jesus, who sits at the right hand of the Power on High, and He has washed away my sins with His own blood! He is, and will always be, the True Love of my life; and I will never give Him up for *anything* this world has to offer!

All praise, honor, and glory unto my LORD Jesus, who is the eternal King of kings and LORD of Lords. World without end! Amen!

I will always be indebted to the LORD Jesus Christ for all that He has done for me; and if you really knew Him, you would feel the same. But I can say with complete confidence that you do not know my God, because if you had really been able to comprehend what the only begotten Son of God did for all of mankind, you would fall on your face and worship Him. Unless of course, your allegiance belongs to another.

My greatest regret since our separation, is when I discovered that we do not serve the *same* God. I had really believed that we did all along, but evidently you love the Darkness more than you do the Light.

II Corinthians 13:5 "Examine yourselves, whether ye be in the faith; prove your own selves. Know ye not your own selves, how that Jesus Christ is in you, except ye be reprobates?"

Liz, I cannot stand the thought of you or any other human being burning in Hell for all eternity; but if you find yourself barred from the Holy City, and cast into the Lake of Fire, you will wish you had listened to *my* LORD Jesus, but *Then It Will Be Too Late.*

Signed and sealed in the presence of a witness on the 17th Day of March in the year of our LORD, One Thousand Nine Hundred and Ninety-Four.

Revelation 22:10-11 "And he saith unto me, Seal not the sayings of this Book: For the Time is at hand.

He that is unjust, let him be unjust still: and he that is filthy, let him be filthy still: and he that is righteous, let him be righteous still: and he that is Holy, let him be Holy still.

And, behold, I come quickly; and My reward is with Me, to give every man according as his work shall be."

EPILOGUE

"Some men's sins are open beforehand, going before to Judgment;
and some men they follow after.
Likewise also the good works of some are manifest beforehand;
and they that are otherwise cannot be hid."
I Timothy 5:24-25

The following dialogue between Cindy's ex-husband's attorney and a former member of La'el Ministries, will help further establish my allegations that the teachings of this Bible study group do indeed fall into the category of the occult.

Please keep in mind that this has been edited, as I have done throughout this Testimony, so as not to reveal actual names and places because I don't want to bring unnecessary attention to innocent people.

I truly care about Evelyn and her family, and I sincerely hope that we will meet again one great and glorious Day!

TRANSCRIPT DATED 17 MAY 1993

Lawyer "Evelyn?"

Evelyn "Yes sir."

Lawyer "Again, my name is... And today is May the 17th 1993, and it's pretty close to 3:30 in the afternoon, and the purpose of my call is to take a recorded statement from you relative to your knowledge of a situation that exists... And particularly as it may affect Rebecca...Do I have your permission to take a recorded statement at this time?"

Evelyn "Yes, you do..."

Lawyer "When did you last live...[there]?"

Evelyn "I moved up permanently, I think it was the middle of February of this year."

Lawyer "Of Ninety-Three?"

Evelyn "Yes sir."

Lawyer "That's when you left...?"

Evelyn "Yes."

Lawyer "...Why did you leave...?"

Evelyn "Oh, the problems that I was having with my husband... We were going to get a divorce and—"

Lawyer "You don't need to go into details now."

Evelyn "Well, it was a personal thing with our family. And then I decided to move somewhere with my son, and that's where I chose to go."

Lawyer "Okay. Did you and your husband get a divorce?"

Evelyn "No sir."

Lawyer "Okay. Now what I want you to do, is just tell me about your knowledge and involvement with this group that's led by [Mr.] Huff. Just talk to me a little bit about it."

Evelyn "Okay, um, I guess I was probably first introduced to everybody...Everybody being the [H's], and [Mr.] Huff, and Liz...and Tom...

And the fall or winter of Eighty-nine...I drove out a few times to the meetings...but it was just too inconvenient, so I didn't see them for a while. And I'm not sure exactly—

Before I moved back out this way—We moved [there] in January of Ninety-Two, and maybe a couple of months before we moved out here I started coming again. And then I would say I was a full time—uh, I attended Wednesday, Thursday, and Sunday."

Lawyer "All right now. When did you become a full-time member?"

Evelyn "I would say it would have been January of Ninety-Two."

Lawyer "And you left in February of Ninety-Three?"

Evelyn "Yes sir."

Lawyer "Okay, so over a year then?"

Evelyn "Yeah."

Lawyer "All right. During that time did you get to know Cindy and Rebecca?"

Evelyn "Yes, I did."

Lawyer "Tell me what you know about the group, and the activities of the group, and what occurred while you were a member."

Evelyn "Well, to the surface it appeared to be just a fellowship of people that had a common faith in God, and loved the LORD.

And we all just wanted to hear more and get closer and know Jesus better.

And it was just nice having the camaraderie, the likeness of people with the same faith.

And we were encouraged not to have unbelieving friends. Like I had, ya know, some friends that I used to spend time with...and stuff like that."

Lawyer "Is an unbeliever a non-Christian, or just a non-member of the group? In other words, I am a member of the Methodist Church, and believed to be a Christian. I believe myself to be a Christian. But would I, based on what you're talking about, would I be considered a non-believer, or an unbeliever?"

Evelyn "Well, they would probably ask me, did you believe in Jesus, and if you said yes, then they would probably just say, ya know, what kinds of things would you talk about, and what kind of things would you do. And they would just warn you to be careful of who you associated with outside the group."

Lawyer "Okay. Basically, they would want you to spend all your time with group members?"

Evelyn "They would prefer that. Yes."

Lawyer "What were some of the activities that you participated in as a group member?"

Evelyn "The worship services that were here at the H's house. I did attend a couple of the ones that were at...(Liz's) house."

Lawyer "Can you describe to me what went on at those meetings, in general terms?"

Evelyn "In general terms—Uh, we would gather, and there would be iced tea, and there would be refreshments.

And what struck me, was everybody but me was a smoker. There would be smoked-filled rooms, and uh, we would have small talk, and then a Bible study session, and then small talk afterwards.

And not until—I don't know how many months ago we started the music, but I much preferred it after we started the singing part of it. And we would sing for about Twenty to Thirty minutes before we had Bible study.

And then when it came to Cathy's house they also started having dinner at least Wednesday and Thursday."

Lawyer "Did you also socialize together at times other than the meetings?"

Evelyn "I spent quite a bit of—You mean on the days of the meeting, or at other times?"

Lawyer "At other times."

Evelyn "Well, during this last year I spent an awful lot of time with Cindy because I wasn't working. She was out of work with her knee. And she and I spent quite a bit of time together. I would take her to...her doctor's appointments. Took her to the hospital, I believe when she had to go in for her knee and stuff like that."

Lawyer "Were you and Cindy friends?"

Evelyn "Yes."

Lawyer "Are ya'll still friends?"

Evelyn "Well, I've spoken to her since I've moved...But when—After the incident, that you know, that initiated the breakup of Cathy from the group. Um, it just came to me to call Cathy, and I did. And so the next day after it happened—"

Lawyer "All right, what incident are you talking about, that caused Cathy to leave the group?"

Evelyn "Um, I don't know what the date is, but when—"

Lawyer "But what was it?"

Evelyn "At a prayer meeting, at a Bible study meeting, uh, the Holy Spirit had some words for Mr. Huff which she spoke, and um—"

Lawyer "Was that the confrontation meeting?"

Evelyn "The confrontation was a couple of days later I believe."

Lawyer "Okay, yes, I know. So in other words, basically in my language, ah, when Cathy got on to him about what he was doing, was when they pretty much forced her from the group?"

Evelyn "Right."

Lawyer "Okay. And so then you contacted—"

Evelyn "I called Cathy the Wednesday after the confrontation, and I said, 'I don't know why I'm calling you, but I—' Ya know, cuz generally I don't like to call Cathy, because she likes to talk a long time. And it cost too much money." (She started laughing.)

Lawyer "And I understand."

Evelyn "She's a talker now."

Lawyer "I know. Cathy and I have engaged in several conversations."

Evelyn "But I said, 'No I got to talk to Cathy.' So I called her, and she said, 'Why did you call, Evelyn?' And I said, 'Well, something just urged me to call.' So she proceeded to tell me everything that had happened.

And then after that time I did call Cindy once. And I called her for the purpose of getting back a vacuum cleaner that I had loaned her."

Lawyer "Okay."

Evelyn "And I told her that I loved her, but I really didn't want to talk about anything that had happened in the group, because I knew that she would try and tell me that Cathy's crazy."

Lawyer "Okay."

Evelyn "And I—Cathy is driven, but she's *not* crazy."

Lawyer "All right. Now let me ask you a couple of things about what you brought up so far."

Evelyn "Okay."

Lawyer "Do you have any personal knowledge of any of the sexual activity that went on in the group while you were a member?"

Evelyn "I did not know about Cathy."

Lawyer "All right, tell me what you do know about."

Evelyn "The only thing that I do know about is an obvious...uh, relationship between Liz and [Mr. Huff]."

Lawyer "Now, how do you know about that?"

Evelyn "Just the way they act towards one another. I've never seen any sex... but they treat one another as husband and wife."

Lawyer "Well, now explain to me what ya mean by that."

Evelyn "They embrace. They kiss. They—"

Lawyer "When they kiss, is it a kiss on the lips?"

Evelyn "Oh, yes sir."

Lawyer "In other words—what's a better word—"

Evelyn "Intimate."

Lawyer "...A real sexual type kiss?"

Evelyn "Well, something that is reserved only for a husband and wife."

Lawyer "I know but—"

Evelyn "Well, I don't believe I've ever seen any passionate kissing."

Lawyer "Okay. All right."

Evelyn "But I would still describe it as a husband and wife type of an embrace."

Lawyer "Have you seen, and I apologize for being so explicit...But any fondling of any kind between the two of them...?"

Evelyn "Na-a—No."

Lawyer "...I guess what I'm saying...in a lot of religious groups, the friendship hug is something that is very traditional."

Evelyn "Yes sir."

Lawyer "And even a kiss on the cheek is a Christian greeting."

Evelyn "Yes sir."

Lawyer "Are you saying that what you have seen on more than one occasion, between these two people, more than that sort of hugging and kissing?"

Evelyn "Yes sir."

Lawyer "Okay. And have they done this in the presence of the children, specifically Rebecca?"

Evelyn "I don't know. For a time they didn't seem to show that much emotion for each other, but towards the last six, seven, eight months they didn't seem like they were trying to hide anything, at all. But in the beginning they wouldn't do even much around me."

Lawyer "Did they do this in front of Tom?"

Evelyn "Oh yes."

Lawyer "Do you have knowledge that they sleep together ah, in Tom's house?"

Evelyn "Um, you mean by admission of either of the two parties?"

Lawyer "That's sufficient."

Evelyn "Well, um, the only conversation and admission of any kind, was maybe after Liz and [Mr. Huff] had gone to—Was it Louisiana? *[She was directing that question at me, but I don't remember my response.]*

They went on a vacation together."

Lawyer "Just the two of them?"

Evelyn "Yes. When she came back she was very upset because she thought she was pregnant."

Lawyer "And she told you that?"

Evelyn "Yeah. She went out and bought a pregnancy test."

Lawyer "And she told you that? And told you she had—That she was afraid [Mr. Huff] was the father?"

Evelyn "She didn't mention his name, but that was the person that she was with."

Lawyer "Okay."

Evelyn "She wouldn't come out and admit it to me. She never did."

Lawyer "All right, have you witnessed any French kissing with [Mr. Huff] and any of the male members?"

Evelyn "No sir."

Lawyer "Okay. Have you witnessed any inappropriate physical contact by [Mr. Huff] or any of the other members of the group and any of the children?"

Evelyn "No, I can't say that I've ever seen him, uh—"

Lawyer "And one of the children in particular that I'm talking about, which I consider a child, is Kim."

Evelyn "Um—Well, I, ya know, she was drawn to him when she first came. She wanted to spend time and be close to him. And I have seen him, ya know, with his arms around her."

Lawyer "Are you aware that they had sexual relations?"

Evelyn "Only by hearsay."

Lawyer "By hearsay, would it have been from Kim or Cindy? Either one of them ever tell ya?"

Evelyn "No."

Lawyer "Only from Cathy? *(There was a delay in her response.)* Or from anybody else?"

Evelyn "Well, I have a stepdaughter...And she lived with us for a period of time. She is Kim's age. She went to...high school, and she palled around with Kim. As a matter of fact, she is the reason that Kim was introduced to the group."

Lawyer "Okay."

Evelyn "She told her friends that he tried—He would put his hands down her pants, and kissed her."

Lawyer "Kim?"

Evelyn "Yes."

Lawyer "Okay."

Evelyn "But she never told me that. She was telling her friends, her peers this. Something Kim had told her, and it got back to me."

Lawyer "Okay, now do you know when this—"

Evelyn "It had to have happened within the first month to two months after she joined the group."

Lawyer "All right, was this while she was...being hidden out? Or was this—"

Evelyn "Prior."

Lawyer "...Do you know where it occurred at? This is while she was living with Cindy, correct?"

Evelyn "I don't know where it was supposed to have taken place. I would assume it would have taken place either at Cindy's or at [Mr. Huff's], but I believe it was before she came to live at Cindy's."

Lawyer "When she was still kind of baby-sitting?"

Evelyn "Yeah, I believe so."

Lawyer "Okay."

Evelyn "Because they...really didn't have all that much to do with one another after Kim went to live in [another city.]"

Lawyer "Okay."

Evelyn "Or wherever she went to live, I was never told where she went to live."

Lawyer "...So, the only—Is that the only knowledge you have of any sexual activity by [Mr. Huff], is with Liz, and also with Kim? Are there any others? I know about Cathy, but are there any others?"

Evelyn "He was inappropriately—Uh, he would try things with me, but I really wouldn't have anything to do with it."

Lawyer "All right, can you explain, and I apologize again—"

Evelyn "That's all right, that's all right."

Lawyer "But what would he try with you?"

Evelyn "Sometimes he would share something with you that got you really emotionally going, and you would cry, and then he would put his arms around you, and comfort you. And it was like—It wasn't like *he* was comforting you, you really felt that the LORD was comforting you. But then he would take advantage of the situation, and try to kiss you in the mouth, and stuff like that, but I would always turn my head, because that didn't seem appropriate to me. And I just said, well, he's just, he's just a sensual person, and he gets carried away, but I'm not going to participate in that."

Lawyer "Would he also attempt to touch you in inappropriate places?"

Evelyn "No."

Lawyer "So really it was just the kissing part?"

Evelyn "Yep."

Lawyer "All right. Ah, now—So you never had any type of a relationship with him?"

Evelyn "No."

Lawyer "Again, I apologize. Did you have any other relationship with any other member of the group?"

Evelyn "No sir."

Lawyer "Okay. The cause of your possible divorce with your husband had nothing to do with your involvement with the group?"

Evelyn "Oh, I believe it had everything to do with the group."

Lawyer "All right...well, explain that to me so I can understand."

Evelyn "Well, when we moved out...[there], um, I spent more and more time with the group. And my husband spent more and more time—He's a hunter and a fisherman. And possibly we had problems, but they were just completely made worse by the situation.

[Mr. Huff] and Liz, non-directly—Now they never did anything directly; but they would put, ya know—They would suggest things...that I didn't need the man, and he was no good for me, and he was a terrible influence on my son. And I would be much better off to raise my son by myself—With their help, with the help of the church. And God really had a plan for my life. And didn't I feel better here anyway? And they would take care of me. And hadn't they pulled through for me before?"

Lawyer "Is that the emotional type experiences that you would be going through when he would attempt to kiss you on the mouth? Is that the type of thing that he'd be doing?"

Evelyn "No."

Lawyer "Okay. All right. Did anybody else witness him attempting to kiss you?"

Evelyn "Possibly."

Lawyer "Such as?"

Evelyn "Probably Cathy."

Lawyer "Okay, any children?"

Evelyn "No, generally something like that would probably have happened after we would pray, or at the culmination of Bible study, which the children would have been in bed."

Lawyer "...As you know, this is a rough type thing to be involved in as far as a child custody battle. Because all we're interested in is Rebecca being in an environment where she can grow up and learn to love the LORD in her own way without being influenced in anything happening to her, such as happened to Kim or anything like that."

Evelyn "Right."

Lawyer "While it is on my mind, did he ever make any advances toward...your stepdaughter? [Mr. Huff]? Or any other member of the group?"

Evelyn "I don't know what he did with her...I know he kissed her, to what extent, she never told me..."

Lawyer "Do you think she would be willing to talk about this if she had to, or is this too emotional for her?"

Evelyn "Oh, I'm sure she'd probably be willing to talk about it."

Lawyer "Because what I'm interested in, again, if there was any inappropriate activity toward her. Because she was a minor. Was she not at that time?"

Evelyn "She turned eighteen in July of Ninety-Two."

Lawyer "So at least a portion of that time she was a minor?"

Evelyn "Right."

Lawyer "Now, talk to me a little about your relationship with Cindy, because what I need to know—

Cuz any testimony that, you know, that would lend itself to show that she was not caring for Rebecca as she should.

Such as any type of sexual activity she may have had that would be improper. Improper or maybe like neglect of Rebecca by leaving her alone or unattended, unsupervised, those type things. Tell me what you know about that."

Evelyn "Everything that—I think Cindy really thought she was doing the best for Rebecca. I knew of no, uh—From the time I met Cindy she wasn't—She didn't have an involvement with any man that I knew of. So as far as Rebecca witnessing something like that I have no idea.

As far as neglect, the only type of neglect would have been what Liz used to do, would always to be on the telephone with her. Cindy was always on the telephone either to Cathy or to Liz. And it wasn't so much that she wasn't there, but they monopolized a lot of her time that she could have spent with her child."

Lawyer "Are you not aware of any boyfriends that, or men friends that Cindy had, that spent the night at the home?"

Evelyn "No."

Lawyer "You're not aware of any of the physical or sexual encounters that Cindy had with [Mr.] Huff?"

Evelyn "No."

Lawyer "You're not aware that she was disrobed on at least one occasion?"

Evelyn "She never discussed it with me."

Lawyer "Okay. All the time that you were friends she never discussed that with you?"

Evelyn "Never."

Lawyer "Is there anything that you can tell me?"

Evelyn "We did discuss at one point that—Because I'd constantly ask Cathy and Cindy; I said, 'How could—' Ya know, I would always question the household that lived together. How could they be believable if they lived that way? And they would always say, 'Well, you just got to trust God.'

And we did talk about the time, about the way [Mr. Huff], the way he kissed. It was more sensual, than just brotherly.

And huh, she said, 'Well, yeah, he does that, but that's just [Mr. Huff].' As far as her offering any information it never went any further than that."

Lawyer "What do you think? I mean as far as Rebecca. Is she being taken care of in a suitable manner by Cindy?"

Evelyn "I think Cindy means well. I don't believe Cindy fully understands what influence that group has on her. I don't think she's intentionally neglecting or anything."

Lawyer "What influence is that group having on Rebecca?"

Evelyn "Well, I would say in some respects it has a good influence because she did make a commitment to the LORD, and I haven't seen her since her mother called to tell me that. That was after I moved...

She was all excited. She said her daughter made a commitment to the LORD and it was great. Cuz she was kind of a rebellious girl—spoiled. And no more spoiled than my son, who is five. Of course, now Liz and I had a lot of discussions about that. She didn't agree with the way I was raising my son. And we butted heads a lot about that."

Lawyer "Do you see any bad influences of this group on Rebecca? Do you feel like Rebecca is in any danger, and needs to be removed from this group?"

I AM SURE THE ATTORNEY HAD A COMPLETE TAPE, but my tape ran out so I did not get the end of the conversation, and I do not remember what her response was to the question. Apparently, the LORD wanted her removed and so did the Judge since he granted full custody to her father.

An interesting development since my leaving this group is that Mr. Huff was divorced from his wife Becky, and married Liz.

Also worth mentioning is that prior to our joining the Bible study group my Husband had visited our neighbor, Mr. Huff, as part of a discipleship assignment when he still lived across the street from us.

His wife answered the door and let him in, but Mr. Huff was not aware that my Husband had entered the room, considering the fact he was viewing a pornographic movie. After Mr. Huff realized that he had an unexpected visitor sitting next to him he immediately turned it off.

Strangely, my Husband had no recollection of this very strange incident even taking place until just recently. And after four years, it came back to his memory that it had even occurred. Ponder that one.

I AM SO AMAZED at how the LORD God Almighty has enabled me to put together these different letters, transcripts, and Bible verses to help show how I came to be *Walking With The Enemy.*

Huff and Liz have continued to try and manipulate me in order to change my view, but nothing has really changed since our separation, except their hatred for me has intensified. We see from a totally different perspective, and we have not come to an understanding, much less any kind of agreement, concerning that eventful night of 28 February 1993.

The following transcript will reveal the fate of La'el Ministries, whose title means "belonging to God" in Hebrew. However, the most important question that begs to be asked is, Which "god?" I hope you are able to see that the "god" they serve is *not* the God of Heaven.

To date, this is the last conversation I had with Mr. Huff, and I have included most of our discussion so you can see what was spoken between us. Considering that I was rather nervous, I left out the more obvious indications of that, otherwise it is verbatim.

CONVERSATION BETWEEN CATHY AND MR. HUFF
SUNDAY 2 MARCH 1997

Child "Hello?"

Cathy "Is Liz there?"

Child "She's resting right now."

Cathy "Oh, she is? Okay. Is [Mr. Huff] there? Is he resting too?"

Child "Ah, just a second."

Huff "Hello?"

Cathy "[Mr. Huff]?"

Huff "Yes."

Cathy "This is Cathy... How are you doing?"

Huff "Fine. How are you doing?"

Cathy "Oh, I don't know. I guess I Am okay."

Huff "Let me uncork my body here. I'm trying to get it up out of a chair."

Cathy "Uncork your body?"

Huff "Yeah, yeah it's not functioning so good these years."

Cathy "I had asked for Liz, but she's laying down. I guess you're just as good. Aren't ya?"

Huff "I reckon. Am I? I doubt it. I'm not very good at all."

Cathy "You're not?"

Huff "Not really."

Cathy "Well, she had sent me a letter last week, and I got an inclination to call ya'll."

Huff "Well, I'm glad you did."

Cathy "You are?"

Huff "Yes."

Cathy "How come?"

Huff "Why not? What am I supposed to be? *Mad? Angry?"*

Cathy "I—I don't know. I haven't seen ya or talked to you since—I guess it's, I don't know, September wasn't it? Rosh Hashanah of last year?

That date stands out for some reason. But—"

Huff "It was about—Let's see, not last year, but about two years ago."

Cathy "Okay. The years are kind of going together these days."

Huff "Oh yes. That, they are."

Cathy "The last time I called you my Husband...was home, and that's why I let him listen in on the phone, because he needs to be aware of whenever I talk to you all. He's asked me not to have contact with you all unless he knows about it.

And I Am recording our conversation so that he can listen later. If that's okay with you? If you'd rather I didn't—"

Huff "It's fine with me."

Cathy "...I really don't know why I'm calling you. I Am concerned about some of the things that she wrote in the letter to me. Mainly, I guess about you.

She was saying that you had said that you're finally getting through this, and recognizing that the things that you did were sins against God? Is that right?"

Huff "Cathy, my whole life is a sin against God! That's the way I look at it. I don't see any good that I've done.

I don't see any blessing that I brought to anybody. And I don't see any good thing that I've done at all.

I wrote somebody a letter a couple years ago and I told him, 'All I was, was death.' And you can record that, I don't care. Because that's about the way I feel."

Cathy "Why is that? Do you, um, do you believe—"

Huff "Well, the best intentions of men and, ya know, just aren't adding up. And no matter what my intentions were; no matter how good I may have thought they were; and what I tried to do; it turned out rotten. And it turned out really bad. And it injured a lot of people. And it hurt a lot of people. And it influenced a lot of lives.

I don't say what everybody has done, in response to that—Liz, me, anybody, you, anything anybody's done—I don't say all those are godly. I don't say all those are right. But I am not the one to judge all that stuff.

To me, if you're going to live it, ya got to live it by the 'word.' And what the 'word' has to say is, 'Thou shalt, and thou shalt not.' It says, 'You put God first.' And you put Him first. Ya know, you worship Him and Him alone."

Cathy "Oh yeah, I believe that."

Huff "And worshipping Him, and in loving Him, you love your fellow man. That means you don't defraud, and you don't take advantage of them. And you don't mislead them or misguide them, or try to build yourself up, or set yourself up above them.

Or any shape, form, or fashion allowing yourself to become the one who is God's spokesmen, or His instrument, or anything else. Because when God chooses to use you, He uses you. If you're yielded to Him and you put Him first.

Well, the fact is, I didn't do that. And I hadn't done that. And because of it, I messed up a lot of people's lives."

Cathy "Do you not believe that it was the Devil leading you though?"

Huff "No, it wasn't the Devil leading me. There's a big difference in being deceived into doing something that you think is right—"

Cathy "I mean if you're in a deception ya know, he could be the one that is doing it."

Huff "You got the 'word' right there before you. What the 'word' says is very plain. It's very clear. God doesn't hide it. He makes it very, very plain for us to see it. Very, very plain for us to follow it. Doesn't make it easy to do it. But it's there."

Cathy "Well, how come you don't think it was the Devil? I mean, he's the Deceiver!"

Huff "If you think for one minute that I'm going to put responsibility for my sins off on anybody else. Or even a devil, *the* Devil, Satan, Lucifer, or the angels of deception or anything like that.

Then I'm not going to stand before God and say, 'Oh God, it was, ya know, the Devil made me do it.' That's not what this is all about. What this is all about is being accountable for your own actions."

Cathy "That's true."

Huff "And what my actions were, I'm accountable for them. It doesn't have anything to do with deception or—"

Cathy "So, you weren't deceived then? Is that what you are saying?"

Huff "No, I wasn't deceived."

Cathy "Oh, so you just knew full outright what you were doing? And it wasn't a deception?"

Huff "Well—"

Cathy "I mean, that's what I Am trying to understand."

Huff "Well, what I am saying to you, I didn't follow the 'word,' okay. As misguided as I may have been, and misled—"

Cathy "Well, you used the 'word' to justify everything?"

Huff "You can use the 'word' to justify anything, Cathy. You can pull scripture apart and dissect it. Take this verse, and that verse, and you can make it all add up to doing what you want it to do."

Cathy "Yeah, I know. A lot of people are doing that these days. I had asked Liz if you all knew anything about that Pensacola thing. You hadn't heard about any of that going on down there?"

Huff "I hadn't heard a word about it."

Cathy "I mean the only way I knew anything was from [WWAR] also. They had a program on it. But I see that as a major deception, and I was hoping that you all did too, because—"

Huff "I hadn't even heard anything about it."

Cathy "It would at least help me to see where you are at, because I've had feelings in my heart about things, and I know that unless someone—

Ya know, I don't judge your heart. And I will never do that. But...what's in your heart, does come out of your mouth. And I know even now, you don't admit that any of that was the Devil working? I mean, he—"

Huff “Look—”

Cathy “I considered—When I look back—La’el Ministries was a cult. I mean it was! The Devil, he was the leader of that group. He was the head ‘man’ that people looked to. I mean, not me. If I felt like the Devil was involved with anything I did, I would not have done it. I think you believe that.

But the things that were done there, that was not God, the Almighty. It was—I believe it was the ‘god’ of this world. Are you saying you don’t believe that?”

Huff “Don’t you see anything that people have to do with this, Cathy? I mean, this isn’t just a battle between God and Satan here.” [Editor’s note: ***Oh yes it is!***]

Cathy “Well, it’s when you submit to sin, which will lead you to walking with the Devil.”

Huff “Cathy, if you do not follow the word of God, if you do not listen to it, and do not heed it—”

Cathy “You fall into a trap. That’s what I consider it.”

Huff “No, if you don’t do it, it’s called sin.”

Cathy “Well, yeah—”

Huff “And sin separates you from God. You know, for whatever purpose, for whatever reasons that people do it, you know, do their own thing. There are certainly evil influences out here. There are certainly satanic forces at work out here that disrupt God’s people; to disrupt the work of the LORD; to destroy people’s lives.”

Cathy “But you know what? In our last conversation, you even said that if I think I can’t be deceived by the Devil, then I already am. Do you remember that?”

Huff “Yeah.”

Cathy “I mean that thought has just come to me; that you said, ‘That if you don’t think that you can’t be deceived by the Devil, then you already are...’ ” *[See page 122 of this book.]*

Huff “Very much so. I mean I’m not going to sit here and say that Satan didn’t have any influence. And Satan didn’t have any ya know, guide, guidance, or something like that involved in the things that took place at La’el Ministries, or at the Bible study, or anything else. I’m not saying that.

I'm just telling you that I'm not going to put the responsibility off on somebody else, because I had a choice."

Cathy "Well, that's true."

Huff "I had the choice to respond godly by the word of God and follow His teachings, or I had a choice not to. There were many times that I chose to, and there were times that I chose not to."

Cathy "Yeah, well, you—"

Huff "Well, we could call it, well, you were deceived. You could say, 'Well, yeah, Lord, I didn't understand all that. And I was misled, and all that.' But that doesn't relieve me for the accountability before the Lord for it."

Cathy "Well, I understand that, actually."

Huff "Ya know, I'm just not going to run around here and call everything Satanic, and deception. And say it wasn't my responsibility, and it wasn't my fault. Those things were my fault. Those things were my responsibility. And I didn't honor that responsibility very well. And because I didn't honor that responsibility, things happened.

Sin got planted and it grew a crop. And when that crop came to fruition it wasn't very pleasant."

Cathy "No, *the Devil's work never is*—" *[Emphasis mine.]*

Huff "But we all have a choice of whether we are going to listen to the word of God and do what He says, or whether we're going to allow ourselves to be tempted into sin; or fall away from the Lord; or seek the things that the flesh desires or whatever. Ya know, we all have that choice."

Cathy "Yeah?"

Huff "But the bottom line is the 'word' has something to say—A truth to say about our conduct, about our thoughts, about our intentions, about our actions, and about the way we live."

Cathy "Oh yeah."

Huff "And we can live according to the word of God if we so choose to. If we choose not to, things happen. Things happen both ways, but that's just how it is."

Cathy "Ya know, this is a four year anniversary of a date that's really important to me. I don't know, do you realize that?"

Huff "No."

Cathy "Oh."

Huff "I don't keep up with days."

Cathy "Oh. Well, I do, actually. Ya know, the 28th of February is the Day that the LORD revealed the Truth to me about [you and] La'el Ministries. And ya know, that's kind of become a bittersweet day for me.

I have to tell ya, that I'm not pleased about the way things have ended up between some people that I really loved. You were among those people, but um, I still would—"

Huff "Cathy, I am not worthy of anybody's respect, or anybody's love. You know, you are doing yourself an injustice by not, ya know, if you have the truth, then you are doing yourself an injustice by not associating with Liz. Because she is a very godly woman. She sees the truth. She knows the truth. Ya know, Cindy listens to Liz, and she knows the truth.

I am not about to begin to have relationships with anybody. Ya know, I'm not having leadership, ministry, discussions, or anything with anybody.

Ya know, I've done this on the phone, but this is the first time in about four years. Because I'm not doing that. That's not who I am."

Cathy "I guess you quit—"

Huff "But you are doing yourself a great disservice. Ya know, you really ought to be before the Lord about whether you need to go ahead and begin to make some contact with her. I told you this two years ago.

Ya know, I didn't call you to try and reconcile yourself to me. Cuz that ain't going to ever happen. But I called you to tell you that ya know, you ought to at least open yourself up to the possibilities of being able to stand upon the truth that the LORD'S given you—"

Cathy "Oh, I believe I already do that."

Huff "And carry that truth to Liz, and you all discuss it. Ya know, because if you're wrong, if you've missed it in some areas or something, ya know, let the Lord open your eyes to that. If she's missed it in some areas you might be the instrument God uses to open her eyes in some areas."

Cathy "Well, can you tell me, do you still have the same opinion of the Twenty-eighth of February of Ninety-Three, as you did when I talked to you last?"

Huff "What was my opinion then? I don't remember."

Cathy "Oh, you don't remember?"

Huff "No."

Cathy "Well, basically, you didn't believe it was of the LORD. It was just Cathy leading, ya know, standing up and saying some things. At first I know Liz had, through a letter, told me that she thought it was of the Devil; and then she changed her mind, and said it was just me—Ya know, what I was doing. Do you still believe that?"

Huff "Well—"

Cathy "That event really is kind of like a turning point in my life. It's kind of like an instrument I use to gauge where people are at with the LORD. Because I know that that was not Cathy... That was not—certainly not the Devil.

It was Jesus Christ coming into that room. And you were a witness to it. And it amazes me, when I think about it, that God would actually show up in such a way. And He did! And it seems like I Am the only one that believes that it was... My family does, they know that it was the LORD. There has never been any question there.

But you and Liz, and even Cindy—I haven't really talked to Wendell about what he really thinks, but you all don't feel like that was God, and I would like to understand why not? Why is there...a major division there?

And that is one of the main reasons why there hasn't been a reconciliation between me and you, or her, and any of you all. That is, I think, *the defining moment in all of it.* Because, you know, everything that happened between me and you, and between me and Liz, and any of you all could be set aside. I believe. *But it's the way that the LORD was treated, is my concern.*

And it's the same—I mentioned in a letter to her that I Am not attending a fellowship right now. And it wasn't meant to imply that she knew my business. It was meant to say that she would understand. I didn't realize, or think that you all had knowledge of what I Am doing. *[Emphasis mine.]*

But I would think that you would understand that *the LORD is not well received among many churches...And He is with me.* I know He is. But He is rejected. Him inside of me is rejected. And when it's just Cathy, she is very welcome. When it's Him though, He is not welcome. And um, I guess I would like to understand why you don't think it was Him?" *[Emphasis mine.]*

Huff "Well—" *[He was very reluctant to answer this question.]*

Cathy "And why do people reject Him so much? I had really hoped in that letter that I wrote to you—I know it was a long letter, and I was trying to work out, even in my own heart and mind, why the things happened between us. And I was hoping that you were so deceived, and deluded, and overcome by the Devil that you came to the point that you realized that. And came out of it; and asked God to forgive you. And I was hoping that *that* is what would happen to you, but apparently it didn't, because you don't even want to—I mean you take credit for what happened, but it's almost like—I don't really understand there."

Huff "What do you want people to do? I mean how do you want— How do you want me to respond to my sin? Do you want me to excuse it away by saying, 'Well, gee Lord, Satan deceived me here?' And ya know, because I was so deceived...I'm not really responsible for my actions?"

Cathy "Oh no, you're responsible and held accountable. Even me, I have been greatly affected by what I did. I have never said that, but I know if I had gone in full well realizing that the Devil was influencing my thoughts and my actions, I wouldn't have done much of what took place."

Huff "Well, I'm not going to sit here and tell you, yeah I sat there and said, 'Well gee, I'm just deceiving these people. And ya know, the Devil's in charge of my life.' That's not what happened at all. I don't think anybody—Well, I don't know, maybe there are. Maybe you believe it, I don't know. I can tell you that that's not the way it was. Ya know, I went in there with the best of intentions of serving God and—"

Cathy "Well, I believe people start out that way...I believe a lot of people start out with great intentions, and they get down the wrong road, and then they end up doing things that they don't understand the ramifications to, or what influence has taken them over.

And it's through sin that they get into that condition. Their own personal sin. But then, it's like you get to a certain point, and then it's definitely the Devil taking control. Do you not believe that?"

Huff "At times that happens. You know, there's a whole spectrum out there. You can't lump everyone into one category. Ya know, some things happen in people's lives. And some people are doing it through the very good heart intentions, and yet are either, by their own lusts, or cares and concerns for other things, ya know, get misled and get off track.

Some people may even have an evil heart. And they do...have a heart of evil. And they masquerade as ya know, wolves, ah masquerade as sheep...wearing all the clothing and the right words, and with all the looks, and the right stuff, but inwardly they are ravenous wolves. Jesus talked about those...

So, you're asking me to define me. Well, that's what I've tried to do. I'm not trying to classify everybody into one particular group of people, or make everything fit a formula for sin occurring in their lives. The whole formula is this—If ya want a formula, ya know, the formula is this.

Ya know, without Jesus Christ and His blood shed on the cross, there's no forgiveness of the sins. And if a person refuses to accept Jesus, and accept that blood sacrifice for an atonement for their sins, then they will die in their sins."

Cathy "Well, are you refusing to accept the fact that He showed up in our living room that night? Do you not believe that?"

Huff "What night?"

Cathy "The 28th of February. The last night you preached in my home. You don't remember that night?! It should have been an eventful night for all concerned. It was for me!"

Huff "Cathy, the events—Ya know, to be honest with you—"

Cathy "I hope you will be."

Huff "I'm not really thinking about what's, ya know, what all that has—I do not remember the specifics, okay?"

Cathy "Well, that night, I mean it was the last night you preached. You have to remember that very well. I mean I started praying in the Spirit. That was definitely not my normal character."

Huff “I remember the night. I remember what happened. You want me to give you my assessment of that? That I—”

Cathy “Yes, I would love to know that.”

Huff “Okay, my assessment was this: You were right on with the fact that there was sin in the camp. That there was sin in my life. That there was...sin leading and misleading, and permeating every aspect of what we were doing. The— It’s not so much that night that I disagree with. It’s what happened after that night.”

Cathy “On the Second of March?”

Huff “No.”

Cathy “That night you all came over to talk?”

Huff “No, it’s what happened with you in beginning to be—In taking on the role, or whatever it was. I don’t know. Ya know, all I know is—”

Cathy “Taking on what role?”

Huff “That you somehow decided that you were going to make everything that had ever transpired, ya know, in all of our lives, a matter of public record. And ya know, the attacks, and the ya know, the degrading of individual people.”

Cathy “What do you mean by that?”

Huff “Well, I mean, you went to other people. You talked. You wrote letters. You shared. Ya know, well, I don’t really know. I mean the only thing I got, is what you wrote to me. Okay? I’m not going by—”

Cathy “Well, go by what you know. Not necessarily—”

Huff “—by hearsay here. But I’m just going on what you’ve written to me.”

Cathy “Yeah?”

Huff “Ah, ya know—”

Cathy “Is anything in that untrue?”

Huff “What the ‘word’ has to say about that is, ya know, if you find your brother in sin, you go to him.”

Cathy “I went to you, don’t you remember?”

Huff “And I got no problem with you rejecting me. And I got no problem with...you blasting me. And calling sin, sin. I don’t have any problem with that, Cathy.

What I have a problem with, is you doing it outside the realm of God's love. Now that may be my personal preference. And that may be my personal choice. But for me...it's almost like the woman caught in adultery, or any sinner that Jesus came to—He reached down to them and said, ya know, thy sin be forgiven thee, go and sin no more."

Cathy "Yeah?"

Huff "And to ya know, to almost treat somebody like, 'Well, I know that you are not going to repent; and I know you are not going to stop sinning; and I know that you're not going to, you know, acknowledge anything here...*then I'll just become your enemy*, and I'll just blast you up one side and down the other.' And—" *[Emphasis mine.]*

Cathy "And that's what you've taken, as what I've done?"

Huff "Well, you asked me?"

Cathy "Well, that's okay. I'd like to understand."

Huff "I just tried to tell you real honestly that I think you were right on with what you said concerning sin. I think you were right on with ya know, your personal assessment of the situation."

Cathy "Yeah?"

Huff "But when it came to reaching out in love—"

Cathy "It's what I've done afterward? That's what your problem is?"

Huff "And not responding—And ya know, a godly response to a sinful person, ya know. I mean it just don't add up in the word of God. That's not what the 'word' says to do. The 'word' says, yeah, if they don't stop sinning—It says to separate yourself from them. It don't say one word about taking them into the judicial courts of the world."

Cathy "I haven't ever done that. You all are the ones who dragged me in there. That wasn't my doing."

Huff "Dragged you where?"

Cathy "To that court room. Don't you remember?"

Huff "What court room?"

Cathy "In [the county]."

Huff "That wasn't—I didn't have anything to do with that!"

Cathy "Well, I didn't either. That was someone else having me come."

Huff “You didn’t feed Steven all that information? Ya didn’t, ya didn’t, ya know—”

Cathy “Yes, well. After—”

Huff “Here you took all the things—”

Cathy “Well, I—If you really want to know what happened. I don’t know if you do or not?”

Huff “Yeah, I’d like to know.”

Cathy “Ya know, after 28 February 1993, that *very* significant date for me; and then on 2 March—it was really obvious that we were against one another in our views. If you want to put it *mildly.*

...That *was* the LORD working in me. And it wasn’t Cathy... saying, ‘Okay I’m going to get at you.’ Because there’s never been a revenge in my heart towards you. I don’t know if you realize that or not? But there has never been.

But I know that based on everything that took place, I felt very inclined for people to know about what had happened to me. And that I had been involved in a cult group for three years. That I was not—That I was definitely being influenced by an evil influence. Not by God.

Because I professed to be a Christian all that time. I professed to be serving the LORD. And there was just something in me that I wanted people to know what I had been involved with. And the only desire in having people know what I went through—

Because I was very willing to go into the adulterous relationship I had with you. Ya know, people that are trying to hide something, they would not have talked about that, but I told everybody what I had done. And I wanted them to know that I was in a deception. I was!

And ya know, Cindy’s family—It was very important for them to know. And [my Husband’s]...family, I told all of them. Ya know, it was on the sixth of March that I got together with Cindy’s family. And it was only—The only purpose in mind there was to warn them of these dangers. And that’s why any of that took place.”

End of Transcript

THE TAPE ON MY ANSWERING MACHINE RAN OUT, so I ended my conversation at that time. The following transcript is a continuation of the discussion that I had with Mr. Huff on 2 March 1997.

CONVERSATION BETWEEN CATHY AND MR. HUFF
SUNDAY 2 MARCH 1997

Liz "Hello?"

Cathy "Hello?"

Liz "Yes?"

Cathy "Is this Liz?"

Liz "Yes, it is."

Cathy "Oh, hi this is Cathy. I guess you got up?"

Liz "Yes."

Cathy "Or did I wake you?"

Liz "No, [Mr. Huff] said you had called. Did you want to talk to him again?"

Cathy "Well, uh, it doesn't matter. I know I was in the middle of a statement, and I told him that I was recording our conversation so that [my Husband]...could listen to it later. Because he's not here right now. He doesn't really want me contacting you all unless he knows about it. And I explained that to him at the beginning. And I was looking for one of those little tapes. And I don't have any more."

Liz "Well, I'm sorry. Did you want to talk back with him?"

Cathy "Um, I guess just for a moment. I guess just to finish what I was saying."

Liz "...telephone." *[Speaking to Mr. Huff.]*

Huff "Hello?"

Cathy "Sorry I took so long. I was looking for one of those little tapes, and I couldn't find one. You know, the kind you put in the recorder? It had run out. I didn't realize I was going to talk to you for that long. I won't keep you much longer. Are you watching a ball game?"

Huff "No. I was just sitting down here. The T.V. was on."

Cathy "Well, I was just mentioning to you what I think about what happened. After I got out of your Bible study group, there was just a real desire in me to let people know what I had been involved with.

And there wasn't a—And there still is not a desire to hurt any of you all, actually. It seems that you see otherwise. And you seem to think I Am not very loving, but I know that the more I see how God is, a lot of what looks to be not loving, actually *is*.

...He knew where I was at when I went to La'el Ministries. And He knew what would happen to me. And He let me go through that place. And actually, that was very loving of Him. Because of the things that happened I—

Kind of what you all said at the beginning, I was very self-righteous. And you remember—I don't know if you remember some of the things that you said that you did?

Like you would cuss in front of me. And that one time when you and Liz had sex right in front of me. You said it was to kind of break me of my self-righteousness. To be accepting of some of the things that go on. And not be so shocked. Do you remember that?"

Huff "Cathy, I remember that a lot of things that took place were ungodly. You want me to focus on the things that were godly; it's very difficult for me to come and see very many things that were right. Or very many things that were godly here.

Now you know God uses any situation that we get involved in. Whether it's His leadership or our own stupidity. Ya know, He guides us, and He leads us. And for the heart that seeks after the LORD, He'll work it out. But ya know, He says—Takes everything that—"

Cathy "And He did too."

Huff "He takes everything and turns it around for good to them who love Him, and for them who are called according to His purposes. Ya know—

I'm going to swap phones here cause I can't hear on this port-a-phone anymore."

Cathy "Is Liz on the other end?"

Huff "I don't think so. But—"

Cathy "But I don't mind. In fact, I wouldn't mind if she is so she knows what you say to me."

Huff "I don't either. I mean, you know, I'm not trying to hide anything here. But there were a lot of things that were wrong.

And ya know, you can't take a bunch of things that are wrong and add them up and make them right.

And you can't look at it from a standpoint of well, they did this right and they did this right, and they did this wrong and they did this wrong. That's not the way I'm looking at it. However other people look at it, it's how they look at it. I don't care. All I know is what I have to do to look at it.

And I don't see righteousness reigning. And I don't see Jesus being Lord. And I don't see goodness coming out of it. Out of what took place at La—At the Bible studies, and all that kind of stuff.

And you know, you're not going—You're going to be hard pressed to come to me and talk about ya know, this happened and this was good. Look, if any good happened, it's not because of me, it's not because of what I can do. Or what anybody else can do.

Jesus said it very aptly, He said, 'Why call Me good, only My Father in Heaven is good.' Anything good that happens comes because of the goodness of God. And Him working in people's lives. Ya know, how He works is His business. Not mine."

Cathy "Well, Liz stated in her letter that you admitted that your relationship with her was wrong from the very beginning?"

Huff "It was. I was married to Becky. And I should have honored that commitment."

Cathy "Have you not ever wanted to get back with her?"

Huff "That's forbidden by the word of God, in case you don't remember. Ya know, you go look to the 'word' and you'll find that that's forbidden."

Cathy "What?"

Huff "That when a man leaves a woman and marries somebody else, it is forbidden for him to go back to that woman. But that doesn't have anything to do with ya know, the relationship now. Ya know, all I'm doing is looking at where I am today. And you know, you can't go back and—

The sin—If you commit sin, it's like an act. Ya know, you go out and wreck your car, you can't stand there and say, 'Oh God, make my car whole again.' "

Cathy "No, you got to get rid of it and start over."

Huff "And you got to—Ya know, there's things that have to be repaired. There are things that have to be fixed. But the fact is that the car's been wrecked. That happens to lives a lot too."

Cathy "Well—"

Huff "My question back to you is what we were talking about, ya know—"

Cathy "What?"

Huff "It's not me here anymore. Because, ya know, I'm not leading anybody. And I'm not *trying* to lead anybody. I'm not out here trying to—"

Cathy "Have you not led anybody, or had a group since the—"

Huff "Right after—A few months after all that happened—Ya know, this one just passed into oblivion, and that's been it."

Cathy "Yeah? So actually the prophecy did come to pass?"

Huff "What prophecy?!"

Cathy "The Twenty-Eighth of February. You seem to think that that's *so* insignificant. Actually, everything that was said that night, by the LORD, *is* coming to pass."

Huff "Well, whatever. I don't care. I mean, I really don't! Ya know, good, or bad, or indifferent. It doesn't make any difference to me!"

Cathy "But you still don't think it was the LORD? Is that right?"

Huff "I never said that, Cathy! I told you that I thought you were right on—"

Cathy "Well, now, now. I know Cathy can be right on if she is with the LORD. But do you still not believe that that was His Spirit coming into our—Into *my* room?"

Huff "There was the Spirit of the Lord there, but there was something else there also."

Cathy "What?"

Huff "There was a spirit of condemnation. And that's not from God. There was a spirit of, of hatred that was there. And that wasn't from the Lord. Ya know, if your brother is in sin, or your sister's in sin, and you really have the heart of the Lord to bring them out of that sin—"

Cathy "You talk to them first, of course."

Huff "Well, now there's an over-riding love that Jesus had in His heart for people that over-rode everything. The whole point here was— I can understand, Cathy, your vengeance against me. I can understand that. I can understand—"

Cathy "I don't have a vengeance against you, actually."

Huff "Look, I can understand your words against me. I can understand you wanting to go here in the society, in the world, and to the Church, and Christians, or families or anything else and saying, 'Look this man is not from the LORD. This man has done this, this, this, and this. I was an eye witness to these things.' I got no problem with that."

Cathy "You don't?"

Huff "No. The point is, here you drug other people into it.

Excuse me, hang on a second.

But you carried it beyond that. You carried it to the innocents."

Cathy "To the what, now?"

Huff "The innocents. Those who were innocent."

Cathy "What do you mean?"

Huff "Other people got caught up into it who were innocent."

Cathy "Like who?"

Huff "Liz is innocent."

Cathy "How is she innocent?"

Huff "She didn't buy into this. She came to you for months, and even years before all this happened and said this ain't right. She was telling you these things from the very beginning and you would never listen. And because of it, Liz today, is branded as a witch in this world!"

Cathy "Really?!"

Huff "Cindy didn't see it. Cindy didn't go along with it. Cindy was listening to, to, ya know, to the truth, and trying to follow that. It didn't have anything to do with them siding with me, or siding with you. It had everything to do with them siding with Jesus. With the truth. And ya know, beyond—Ya did go out. And March the sixth as you just said, you went. And you talked to an ungodly family. Who took Cindy to court. And took her daughter away from her. And now that daughter is in worse shape than you could ever imagine."

Cathy "How's that?"

Huff "How's that?! She sold herself to the world, because she has no godly influence in her life."

Cathy "Well, they go to church don't they? I don't know Steven very well—"

Huff "Cathy, you've been around out there, in the church world, enough to know that people that go to church are not necessarily godly, spiritual people."

Cathy "Well, I Am quite aware of that, yes."

Huff "Well, these aren't godly spiritual people. But yet, because of your desire to share everything, and tell everything; you went beyond where you needed to go. That wasn't from the Lord. That wasn't from God.

Cathy, Cindy never did anything to you. Neither did Liz. She—They warned—They got together with you and prayed for me to see the truth. It wasn't any of this, 'Oh we're siding with him, and you're totally wrong.' "

Cathy "Well, actually, Liz used to always accuse me of enticing you, and being a bad influence, and that I was doing things to—"

Huff "Well, were you?"

Cathy "No."

Huff "You never had any, in all that? You never had any desire—You never let your flesh, or your lust, or anything rule?"

Cathy "No, no that's exactly what *was* ruling. That's the problem."

Huff "That's the point she was trying to make to you. That was the whole point of what she was trying to come to you, and say look—"

Cathy "It was definitely lust..."

Huff "That's what she was saying to you. So she was—"

Cathy "Yeah, but I didn't understand that. And if she was so *spiritual* she should have—"

Huff "Cathy, she tried hundreds of times to talk to you about that. Your flesh just didn't want to hear it."

Cathy "Obviously."

Huff "Neither did mine. I mean let's be totally honest about it. Ya know, the whole point is that the flesh was ruling..."

Cathy "Well, do you remember that conversation when I first came there? You had asked me who you were to me."

Huff "And that was as ungodly as all get out."

Cathy "But you know what? I *did* hear those things that—"

Huff "I'm sure you probably did hear those things."

Cathy "—that you had suggested that I heard. Of course, the first thing was that you would be my teacher. I mean, not actually teacher, that 'I would learn a lot from you,' was more accurate. And so we deduced from what I heard, that you would be my teacher.

But also the fact that you would be my husband. And that...was the seed planted that kind of helped lead the other stuff on. *But I heard those things. Those were real voices. [Emphasis mine.]*

And uh, do you not admit that you can pray and cause people to hear voices? Ya know, because how would you know that I would hear the same thing?"

Huff "I'm not going to pray—I don't have that kind of influence in people's lives! I can't pray and ask God to reveal some voice in somebody's head that's ungodly!

You got a scripture sitting right there that says be the husband of one wife. I mean that is what the scripture has to say. It doesn't say go out here and attract unto yourselves women and men who call you their, ya know, husband. That's not what the scriptures say. We have the 'word.' The 'word' is the guide."

Cathy "You used to bring David into it. Remember him and all his wives? That He would give him all those thing?"

Huff "Absolutely. You can take the word of God and justify anything you want to do with it.

But that don't necessarily make it true. Doesn't make it godly. And it don't make it right on with the Lord. And what I'm just saying to you is, that ya know, the things—

I didn't have any problem with you standing up and saying—I mean, well, my flesh did, but looking back on it four years later, I'm saying, 'No this woman was right on when she said, Yes, that there's sin in the camp. Yes, there's things that need to be taken care of.'

But instead of allowing the Lord to take care of it, *you took the Sword up in your own hand. [Emphasis mine.]*

And you somehow heard, and—Ya know, you ought to—Need to remember, if you heard a voice that told you something that was ungodly such as, 'He's your husband,' that you could also hear a voice that, that—There's also another possibility, that you could hear a voice that says, *'You need to go out here and reveal this truth to everybody.'*

Because what happened in the long run of revealing the truth, was you not only isolated yourself, and alienated yourself from people who could probably benefit from a loving, kind, gracious, humble spirit; and teaching them how to avoid sin in their life. But in the process, a lot of other people got affected by it. *A lot of other people became victims of that Sword. [Emphasis mine.]*

Liz never did anything to you except encourage you, love you, care for you, talk with you, plead with you, pray with you, and beg you to listen to the word of God, and flee from sin.

And yet she's branded as a witch in this entire community because of some of the things that have been written and said about her." *[Emphasis mine.]*

Cathy "Because of me?"

Huff "Yes. I mean no one—Cathy, when you offer a Testimony to people in a letter that says the spirit of anti-Christ, what do you think ungodly people are going to do with that?"

Cathy "Well, they are going to have to take it before the LORD and let Him—"

Huff "They're ungodly! How are they going to take it before the Lord?"

Cathy "—and know if it's true or not.

Well, that night, the second of March, which is exactly this date four years ago—*Do you remember when I accused you of being of the anti-Christ?* And you would not deny it? You didn't deny it! You didn't deny it that night, and are you denying it tonight, or today? Do you deny that the spirit of anti-Christ led you in the activities that took place when I was with you for those three years?" *[Emphasis mine.]*

Huff "What do you want me to do, Cathy?! Which gate do you want me to go out so everybody can stone me?! So you can prove the point that I'm of the anti-Christ. Which one?! I'd be glad to! My life don't mean squat to me!"

Cathy "Well, do you remember what you used to tell me? That your life would be one of suffering and pain, and that you would die for your faith? Do you still believe that? Remember? That's what you used to tell me. And I—"

Huff "Yep."

Cathy "I used to be so concerned about that. And I used to even hate the way people would treat you."

Huff "That was nothing more than a fleshly ploy to get people to be sympathetic with me. And to get me what I perceived that I needed. And convince them that that's exactly what they ought to do. Not *knowingly* doing that. I mean, I'm not going to sit here and tell you that boy I had this wonderful plan. Cause that wasn't the plan. But instead of committing—"

Cathy "But you know what? You know what would make all of this more credible...? Is if you *did* admit that it was of the Devil. I mean good grief!"

Huff "Cathy, what it—I mean I—"

Cathy "I mean, it was! It had to be!"

Huff "That everything that I did was opposed to God?! That everything that I taught, preached, lived—"

Cathy "Well no, it was truth mixed with lies."

Huff "—was totally outside of the word of God?! And you want me to confess—Make some kind of confession that the Devil made me do it?! And I'm not going to do that to you! ... I told you that I'm not going to give Satan credit. I know that Satan had an influence here. And I know that he corrupted me. And he corrupted a lot of things that I did. And he, ya know, in his influences, and his demonic spirit world, and all the spiritual ramifications of evil took hold here. I know that. But if you think for one minute that I'm going around confessing before the world that *I'm some kind of anti-Christ—" [Emphasis mine.]*

Cathy "Well, what's anti-Christ? It means against—"

Huff "Cathy, the spirit of anti-Christ is denying Jesus Christ as Lord! Denying that He is the Son of God! That He died on the cross for man's sins! It is trying to get people to acknowledge that there is another "god" out there, other than Jesus Christ. I have not done that! And I never even did that! I never preached that! I never said deny Jesus!"

Cathy "...Something that I Am reminded of—It was a dream that I had about you, that I was telling Liz about. Do you remember that dream?"

Huff "No."

Cathy "It was a very strange dream. And it was like you were fixing to bow your knee to the Devil. And she freaked out when I said that. I brought that up in that letter. I know it was kind of long. I don't know if you got back to the—Did you read the whole letter?"

Huff "Yes."

Cathy "It was brought up in that."

Huff "It's been a while."

Cathy "But, you know, I actually dreamed that you were going to do that. And I know that there's people that do, do that. And I—"

Huff "But I don't! And I haven't! Not knowingly, willingly, with all the faculties, and senses, and intelligence, or lack of, that I have, or don't have, have never gone out to worship Satan. I have never bowed my knee to the Devil!"

Cathy "Yeah?"

Huff "But the ramifications of the things that I've done are exemplified by evil. Which means that I was not listening to God. That I was not following the 'word.' No matter how pretty it sounded. No matter how great it might have come across. Now if that ain't enough for you—For a man to admit that he's sinned before God. That he's sinned against God, that he's sinned against humanity.

Then ya know, I don't know anything I can call it beyond that. It's a spirit of revenge, or anger, or bitterness, or resentment, or something.

Because that's all that God asks us to do. That's all that Jesus said for us to do, is repent of your sins, confess your sins before God, and He's faithful to forgive you of those sins.

Well, let me tell you, I've spent a lot of time before the Lord confessing my sin; and I still have to spend a lot of time before the Lord. *And I have to live with what I have done. My sin, like David, is ever before me. I live with it every day. Day in and day out." [Emphasis mine.]*

Cathy "Have you not been forgiven?"

Huff "Yes, I have been forgiven! But that doesn't mean that I can ever attain to the positions, or fulfillment of the plan that God had for my life, because of the kind of sin of standing up proclaiming myself to be some kind of spiritual leader and teacher to other people, have them to follow me, only to find that we're all in the same *pit* together.

The blessed thing about it, is that if it—If there's anybody in a pit, I'm the only one in it. Everybody else has seemed to get out of it. Which is a blessing."

Cathy "For them or you? It's not a blessing to you?"

Huff "Yeah, it's a blessing to me. I'm glad people aren't wrapped up in me. I'm glad people aren't sitting there going ew, ah, come on, ya know, wup tee do. I'm glad they're not there. I rejoiced that people could find Jesus.

But I also will not stand behind something that says I'm being godly when *the things that I've done out here caused nothing but destruction. [Emphasis mine.]*

And what I'm saying to you is perhaps, there are things that have taken place because of the things, even you have done, with a godly intention, and yet have backfired out here. And virtually caused misery, grief, pain, anguish, suffering, and untruth to be placed in the lives of other people."

Cathy "Now I don't believe untruth. Anything that I have spoken or written has not been untruth."

Huff "Well, I'm not going to argue with you on that one, because for the most part I can't even remember what you've written. And I mean the letters are here, but I don't go back and read them. And I—Ya know, I read them when they came, and that's it."

Cathy "Well, I—That is something that I do not ever want to believe, is a lie. And I know I did when I was with you all. I believed a lot of lies. And something that I will always stand for is the Truth.

And if I should speak a lie, I would not mind it being brought to my attention. In fact, I would welcome that. *If I speak lies, I would have no problem with someone addressing that with me...*

You seem to think that, just by what you are saying, that I have vengeance and hatred. And *actually my hatred is more towards the Devil,* because he—"

Huff "Well, I tell you what, Cathy! If you don't have hatred and vengeance in your heart...Then you go to the godly people. The people who really seek after the Lord. Who are really earnestly seeking after—"

Cathy *"I would like to find them actually." [Emphasis mine.]*

Huff "Well, there's one of em right here! There's two of em right here. Liz and Cindy. If you really want to know the truth, then you prove it! I've proved it! I've proved that—That I will not preach lies, and deceit, and ungodliness, and untruth out here. By backing off, by not accepting any kind of speaking engagements, by not trying to organize any kind of ministry. In fact, I don't have one. I've done that."

Cathy "So, you don't have La'el Ministries anymore?"

Huff "I don't have nothing!"

Cathy "Ya'll quit doing anything to do with—"

Huff "That's what I'm telling you. I'm not doing anything!"

Cathy "Is Liz not considered La'el Ministries?"

Huff "Liz never was La'el Ministries. *I* was La'el Ministries."

Cathy "Oh."

Huff "That was it. But you mistakenly thought everybody else was. And they aren't. And they never were."

Cathy "Well Liz, on her little booklet that she published had La'el Ministries in the address."

Huff "Yeah, she published it under my leadership and my guidance. It didn't have anything to do with her being La'el Ministries.

But what I'm saying to you, if you really, honestly want me to believe, or want anyone else to believe it—That you really are after the truth. And that you do have the truth, then you go to the people who are seeking that same truth. And be reconciled to your brothers and your sisters.

And find ya know, a common ground to stand on here. And go to them. And share with them. And listen to them. And learn."

Cathy "Well, I have read her letters. And I have read some of the stuff she sent me, and I do want you to know that I don't think that...I can't hear evil spirits. Because I know I can.

And I know if I get into that self-righteous mode again, I will certainly fall again. And I hope that I don't.

But everything that I do, I feel led by the LORD. In fact, I felt led to call you. I was very nervous at the thought of speaking with any of you all. *Because I do believe that much of what took place was the workings of Satan. And even though I despise him, I respect him. [Emphasis mine.]*

And my hope is that people can learn from my mistakes. Because I have made many in my walk with the LORD. But ever since the 28th of February, I have been walking in a completely different Light than I have ever in my life. And I was hoping that maybe your view of that Day, that very *important* Day to me, was different. But I see that it is not.

And I do not have a vengeance for you. God will be the one that exacts His vengeance upon those that do not love Him, and those that have evil motives. And He is the one that will determine everything. I don't.

And I do want you to know, that what I do, is because I truly feel like He is leading me. It is not because I Am out to hurt you, or hurt Liz, or hurt Cindy. I have no desire for that. Actually, my desire right now would be to move away and never come back. That is really what I would like to do right now. And if the LORD desires for that to happen, it will."

Huff "Maybe the Lord desires for you to reconcile with your sisters, who never did anything to you in the first place."

Cathy "Well, I don't know, uh, I know Cindy—I don't feel like she ever had any evil motives toward me. I don't really know. But you know, I Am just basing things off of the results of what has happened, and what has taken place."

Huff "What are you basing it on? What has taken place? What—"

Cathy "Well, do you remember the night when you all came over on the Second? The night that you know—The 28th wasn't really a day that I feel like we broke-up. There was a revealing of some things that night, but the Second of March is when we got together. And privately I—It was still very private on the Second. It didn't become public until the continued refusal of wrongdoing. But on the Second, she was very mean towards me that night. Very, very hostile. And quite agitated at me because I wanted to bring up to Wendell, and to Cindy, and to my husband that what had taken place between me and you was absolutely wrong.

> But you tried to deny everything that night. Even with Kim and everything, when Liz and Cindy had already admitted to it... And you still were denying it until you saw that it was completely over. And that night she was even, ya know, wanting to deny it. And I guess it's—"

End of Transcript of 2 March 1997

THE TAPE RAN OUT, so I was not able to record the ending. When I called to speak with Liz on that Sunday afternoon of 2 March 1997, I did not realize that I would actually be speaking with Mr. Huff, but God did.

God also knew that Mr. Huff would confirm all the accusations that I made against him over four years ago on 2 March 1993, during our confrontational meeting. If you noticed, he was never able to admit that the One who appeared in my home on that night of 28 February 1993, was Jesus Christ who "is come in the flesh." (See I John 4:1-3)

Mr. Huff and Liz have tried not to allow their true colors to come through, but these next excerpts will show exactly how Liz feels about what God has led me to do since our separation. The following was her response to an open letter I sent out, of which she was included.

EXCERPTS FROM LETTER FROM LIZ DATED 5 MAY 1997

...Cathy, I am continually amazed by your words and actions! ...The unfortunate truth is that everyone knows your words, your "prophecies," and your actions do not conform to God's Holy Word.

"True Light Ministries" is an embarrassment. How can you adopt the title "True Light" when practically every written word you send out contradicts the direct words of Jesus as well as those of His followers.

I grimace in pain as I watch you condemn and judge yourself for "by your own words you are justified and by your own words you are condemned." You speak as the self appointed oracle of God, condemning, "God is against you and against WWAR." Jesus plainly stated in Mt. 7:1,2 "Judge not that ye be not judged, for with the same judgment you judge, you shall be judged and with what measure you mete, it shall be measured to you again."

You, Cathy, seal your own fate. Since that dreadful day, Feb. 28th, you have uttered only judgment, fault, and disagreement with every brother you come in contact with. It appears that from the 20th century, only Cathy...has felt the cleansing blood of Jesus! That is your viewpoint not the rest of Christ's Body.

You had no problem going to WWAR to tell them of your deliverance from your "cult," only to turn on them as you have every church you have visited since!

WWAR has wonderful programs and music. I heard your own testimony over their airways, praising them for the blessing they had been in your life. I certainly cannot say I agree verbatim with every word of every program, but they spread the gospel of Jesus Christ daily to many who could not otherwise receive food and drink from God's table.

I myself disagree with some aspects of Promise Keepers—the fact that many men spend 2 or 3 entire weekends away from their families—that it's closed to women and children.

But I have also seen the magnitude of good that Promise Keepers[49] *has accomplished in the lives of many men. Marriages have been saved, men have come to know Jesus, men have learned to be accountable to spiritual authority and the list goes on and on...*

One thing is certain, Cathy, no matter how many negatives, Promise Keepers preach Christ Jesus! And I therein rejoice and so should you! This is yet another example of your over eagerness to judge, knowing that it brings God's judgment upon yourself. God is simply not against...WWAR! Those are words of false prophecy! God plainly says that prophecy is not wrong but it should be for the edifying (that means building up, not tearing down of His Body). Paul also instructs that the Prophets should judge the prophecy of one another. Where dear sister, is your corroboration in this matter?

The truth, Cathy, is that you are accountable to no one—no pastor, no prophet, no one! You do not see fit to join yourself in the unity God's word commands to be part of any Body! You are accountable only to the voices in your head and they sadly lack scriptural basis for being from God's Holy Spirit!

Paul sternly warns in 1 Cor 4:5 "Therefore judge nothing before the time, until the Lord come, who both will bring to light the hidden things of darkness, and will make manifest the counsels of the hearts, and then shall every man have praise of God." The Lord hasn't come and He alone reserves the right of judgment. How you believe you are scripturally justified in your crusades startles me.

Jesus said judge their fruit. ...WWAR, and Promise Keepers all produce Godly visible ripe fruit. You, Cathy, on the other hand, produce strife, variance, scorn, and anger. Your fruits do not pass the Biblical standard. You are not united to Christ's Body, nor do you believe that "in any area one is lacking, God will reveal."

You use the term I AM in reference to yourself, and think your actions glorify the one and only True and Living God. They do not.

A careful reading of His word would reveal this if your eyes were not so totally blinded. How I grieve that even the uncorruptible word of God fails to convict your own heart.

God is a truly blessed God, Cathy. He will allow you to continue to condemn His children and His word regardless of the damage it causes to others, but Praise His Holy Name, He Will hold you accountable for every word. Yours will be a high price to pay—when He comes and when He brings all things to light. Unfortunately for you, it will be too late and all your sorrow will not save you, Cathy. It is a fearful thing to fall into the hands of the Living God!

...You chose to ignore God's written commands to you and hide behind "True Light" which is really nothing but darkness. Satan does come as an angel of light, but his tactics bring lies and his whispers condemn others and fall far short from God's Word—the 'Word' that you claim to cherish.

Jesus said, "You will know My disciples because of the love they have one for another." Again Cathy, I ask you, as I asked you on Feb. 27th 1993, [She got her date wrong, it should be Feb. 28th 1993.] "Where is your love?" You attack the brethren, Cathy. You criticize every word anyone speaks. You have a ready-made prophecy for everyone you come in contact with.

Certainly no one outside, or inside for that matter, Christ's Body would know you for your love—even though you will no doubt argue that love points out one's faults. God's word says love is long suffering—you attack the first discrepancy you think you see. Love is not prideful, you judge and then send copies of your judgment to a mailing list. Love thinketh no evil and yet you believe the worst of others even when they confess and demonstrate the opposite. How many people, exactly, have you led to Jesus through your love?[50]

...Your anger drives you, Cathy. The same anger you profess that is absent within your heart. Your words and actions prove otherwise. ...For the first time, I can honestly say I have no desire to reconcile to you in your present condition. Until you see the "true light," confess your sin before God, and make restitution to those you have falsely accused, I have no desire for any type of relationship with you, Cathy. You have and continue to hurt multitudes of God's children with false prophecy and condemnation. God is not pleased nor am I! I love you, and continue to pray that somehow God will break through the darkness and your blindness. And yet, I realize that you have to want "true light" instead of power. You finally got your power, but it comes from the WRONG source!

The reason I said that your letter to WWAR was an answer to my prayers is because I have earnestly prayed for you, and since the last conversation you had with [Mr. Huff] (2 March 1997) I had asked God if the blindness you had experienced over the last 4 years was finally being broken or not. Your letter answered all my questions beyond a shadow of doubt.

I pray that you will back off your hateful campaign—not because you're really hurting those you attack, everyone who gets your letters pays not the slightest bit of attention because they know you are not speaking God's words. The only reputation you've acquired is one of being nuts! No one thinks you are the least bit spiritual—your words prove that!

I pray you will abandon this hateful treatment of others to spare yourself even harsher judgment on that Dreadful Day! That, of course, is your choice, but you will give account for refusing to heed God's word, His Spirit's leading, and the multitude of counsel that has spoken truth to you all along the way.

God have Mercy on Your Soul Cathy,

Liz

PS. Don't bother sending me any more of your "prophecies"

I'm not interested!

THAT WAS AN EIGHTEEN-PAGE, HAND-WRITTEN LETTER. The next day I received an eight-page typed letter from her. I have not included her entire letter, but I have referenced her first and last statements.

Cathy, *6 May 1997*

Since I'm sure you are still fuming from yesterday's letter, I will begin by assuring you that this is my FINAL letter to you.

I greatly debated over whether or not I should send it or not, knowing that my words are nothing more to you than silent winds that have no direction or meaning.

The reason, therefore, for this final correspondence with you is to fulfill my own responsibility before you and God over a teaching I gave you—one on which you have founded your entire new life—blasphemy of the Holy Spirit...

You SAY you don't want to be in the spotlight, but everything you do PUTS you directly there, Cathy! You say you don't like having to tell people the things God tells you to say, and yet, you not only say them—you mail copies to everyone you can think of! Of course you again say, GOD TOLD ME TO!!!

Let me tell you something, Cathy, if God wants you to do something, there will be complete peace inside your heart! And He will NEVER, EVER, EVER, command you to do something that violates His written word. Practically EVERYTHING you have done since Feb. 28, 1993, has directly violated His written word.

If you don't believe me, go talk to some pastor who knows of none of this, take your letters, our letters and tell him what you have done and ask him if he believes your actions have aligned to the written word of God. GET that multitude of counsel, Cathy!!!

Get 3 or 4. Believe me, I HAVE! I found many areas I was wrong in and many that I was not. The areas I was wrong in I confessed and turned from. Are you willing to operate in such a Biblical manner as this? Or are you determined to continue trusting the voices in your head?

If you are sure you're right, go get counsel!!!! What harm will it be for you to confirm yourself? Be honest, TAKE YOUR LETTERS!!!!! If your actions are truly from the Holy Spirit, you should have NO problem getting confirmation from a MULTITUDE of counsel!!!

May God bless you with eyes to see and ears to hear so that you may not grieve His Blessed Holy Spirit.

Liz

THAT WAS NOT HER FINAL LETTER TO ME. Included is excerpts from a subsequent letter that she had sent me several months later. Please keep in mind that her view is from the Darkness and *not* the Light.

Dear Cathy, *21 October 1997*

...This summer has been perhaps the most hectic of my entire life. Bobo (who was her grandfather) found a long-lost girlfriend he had before he met and married Mamaw. This woman was a nightmare! She hated him!

She took over $40,000.00 and then would not even speak to him. This was the reason he took to his sick bed in April and refused to get up. He was actually better physically than he had been in years, but he was so depressed and lonely for someone who hated him that he eventually killed himself...I found him. It was a mess! I didn't let Mother or the girls in to see him. I didn't want them to remember him that way. Dad and I cleaned up the mess after the coroner took away his body. Mother took it really hard.

He had threatened for 35 years to kill himself—just as his Daddy had before him. No one ever dreamed he'd do such a thing because he was so afraid of death. Mother and I spent the next 6 weeks cleaning up the house and getting his estate settled.

Seven weeks from his death, Dad's accident occurred. This was not unexpected, as I told you before, but it was nonetheless traumatic for everyone. I didn't miss a day of work. I closed at noon the day of the funeral and was back the next morning. [Liz worked for her father at their family business as a secretary.]

[Mr. Huff and I]...have been in counseling for over 3 months now with the assistant pastor...We meet with him 3 hours a week on Wednesday evenings and attend a marriage group on Sunday evenings. Things are getting dealt with finally.

[Mr. Huff] is finally beginning to come to grips with his own sin and being able to face all this head on. It has been extremely difficult for him as I'm sure you can imagine, but he has submitted to Doug (the assistant pastor), and Doug has been very firm with him.

Last week we dealt with our original sin in beginning our relationship. The next meeting, we are dealing with what happened between you [two] during the Bible study group. I'm expecting another emotional meeting for [him], but he is finally allowing God to deal with some sensitive issues he has refused to face until now.

...[Mr. Huff] had a close call two weeks after Dad's death. He was having such a hard time facing some things from the past that I was discouraged myself, and I had asked God if He knew that [he] was not going to be able to face the past, admit his sin, repent and be the man that I know God desires him to be, that God would call him home rather than allow him any further spiritual deterioration.

I know this sounds terrible, but I truly love the Lord and want to walk in Godliness. My relationship with [Mr. Huff] has suffered so over the years due to the sinful manner in which our relationship began, that I had pretty much given up hope of ever having any type of intimate loving relationship with [him].

We didn't fight, argue, disagree, or anything, we merely existed together. There has been no passion or desire on my part for [Mr. Huff]. I can live in this manner for the rest of my life, but [he] has agonized over our lack of intimacy and love. As a result, he has pushed in many areas, trying to get that back.

I knew I could never love and respect a man who could not face the past, deal with it honestly and admit his own responsibility for the destruction he has caused so many others—you included.

My respect, love, and trust of him has been shattered, and only a total turning to God in repentance could ever change the emotional damage that has resulted in my own heart over the past.

So, in desperation and fatigue of [Mr. Huff's] insistence that we just simply forget the past and start over from here, I asked God for His intervention. I increased his life insurance, took out burial insurance and waited. His blood pressure was through the roof. He's taking medication that doesn't even seem to touch it.

Then 2 weeks after the funeral, we were all out at the farm installing a field line for Julie's (Liz's sister) trailer. [Mr. Huff] jumped on Daddy's tractor and made a run through the pasture where Ken (Liz's brother in-law) was going to dig the line with the back hoe to bush hog the area, and when he got back to the edge of the property and turned around—at the edge of a 14' creek bank—a small sapling got caught in the bush hog and the tractor was pulled backward, flipped completely over, and fell 14' into the creek with [his] head buried in the mud UNDER 4' of water.

Fred (Sherry's husband and our local fire chief) ran the 1/10 of a mile to get to [Mr. Huff] and found him climbing up the steep bank, soaking wet, covered with mud from the creek bottom with only a scratch on his hand, one on his side, and one on his back.

Fred said he had NEVER seen anyone survive an accident even a fraction of the intensity of this one! It was truly a miracle.

I had so many mixed emotions at that time that I'm honestly embarrassed to admit them to anyone except my Father who knows already, but I was not relieved that he was alive. I was scared stiff that God HAD answered my prayer, and that it was not the answer I expected or had hoped for. He was going to be healed and I shuddered to think that I too would need immense healing as well!

The week before this accident, Doug had a word from the Lord for [Mr. Huff] during the service—which in itself is MOST unusual for our church, but he told [him] that God had instructed him to tell [him] that His desire for him was life and not death—that he would live and not die.

At this point, I was still skeptical, but that morning, I KNEW that Doug had clearly heard from God.

Four weeks after the accident, [Mr. Huff] was still so shaken from his near death experience that it was all he could talk about. He said it was not that he was not ready to die, he said, he longed for death—It was the shock that God had demonstrated beyond a shadow of a doubt that his work on this earth was not complete. [Mr. Huff] has struggled with many things since that Feb. evening.

On the one hand, he felt that he had been disqualified and that God would not forgive his sin, on the other, he would admit only partial responsibility for the things that had happened, but it was still not enough for him to ask God's forgiveness. He seemed caught in a paradox and would not be moved.

After this incident, however, [Mr. Huff] had to face the fact that God demanded him to face the past and move forward. The past few weeks of counseling have been the most intense as a result.

Surprisingly, my greatest concern wasn't [Mr. Huff's] adultery or unfaithfulness, but his refusal to take full responsibility for the destruction he had caused so many people—namely YOU! He admits that he was wrong, that he sinned against God, me, you, and himself, but he still wanted to blame others. His confession was incomplete, his repentance half-hearted.

I have never been able to forgive him for the pain he caused you and others because of his selfishness. I have not been able to forgive him for not taking responsibility for the situation and repenting whole-heartedly before God with tears through anguish of soul. I know what this means because I spent a year in this state before I was able to move forward.

I was so grieved about my own sin, my part in all this, that I went into a deep dark depression. It was not until I was able to counsel with a local minister that God was able to bring healing and soothe my aching soul. I know [Huff] has not felt that anguish. He's felt the anguish of failure, of disgrace, of loss—but he's not felt anguish because of his own sin and the effects that sin had on the lives of others until now.

It has been very difficult for him as it was for me. He's not through it yet. I'm sure it will not come in an instant, but it will come, and the anguish of true repentance is necessary and healthy for healing to come.

Like I said, our next meeting will be another emotional session because it deals with my hurts over [Mr. Huff's] treatment of you and our broken friendship.

I know that this meeting will be difficult for me as well because I have ALWAYS wanted [Mr. Huff] to shoulder ALL the blame. And from HIS perspective, he MUST, but I must be able to see both sides—his and YOURS.

Although I still truly believe you were deceived in your relationship with [Mr. Huff], I also know that you were clearly warned and refused counsel concerning your relationship...I have been angry at [him] for years now that I lost a dear and precious friend in you.

I have insisted that HE carry ALL the weight of the guilt. I do not look forward to having to forgive him, and see your part in that relationship in clear terms.

I just wanted him to make everything all right between us, no matter what that took from him. I now understand that one reason that you cannot go on where this relationship is concerned is because you too, want [Mr. Huff] to carry ALL the responsibility.

Like [Mr. Huff], you admitted your part in all this with your mouth, but your heart still relegates ALL the blame to [him]...even though YOU insisted that God told you, you were to be a wife to [Mr. Huff]...He wasn't the only one who pushed, but in your heart, it is easier to blame someone else, just as it has been for him to blame someone else.

You will never know the anguish I am presently facing as God deals with my heart concerning your part in all this, Cathy. Certainly [Mr. Huff] was MUCH MORE responsible here because he was a leader—one entrusted with God's Holy Word—one entrusted to lead God's chosen people, but you did not submit to this relationship without knowledge of God's word, without warning from MANY others, nor with a clear conscience. To me, THAT STINKS!!! I STILL want to blame [Mr. Huff] and not YOU!!! Please pray for me that I may be strengthened to receive God's direction and that I may once and for all forgive [him]...

You are never far from my thoughts or prayers...I love you and hope you continue in grace and wisdom, walking in the strength of the Lord, directed by His will for your life.

Love,
Liz

HER USE OF FLATTERY, CONDEMNATION, GUILT, FEAR, LIES, HYPOCRISY, vain words, false humility, deception, sympathy, and anything else she has tried to use in order to persuade me to come back, has not worked.

Sin is the doorway into Darkness, and should I ever get lifted up in pride and arrogancy again, I would once more be blind to the Truth, something of which I earnestly pray will never happen.

I wrote the following letter in response to the suicide of her grandfather (6/12/97), and the sudden death of her father (8/18/97), who died from the fatal injuries that he sustained after being thrown from an elevated platform on top of a forklift where he had been standing.

Liz personally informed me of the details of his hospitalization and death because she wanted to make sure I heard the correct story. She said God had told her it was going to happen, and strangely, she did not even have a hint of sorrow in her voice while she spoke to me about it.

Liz told me that her father and his crew knew the forklift had defective breaks prior to his headlong fall into the cement pit; and I Am sure they deeply regret that they did not heed the warnings.

Dear Liz, *22 October 1997*

I find it very difficult to be as open with you about my life as you seem to be with me; and even though you have expressed in a past letter that you really have no desire to hear from me ever again, I do feel compelled to at least respond to your recent letter that I received today. However, I will try to be as brief as possible.

You don't seem to trust my words, and I do understand, but I did want to say that I Am sorry for what your family has been going through. I know that it has been very hard on all concerned.

If the end result has caused people to seek the LORD, then God's word has been confirmed again. "And we know that all things work together for good to them that love God, to them who are the called according to His purpose." Romans 8:28

I just praise God that He has allowed me to be a recipient of His love and mercy. Regardless of whether you believe me or not, I do take complete responsibility for my actions while I was with La'el Ministries. I know God will judge each one of us individually, and I do not blame you, Mr. Huff, or Cindy for anything that happened with me. It was my sin that blinded me to the Truth. It was my sin that caused me to do some things that I Am extremely ashamed of—And I will take that shame to my grave.

I Am just so thankful that God is so forgiving and so wonderful that He does not hold our sins against us if we are truly sincere and repentant.

I do want to say that I still make mistakes, and I Am certainly not perfect. If I find I have been wrong or presumptuous in my treatment of any of you, I will be the first to ask for your forgiveness. But you know me, if I truly believe that I Am right in God's eyes, no "man" can persuade me otherwise. Although, I Am sincerely sorry if I have ever responded to any of you in an unbiblical way. I truly want to live by every word that proceeds from the mouth of God.

That's been my desire ever since I first committed my life to the LORD over seventeen years ago, but self-righteousness and pride has always been a great hindrance. (You even confirmed that to me when I first met you nearly seven years ago.)

One of my most earnest prayers before the LORD is that I won't be found guilty of that sin, or any other sin, when I finally get to stand before my God face to face.

I was intrigued with your final statement in the eulogy for your father that you sent me: "Walk with Him faithfully for we do not know at what time He may come for us."

I look forward to that great Judgment Day with mixed emotions, but I look forward to it nonetheless. May God's people truly be prepared for the great and dreadful Day of the LORD, as it is closer than it has ever been!

Signed and sealed in the presence of a witness on the 31st Day of October in the year of our LORD, One Thousand Nine Hundred and Ninety-Seven.

I DID NOT GET A RESPONSE FROM LIZ right away as I usually do, but when I did hear from her, she was obviously very angry with me. It just proves to me that her hatred is still there, and I believe it always will be.

A FINAL NOTE

In light of the fact that the Devil has such a tremendous knowledge of God, he is able to mix just enough truth with his lies in order to lead people astray in an evil way. And many sincere people have fallen into that trap, of whom I Am one.

Moreover, I know if I ever get so prideful or over-confident to think I could never fall again, is when I really need to take heed. Thus, my earnest prayer before God is that He will reveal to me anything that would hinder my relationship with Him.

The scripture, *"Many are called, but few are chosen,"* confirms to me that God *is* calling certain ones to accomplish specific tasks, but He will not force His will upon them. And if you are one that God has been calling, please heed that very important call. You won't be disappointed!

A few thoughts for you to prayerfully consider: It is written, *"The LORD so cometh as a thief in the night..."* Based on that passage, if you are "asleep" and remain at His coming, you may only see the results of His visit here, but have no knowledge or understanding of what happened.

If you are abruptly awakened out of your sleep, the results could be devastating depending on where you are at, and what you are doing. Thus, the condition of your heart will affect how you respond to Him, and more importantly how He will respond to you.

But if you are eagerly awaiting and prepared for the LORD when He comes again, you may have a wonderful Testimony to share with this lost and dying world that really does need to hear from God!

I Thessalonians 5:1-10 "But of the times and the seasons, brethren, ye have no need that I write unto you. For yourselves know perfectly that the day of the LORD so cometh as a thief in the night.

For when they shall say, Peace and safety; then sudden destruction cometh upon them, as travail upon a woman with child; and they shall not escape. But ye, brethren, are not in Darkness, that that day should over take you as a thief. Ye are all the children of Light, and the children of the Day: we are not of the night, nor of Darkness.

Therefore let us not sleep, as do others; but let us watch and be sober. For they that sleep sleep in the night; and they that be drunken are drunken in the night. But let us, who are of the day, be sober, putting on the breastplate of faith and love; and for an helmet, the hope of salvation.

For God hath not appointed us to wrath, but to obtain salvation by our LORD Jesus Christ, Who died for us, that, whether we wake or sleep, we should live together with Him."

In Conclusion...

I would like to address those who have rejected the LORD or have fallen away from Him for whatever the reason. Whether it's based on a misunderstanding because of your own perceptions, or that of another; either way, the end result is the same: YOU NEED THE LORD!

Or, you may even possibly be someone that was also deceived, deluded, or misled into believing lies in place of the Truth; either way, the end result is the same: YOU NEED THE LORD!

Or, maybe you are one that has rejected the Church altogether due to an encounter with an improper representative of Jesus Christ; either way, the end result is the same: YOU NEED THE LORD!

Regardless of your individual circumstances, if you have never experienced the grace of God, and His incredible forgiveness, the end result is the same: YOU NEED THE LORD! And I hope you have come to that *same* conclusion.

I have made many mistakes during my walk with God; and even now I still have times that I feel so unworthy to be called a servant of the Most High God, but it just reminds me of how much I NEED THE LORD!

If you ever meet up with the one, true, and only living God, He can, and He will, fill the void in your life if you call upon the name of the LORD Jesus Christ from a sincere and repentant heart.

God will replace despair with hope; emptiness with purpose and meaning; hatred and bitterness with love and joy; discontentment with satisfaction; along with an abiding peace that nothing or nobody in this world could ever give you—Only Him!

All of us have an inner desire to love and to be loved, and only "True Love" that will last forever comes from Almighty God. He purposefully meant it to be that way, so that if we ever left Him out of our lives we would realize that something was missing; and hopefully we would go searching for Him.

But I Am so sorry to say that most people are looking for the love and joy that only God can give in all the wrong places.

God sent His Son to this earth to reveal the Truth about Him, His kingdom, and eternity, but so many people are too busy to even pursue a relationship with God, or they just outright reject Him.

Since God has begun to allow me to understand more fully what took place as He watched His Son live out His time on earth, one of the hardest things for me to deal with, is the pain and anguish that I Am sure my Heavenly Father went through while He stood by and watched as they made a mockery of His dear Son.

Could you imagine what it must have been like? Which of us would even consider giving up our only son with the knowledge that he was going to be ridiculed and laughed at by the entire world, beaten almost to the point of death, and nailed to a cross as a criminal, even though He was totally innocent!

But God knew it all! In fact, He planned it all! He knew that His supreme sacrifice was the only way to win the ultimate victory over sin, death, and Satan. That's what His love is all about—To love someone so much that you are willing to give up everything you are, everything you own, even your very life, so as to prove your love to the whole world. What an awesome God He is!

And you must know that has to be the most heartbreaking of experiences for a Father to stand by and watch the misuse, the abuse, and the eventual murder of His only begotten Son; unless of course the same was to happen to His wife. And I Am here to tell you that He has experienced that sorrow as well.

But just as the horrible death of His only begotten Son was not in vain, because Almighty God was able to raise Him up again; so too shall He bring back to eternal life His glorious bride that shall rule and reign with Him forever and ever, world without end. Amen!

My LORD and my God has most certainly endured great pain, suffering, and sorrow, and if you have not yet begun to know and truly understand why He would do all that He has done for all of mankind, then you really don't know the LORD God Almighty very well.

Nonetheless, the most important thing for you to prayerfully consider is whether or not you will be allowed entry into His glorious kingdom. And it all hinges on what you do while it is still called Today.

I ask you, who are you going to follow? There are only two choices. There is no middle ground in this battle for your soul. Satan would love for you to walk with him in his Kingdom of Darkness, but my dear Father would rather you joined Him in His Kingdom of Light.

And He proved it by giving you a way to be reunited back to Almighty God through His Son, Jesus Christ. And you *must* come through that Door! There is no other way to God and His Holy City.

God will forgive you for any rejection of Him because of your ignorance of the Truth, but if you purposefully reject the voice of God, and blaspheme His Holy name, you will not be forgiven in this world, nor in the world to come. Please consider what I Am saying.

It would be such an honor if God would use my Testimony to show the world that they need to be saved from Hell and eternal death, and only until you receive the free Gift of Life can it ever happen.

I will never forget the most wonderful gift that I was given by a young Marine in Yuma, Arizona. Even though I was a complete stranger, he just came up to me, handed me the word of God, and said, "Here, I think you need to read this." And praise God, I did!

I have told my children that the greatest gift I could ever receive from them, is if they would truly love, honor, and obey the LORD God with all their heart, soul, mind, and strength; and to love their neighbors as themselves—It would please me immensely.

And the same holds true for you! If you were to willingly give your allegiance to the one, true and only living God, and sincerely worship Him in Spirit and in Truth, due to the Testimony of Jesus Christ in my life, that would bring such a tremendous joy to my heart; and not to my heart only, but more importantly, to the heart of God!

Jeremiah 9:23-24 "Thus saith the LORD, Let not the wise man glory in his wisdom, neither let the mighty man glory in his might, let not the rich man glory in his riches:

But let him that glorieth glory in this, That he understandeth and knoweth Me, that I Am the LORD which exercise loving kindness, judgment, and righteousness, in the earth: For in these things I delight, saith the LORD."

To God's People...

I just could not conclude this book without saying that I Am so thankful to the people that God has allowed to be a part of my life, especially since being released from my Enemy's control.

That is not to say that I Am completely over my experience with those of La'el Ministries, but I have come to terms with how and why I came to be in that group, and I can actually say that I Am a much stronger person because of my walk with the Enemy.

Not because of the Devil's repeated attempts to lead me astray, but because of what I saw the LORD God Almighty do in spite of what Satan and his evil workers of iniquity intended.

You may not be aware of the ways that you help those in need, but always realize that if you are truly led by the Spirit of Christ, whether it be through word or song, you are making an impact on this evil world, and making a difference in the lives of those who belong to God.

If you are one who truly loves the LORD God Almighty, always remember and never forget, we will never be alone in this world; and even though we may be scattered about, it won't always be. We *must* always look to the "Author and Finisher" of our faith!

The LORD Jesus desires to be our strength in Time of trouble, but He can't be if we don't learn to lean on Him and His Holy Word. And if you have not yet fully trusted Him for your life, I pray you will.

I can attest to the fact that *He is* One that can be relied upon, and I Am certain that *my* God will never, ever, let me down. And if He is truly your God, the same holds true for you.

God's word is so amazing! When it is sincerely spoken in Truth, it can affect the hearts of men. Depending on your own heart condition, it will either strengthen you because it establishes the Truth more fully, or cause your heart to grow faint because it convicts you of sin.

And it is so important to acknowledge and repent of your sin *while there is still time.* The shame and disgrace that you experience now, cannot even be compared to what will happen should you stand before the LORD God Almighty condemned.

My last word to you is this: No matter what your situation is, don't give up! The LORD knows exactly what you are going through for His namesake, and He will reward you accordingly.

Keep contending for the faith! And know, if God be for you, it doesn't matter who is against you. His eternal Truth will prevail! Praise the Holy name of Yeshua HaMashiach—Jesus the Christ!

Luke 4:17-21 "And there was delivered unto Him the book of the prophet Esaias (Isaiah 61). And when He had opened the book, He found the place where it was written, The Spirit of the LORD is upon Me, because He hath anointed Me to preach the gospel to the poor;

He hath sent Me to heal the brokenhearted, to preach deliverance to the captives, and recovering of sight to the blind, to set at liberty them that are bruised, to preach the acceptable year of the LORD.

And He closed the book, and He gave it again to the minister and sat down. And the eyes of all them that were in the synagogue were fastened on Him. And He began to say unto them, This day is this scripture fulfilled in your ears."

HEAR, O ISRAEL: THE LORD OUR GOD IS ONE LORD! And may YHWH[51], the Holy One of Israel, truly bless those who love Him with all their heart, with all their soul, and with all their might! Amen.

Sincerely,
A servant of the Most High God,
C. Read

Signed and sealed in the presence of God as my witness,
on the 12th Day of May in the year of our LORD,
One Thousand Nine Hundred and Ninety-Four.

APPENDIX ONE

I sent the 27 August 1992 Prophecy to several others as I was led by the LORD, and this is the cover letter that I sent with it.

My Dear Fellow Saints, *26 June 1993*

To those that truly love the LORD God Almighty with their whole heart, soul, and mind. To those that truly love the LORD Jesus Christ from a pure and sincere heart. To those that sincerely love their neighbor as they do themselves. To those that truly desire to worship the LORD God in Spirit and in Truth. And to those who are willing to lose their life in this world so that they will gain more abundant Life in the world to come.

My sincere prayer for you as you read these Words is that the LORD will truly prepare your hearts to receive only His Truth. And may the eyes to your understanding be enlightened so that you can truly understand and experience the great love God has for us, and for all the world.

And as you experience His great love, my prayer is that you will share that love with others. And I pray that Almighty God will continue to pour out His abundant mercy and grace on us individually and collectively as the Body of Christ.

The LORD so desires to have a very personal relationship with each one of us. He so wants to share all that He is with us, but sin stands in the way. That's why I have found that it's so important to stay before the LORD God Almighty in His word and by prayer, so that He can reveal to us the things that are keeping us from fellowship with Him.

He has so freely given of Himself, but the world, and even some professing Christians, just throw His love back in His face. There is such a sorrow in my heart because as the LORD reveals Himself to me, I have started to truly understand who He is, and what He really did for us at Calvary. It so saddens me that I could have ever sinned against Him.

He is everything that is wonderful, and beautiful, and precious. And all He wants to do is love us and share His glorious Kingdom with us. And now, it's so hard for me, after having walked with Him for thirteen years, to understand why anybody would ever want to reject that.

But for some I realize it's because of their lack of knowledge of Him. And that is what this War is all about.

I have personally determined in my own heart that I want to serve Him no matter what that may entail. I so desire to be a vessel unto honor so that He can use me for any good work, if and when He desires.

My stand with Him is: not my will, but Yours be done LORD. And my main objective is to keep on growing in a more intimate relationship with our Creator, and try to be very sensitive to His Holy Spirit inside of me.

I truly love and adore Him; not because of anything I did, but because of everything He did. And I would like to share with you an experience I had with the LORD that took place 10 months ago from this date. At the time I was a member of La'el Ministries.

The meetings were held in my home. I had been walking with them approximately two and half years. It was after a Thursday night Bible study. Everyone had already left and it was just me and the LORD.

I would also like to mention that we used to pray on Wednesday nights together as a group, but I had a very difficult time praying with them. It was very much of a struggle from within to pray in their presence. So I prayed many nights after everyone left.

This particular night, I was just sitting on my couch downstairs in the room where we met for services, just talking to the LORD. As I was speaking, He interrupted and said get up and get a piece of paper, and write down what I speak to your heart. So I did.

And I testify this to be an accurate statement written by me...as the LORD God Almighty spoke to me by His Holy Spirit.

Signed and sealed in the presence of a witness on the 27th Day of June in the year of the LORD, One Thousand Nine Hundred and Ninety-Three.

SEE THE 27 AUGUST 1992 PROPHECY in *There is Still Time,* on page 234 of this book. Also, in the Scripture Index you will find several Bible references to confirm what the LORD God spoke to me on that night.

APPENDIX TWO

God said on 28 February 1993: *"You have been taught truth mixed with lies, and the* L*ORD says it will go on no longer...He will not hold your sin against you if you repent. And if you do not you will die...*

Light will overshadow Darkness and Darkness will not be able to stand in the presence of God!"

Please prayerfully consider these passages in Light of that Day.

Jeremiah 2:28 "But where are *thy gods that thou hast made thee? Let them arise, if they can save thee in the time of thy trouble: for* according to *the number of thy cities are thy gods, O Judah."*

Daniel 2:28 "But there is a God in Heaven that revealeth secrets, and maketh known to the king...what shall be in the latter days..."

Joel 2:28-29 "And it shall come to pass afterward, that *I will pour out My Spirit upon all flesh; and your sons and your daughters shall prophesy, your old men shall dream dreams, your young men shall see visions: And also upon the servants and upon the handmaids in those days will I pour out My Spirit."*

Mark 2:28 "Therefore the Son of man is LORD also of the Sabbath."

Luke 2:28-32 "Then took he Him up in his arms, and blessed God, and said, LORD, now lettest thou Thy servant depart in peace, according to Thy word: For mine eyes have seen Thy salvation,

Which Thou hast prepared before the face of all people; a Light to lighten the Gentiles, and the glory of Thy people Israel."

Acts 2:28 "Thou hast made known to me the ways of life; Thou shalt make me full of joy with Thy countenance."

Romans 2:28-29 "Fore he is not a Jew, which is one outwardly; neither is that *circumcision, which is outward in the flesh: But he* is *a Jew, which is one inwardly; and circumcision* is that *of the heart, in the spirit,* and *not in the letter; whose praise* is *not of men, but of God."*

Philippians 2:28 "I sent Him therefore the more carefully, that, when ye see Him again, ye may rejoice, and that I may be the less sorrowful."

I John 2:28 "And now, little children, abide in Him; that, when He shall appear, we may have confidence, and not be ashamed before Him at His coming."

Revelation 2:28-29 "And I will give him the Morning Star. He that hath an ear, let him hear what the Spirit saith unto the churches."

Proverbs 8:35-36 "For whoso findeth Me findeth life, and shall obtain favour of the LORD. But he that sinneth against Me wrongeth his own soul: All they that hate Me love death."

REFERENCE INDEX

AMERICAN HERITAGE DICTIONARY: Copyright © 1992 Houghton Mifflin Company. Adapted and reproduced by permission from *The American Heritage Dictionary of the English Language, Third Edition.* Pg 195, 272

CONGRESS OF THE UNITED STATES OF AMERICA: Pg 265

Capitol Hill Switchboard Phone Number: (202) 225-3121

GSUSA / HORNBLOWER: Middle Miss. Girl Scout Council. Pg 260-261

ISRAEL MY GLORY MAGAZINE: (ISSN 8755-402X) Published bimonthly by *The Friends of Israel Gospel Ministry, Inc.* Copyright © 1997/Volume 55, Number 5, October/November 1997. Pg 343

MASTERLIFE: Discipleship Training for Leaders. Copyright © 1980, 1982. Produced by the Church Training Department of The Sunday School Board of the Southern Baptist Convention; Nashville, TN. Pg 74, 238, 335, 346

A NIGHT TO REMEMBER: by Walter Lord Copyright © 1955, 1956 by Bantam Books. Pg 116, 348

THE QUEEN: A Biography of Elizabeth II by Ben Pimlott Copyright © by Ben Pimlott. First published in the U.S. by John Wiley & Sons, Inc., 1997. Pg 349

WATCHMAN NEE: Author of *The Spiritual Man* Copyright © 1968 Christian Fellowship Publishers. Pg 175-186, 196, 349

FRANK E. PERETTI: Author of *This Present Darkness* Copyright © 1986 Published by Crossway Books. Pg 85, 347

HOSTAGE: My Nightmare in Beirut by David Jacobsen Copyright © 1991 by David Jacobsen and Gerald Astor. Pg 342

MEDIA SPOTLIGHT: by Albert James Dager Copyright © 1995. Pg 349

REPORT OF THE DEPARTMENT OF THE TREASURY of the Bureau of Alcohol, Tobacco, and Firearms Investigation of Vernon Wayne Howell also known as David Koresh. (9/93) Published by the GPO, Washington, DC. Pg 341, 342

UNITY SCHOOL OF CHRISTIANITY / SILENT UNITY: Unity Village, MO. *The Adventure Called Unity* by Charles R. Fillmore and *What Unity Teaches* by Elizabeth Sand Turner / *A Manual of Prayer.* Pg 130-137, 336

WALKING IN THE TRUE LIGHT: A Testimony: Published by True Light Ministries® Copyright © 5 September 1997. Pg 30, 44, 344

TIMELINE INDEX

HOLY SCRIPTURE INDEX

27 AUGUST 1992
PROPHECY REFERENCES

Amos 3:7
Amos 9:6
Colossians 2:11
I Corinthians 3:13
I Corinthians 7:18-20
I Corinthians 12:11, 18
II Corinthians 3:13-16
Daniel 4:35
Deuteronomy 10:16
Deuteronomy 30:6
Ezekiel 28:18
Ezra 2:59
Hebrews 2:3-4
Hebrews 12:29
Isaiah 4:4
Isaiah 33:14
Isaiah 42:9
Isaiah 47:14
Jeremiah 4:4
Jeremiah 9:26
Jeremiah 16:15
Jeremiah 23:29
Jeremiah 31:22
I Kings 18:24
John 4:23-24
John 6:37
John 6:63
John 13:19-20
John 14:3
John 16:13
Luke 9:50
Luke 12:49
Mark 1:34
Matthew 3:11
Matthew 10:1
Matthew 11:29
Matthew 12:30
Matthew 16:24-27
I Peter 1:7
I Peter 4:1-2
Philippians 3:3
Proverbs 8:35-36
Proverbs 13:13
Psalms 18:17
Psalms 57:4
Psalms 68:11
Revelation 4:5
Revelation 22:16
Romans 1:3
Romans 2:28-29
Romans 10:12-13
II Thessalonians 1:8
I Timothy 3:15
II Timothy 2:3-5
II Timothy 2:8-9
Zechariah 11:8
Zechariah 13:8-9
Zephaniah 1:18
Zephaniah 3:8

28 FEBRUARY 1993
PROPHECY REFERENCES

See Appendix 2 pg 334

"BORN AGAIN"
SCRIPTURE REFERENCES

Galatians 4:27-29
I Peter 1:22-23
John 1:9-13
John 3:3-9
I John 3:9-10
I John 4:6-13
I John 5:1-18

See pg 343/End Notes

From the Author

Dear Readers, 27 September 1994

I could not have accomplished this momentous task without the LORD God Almighty working through the body of Christ, and many others, in order to fulfill His purposes and His plan. So I have to say that I take no credit for this great work of God. I Am just a vessel for Him to use in whatever manner that He may choose.

My primary purpose is to get the true message of Jesus Christ to as many people as possible, and if that is also your desire, please feel free to help in whatever way you believe the Spirit of the Most High God may be leading and guiding you in your endeavors to serve Him.

But before you proceed with anything, please earnestly seek the LORD God and ask Him what He would have you to do. That way when He blesses and equips you to be prepared to carry out His work, you will be able to give Him the thanks and praise for all the glorious things He has done for those who love and belong to Him.

I just thank the LORD that He has equipped me with everything I have needed to carry out His will, and I will continue to trust Him for anything and everything in connection with this pursuit.

And as long as the LORD God Almighty gives me the strength, the ability, and the means to fulfill His commands, I pray that I will remain "Always Faithful" to Him and what He asks of me.

One last thing I must mention, that we need to keep in the forefront of our minds—is that, even though we start out our walk with the LORD with the best of intentions, we must never forget that we have an Enemy who wants to get us off the right path in an attempt to cause disgrace to ourselves, and dishonor to Almighty God.

The Devil may succeed in leading you astray for a Time, but if you truly love the LORD God with your whole heart, soul, mind, and strength He will deliver you from the power of Darkness.

May Almighty God truly bless all those who love and worship Him in Spirit and in Truth, with His love, joy, and peace! And may you always have a heart to serve Him—He is so worthy of our adoration!

I genuinely welcome any comments and concerns you may have in regard to anything I have spoken or put down on paper. But first, I ask that you seriously consider all that I have written, and then earnestly pray to the LORD for the grace and the wisdom to truly understand.

C. Read

"...I AM ALPHA AND OMEGA,
THE BEGINNING &
THE END..."

END NOTES

[1] APOCRYPHA, meaning "things that are hidden," is a collection of writings that are considered to be unbiblical by some, yet they are considered to be of divine origin by others. These writings are of great historical value, and were included in the 1611 version of the King James Holy Bible, and appointed to be read in the Churches.

I would like to quote a passage that has special meaning for me from the book of: *I Maccabees 1:44,49 "For the king had sent letters by messengers unto Jerusalem and the cities of Judah, that they should follow the strange laws of the land...To the end they might forget the Law, and change all the ordinances."*

That has been Satan's objective from the beginning, unto this very day—to cause God's people, whether Jewish or Christian, to forget God and His Holy Commandments. Just a few examples: The Sabbath has been changed from the last day of the week to the first day. The Holy Days that Jesus celebrated are not kept as God has commanded. God's people eat things that He has forbidden in His word.

Even though there is no scriptural justification for any of these practices, people will justify why these things are acceptable under the New Covenant.

The inspired word of God will not contradict itself, and if there seems to be a disagreement, then obviously there was a problem in the translation process. Thankfully, through Christ we have access to the Holy Spirit—the One who can show us the Truth about God, and can clarify any supposed contradictions.

Since Jesus is our example to follow, we should do what He did, and so should all those who claim to love the God of Abraham, Isaac, and Jacob. (Pg 4)

[2] PROVIDENCE HOUSE was the original printer/publisher for the First Edition of *Walking With The Enemy*. I mailed *Providence* my manuscript on 31 October 1994, my Enemy's most sacred holiday—Halloween! Amazingly, I received my first perfect bound book on 28 February 1995, which was exactly two years to the very day that I was delivered from my Enemy! (Pg 14)

[3] YESHUA HAMASHIACH: Yeshua, is the Hebrew translation for Jesus, which means "YHWH is salvation." YHWH is the four consonants that make up the Holy name of the God of Israel, who is the Most High God, the Great I AM! HAMASHIACH is the Hebrew word for Christ, meaning "Anointed One." [Pg 15, 147, 331, 342, 343]

There are those who would cast a dark shadow over Jesus' name, but it's not how you pronounce the "Name," or what language you use that really matters, but what's important is if you know the Messiah—the LORD Jesus Christ. (Pg 15)

[4] BRANCH DAVIDIANS: Cult group led by David Koresh whose real name is Vernon Wayne Howell. He formally took on another name in 1990, and according to the court records, Koresh changed his name because he said that he was an entertainer, and wanted to use the name for publicity and business purposes.

The Branch Davidian movement, started by some members from the Seventh Day Adventist Church, was taken over by Howell in 1987. His followers were extremely devoted to him. They had an excessive dedication and loyalty to him and his teachings, especially regarding the book of Revelation. (Pg16, 25)

[5] MOUNT CARMEL was the name given for the Branch Davidian Compound near Waco, Texas, which was located on 77 acres, with the main structure having a fortress-like construction. Prior to Koresh leading the group, there were separate housing units lined along the road, but he had them dismantled after he took over.

The Compound that he had constructed did not have indoor plumbing, air conditioning, or heating. However, in the room where Koresh slept, it was equipped with air conditioning, heating, a stereo, a television, and other amenities.

Ironically, Mount Carmel was the place in the Scriptures whereby Elijah the prophet prayed for God to reign down fire upon his sacrifice, rather than on the sacrifices of the prophets of Ba'al, in order to prove that they were false prophets.

Elijah's prayer was answered, and the fire of the LORD fell and consumed only his sacrifice and everything surrounding it, which caused God's people to acknowledge that the LORD God Almighty is the One, True, and only Living God.

Elijah made sure that none of the prophets of Ba'al were able to escape, and they were subsequently killed. I Kings 18:17-40 (Pg 16)

[6] WWAR is not the actual call letters to this radio station. It is purely a fictitious name that was chosen due to the symbolism it represents. (Pg 16)

[7] 28 FEBRUARY 1993: This was the exact day that David Koresh and his religious cult in Waco, Texas was exposed to the world during the failed ATF raid. (Pg. 16)

[8] RAID ON THE BRANCH DAVIDIAN COMPOUND: ATF agents were attempting to execute lawful search and arrest warrants at Mount Carmel, the Branch Davidian Compound at approximately 9:55 a.m. on 28 February 1993. The ATF agents, a force of 76, were ambushed by the members of this religious cult, led by David Koresh. The Davidians opened fire with assault weapons before the agents even reached the door. The gunfire continued until the Branch Davidians agreed to a cease-fire. This unsuccessful raid near Waco, Texas resulted in the deaths of two cult members and four courageous ATF special agents, who are: Conway LeBleu, Todd W. McKeehan, Robert J. Williams, and Steven D. Willis. (Pg 25)

[9] PRINCE OF THE POWER OF THE AIR: Another name for the Devil. In Ephesians 2:2 the Devil is referred to as the *"prince of the power of the air, the spirit that now worketh in the children of disobedience:"*(Pg 26)

[10] UNITED STATES MARINE CORPS: During the 3 ½ years that I was enlisted in the United States Marine Corps, many significant changes took place in my life. For one, I had the once in a lifetime chance to live in Paradise (Hawaii) for three years.

Another momentous event was when I was on a temporary assignment in Yuma, Arizona, and the Iranian students seized the American Embassy in Tehran on 4 November 1979 and took fifty-two Americans hostage.

Subsequently, the United States Marines that were stationed in Japan were placed on Red Alert—my boyfriend being among them. I was so worried about him way over there, because he could have been sent to Iran at a moments notice, but thank God, he did not have to go. And finally, on 20 January 1981, the Fifty-two American hostages were released by Iran.

Moreover, just as 11 September 2001, was a devastating event that affected almost everyone in this Nation, so too was the Iranian crisis a Day of Reckoning for so many people, including myself. I was definitely headed in the wrong direction, and due to the distressing state of this world, my priorities dramatically changed.

But praise God He sent one of His servants to direct my way back to Him during this difficult time in my life, when my heart was crying out God. And in November 1979 I gave my heart to the LORD, and I have been walking with Him ever since. And only by His grace will I continue unto the End. (Pg 28)

[11] BORN AGAIN: There is much debate over this subject and what it truly means to be "born again" of God's Spirit. I have included the pages whereby "born again" has been mentioned in this book, along with the Scripture references, so you can allow the Holy Spirit of God to confirm the Truth to you.

Bible References: John 1:9-13; Galatians 4:27-29; I Peter 1:22-23; John 3:3-9; I John 3:9-10; I John 4:6-13; and I John 5:1-18.

Book References: Pg. 28, 83, 130, *176, *177, *179, *180, *182, *183, *185, 187, 210, & 240. [The * denotes the words of my Enemy.] (Pg 28)

[12] 11 JUNE 1993 is very significant for me, because that is when God prompted me to have my 5 June 1993 letter notarized at the Chancery Clerks Office. I have since discovered that 11 June 1967 was when the Six Day War that began on 5 June 1967 between Israel and the Arab Nations was ended.

At that time, it had only been 19 years since Israel had been "re-born" as a Nation (15 May 1948), after centuries of not having their own homeland. Hence, the surrounding countries were quite angry when Israel re-claimed their right to this land as given by Almighty God. Subsequently, Egypt, Syria, and Jordan proceeded to devise a plan to destroy this very small Nation.

With no other choice but to defend themselves, the Israeli Air Force attacked Egypt on the morning of 5 June 1967, and amazingly destroyed almost the entire Egyptian Air Force (more than 300 planes) in less than three hours!

On that same day of 5 June 1967 Israel's armored divisions, under the leadership of Ariel Sharon destroyed more than 800 Egyptian tanks and took thousands of prisoners in just three days!

The second phase of this Six Day War resulted in the capture of East Jerusalem, to include the Old City, which prior to that had been controlled by the Arab Legion. When under Jordanian control they decimated the Jewish Quarter of the Old City, blowing up its synagogues and destroying every vestige of Jewish life there. Jewish gravestones on the Mount of Olives had even been used to pave roads!

By 8 June 1967, Israel now had access to the Western Wall—the remnant of the wall that once surrounded the ancient Jewish Temple. Israel also won back the ancient towns of Shechem, Shiloh, Bethel, Bethlehem, and Hebron—very holy sites from Biblical history.

Finally, on 10 June 1967, Syria accepted a cease-fire and Israel was now in control of the Golan Heights—a most strategic position. Strangely, Israel has given back much of what the brave men and women fought for during this Holy War—all in the name of Peace. And they have even talked about giving back the Golan!

Through the Oslo Accords (13 September 1993-28 September 2000), Israel was promised peace and safety, but they have no peace or safety—only destruction.

I just pray for the Day that the people of Israel will truly call upon the Most High God with a sincere and repentant heart, and be willing to depart from all that is evil in order to be the Holy Nation that God intended for them to be.

May the people of Israel, from the least to the greatest, truly call upon the Name of Yeshua HaMashiach, who is the true Prince of Peace—the Messiah, the Holy One of Israel. And then, and only then, will the State of Israel genuinely be a "True Light" to the Nations of the world! [References: Israel My Glory Magazine, October/November 1997 Issue] (Pg 29, 335)

[13] CHARISMATIC CHURCHES: These are usually non-denominational churches that are characterized by "Praise and Worship" music, along with prayer services whereby the "worship leaders" pray and "lay hands" on the people to "fill" them with the "spirit," similar to what took place with me at La'el Ministries.

The "Charismatic" type churches should be avoided at all cost, no matter how much their "ministers" say they love you, God, the Bible, and Israel. People really need to beware, regardless of how good you feel while in these churches. It's not the feeling that's important, but what "spirit" is behind the words and actions of the preacher, the leadership, and its members. Christ or anti-Christ? (Pg 30)

[14] "WALKING IN THE TRUE LIGHT" was originally published on 5 September 1997 by *True Light Ministries®*. This book goes into great detail about a "revival" meeting that took place in Pensacola, Florida on Father's Day of 1995. I learned about this "event" on WWAR during an interview they had with a pastor on 5 September 1996, who was heavily involved with the "Brownsville/Pensacola Revival."

Based on this interview with the Pastor on WWAR I thought the revival sounded great, but when I saw what happened during the services, it reminded me of what took place at La'el Ministries, but on a much wider scale. (Pg 30)

[15] WINKED AT: Is an archaic word which means to overlook. It is worth noting that there are several words in the 1611 version of the King James Bible that mean different things in our modern day language, which is why it is helpful to use a Concordance of the Holy Bible to look up the true meaning of the original words in order to gain a better understanding of the Holy Scriptures. (Pg 31)

[16] QUICKEN is an another archaic word which means, "To give Life." (Pg 31)

[17] THE FOLLOWING IS THE MESSAGES that Liz and Cindy left on my answering machine after they received a taped message that I recorded on 7 July 1993.

11 JULY 1993 "This Liz. It is 11:15PM and I had gone to bed and just couldn't quit thinking about you tonight. I just wanted to call and tell ya that I love you. And I hope if you are there, that you would just pick up and say hello. And I do miss you. And I am not angry at you, and I don't despise you. I could never hate you darling. I guess there has never been anyone that I have loved more than you. I do love you. I just wanted to get in the car tonight and knock on the door. I was afraid you wouldn't come to the door if you saw that it was me. But I do love ya. And I hope you'll call me." [I picked up and said, "Liz?" And she said, "What?"]

14 JULY 1993 "Hi Cathy, this is Cindy. I am sorry I'm calling so late. I have wanted to call you all week. I got your tape last week, and I just wanted to call you and hope that you would pick up the phone and talk with me. I just wanted to tell you that I love you very much and that I have really missed you, Cathy.

It has been really hard being separated from you. And I just want you to know how much I do love you. And I do miss you. There is not a single day that goes by that I don't think about you, and I don't long for the time that we spent together. And I just wanted you to know that.

If you are awake and you want to call me back, I am still up. I don't like talking to an answering machine because it is so impersonal. I am here, and I am awake. And I really love you. Bye." [I picked up the phone and said, "Cindy?" And she said, "Yes."] (Pg 33)

[18] KIM: A young girl who was only seventeen when she joined the group. Sadly, she stayed with the group even after she was warned about Huff and Liz. I was told that Cindy had adopted her as her own child, but I really don't know if it was an actual adoption through the court system. (Pg 36)

[19] "WHAT IF YOU ARE WRONG?" I posed this question to the Rabbi during a three-session introductory course on Judaism, which members of La'el Ministries and I attended during the month of February 1993, right before God intervened on behalf of those who are walking in Darkness, and know not where they are going.

My question was referring to his rejection of Jesus Christ as being the true Messiah of Israel that was sent by God to redeem mankind. I don't remember his response to me, but I was quite sincere in my inquiry.

Some Jewish folks have quite a hostility towards Christians, especially in regard to Jesus Christ being the Messiah, as foretold in the Scriptures, but I Am certain that one day God will take the blinders away from the eyes of those who sincerely love Him, and give them "eyes to see and ears to hear" the Truth. (Pg 37)

[20] GREAT WHITE THRONE: There is a lot of speculation as to who will be judged at the Great White Throne, as referenced in Revelation 20:10-15. I Am reluctant to be totally definitive as to what exactly will happen on that Day, but obviously there are two sets of people being judge—those who belong to God, and those who do not.

God has said that you must be "born again," in order to see Heaven, and how you respond to God and His word will determine your destiny. It's not your bloodline that matters, but whether your name is inscribed in the *Book of Life.*

I Peter 4:17 "For the time is come that Judgment must begin at the house of God: and if it first begin at us, what shall the end be of them that obey not the Gospel? And if the righteous scarcely be saved, where shall the ungodly and the sinner appear?"

Apparently, obedience is very important to God. I know that it is with me in regard to my children; and I Am sure it is even more so with God. Although, it must be submission of the heart, and you must be willing to do whatever God says.

If you bow before the LORD God Almighty with a sincere desire to obey Him, because you love Him, then that is the soul that God's grace will be upon. *"For by Grace are ye saved through faith; and that not of yourselves: it is the gift of God: Not of works, lest any man should boast." Ephesians 2:8-9* (Pg 38)

[21] BLASPHEMY OF THE HOLY SPIRIT is mentioned at least three times in the New Testament by three separate witnesses, in Matthew 12:31-32, Mark 3:28-29, and Luke 12:10. They all state that it is the only unforgivable sin. (Pg 38)

[22] THE LAODICEAN CHURCH is among the seven Churches addressed in Revelation chapters 2-3. Based on Revelation 3:14-22, God was greatly displeased with the Laodicean Church and its people. They had become apathetic, lazy, boastful, arrogant, and very self-righteous—the very condition of the present day Church.

God loves His people and He will warn us if we are going the wrong way, but you have to be able to hear His voice. When God warns the Churches He addresses the Angel's rather than "men" because God is a Spirit, and those who worship Him must worship Him in Spirit and in Truth. *I Corinthians 2:14-15 "But the natural man receiveth not the things of the Spirit of God: for they are foolishness unto him: neither can he know them, because they are spiritually discerned. But he that is spiritual judgeth all things, yet he himself is judged of no man."*

All of this gets back to the necessity of being "born again." I hope you will read the Scriptures that I have referenced regarding being "born again," and listen very carefully, so that maybe you will be able to hear the Voice of God.

God is knocking at the Door. Will you let Him in? If you do, may He give you "eyes to see, and ears to hear," what He is saying unto the Churches. (Pg. 44)

[23] PENSACOLA REVIVAL LETTER: In December of 1996 I sent out a letter to a Messianic Jewish Rabbi, which is a Jew who believes in Jesus as the Messiah. I asked him in the letter as to what was his opinion of "the Pensacola Revival which appears to be connected to the Toronto Outpouring?" He responded in a very lukewarm way, but due to this letter, I started sending out the same question to other Christians, Jew and Gentile alike, especially those in leadership positions.

Almost everyone I wrote, responded to me, and the results were quite interesting. About a third were for it, another third were against it, and the rest could go either way. But very few saw these "revivals" for what they really are, which is the *"working of Satan with all lying wonders."* II Thessalonians 2:9. (Pg 44)

[24] RUTH was a former member of the group prior to me joining. She was also very deceived by them, but thankfully, she got out before they destroyed her. (Pg 50)

[25] DAIRY QUEEN INCIDENT: Liz, Cindy, Pastor Huff and myself had gone to Dairy Queen for something to eat before going to the Synagogue for our Judaism course. While the girls and I were in the bathroom, something really strange seemed to be happening to me. It was as if there was a very strange presence with us. Liz told me that it was a demonic attack, and she and Cindy started praying for me. Even after we got to the Synagogue, I still felt this unusual presence with us, which was causing me to be very anxious and even fearful. Thank God, the feeling did not last, and it left me after I got home and I was no longer in the presence of Huff or Liz.

In retrospect, I believe the LORD was starting to open up my spiritual eyes to be able to discern when I was in the presence of evil. (Pg 50)

[26] BAPTIST BOOK STORE: Name changed to *LifeWay Christian Stores*. (Pg 55)

[27] ELISHA: Even though everyone else called her Liz, I felt that "God" said that her name as given by Him was to be Alisha, however she informed me that the correct spelling was Elisha, the same as the Prophet Elisha in the Bible. So when Liz, Alisha, and Elisha are mentioned in this book they all refer to Liz. (Pg 58)

[28] MASTERLIFE was a discipleship program. See the Reference Index. (Pg 74)

[29] LIZ used to tell me about the nightmares she would have, and how she could actually see and feel demons touching her. There was one incident that happened during a prayer meeting, right before I got out of the group, that is worth noting. Liz was just sitting there, when all of a sudden she started screaming as if she was in horrible pain. It went on for a few minutes, until she finally stopped. We never discussed what happened, but I believe she was being tormented by evil spirits.

[30] SUE was with the Bible Study group almost the whole time that I was, but soon before the group broke up she had quit coming. (Pg 85)

[31] 9 JUNE 1991: This message came to me early on in my walk with the Enemy, and I have continued to have doubts as to whether it was truly from the LORD. But I Am convinced that it was the Devil trying to sound as convincing as he possibly could to make me think that I could actually hear the Voice of God. (Pg 94)

[32] "IS JESUS ENOUGH?" This was an eleven-page booklet that Liz wrote and had photocopied. When Liz counseled group members, many times she would ask us, "Is Jesus Enough?" And it would usually be in a condemning way.

She gave me several copies of her booklet to distribute, and I sent many as gifts that year. The following is excerpts from her booklet: *"I sat under a man of God once who offended me so much that I began to hate the very words that he seemed to live by—Jesus is enough. He's all I need. Let's be real. If I didn't think Jesus was enough, why in the world would I be at Bible Study anyway? This man just didn't have any balance in his life...*

I began to examine the life of this man who plainly stated that Jesus was enough for him. I was amazed to see that he had even more problems in his life than most Christians. He was persecuted for his beliefs. He wasn't really accepted by many professing "Christians" and yet there was one major difference in his life.

No matter what was going on around him, there was always a joy and a peace in his heart that I had never before seen in anyone. He was just plain different.

Something gave him this peace, joy, and overwhelming love for others that I hadn't yet found. The only thing I knew for certain was that I didn't have this in my life, and I wanted it, no matter what the cost might be."

Well Liz got what Huff had alright, and she sold her soul to get it—the spirit of anti-Christ—a seducing, deceiving, demonic spirit working in her life.

Liz's words are spoken and written in such a way so as to manipulate people's thinking, rather than it being the way she really felt. The rest of this booklet was truth mixed with lies, just like what the LORD God warned us about. The truth is what got me because Satan has to use the truth to ensnare those who are seeking God; otherwise, it would be all too obvious as to who the Devil is.

Both Huff and Liz were aspiring writers. Huff had given me a manuscript entitled "Fulfilling the Call," and he was working on another manuscript similar to Frank Peretti's books. I don't know if either of them tried to publish their writings, but I believe their "works" have gone unpublished—that is, until now.

And may this Testimony of Jesus warn unsuspecting souls of the dangers that lie behind the words of deceptive, manipulative men and women! (Pg 100)

[33] 27 FEBRUARY 1992: At the time I heard these words, it was as if I was surrounded by a dark presence, and considering the doubt and confusion in my heart and mind, I should have known that something was just not right.

Looking back, I now realize that these were the very words of the Devil himself! It was also truth mixed with lies, just like the LORD warned me about on 28 February 1993. I just praise God that He can, and will, use whatever the Enemy intends for evil, and turn it around for my good, and the good of those who truly love and belong to Him. (Pg 102)

[34] THE MEETING when I went to Liz's home, where Huff also lived, and confronted "Pastor" Huff about his lustful behavior. I asked Cindy and Liz to be there as my witnesses, in accordance with the Scriptures in Matthew 18:15-16. (Pg 107)

[35] TREE OF LIFE: *Genesis 3:22 "And the LORD God said, Behold, the man is become as one of us, to know good and evil: and now, lest he put forth his hand, and take also of the Tree of Life, and eat, and live for ever:"* (Pg 108)

[36] HUFF and some of the other men from the group came to get their piano the following Sunday after I left the group. They were transporting it in a pickup truck, and they were slowed down quite a bit because the piano was so heavy.

Their truck was barely able to creep through my yard, and as a result, I circled the vehicle several times and followed them all the way to the end of my driveway while I continually repeated the statement, "*If any man preach any other gospel besides the gospel of Jesus Christ, let him be accursed!*" (Pg 112)

[37] 19 APRIL 1993 is the day the Branch Davidian Compound in Waco, Texas was engulfed in flames after a 51-day standoff with the FBI and the ATF, where more than 70 cult members perished in the fire. Many had gunshot wounds inflicted by fellow cult members, or possibly by their own hand. (Pg 113)

[38] RMS TITANIC FACTS: 10 April 1912 at 12:00 noon, *Titanic* leaves Southampton, and narrowly escapes a collision with the *New York*—an American ocean liner.

14 April 1912 receives numerous ice warnings: 9:00 A.M. the *Caronia* reports ice; 1:42 P.M. the *Baltic* reports ice; 1:45 P.M. the *Amerika* reports ice; 7:00 P.M. the temperature is 43°; 7:30 P.M. the *Californian* reports ice; 9:00 P.M. the Temperature is 33°; 9:40 P.M. the *Mesaba* reports ice; 10:30 P.M. the Temperature of the sea is 31°; 11:00 P.M. the *Californian* warns of ice, but is told to shut up and is cut off by the wireless operator before the wireless operator of the *Californian* gives the location. This sixth warning never reached the bridge. 11:40 P.M. *RMS Titanic* collides with iceberg at Latitude 41° 46´ N, Longitude 50° 14´ W.

15 April 1912 at 2:20 A.M. the *Titanic* sinks. 4:10 A.M. First survivors rescued by the *Carpathia*; 8:30 A.M. Last survivors rescued by the *Carpathia.* The lives lost varies depending on where you get your information. As many 1635 souls, to as few as 1490 souls, were lost on that *Night To Remember*, with 705 survivors. The sad fact remains: It didn't have to be, had they heeded the warnings. (Pg 116)

[39] ROSH HASHANAH: According to Leviticus 23:23-25 this Day is signified by the blowing of the Trumpets, or a Ram's horn, as a wakeup call for all of God's people to prepare for the Judgment Day. It is to take place on the 1st day of the 7th month of the Jewish Calendar (1 Tishrei). It is to be a Holy Day unto the LORD, and no work is to be performed on that Day. (Pg 116)

[40] DAY OF ATONEMENT: The Holiest of all biblical holidays, which is also known as Yom Kippur by Jewish people. It takes place 10 days after the Blowing of Trumpets. It is a very special Day where God asks His people to fast and repent of all their sins, so that hopefully their names will be inscribed in the Book of Life. (Pg 126)

[41] DEBORAH is the same lady mentioned earlier in this book. We have never met face to face, but we did correspond and spoke over the phone on a few occasions. I only heard from her once after this letter. She left a message on my answering machine to let me know that she got my letter, and she seemed very sad. (Pg 129)

[42] COURTROOM: Kim's real mother took Huff and Liz to court to force them to divulge where her daughter was, who was a minor at the time. All the members of La'el Ministries were ordered to come to a local court proceeding to testify as to our knowledge of the whereabouts of Kim, who had obviously been hidden out.

All the members of the Bible Study group showed up except for Evelyn, who had stayed at my house with all the children. Kim, was not there of course, but Cindy's ex-husband, Steven, was there along with his wife, Lynn.

Liz prepared a note for me which said, "I refuse to answer on the grounds that I may incriminate myself." She told me to repeat that statement when I was questioned, but for some reason, no one from the group had to testify. (Pg 144)

[43] MATTHEW 7:6 *"Give not that which is holy unto the dogs, neither cast ye your pearls before swine, lest they trample them under their feet, and turn again and rend you."* This a verse that came up a lot when I first started coming to the Bible study group, and Liz would always try to help me understand passages from the Bible that were hard to comprehend. Of course, she didn't mention that this particular passage was actually referring to her, and that she was seeking to destroy my life. However, if I had known how to truly discern the Voice of God I would have turned around and never gone back to another one of their Bible study meetings. (Pg 145)

[44] 12 MAY 1993, is another very important date for me. It is the day that the LORD commissioned me to be His servant, of which I consider the greatest of honors.

The 12th of May is also a very significant day for the British Royal Family. I have discovered that 12 May 1937 was the Coronation date of King George VI, who is the father of Queen Elizabeth II of Great Britain. (Pg 144-146)

[45] SCRIPTURES: After my release from the Enemy, I had an insatiable desire to read through the Scriptures without being under an evil influence. I even purchased a new Bible (KJV) because I felt like the one Liz had given me was cursed. By the time I had received Liz's letter I had already read almost the entire Bible. (Pg 148)

[46] CINDY left the Bible study group to go live with Liz's brother soon after I joined La'el Ministries. After she attended Huff's birthday party in December of 1990, she repented of that sin and came back after being away for eight months. (Pg 168)

[47] "THE SPIRITUAL MAN" by Watchman Nee was read by Liz during the Bible study meeting on 4 February 1993. She read pages 64-68 of Nee's book. (Pg 175)

[48] MEETING WITH CINDY'S FAMILY ON 6 MARCH 1993: Steven is Cindy's ex-husband; Lynn is Steven's present wife; Katie is Cindy's half-sister; Ronald is Cindy's brother in-law; Mandy is Cindy's youngest half-sister, who is married to Ronald; and Bob is Cindy's step-father. Cindy's mother and Katie's husband was also present, but they never spoke up so their names were not mentioned within these pages. And Rebecca is Cindy and Stevens only child. (Pg 211)

[49] PROMISE KEEPERS: Is a men's movement founded by a coach from Colorado. The first conference was at the *Coors Event Center* in Boulder, CO in 1991 with 4,200 men in attendance. The next conference in 1992, drew 22,000 men. In 1993, 50,000 men attended the *Promise Keepers* Conference; and the numbers continued to grow until 1997, when it was revealed that the founder of this organization was not *really* a "Promise Keeper." His book reveals some of the reasons why. (Pg 318)

[50] "HOW MANY PEOPLE HAVE YOU LED TO THE LORD?" I was asked this question by another minister in an attempt to discredit me, just as Liz tried to do. Moreover, it is such an unfair thing to ask someone, because there is no way to know on this earth how many people we may affect by our Testimony for the LORD Jesus Christ. Even the smallest gesture of genuine love and concern for a stranger can cause them to call out to God. So I guess I will just have to wait until we get to Heaven to know the answer to that question. I just pray that it will be a very great number! (Pg 319)

[51] YHWH: The four consonants that make up the Holy name of the God of Israel, who is the Most High God, the Great I AM! (Pg 331)